WRITING AND ANALYSIS IN THE LAW

Seventh Edition

Helene S. Shapo

Professor of Law, Emeritus
Northwestern University School of Law

Marilyn R. Walter

Professor of Law, Emeritus
Brooklyn Law School

Elizabeth Fajans, Ph.D.

Associate Professor of Legal Writing
Writing Specialist
Brooklyn Law School

FOUNDATION
PRESS

© 1989, 1991, 1999, 2003 FOUNDATION PRESS
© 2008 THOMSON/FOUNDATION PRESS
© 2013 LEG, Inc. d/b/a West Academic Publishing
© 2018 LEG, Inc. d/b/a West Academic
    444 Cedar Street, Suite 700
    St. Paul, MN 55101
    1-877-888-1330

West, West Academic Publishing, and West Academic are trademarks of West Publishing Corporation, used under license.

Printed in the United States of America

ISBN: 978-1-68328-237-2

To our families—
Marshall, Benjamin, and Nathaniel Shapo
Ron, Amy, and Alison Walter
Bob, Nicholas, Rachel, and Paul Zimmerman
For the love, support, and advice they have
given us before and during the preparation
of this book's many editions.

PREFACE

Many people find writing a difficult and frustrating process. As a result, they put off writing projects in the hope that they will eventually be struck by inspiration. Unfortunately, few professions, especially the legal profession, are willing to postpone business in anticipation of this happening.

This book is devoted, therefore, to taking control over the writing process away from chance and investing it in ourselves. We have tried to break the legal reasoning and writing process into manageable components to enable you to be conscious of that process and to be master of your thoughts and their expression. We hope this awareness of the writing process will also make you less anxious when writing and more satisfied with your work when finished.

Writing and Analysis in the Law is a collaborative effort. Decisions about the scope of the book and the focus of each chapter were made jointly. In addition, the authors edited each other's chapters extensively, making both substantive and stylistic contributions to each chapter. We have learned much from each other and hope the book confirms our belief in the benefits of editing and rewriting.

ACKNOWLEDGMENTS

We would like to acknowledge and thank our students. Their progress marks our success as teachers and their questions spur our own development. Our thanks go out to those students we acknowledged in past additions as well as our past research assistants. We are grateful to Kara Higgins and Nicole Hopkins for their helpful assistance on the seventh edition.

We are also indebted to our colleagues. They generously allowed us to base examples and exercises on problems they developed for their classes. Our thanks go out to those we have previously recognized. We welcome the chance to acknowledge Mary R. Falk for her work on the sample appellate brief. Professor Terri LeClercq graciously allowed us to adapt her plagiarism hypotheticals. Professor Cynthia Grant Bowman of Cornell provided us with the memorandum on which Appendix E is in large part based. We also thank Westlaw for allowing us to reprint *Sinn v. Burd*.

We would like to express our gratitude to Brooklyn Law School and Northwestern University School of Law. These institutions not only gave us general encouragement, but also invested in our initial project by granting us research stipends.

Finally, Marilyn Walter and Elizabeth Fajans would like to thank Erica Soto and Debra Richards for their efficient assistance on this latest edition. Similarly, Helene Shapo would like to thank Shona Bonds for her work on this edition.

SUMMARY OF CONTENTS

TABLE OF CONTENTS

WRITING AND ANALYSIS IN THE LAW

Seventh Edition

CHAPTER 1

INTRODUCTION TO THE LEGAL SYSTEM AND LEGAL WRITING

STUDENTS DECIDE TO COME TO LAW SCHOOL for many good and diverse reasons. However, despite our numerous years teaching in law schools, we have never heard new students say they have come to law school because they like to write. Yet lawyers write all the time. They write to colleagues; they write to clients; they write to adversaries in a law suit; they write to third parties to request favors or information; they write to judges. They write documents for many different purposes: to persuade a court to rule in a client's favor; to answer a client's questions; to analyze a client's case; or to inform an adversary that a client is open to settlement but willing to litigate if pressed too hard. They draft contracts and wills. To be a good lawyer, you must be a good writer. And to be a good legal writer, you must have both a good understanding of law and a good grasp of principles of writing.

This book is about good legal writing. It introduces you to the sources of authority with which a lawyer works and upon which a lawyer's writing revolves. It introduces you to legal analysis and some forms of legal writing. Finally, it tries to integrate those lawyerly enterprises with that which all good writing must demonstrate, namely, a clear sense of audience, purpose, organization, and paragraph and sentence structure.

I. THE PRIMARY SOURCES OF LAW

WHEN YOU WERE AN UNDERGRADUATE OR GRADUATE STUDENT, you probably read a variety of primary and secondary sources to get the information you needed to write papers. As a lawyer you will also use many different sources of information to acquire the necessary background information to analyze a legal question. But a lawyer's most important sources of information are primary sources.

Primary sources in law include both case law (judicial decisions) and enacted law (statutes, constitutions, and administrative regulations). Although you may not study administrative and constitutional law until the second or third year of law school, you will need to use case law and statutory law throughout your first year. That is because in our legal system, analysis of a problem is controlled by enacted law that regulates the subject matter of that problem, and judicial decisions that involve issues and facts similar to those in that problem. Because most of your first-year classes emphasize case law, we begin with judicial decisions. You should be aware, however, that enacted law forms a significant part of the body of law in our country. Consult these sources first when you do research for a problem because constitutional provisions and statutes take precedence over case law. However, even when you find an applicable statute or constitutional provision, you will need to search for cases that have interpreted the particular statute or constitutional provision. Then, you will need to analyze how they are or are not relevant to your problem. When no statute or constitutional provision applies, however, you must rely solely on case law to provide the law on the subject. Those cases provide a source of enforceable rules called **the common law**.

The United States is a common law country in that rules of law come from the written decisions of judges who hear and decide litigation. The common law is judge-made law. Judges are empowered by statute or by constitutional provision in every state and in our federal system to decide controversies between litigants. When a judge decides a case, the decision attains the status of law, and it becomes a precedent for future legal controversies that are similar. Our common law system, like the English system from which it came, is a system of precedent. In the simplest sense, precedents are just the decisions of judges in previous litigation. Those decisions, however, play a dual role. First, the decision resolves the litigation that is before the court. Second, if that decision is published, it becomes available for use by judges in later litigation. According to the doctrine of precedent, judges should resolve litigation by taking into account the resolutions of similar cases in the past.

II. STRUCTURE OF THE COURT SYSTEM IN THE UNITED STATES

A. The Vertical Structure of Our Court System

CASE LAW IN THE UNITED STATES comes from litigation conducted in many court systems. Each state, as well as the District of Columbia and the federal government, has its own system of courts. Each is a separate jurisdiction. For our purposes, a jurisdiction is the area over which the courts of a particular judicial system are empowered to resolve disputes and thus to enforce their decisions. Jurisdiction is determined by a geographic area, like a state, and it can also be based upon subject matter. Subject matter jurisdiction is the authority of a court to resolve disputes in only a particular subject area of the law, such as criminal law.

The structure of the court system within each jurisdiction is a hierarchical one. Courts are organized along a vertical structure, and the position of a court within that structure has important consequences.

1.   Courts of Inferior Jurisdiction

Courts in which litigation begins are called courts of original jurisdiction. In many states, the lowest rung of the courts of original jurisdiction is occupied by a so-called court of inferior jurisdiction. This court has the power to hear only limited types of cases, such as misdemeanor cases or cases in which the amount of damages the complaining party (the plaintiff) demands from the party sued (the defendant) does not exceed a specified sum. These courts have various names, such as courts of common pleas or small claims courts. Other courts of inferior jurisdiction are limited to deciding cases about one particular subject matter, for example, juvenile, or family law. Courts of inferior jurisdiction may be conducted informally. For example, in small claims courts, the parties often represent themselves and the court does not follow the formal rules of evidence used in higher courts. The decisions of these courts are not published and they have no value as precedent to future litigants.

2.   Trial Courts

The next rung up from the courts of inferior jurisdiction is occupied by the trial courts, where litigation often begins. Trial courts are usually courts of general jurisdiction, that is, they may hear cases of all subject matters. Thus, a trial court may hear civil litigation, which is litigation between private parties who are designated as the plaintiff and the defendant. It may also hear criminal cases. Criminal litigation is brought by the state, which prosecutes the criminal charges against a defendant or defendants. There is no private party plaintiff in a criminal case.

A trial court is presided over by one judge. It is the particular province of the trial court to determine the facts of the case. The trier of fact, either judge or jury, "finds," that is, determines, the facts from the evidence at trial, the examination of witnesses, and the admissions of the parties. For example, one issue in a case may be the speed at which a vehicle was travelling. This fact may be disputed by the parties. The trial judge or the jury, if the question is put to a jury, will resolve the dispute and "find," for example, that a party traveled at 75 miles per hour. The court then decides the case by applying the applicable law to that fact.

Often the trial court judge will decide a case by procedures that preclude a trial. For example, one of the parties may bring a motion for the court to take a particular action. Some types of motions, if granted, will result in a decision that eliminates the need for a trial. You will learn about those types of motions in your civil procedure course. Often, the attorneys submit a written document to the court, usually called a trial brief or a memorandum of law. If a case is not ended on a pre-trial motion, and the parties do not voluntarily settle their dispute, then the case will go to trial.

3.   Appellate Courts

The next step up the hierarchy of courts from the trial courts is occupied by the appellate courts. The party that lost at the trial level, either by motion or by a decision after trial, may ask for review by a higher court. This review is known as an appeal. The party who appeals is usually called the appellant and the other party, the appellee. The appellate court determines whether the lower court committed any error significant enough to require that the decision be reversed or modified, or a new trial be granted.

Most states provide two levels of appellate courts. The first is an intermediate court of appeals. The second is the highest court of appeals and is usually known as the state's Supreme Court, although some states use other designations. Generally, the intermediate appellate court hears appeals from the trial courts, and the Supreme Court hears appeals from the intermediate courts of appeals. In many states with intermediate courts of appeals, however, the Supreme Court must hear appeals for certain types of issues directly from the trial courts. There is no further appeal of the decisions of the highest state court as to matters of state law.

Some states, although a decreasing number, have no intermediate court of appeals. In those states, trial court decisions will be reviewed directly by the highest court. In either system, except for certain types of cases, the highest court need not hear every case for which an appeal has been requested. Rather, the court has discretion to choose which cases to hear.

In many states, the intermediate appellate level consists of more than one court. For example, the state may be geographically divided into appellate districts, with each district having its own court of appeals. That district will contain several trial courts, the appeals from which all go to the one court of appeals for that district. Each court of appeals in that state is a co-equal, that is, each occupies the same rung on the court hierarchy as the others. The state will have only one supreme court, however, and that court is superior to all other state courts.

An appeal is heard by more than one judge, and because the appeal should be heard by an odd number of judges, all appellate courts require three or more judges. The judges decide the case by voting and usually one of the judges from the majority writes the decision. A judge who disagrees with the majority may write his or her own opinion, called a dissenting opinion. In addition, a judge who has voted with the majority as to the outcome of the case may write a separate opinion to express his or her differing views about certain aspects of the case. This decision is a concurring opinion ("concurring" because the judge concurred in the outcome of the case). The name of the judge who writes an opinion appears at the beginning of that opinion. Sometimes the opinion of the court does not bear the name of an author, but is designated a "per curiam" decision. This means a decision "by the court" and may be used for a shorter opinion on an issue about which there is general unanimity.

The procedure of an appeal differs from proceedings before a trial court. An appeal does not involve another trial before the panel of appellate judges. That is, the parties do not submit evidence or examine witnesses, and the court does not empanel a jury to re-examine factual issues. Rather, the parties' lawyers argue to the appellate judges to persuade them that the court below did or did not commit an error or errors. Typically, this argument is made by means of written documents called appellate briefs that the attorneys submit to the court. The attorneys may also argue orally before the judges, although not all appeals involve oral argument. In addition, the appellate court reviews the record of the proceedings below. Many, but not all, appellate decisions, are published both in volumes called case reporters and online.

B. The System of Courts: The Federal Courts

The hierarchical nature of the federal court system parallels the vertical structure of state courts. The trial courts within the federal system are called **district courts**. There is at least one United States District Court within each state. A district court's territorial jurisdiction is limited to the area of its district. A state with a small population and a low volume of litigation may have one district court and the entire state will comprise that district; for example, Rhode Island has one district court called the United States District Court for the District of Rhode Island. The volume of litigation in most states, however, requires more than one court in the state and thus the district is divided geographically. For example, Illinois is divided into three federal district courts: The United States District Court for the Northern District of Illinois, the United States District Court for the Southern District of Illinois, and the United States District Court for the Central District of Illinois.

Each intermediate appellate court in the federal system is called the **United States Court of Appeals**. For appellate court purposes, the United States is divided into thirteen circuits, so there are thirteen United States Courts of Appeals, eleven of which are identified by a number. Thus, the complete title of one court is The United States Court of Appeals for the First Circuit. The eleven numbered circuits are made up of a designated group of contiguous states (and also may include territories). The United States Court of Appeals for the Seventh Circuit, for example, is made up of the states of Illinois, Wisconsin, and Indiana. The other two courts of appeals, designated without numbers, are the United States Court of Appeals for the District of Columbia Circuit, and the United States Court of Appeals for the Federal Circuit.[1] Appeals from the district courts within the area that makes up a circuit go to the court of appeals for that circuit. A case that was litigated in the United States District Court for the Northern District of Illinois, for example, would be appealed to the United States Court of Appeals for the Seventh Circuit.

The highest court in the federal system is the **Supreme Court of the United States**. This court hears cases from all the United States Courts of Appeals and, for certain issues, from federal district courts and from the highest courts of the state systems. The Supreme Court must hear certain types of cases and has discretion to hear other requests.[2]

III. OVERVIEW OF A CIVIL CASE

THE ATTORNEY-CLIENT RELATIONSHIP typically begins when a client comes to the attorney to discuss a problem. This relationship may involve business matters, such as drafting a contract, or it may involve personal matters, such as drafting a will, or the relationship may begin with a client's legal problem that involves civil litigation. The attorney interviews the client to

---

[1] The United States Court of Appeals for the Federal Circuit hears certain specialized cases such as international trade, patents, trademarks, and government contracts.

[2] The United States also has courts of limited jurisdiction, that is, courts that are competent to hear only specialized subject matters, such as tax courts. You will rarely read cases from these courts in your first year of law school and we will not include them in this discussion.

determine the nature of the client's legal claim, that is, the client's cause of action,[3] and to gather as many facts as possible. At this point, in order to keep a written record of her work and conclusions about the client's case, she may write a short memorandum for her files or for another lawyer in the firm with whom she will be working. She will then research that claim in order to gather the relevant statutes and cases to understand its legal requirements. The attorney may then write a full office memorandum analyzing the law and facts,[4] or may email another attorney summarizing her research and conclusions. She may also write to her client by letter or email to explain her analysis and recommendations.[5]

A.   Pleadings: Complaint and Answer

When the attorney and the client are ready to begin the lawsuit, the attorney will file a complaint with the appropriate trial court,[6] and arrange to serve the defendant with a summons and a copy of the complaint. These documents notify the defendant of the lawsuit against him or her. The complaint must set out enough of the facts that form the basis of the cause of action to give the defendant notice of the plaintiff's claim.[7]

The defendant then, within the time limits required in that jurisdiction, responds either with an answer to the complaint or with a motion. If the defendant answers the complaint, the defendant's answer responds to each of the allegations in the complaint. The answer may also allege facts that would provide an affirmative defense to the plaintiff's cause of action. For example, if the plaintiff's complaint alleges a cause of action for trespass, the defendant's answer may allege facts that set up the defense of license, that is that the plaintiff had authorized the defendant to go on the plaintiff's land. A person whom the plaintiff authorized to enter his land is not liable in trespass for that entry.

---

[3]   We discuss interviewing clients in Chapter 12.

[4]   We discuss the office memorandum in Chapter 7.

[5]   We discuss writing to clients in Chapter 14.

[6]   See Part II of this chapter.

[7]   Most jurisdictions require only "notice pleadings," that is, in the words of Federal Rule of Civil Procedure 8, a complaint that includes a "short and plain statement of the claim showing the pleader is entitled to relief." The other jurisdictions require "fact pleading," and require that the complaint alleges enough facts of a particular kind to state a cause of action. However, the Supreme Court has held that bare notice pleading is no longer sufficient in federal courts. Plaintiffs must now provide more detail of the allegations in a complaint sufficient to plausibly satisfy the elements of a cause of action. *See Bell Atlantic Corp. v. Twombly*, 550 U.S. 544 (2007); *Ashcroft v. Iqbal*, 556 U.S. 662 (2009).

B. Motion Practice and Discovery

1. Motions to Dismiss

Instead of answering a complaint, the defendant may decide to enter a motion, which at this stage is most likely a motion to dismiss for failure to state a claim upon which relief can be granted.[8] In some states, this motion is called a demurrer. This motion asks the court to dismiss the complaint because even if the plaintiff's alleged facts are true, the facts do not establish any cause of action, and do not provide any relief recognized by the law. The defendant will likely accompany the motion with a memorandum of law to the court that explains the reasons for the motion. This memorandum is an advocacy document written to the court to persuade it to grant the motion. It differs from the office memorandum referred to above, which is an analytical memo usually kept within the law firm. The plaintiff will then file her own memorandum of law, but one in opposition to the defendant's motion.

If the defendant argues successfully, the court will grant the motion and dismiss the plaintiff's lawsuit. The plaintiff may then appeal this decision to a higher court. If the defendant loses at this stage, however, the defendant must file an answer to the complaint, and the litigation continues.

2. Discovery

The next step in the litigation process requires the parties to gather information for the lawsuit by a process called discovery. They will often use procedures formalized in the jurisdiction's rules of civil procedure. These procedures commonly involve, first, depositions, which are an attorney's oral examination of the opposing party who is under oath and of witnesses who are also under oath. The deposition is transcribed by a court reporter. Second, attorneys submit interrogatories, which are written questions to the other party. Attorneys may also take affidavits from the parties and others and request relevant documents. An affidavit is a written declaration of facts that the person (the affiant) swears to under oath.

3. Summary Judgment Motions

After the parties have gathered what they consider enough evidence to go forward, one or both may move the court for summary judgment. A motion for summary judgment asks the court to decide the case without a trial by applying the controlling

---

[8] We discuss motions in Chapter 15.

law to the facts gathered through discovery. The parties again will submit memoranda of law in support of or in opposition to the summary judgment motion. A court cannot grant this motion if there is any conflict over material facts; if there are disputed facts, there must be a trial where a jury or judge "finds," that is, determines, the facts. If the court grants either party's summary judgment motion, the losing party may appeal that decision. If neither motion is granted, the case moves on to trial.

C. The Trial

At any point the parties may negotiate and settle the case between themselves, thus avoiding the time, stress, and expense of litigation. The parties may even settle the case during the trial and avoid the case going to judgment. If the parties do go to trial, however, they may submit a variety of motions during and after the trial. If the case goes to judgment, the losing party may appeal, first to an intermediate court of appeals, and then to the jurisdiction's highest court.

D. The Appeal

At the appellate stage of these proceedings, the attorneys produce formal written documents for the court, known as appellate briefs. These briefs explain the facts and the law as the party analyzes them. The party that appeals the lower court's decision (the appellant) also explains that the lower court made errors that require that the appellate court reverse that decision. The other party (the appellee) explains that the decision in the lower court was correct and should be affirmed (upheld).[9] The appellate court may make a final decision in the case or send it back (remand) to the lower court for further proceedings in accord with its legal ruling and the reasons for that ruling. Besides the formal briefs to the court, the attorneys may also have written less formal documents for their files, and letters to their clients explaining the status of the litigation and its outcome.[10]

Thus, at every stage of the process, the attorneys will write for different audiences and for different purposes. The quality of those documents will be crucial for the attorneys' success in negotiations and in court, and important to their professional relationship with their clients.

---

[9]   We discuss writing to the court in Chapters 15 and 16.

[10] We discuss status letters to clients and other types of letters in Chapter 14.

IV. THE DEVELOPMENT OF THE LAW THROUGH THE COMMON LAW PROCESS

A. Precedent and Stare Decisis

SOME CASES HAVE GREATER AUTHORITATIVE value than others because of the American system of precedent and its companion doctrine, stare decisis. That term is a shortened form of the phrase stare decisis et non quieta movere, which means "to stand by precedents and not to disturb settled points." In this country, stare decisis means that a court should follow the common law precedents. But the doctrine also means that a court must follow only those precedents that are binding authority.

Precedent becomes "binding authority" on a court if the precedent case was decided by that court or a higher court in the same jurisdiction. If precedents on a particular point of law exist, those precedents constrain a judge to decide a pending case according to the rules laid down by the earlier decisions or to repudiate the decisions. Cases decided by courts that do not bind the court in which a dispute is litigated, such as a court of another state, are "persuasive authority" only. When an authority is persuasive, the court deciding a dispute may take into account the decision in the precedent case, but it need not follow that decision.

When you search for case authorities to help you answer the issue before you, you will search first for precedents that are binding on the court where the dispute will be decided because these cases provide the constraints within which you must analyze the problem. If the issue has never been litigated in the jurisdiction of the dispute (sometimes called a "case of first impression"), you should familiarize yourself with how courts in other jurisdictions have analyzed the problem. Those precedents, even though not binding on the court, may nevertheless persuade the court to decide your case in a particular way.

Even if there is relevant case law in the jurisdiction in which your dispute will be litigated, you may still want to familiarize yourself with case law in other jurisdictions. This is especially so if those cases are factually similar, well-reasoned, or particularly influential decisions.

B. Binding and Persuasive Authority

Because the United States is composed of many jurisdictions, including each of the states and the federal court system, it is important to determine which precedents a court in each jurisdiction must follow besides its own prior decisions.

1.   State Courts

A state court must follow precedents from the higher courts in the state in matters of state law. For example, states have their own law on gun control, torts, and marriage and divorce. Thus, a trial court must follow those precedents of the state's highest court. If the state court system includes a tier of intermediate appellate courts, as most state systems now do, the trial court must also follow the precedents of the intermediate courts of that state. Depending upon the rules of procedure of the particular state, the trial court may be bound only by the intermediate court that has the authority to review its decisions, or it may be bound by the decisions of any of that state's intermediate courts of appeals that are not in conflict with the court that reviews its decisions.

An intermediate appellate court also must follow the decisions of the state's highest court, but it is not bound by the decisions of the other intermediate courts because those courts are not superior to it, although these decisions usually will be very persuasive.

In addition, a state court is bound by the statutes of that state, as interpreted by its courts. Like case law, the statutes of one state do not bind the decisions of the courts in another state. If another state has a statute that is the same as, or has language similar to, the statute that controls your case, the interpretations given to that statute by the courts of the other state may be persuasive to the court of your state. However they are not binding on it. If your case is not governed by either a statute or a judicial precedent from your jurisdiction, then look to precedents in other states, even though those precedents are persuasive only.

2.   Federal Courts

The decisions of the Supreme Court of the United States are binding on all courts in all jurisdictions for matters of constitutional and other federal law. The decisions of the courts of appeals do not bind each other, even in cases in which the appellate court has interpreted a federal statute. For matters of federal law a court of appeals is bound only by its own decisions and those of the Supreme Court. A federal district court (the trial court) is bound by its own decisions, the decisions of the court of appeals of the circuit in which the district court is located, and the decisions of the Supreme Court. The district court is not bound by the decisions of any other district court, nor by the decisions of other federal courts of appeals.

The federal and state systems intertwine at certain points. Questions of state law, either common law or statutory, often come to the federal courts in lawsuits between parties from different states, known as "diversity suits." In diversity suits, the federal court must apply state law and thus follow the state courts' decisions on state substantive law questions. A detailed discussion of problems related to federalism, that is, the relationship between state courts and federal courts and state law and federal law, is beyond the scope of this introductory explanation.

3.   The Binding Nature of a Statute

The statute and the case law interpreting its language are binding. The binding nature of a statute is somewhat different from that of a case because the entire statute is binding authority, and all the statutory requirements must be satisfied. As indicated earlier, there may be case law interpreting the statute that tells you how to interpret the statutory language. For example, the statute may contain internal contradictions that a court may have reconciled, or a court may have decided that the legislature meant an "or" instead of an "and" in part of the statute. These interpretations affect the manner in which the statutory language is binding.

4.   Holding and Dicta

A judge may decide to be bound by a precedent and to reach the same outcome in a case before the court when the causes of action are the same, the issues presented to the court for decision are the same, and the material facts are similar enough so that the reasoning of the earlier case applies. Even if there is such a similar case from a court that is binding on the judge's decision, that judge is bound only by the holding of the previous decision. This is another limitation on the binding force of precedents in addition to the limitation that arises from a judge's ability to overrule an earlier decision.

a.   The Holding of a Case Generally

The holding of a case is the court's decision on the issue or issues litigated. The holding has been defined as the judgment plus the material facts of the case.[11] Several other definitions of the holding exist. But whichever definition is used, the holding of a case must include the court's decision as to the question that was actually before it. That decision is based on the important facts of the litigated case and the reasons that the court gave for deciding the issue as it did based on those facts.

Thus, the holding is different from general rules of law and from definitions. If a court in a contracts case says "a contract

---

[11]   *See* Glanville Williams, *Learning the Law* 72 (8th ed. 1969).

requires an offer and an acceptance," that is a rule that has come
from many years of contract litigation, but it is not necessarily a
statement of the decision in the particular contract case before the
court. In deciding a case, a court identifies the particular rule that
controls the issue being litigated.[12] Then it analyzes whether the
facts of the case satisfy the requirements of the rule.

Rules come from many places. In addition to rules like the
contracts rule just mentioned that comes from common law
adjudication, rules may come from enacted law like statutes and
administrative agency regulations. Rules also come from private
documents like contracts, deeds, and leases.

For example, a particular contracts case may require the court
to decide the issue of whether the defendant offered to sell goods
to the other party. If the defendant did, and the other party
accepted, then the general contracts rule of offer and acceptance
requires the court to decide that the parties had entered into a
contract. The court may also define some of its terms. If the court
says, "an offer must manifest definite terms," the court is defining
an offer, one in keeping with a long line of litigation, but is not
giving its holding. The holding might be "the defendant's letter
describing his goods and saying, 'I am considering asking 23¢ a
pound,' was not an offer." This statement decides the question
before the court in terms of the facts of the case. A holding that
includes reasons would add, "because the defendant did not convey
a fixed purpose and definite terms." The court is deciding that
those facts did not fulfill the definition of an offer.

b. The Importance of Facts

Parties rarely agree to any one formulation of a holding of a case.
Indeed, there is no one correct way to formulate a holding. One
source of difficulty is to determine which facts are essential to the
decision. For example, in a false imprisonment case, the plaintiff
may have been kept in a corner of a room by a black and white
bulldog that growled. Your statement of the holding would not
include the dog's color because these facts would not have been
necessary to the decision that the plaintiff was imprisoned. The
breed of the dog may have been important, however, if its ferocity
led the plaintiff to believe that the dog would bite if he moved out
of the corner.

Another source of difficulty is how to describe the facts, that
is, whether to describe them narrowly as they were in the case or
to describe them more broadly. For example, a broader descriptive

---

[12] Sometimes the court first will have to decide what rule is the appropriate one to
apply to the case.

category for the growling bulldog is as a dog, or broader still as a noisy household pet. These terms are broader because they include more types of animals and behavior than do the more narrow categories "dog" and "growled." When you describe the facts too broadly, however, your description will include facts that may raise considerations that are different from those that the court took into account when it made its decision. For example, the description "household pet" includes a rabbit. And although a rabbit may cause fear in a person who hates rodents, the issue of whether that person's fear is reasonable raises questions about phobia that are different from considerations about a dog's ferocity.

Frequently, common sense will take you a long way in deciding how to determine a holding. Common sense will tell you that the fact that the defendant's dog was black and white should not be important to the decision in the false imprisonment example, but that the breed of dog could be important because of its size or ferocity. Common sense will also tell you that "household pet" is probably too broad a description for false imprisonment purposes because the term includes white rabbits and goldfish.

c.   *Formulating the Holding*

If you are recording the holding for objective purposes, such as in a case brief for class (see Chapter 2) or just to describe a case, then you may want to use more specific facts rather than broad categories. Often, however, you will describe a holding more generally. When you want to persuade a court that it is bound in a particular way by a precedent's holding, you may need to describe the facts more generally in order for them to encompass your client's situation. Courts have a good deal of freedom to decide what a precedent stands for, that is, what its holding was, and an important skill of the attorneys appearing before those courts is to formulate a holding in a way that is favorable to the client's case.

Sometimes the court itself will announce its holding. You should not always accept that court's formulation, however. Make sure that the judge has not stated the holding too broadly or too narrowly and that the principle the judge has articulated was actually required for the resolution of that case. For example, if the court deciding the hypothetical false imprisonment problem had written, "We therefore hold that the defendant's dog's growling at the plaintiff was sufficient to constitute false imprisonment," that court would have stated its holding too broadly. A literal application of this statement of the holding would permit liability if a person's dog growled at someone on the street. The statement must be read in conjunction with the facts of the case that the plaintiff was kept immobilized in the corner of a room.

d. Dicta

There are many statements in a judicial decision that are not part of the holding and are not binding on later courts. These statements are called dicta. For example, the statement "but if the defendant's cat had trapped the plaintiff in the corner of the room, the defendant would not be liable," would not be part of the holding of the false imprisonment case we have hypothesized. This is because the plaintiff was not trapped by a cat, and so that is not a material fact of the case. The court was merely illustrating the extent of its decision. Therefore, dicta about a cat in an earlier case concerning a dog would not bind a judge who had to decide a later case in which a defendant's hissing cat had kept a plaintiff in a corner of a room.

Statements that are dicta are not always unimportant, however. Sometimes the dicta in a case become more important in later years than the holding of the case. Dicta is analogous to persuasive authority in that the statements may be persuasive to a later judge, but the judge is not bound to follow them. If the court later had to decide a false imprisonment case involving a cat, the court's dictum in the earlier case would be important to the later court's decision.

When you write about judicial decisions, you will have to describe the action that the court took by saying that the court said something, or held something, or found something. Be careful to use the correct verb. It would be incorrect to say "the trial court held that the defendant's car was traveling at ninety miles per hour" if this sentence states a finding of fact by a court. In that case, the sentence should be written, "the trial court found that the defendant's car was traveling at ninety miles per hour." A sentence correctly describing the holding of this case might be written, "the court held that the defendant was guilty of reckless driving for driving ninety miles per hour in a forty-mile-per-hour zone."

To describe a court's dicta, you could use a verb such as "said," or "stated," or "explained." For example, the hypothetical dicta used in the false imprisonment example, "but if the defendant's cat had trapped the plaintiff in the corner of the room, the defendant would not be liable," should not be preceded by the inaccurate statement "the court held," but by a statement such as "the court said," or "the court hypothesized," or "the court limited its decision."

Read the case decision below. Then choose the best statement of the holding from the five choices.

In re Gaunt

Silver, J. John Gaunt was having coffee with his nephew Felix. John told Felix that he was giving him a gift of his gold watch, which he kept in a safe deposit box in his bank. He said he would get the watch for Felix the next time he went to the bank. John died that night, without going to the bank. Felix has demanded the watch be delivered over to him as his gift. The administrator of John's estate is keeping the watch as part of John's estate.

Felix's demand must be refused. A completed gift requires first that the donor intend to give the gift, second, delivery of the item of gift, and third, acceptance by the donee. Only then does the intended donee have title to the item. John probably did intend that Felix have the watch. The watch had been John's grandfather's and Felix is the next male heir in that family. We can assume that Felix would have accepted the watch. Sentiment aside, it is a valuable piece of jewelry. John, however, never delivered the watch to Felix, and Felix never had possession of the watch. If he had given him the key to the safe deposit box, that may have been a constructive delivery, effective to create a gift. As it is, without delivery, John made only an unenforceable promise. A court will not enforce an uncompleted gift.

Which is the best statement of the holding in *In re Gaunt*?

1. The court held that delivery of a key to a safe deposit box is a delivery of the item kept in the box because it is a constructive delivery.

2. The court held that there are three requirements for a valid gift: intent to give, delivery, and acceptance.

3. The court held that a decedent's jewelry remains part of his estate at death if he has not given it away during his life.

4. The court held that a decedent had not made an effective gift of personal property during his life where he made an oral promise of the gift, but had not delivered possession of the item to the intended donee (the person receiving the gift).

5. A court will not enforce an incomplete promise of a gift.

Sentence four is the best statement of the holding.

1. Sentence 1 is a statement of dicta in *In re Gaunt*. John did not give the safe deposit key to Felix. The court used

---

> that fact as a hypothetical of what may have been a delivery for purposes of satisfying the requirements of a gift.
>
> 2. Sentence 2 is the general rule of the three requirements for a gift that had been formulated before this case was litigated. Not all three were disputed in this case.
>
> 3. Sentence 3 sounds as if it could be the holding, but it is really a general rule of property law that tells the result of the decision in this case.
>
> 4. Sentence 4 is the holding that decides the question in this case of whether John Gaunt had given away the property during his lifetime if he had not delivered the watch to his nephew. If he had not, then John still owned the watch and the result described in Sentence Three occurs.
>
> 5. Sentence 5 is a reason for the decision in the case.
>
> The holding could be made broader or narrower by describing the intended item of gift differently. The gift could be described as
>
> 1. property (which includes real and personal property)
>
> 2. jewelry
>
> 3. a gold watch
>
> 4. a family heirloom
>
> Which of these items is the broadest? Which is the most specific? Could you describe the parties involved as an uncle and nephew instead of a decedent and a donee?

5. Writing About Legal Authority

a. *Weight of Authority*

Because the common law and statutes of a jurisdiction are binding on future litigation within that jurisdiction, when you write an analysis of a legal problem you should always first identify and explain the binding law on the issue of the problem. Begin first with relevant statutes, if there are any, and the cases that interpret the statutes. Explain relevant case law first from the highest court of the jurisdiction and then other reported decisions from that jurisdiction's lower courts.

If there is controlling law from the jurisdiction of the problem, you should not begin by writing about the law in other jurisdictions or with explanations from other sources such as legal encyclopedias or a law dictionary.

Read the two examples below, which are introductory sentences to a discussion about a false imprisonment problem in the state of Kent. What is the difference between them? Which is the better way to begin the discussion? The italicized words are the names of the cases from which the quotes were taken. All are cases from the state of Kent.

---

1.   In most states, the definition of false imprisonment requires that the defendant intend to confine the plaintiff within boundaries set by the defendant. Some other jurisdictions also require that the plaintiff be aware of the confinement.

     The definition of false imprisonment in Kent is "the intentional unlawful restraint of another against that person's will." *Jones v. Smith.*

2.   In Kent, false imprisonment is "the intentional unlawful restraint of an individual's personal liberty or freedom of locomotion against that person's will." *Orange v. Brass.* A person need not use force to effect false imprisonment, but may restrain by words alone. *Arnold v. Rocky.* "Against that person's will" requires that the person be aware of the confinement. *Jones v. Smith.*

Example 1 incorrectly begins with the law of other states. Example 2 correctly begins by setting out the law of the jurisdiction of the problem.

b.   Evaluating Case Law

Besides the judgments involved in determining the holding and the dicta of a case, and therefore which part of that case is binding, you must make other judgments in using precedents. For example, where there are many relevant cases, you will have to decide which are most important to your problem and will have the most weight with the court deciding your own case. Several factors can determine the weight of an authority.

- If there is no binding authority, the decisions of the courts within the jurisdiction, even if not binding (such as decisions of another court of appeals), are important.

- The level of the court that decided the previous case is important. A case decided by a state's Supreme Court is more authoritative than one decided by a lower state court.

- An opinion written by a particular judge may be important because of the excellent reputation of the judge. In addition, decisions from a particular court in a particular era may carry extra weight because of the membership of the court during those years. Exemplary are the New York Court of Appeals (the highest court in New York) during the time when Benjamin Cardozo was a member of the court, and the California Supreme Court during the service of Justice Roger Traynor.

- A case decided by a unanimous court or a nearly unanimous court may be more persuasive as a precedent than one in which the court was closely divided. And statements from concurring or dissenting opinions will usually not carry as much weight as statements from majority decisions, although exceptions exist.

- The year of the decision is important. If a case is old and the decision reflects policies or social conditions that are no longer as important as they once were, then the precedent will have little weight even if the facts of the case are very similar to your problem. If, however, the decision is based on reasoning that is still valid, the age of the case may not be important.

- Decisions from states that are geographically close and that have similar social or economic conditions that relate to the litigation may be favored by some courts. In addition, a decision that interprets a statute may be persuasive to another court in a case that involves a similar statute.

- A case in which the issue received the full attention of the previous court and was fully and articulately discussed will be more important than one in which the question received cursory attention. And well-reasoned decisions with careful explanations will probably already have achieved deserved respect in the field.

As to the weight of authority of cases from all jurisdictions, the similarity of the facts between the precedent and your problem is important. The more similar the specific facts between the cases, the greater weight the precedent will have for your own problem.

C. Stare Decisis and Overruling Decisions

Although stare decisis implies that following precedent within a particular jurisdiction is mandatory, the doctrine as applied in the United States does not produce rigid adherence to prior decisions. Instead, a court has freedom to overrule its previous decisions and thus decide a case by a rule different from the one it had previously adopted.[13]

One reason that a court may overrule a case is that the earlier decision has become outdated because of changed conditions. Other reasons are that the existing rule has produced undesirable results, or that the prior decision was based on what is now recognized as poor reasoning. Sometimes a changed interpretation reflects a difference in the views of the present judges on the court as compared with those of the previous court.

When a court overrules a previous case, that change in the law has no effect on the parties to the litigation that produced the prior decision, or on other parties whose rights have been determined under that precedent. Those results became final at the time of the last decision in those cases. Indeed, sometimes the change in the law will not affect the parties in the very case in which the court overrules the earlier decision. This result occurs when the court makes the new rule prospective, that is, applicable in future cases only.

Another means of overruling a judicial decision is by legislation. The legislature may change by statute a rule that came from a particular decision or a common law rule of long standing. This change in the law binds the courts within that jurisdiction.

A more literal interpretation of stare decisis would lead to a more rigid system of law than now exists in this country, or would require frequent appeal to legislative bodies to correct by statute undesirable or outdated judicial decisions.

Exercise 1-A

Read the following decision in the case Sosa v. Lowery.

Singer, J.

The plaintiff John Sosa rented an apartment from Tim Lowery. Lowery required a security deposit of one month's rent. The lease provides that Lowery must return the security deposit within 30 days

---

[13] A court will not overrule the decision of a higher court, although cases exist in which a lower court did not follow a rule from a controlling higher court because that rule was very old and out-of-date. If a judge of a lower court were to refuse to follow the decision of a higher court, that judge's decision would no doubt be appealed.

of the expiration of the lease, but could deduct for damage to the property beyond reasonable wear. Lowery deducted $400 from Sosa's deposit to replace the living room carpet, which, during Sosa's tenancy, suffered several cigarette burns. Sosa claims that the burns are the result of reasonable wear. We disagree. Cigarette burns result from a careless act rather than from accumulated use. Frayed spots from walking on the rug would be reasonable wear. Lowery properly deducted the $400.

1. What is the rule for when a landlord may deduct from the tenant's security deposit? Where does this rule come from?

2. The court used this rule to decide the question before it, that is, to reach its holding. What is the court's holding regarding Sosa's deposit?

3. What is the court's dicta about what type of use might be reasonable wear of the carpet?

Exercise 1-B

Miller v. Adam

Stevens, J.

Jane Miller, a college student, has sued Adam, the owner of a campus restaurant, for false imprisonment. Adam believed that Miller was leaving without paying her bill. Miller in fact had left the money on her table. Adam told Miller that she could not leave until someone verified that she had paid. Adam took Miller's pocketbook in which Miller had her keys, money, credit cards, and phone. The restaurant was very busy and understaffed. Miller stayed with Adam for twenty minutes until Adam found an employee to see if Miller had left the money on the table.

Although Adam never physically prevented Miller from leaving, and Miller could have walked out of the restaurant at any time, Adam is liable to Miller for falsely imprisoning her. A person falsely imprisons another by unlawfully confining her within fixed boundaries if he acts intending to do so. Adam confined Miller in the restaurant by telling her she could not leave and by taking her pocketbook. Confinement may be effected by duress, even duress that is not the product of threatening behavior. Miller could not leave the restaurant because she believed that she could have lost her pocketbook with its valuable contents if she did so. Thus, she was unlawfully confined. She acted reasonably by remaining in the restaurant until she recovered her possessions.

Which is the broadest formulation of the holding? The most narrow?

1. *The defendant falsely imprisoned the plaintiff by duress when he took an item from the plaintiff in order to have her remain on the premises.*

> 2. *The owner of a restaurant unlawfully confined his customer when he told her she could not leave and took her pocketbook and its valuable contents away for twenty minutes until he could verify her payment of her bill.*
>
> 3. *The defendant falsely imprisoned the plaintiff by means of duress although he did not use physical force when he took an item of value belonging to plaintiff in order to have her remain on the premises.*

V. STATUTES AND THE RELATIONSHIP BETWEEN CASE LAW AND STATUTES

A. Statutory Enactments

ALTHOUGH THIS INTRODUCTION HAS FOCUSED ON case law, remember that enacted law, especially statutory law, forms an ever greater part of the body of legal authority in our country. In fact, enacted law should be the first source in which you research a legal problem.

Statutes are enacted by legislative bodies that are constitutionally empowered to exercise the legislative function within a jurisdiction. The federal legislative body is the United States Congress. Each state has its own legislature and also has municipal and, perhaps, county forms of legislatures. In addition, state and federal administrative bodies may have limited legislative functions in that they are empowered to enact regulations concerning the subject matter of their administration. These regulations provide another form of enforceable law.

Enacted law, like case law, falls along a vertical hierarchy. At the top of that hierarchy is the Constitution of the United States. Next are both federal statutes and treaties. Federal statutes, when enacted within the powers conferred by the Constitution, take precedence over statutes of other jurisdictions. Then come federal executive orders and administrative regulations, state constitutions (a constitution, however, is the highest authority within a state as long as it does not conflict with federal law), state statutes, state administrative regulations, and municipal enactments.

A jurisdiction's constitution and its statutes are the highest authority within that jurisdiction, and the courts are bound by them. A legislature may change the common law by passing legislation that changes the common law rule. That change then supersedes the old rule. A court cannot in turn overrule that legislative enactment and say it will not follow it (although it can invalidate it on the ground of unconstitutionality). The legislature may also create new causes of action that were not available in the common law but which result from the legislation, such as worker's compensation laws and employment discrimination laws. A legislature may also enact a common law rule into statute; for example, many criminal statutes have codified what were previously common law crimes. Then the case law interpreting that common law rule may still be valid.

Because a jurisdiction's constitution is more authoritative than its statutes, the legislature may act only within its constitutional powers. Although a court cannot overrule legislation, that is, it cannot decide it will not follow the law imposed by the particular statute, a court may review a statute's validity. Legislation may be challenged in court on the ground that the legislature exceeded its constitutional powers. A reviewing court may then decide a statute is unconstitutional and is invalid.

Courts are constantly deciding statutory issues because statutes must be enforced and frequently must be enforced by litigation. A person's challenge to the constitutionality of a statute, for example, will usually arise during litigation in which the government attempts to enforce the statute against that person.

B. Statutory Interpretation

More often, however, a court must decide not the validity of the statute, but how to apply the statute. As a necessary step in this litigation, the court may have to interpret the meaning of the statutory language in order to apply and enforce it in a specific situation. Cases that interpret and apply statutes are case law and become precedents in that jurisdiction. But they are not common law because the legal rule that is being enforced originates with the legislature. Common law rules originate with courts.

By its nature, legislation is cast in general terms, that is, in broad categories, because it is law written to affect future conduct, rather than law written to decide a specific case. General legislative language must then be applied to individuals and to the particular controversy being litigated. Statutory language may also be vague; for example, businesses cannot act in "unreasonable restraint of trade." Thus, a good portion of a court's work is deciding questions that involve the interpretation of statutes. The legislature could still have the last word, however. If it does not agree with the court's statutory interpretation, it can amend the statute. In reality, however, a legislature rarely gives attention to the course of judicial interpretation of a statute, and even more rarely reacts to judicial interpretation by amending the statute.

(An exception is the United States Congress when it disagrees with the Supreme Court's interpretation of a federal statute.)

When you are writing about a problem that is controlled by a statute of that jurisdiction, always include the exact statutory terms at issue and an explanation of those terms. The explanation usually should be at the beginning of your written analysis. Do not start writing about the problem as if the reader knows the statute's terms unless you have been instructed to do so.

Exercise 1-C

What is the difference between the two examples below? Which is the better introduction to a discussion of a statute?

1. *Under Kent criminal law § 10(a), a person is guilty of burglary in the third degree if he "knowingly and unlawfully either enters or remains in a building, with the intent to commit a crime."*

2. *Smith is guilty of a burglary in the third degree because he fulfills all of the elements of the crime*

VI. CITATION

ONE CONSEQUENCE OF RELYING ON legal authorities in your written work is that you will have to provide citations to those authorities. In legal writing, you use citations for many purposes:

- to demonstrate that your assertions are supported by other authority

- to supply the bibliographic information a reader needs if she wants to look up that source herself, and

- to attribute borrowed words or ideas to their sources, thus avoiding plagiarism.

A. Citations to Provide Authority and Bibliography

Citation is important to all types of writing, but you probably will use more citations in your legal writing than you are accustomed to using. Because of the doctrine of precedent, lawyers analyzing a common law action constantly rely on case law to prove that the legal theory offered as the governing rule of law is valid and has been applied in similar situations. In a statutory action, lawyers quote or refer to and thus cite the statute that supplies the governing rule of law. They also use cases to help interpret what the statute means. Thus, a legal argument requires identifying the sources of the governing principles of law as well as analyzing what they mean. The writer must cite to those sources each time they are mentioned or relied upon. Lawyers also use secondary authority, such as books and periodical articles, as support for their legal analysis. These sources also must be cited.

Legal citations tell the reader many things A citation to a case tells the reader that there is legal authority for the previous statement and where the reader can find that authority. The presence of a citation tells the reader that the preceding text is based upon information from another source and is not original with the writer. A citation provides information that helps the reader evaluate the weight of the precedent. For example, the citation tells which court decided the case.

Most law schools and lawyers use a specialized citation form found either from *A Uniform System of Citation,* known as the *Bluebook,* or from the *ALWD Citation Manual.* Some lawyers adhere strictly to the citation rules; others make changes to suit their own practices or to comply with the rules of a particular court or agency.

Besides learning correct citation form, you should also become familiar with certain conventions of legal citation. In legal memoranda and briefs, which are typical law school writing assignments, you will put citations in the text right after the material for which they provide authority, rather than in footnotes. You must use citations to authority for direct quotations, for text that paraphrases the authority, and for text that is based on information in the authority, although not quoting or paraphrasing from it. Notice the citations in the following paragraph.

> The law of battery in this state is adopted from the Restatement of Torts. *Gaunt v. Felix*, 659 N.W.2d 10 (N.D. 2010). A person may be liable for battery if the person directly or indirectly causes a "harmful contact" with another's person, and the person intends to cause the contact. *Id.* at 12; Restatement (Second) of Torts § 13(1)(a) (1977). Under this definition, Smith will not be liable because she did not act with the required intent.

The first citation, to the case of *Gaunt v. Felix*, supplies the authority for the statement about the state's law of battery. It tells you that the court that decided *Gaunt* is the court that adopted the Restatement definition. The second citation provides the source of the definitions. These sources are the case already cited (*Id.* means that the citation is the same as the previous one) and the Restatement (Second) of Torts.

Exercise 1-D

Where do citations belong in the following paragraphs? Why?

1. *The test for determining whether a plaintiff is entitled to attorney's fees involves four factors: whether the litigation provided a public benefit, whether the plaintiff gained financially from the litigation, whether the plaintiff had a personal interest in the materials sought, and whether the government unreasonably withheld the materials. The factors usually have equal weight. However, if the government acted particularly unreasonably, the last criterion may be most important.*

2. *The Kent statute permits an unwitnessed will. This type of will is known as a holographic will. To be valid, a holographic will must be entirely written and dated by the testator. The courts have interpreted "dated" to mean month, day, and year.*

Once you become accustomed to using legal citations, you will find that they can contribute to your legal writing style by keeping unnecessary information out of your text. For example, one common writing weakness of lawyers is to explain textually the information that is available in the citation, instead of using the citation to provide that information. Notice the differences in these three sentences.

1. In an old 1960 New Jersey case, the New Jersey Supreme Court held that an express warranty that limits an auto manufacturer's liability to replace defective parts is against public policy. *Henningsen v. Bloomfield Motors, Inc., 32 N.J. 358, 161 A.2d 69 (1960).*

2. An express warranty that limits an auto manufacturer's liability to replacement of defective parts is against public policy. *Henningsen v. Bloomfield Motors, Inc., 32 N.J. 358, 161 A.2d 69 (1960).*

3. New Jersey is the first state in which a court held that an express warranty that limits an auto manufacturer's liability to replacement of defective parts is against public policy. *Henningsen v. Bloomfield Motors, Inc., 32 N.J. 358, 161 A.2d 69 (1960).*

The writer of sentence 1 has supplied two facts in the text that are provided in the citation, that the case was decided in 1960 and that the highest court in New Jersey decided it. (If the citation does not specifically include the name of the court within the parenthesis and the court is not otherwise identifiable by the citation, the case was decided by the highest court of the state). Unless the writer had a particular reason to include those facts in the text, they are unnecessary, and the sentence is better written as in sentence 2. If the writer wanted to emphasize that the rule is a leading case one, sentence 3 provides more specific emphasis than sentence 1.

Although the examples may seem strange to you now, citation will become an important and familiar aspect of your writing about legal materials.

Exercise 1-E

1. *You are doing research for a state law problem on environmental protection. Your research uncovers some cases similar to the case you are working on, which you are appealing to the intermediate appellate court of your state. These cases are from the following:*

   a. Another intermediate appellate court of the state

   b. A diversity suit in a federal district court in the state, applying the state's law on that issue

   c. The federal court of appeals for the circuit of your state in an appeal from a district court from a diversity suit applying the law of a different state

   d. A state trial court's judgment entered in a decision that was not published but which you know about

   e. The highest court of the state

   What weight would you assign to these authorities? Evaluate how important each is as a precedent.

2. *You are litigating a New York law relating to cyberbullying in the United States District Court for the Eastern District of New York based on diversity jurisdiction. In which sources of primary law would you do your research? Why? Evaluate these in terms of efficient use of your research time.*

   a. United States Supreme Court cases

   b. Cases from the New York Court of Appeals (the highest court) and intermediate appellate courts

   c. Cases from the United States Court of Appeals for the Second Circuit (New York state is in the Second Circuit)

   d. Cases from the other three United States district courts in New York state

e.   Cyberbullying law cases from other states

3. *You are doing research for a state law problem about the liability of owners of recreational land to people who use those premises. Your client has sued a landowner for the death of his sons, aged 6 and 8, who drowned in a pond on the landowner's property. There are two questions involved, whether the land is "recreational land", and if so, whether the landowner did not fulfill his legal duties.*

How relevant are the following authorities to your analysis of this problem?

a.   A newspaper article about accidents in parks

b.   A statute of the state that limits the liability of owners of recreational land

c.   The regulations of a state agency requiring safety features on recreational land that is open to the public

d.   A brochure printed by the owner of the recreational land

e.   Case law from the state's intermediate appellate courts interpreting the statutory term "recreational land"

f.   Case law from the highest court of another state that has an almost identical statute, interpreting the term "recreational land"

g.   A case from your state's appellate court that interprets the term "recreational area" in a different statute in that same state about licensing for privately owned recreational areas

h.   The notes of the drafters of a uniform act about liability of owners of recreational areas, an act that your state has adopted

B.   Citations to Provide Attribution and Avoid Plagiarism

Citation to sources is essential in legal writing not only to show authority for your reasoning, but to avoid plagiarism. Although the Rules of Professional Conduct do not specifically forbid plagiarism, the Rules do forbid dishonest, fraudulent, or deceitful conduct.[14]

1.   Plagiarism Defined

a.   *In Law School*

Law schools define plagiarism differently, so it is important to become familiar with the one used by your school. In general, however, **plagiarism occurs when you use another's ideas or words and pass them off as your own, that is, when you do**

---

[14]   Model Rules of Professional Conduct Rule 8.4.

not cite to the source. One important difference among definitions is whether plagiarism requires the element of intentional conduct. Some schools consider plagiarism to have occurred only when done intentionally. Other schools do not require the writer to have acted intentionally; careless research and note-taking that result in the negligent failure to attribute work is enough to sustain a charge.

Although these schools punish careless attribution, inadvertent plagiarism may be met with less severe sanctions than intentional conduct. Nonetheless, you should be aware that the sanctions for plagiarism can be an oral reprimand, an F in a paper or in a course, a disciplinary letter in your file (which will go to the ethics committee of your state Bar), or any other penalty or combination of penalties deemed appropriate. You should refer to your school's code of academic conduct for precise information.

b. In Practice

When you become a lawyer in practice, you will find that attitudes toward plagiarism are different from those in an academic setting.[15] In practice, lawyers cite to cases and statutes and to other materials to add precedential value to their arguments and to help their readers to find the sources. Lawyers also provide citations for quotations. However, lawyers typically use in-house office materials without attribution. This is because law firms often consider work done by its employees as proprietary, that is, as the property of the firm, not the author. Indeed, a brief written for one client may include ideas and even verbatim material from the work for another client. Similarly, judges often use material directly from a party's brief without attribution. The attorney who wrote the brief would never accuse the judge of plagiarism, however; instead, he or she would likely feel complimented that the judge was persuaded by the brief's language and arguments. Where you are receiving academic credit for work, however, plagiarism is an unacceptable practice.

2. Causes of Plagiarism

Inadvertent plagiarism often results when you do not include citations or quotation marks in your drafts. As a result, you may forget what material comes from another source or which source you got it from. In today's electronic, internet-fueled environment, the relative speed and ease of cutting and pasting may cause you to forget to enclose the copied language in quotation marks and to

---

[15] Nonetheless, courts have reprimanded attorneys for plagiarism. *See Iowa Supreme Court Bd. of Prof. Ethics & Conduct v. Lane*, 642 N.W.2d 296 (Iowa 2002) and Matthew C. Mirow, "Plagiarism: A Workshop for Students," Lexis-Nexis.

cite the source, especially when you are up late at night, furiously trying to finish your paper. To avoid this, you can change the font or highlight the text, so that it looks different from the other text in your draft. Even then, you will save yourself the time and trouble of combing through your sources a second time if you include cites in the first draft—even if they are not in *Bluebook* or *ALWD* form.

Plagiarism is a particular danger when you paraphrase material. If you use quotation marks, even if you don't have citations, you are at least alerted to the fact you need to find and cite the source. With paraphrases, however, you may not remember you took the material from someone else. You can avoid this problem if you introduce your paraphrases by announcing where the material comes from. You can give the reader the name of the source ("In *Elliott v. Krear*, the court said"), or you can refer directly to the author ("As Professor Doe argues," or "As one commentator notes"). These references will remind you to attribute the material.

Plagiarism also occurs because writers are unclear about the difference between a paraphrase and an altered quotation. It is important to realize that changing a few words in a quotation does not turn a direct quotation into a paraphrase. The phrase is really an altered quotation and should appear within quotation marks with changes indicated with brackets or ellipses.

A related problem, inaccurate attribution, results when you use the *id.* citation in drafts because as you write, and cut and paste, your *id.* cites may no longer refer to the correct source. Do not use *id.* until your final draft. Instead, use the full citation.

3. Rules of Attribution

a. What to Cite

The basic rules of attribution require that you cite (i.e., attribute) all ideas taken from someone else and all words taken from someone else. Ideas include more than just arguments and conclusions. You also need to attribute novel methods of procedure like the list of steps in a process, as well as audio-visual media to which you have referred. You must provide citations for visual media like artwork, graphs and tables you have reproduced, and for information gathered from internet sources, listservs, email, lectures, and conversations. If you use unpublished material, you need get permission from your source.

In your undergraduate work, you did not have to attribute "common knowledge,"[16] that is, ideas not unique to an author. Common knowledge includes factual information in the public domain, information like the dates of historical events or the author of Hamlet. But in both college and law school, cites are needed for facts unknown to the writer before his or her research or for facts that may be unfamiliar to your readers. Thus, you would not have to provide a citation for the fact that there was a terrorist bombing of the World Trade Center on 9/11. You would have to provide a citation, however, for the number of lives lost or for the security procedures in place at the airports on that date.

There is an important difference between general common knowledge and legal "common knowledge," however. Law school practice requires citation for legal "common knowledge" as well as for unique ideas or language. For example, it is commonly known that a contract requires an offer and an acceptance, but were you to write that statement in a legal memorandum, you would cite one or more authorities. This is not really a matter of plagiarism, however, but of providing legal support for your proposition of law. Your writing professor will not likely report you to the school for violation of an honor code for failure to cite. The professor will probably note that the statement needs a citation to show its acceptability as a general rule of law.

b. How to Cite

- **When you borrow someone's language**, whether the source is print or electronic, published or unpublished, you must provide a citation.[17] But citations alone are insufficient. You must also use quotation marks for borrowed language of less than fifty words and block quotes for quotations of fifty words or more.

- **When you paraphrase an idea**, you should make it clear where the borrowed material begins and provide a citation.

- **When a phrase is really an altered quotation**, it should appear within quotation marks with changes indicated with brackets or ellipses. Use brackets to indicate the addition of a letter, a change in case, and an insertion or editorial comment. Use an ellipsis when omitting one or more words in a quotation.

---

[16]   *See, e.g.,* MLA Handbook for Writers of Research Papers § 1.8 at 33 (1999).

[17]   If you copy someone's string cite or parenthetical description of authority, you must also provide a citation.

Although you do not use an ellipsis at the beginning of a quotation, you need to indicate elided material in the middle of a quotation or at the end of a sentence. You also need a citation.

> **Example:** Exhibits A through E show that a number of tenants were "bitterly opposed to the way in which they perceived the agent[s] managed their buildings. . . ." *Cite.*

> **Example:** Exhibits A through E show that a number of tenants were "bitterly opposed to the way in which they perceived the agents[s] managed their buildings. . . and [the tenants] intended to explore available legal remedies for redress." *Cite.*

As noted above, changing a word or two in a direct quotation is not a paraphrase but an altered quotation. If you wish to paraphrase a source, make sure you change its language and organization significantly. Examine the sample that follows and ask yourself whether it uses its source correctly.

> **Source: *Kirk v. Wood*, ___ N.E. 2d 1062, 1065 (Mass. App. Ct. (20__)**
>
> These cases demonstrate that previous courts decided provocation by looking at the incident from the perspective of the animal. The cases tend to focus on how an average dog, neither unusually aggressive nor unusually docile, would react to an alleged act of provocation.

> **Student Paper**
>
> To determine provocation, prior cases considered the perspective of the animal. Courts focused on how an average dog would react to an alleged act of provocation.

The first sentence in the student paper changes a lot of the language and is, therefore, a legitimate paraphrase, although the phrase "perspective of the animal" should be in quotation marks and cited because it is the court's standard. The language in the second sentence is identical and the sentence should be written as an altered quotation, using quotation marks and an ellipsis.

> **Rewrite:** Courts "focus on how an average dog. . . would react to an alleged act of provocation." *Cite.*

- **You need not turn your writing into a bibliography, however.** If a book or an article leads you to cases and statutes and you yourself read those materials and discuss their facts or language in your written work, cite to the cases and statutes. You do not also have to cite the source that led you to the cases and statutes, even if that source describes their facts and language.

- **You do cite the source for any of its ideas or theories that you use.**[18]

See Appendix A for additional information on the mechanics of quotation.

---

[18] In more advanced writing, you should cite the source that has led you to other sources if the first source uses the other source in an unusual way and you use the other source in the same way. That type of citation is usually not necessary in memoranda and briefs, but may be.

CHAPTER 2

ANALYZING LEGAL AUTHORITY: CASE LAW

I. INTRODUCTION TO READING CASES

IN YOUR FIRST YEAR OF LAW SCHOOL, you will be analyzing cases in two contexts. First, you will be reading judicial opinions in casebooks for your doctrinal classes, and second, you will be reading cases in reporters[1] for your legal writing classes. Decisions in casebooks and decisions in reporters look different. Opinions in casebooks are edited and omit research tools that publishers insert and arguments irrelevant to the author's purpose for including the case. In addition, the purpose of reading cases in a doctrinal class differs from the purpose of reading cases in legal writing classes—and indeed in legal practice.

A. Case Reading for Doctrinal Courses

One purpose in reading an opinion in a casebook is to understand that particular case in the event your teacher asks you about it in class. There are other equally important purposes:

- to understand the prevailing principles and exceptions in that area of law,

- to see how those principles evolved over time,

- to identify the conflicts in that area of law and the reasons and policies important to the courts' resolutions, and

- to apply the decision in that case to hypothetical facts.

Thus reading in a doctrinal class requires you to put the case in context. You can begin to do this by examining the casebook's table of contents to determine the topic and subtopic under which the case falls and the relation of that case to others in the section. It is useful to read the background information at the beginning of the section since it may provide an overview of the legal, historical, social, and political context of the cases. Equally helpful are the 'Notes and Questions' at the end of each section. These alert you to some of the issues and conflicts in that area that have led to

---

[1] Judicial opinions are collected and published in volumes called reporters. They are also found online. We refer to both as reporters.

different resolutions or evolving trends. They also supply suggestions for added reading that may flesh out that area of law.

B. Case Reading for Legal Writing Classes and Legal Practice

Your purpose in reading cases in practice and in legal writing classes is somewhat different from reading cases in your other classes. Here, you read to see what impact a case will have on your client or on a hypothetical fact pattern in legal writing classes. As in a doctrinal class, you need to understand the case, but your primary interest is in predicting what effect that case might have on your client. Reading with this specific goal is both easier and harder than casebook reading. It is easier because you focus on cases within a particular jurisdiction. There is a good chance that there is more consistency in the rules and standards within that jurisdiction than in opinions in a casebook, which span jurisdictions.[2] On the other hand, it is harder because the cases in reporters are unedited and may include several issues, some of which may be irrelevant to your problem. Thus you must learn to read selectively, focusing only on the issues in a case that bear on your problem.

II. READING STRATEGIES

FOR A BEGINNER, READING LAW IS HARD. The cases may contain legal terms that are foreign to you and they may have an unfathomable structure. Moreover, because you are not familiar with the subject matter, you may have difficulty in recognizing and separating complicated procedural issues from complicated substantive law issues, or main points from minor arguments, or holding from dicta. Thus try to develop reading strategies that will help you navigate the text.

A. The Structure of a Case in a Reporter

You will be able to understand a case more readily if you understand its structure and organization.

- The first thing you read is the **caption**. The caption gives you the name of the case (meaning the parties), the court, and the date of the decision.

- After this comes a **synopsis** of the case. The synopsis is written by the publisher, and because it is not part of the opinion proper, it should never be quoted or

---

[2]   For more on the differences between reading casebooks and cases in reporters, and for an extended discussion of reading strategies, see Ruth Ann McKinney, *Reading like a Lawyer* (2005).

cited as authority. Use it instead as a research tool that may help you decide if the case is relevant to the issue you are researching.

- Following the synopsis comes another research tool publishers like West insert, namely, the **headnotes**. Each West headnote is categorized by topic indicated by a name and number (e.g., negligence 272) and subtopic indicated by a key number (e.g., 1024 preceded by a key sign). The headnote then summarizes a legal issue in a few sentences. Experienced lawyers skim the headnotes to decide if the case is on point and then may use the Westlaw key numbers digest system to find more cases on point. In the West research system, each topic and key number will lead you to other cases on that particular topic of law.

- Below the headnotes are the names of the **attorneys** of record.

- This is followed by the name of the **judge** who wrote the decision.

- The **opinion** itself begins after the judge's name.

Although the structure of opinions differs, most decisions have a basic pattern.

- They begin with an **introductory paragraph** that articulates the issues and the court's disposition of the case.

- This paragraph is usually followed by the **fact statement**, which includes the facts that created the dispute, as well as the procedural history of the case and the decisions of the lower courts.

- Only after the facts does the court begin its **analysis**.

The analysis often begins with a summary of each party's arguments, although sometimes only the losing party's arguments are given, as well as the court's reasons for rejecting them. At other times, however, the analysis begins with an introduction to the issues and then proceeds to analyze the issues one by one. The court usually begins with the relevant legal rule or rules and follows with its rationale. The rationale may include discussion and application of relevant legal authority as well as policy arguments. Among the policy arguments that a court might raise to bolster its decision are the following:

- Social goal arguments, which ask whether a rule advances or undermines moral principles, social goals, or justice.

- Economic arguments, which are concerned with the efficient allocation of resources.

- Institutional competence arguments, which examine the proper role of government branches.

- Judicial administration arguments, which assess the practicality or impracticality of a rule.

(For more on policy arguments, see Chapter 11, Part IV.)

You should also attempt to discern those parts of the analysis that are dicta, that is, statements about issues tangential to the case before the court and unnecessary to its decision. Although dicta is not binding, you may want to use it as persuasive authority. It provides guidance as to what future courts may hold.

What follows is an annotated, abridged opinion, reproduced from its online publication. The material in the right margin outlines its parts, structure, and types of arguments. The issue is whether a **bystander may recover for negligent infliction of emotional distress when the bystander is outside the zone of danger of being struck by the negligent force.**

486 Pa. 146, 404 A.2d 672	**Case citations in state and regional reporters**
Supreme Court of Pennsylvania. Robert G. SINN and JoAnne Marie Sinn, Administrators of the Estate of Lisa Anne Sinn, Deceased, Deborah Frances Sinn, a Minor, by Robert G. Sinn, Her Natural Guardian, and JoAnne Marie Sinn	
v.	**Caption— identifies the parties, court deciding case, and date of decision**
Brad Lee BURD.	
Appeal of JoAnne Marie SINN.	
July 11, 1979.	
Reargument Denied Aug. 22, 1979.	
Action was brought against driver of automobile, which struck and killed child, to recover under wrongful death and survival acts, to recover for psychological damages sustained by child's sister and to recover for damages sustained by child's mother due to emotional stress arising from fact that, while she was outside zone of danger of any physical injury to herself, she observed the child	**Synopsis— publisher's case summary. Not part of opinion. Do not quote.**

being struck and killed. The Court of Common Pleas, Civil Division, . . . sustained demurrer to count seeking to recover damages sustained due to mother's emotional stress, and appeal was taken. The Superior Court, . . . held that: (1) recovery of damages for negligently caused mental trauma suffered by bystander is not to be precluded merely on basis of fact that he was outside zone of danger of being struck by the negligent force, and (2) the count in question stated cause of action on which relief could be granted, in light of fact that such emotional distress on part of mother was a reasonably foreseeable injury.

Order reversed, and case remanded.

West Headnotes

[1] Pleading 302 ◌⌐214(4)

302 Pleading

 302V Demurrer or Exception

  302k214 Admissions by Demurrer

  302k214(4)(k). Inferences and Conclusions of Fact. Most Cited Cases

302 Pleading

 302V Demurrer or Exception

  302k214 Admissions by Demurrer

   302k214(5)(k). Conclusions of Law and Construction of Written Instruments. Most Cited Cases

Conclusions of law and unjustified inferences are not admitted by preliminary objection in the nature of demurrer. (Per Nix, J., with one Justice concurring, one Justice specially concurring and one Justice concurring in result.)

[2] Pleading 302 ◌⌐193(5)

302 Pleading

 302V Demurrer or Exception

  302k193 Grounds for Demurrer to Declaration,

Complaint, Petition, or Statement

302k193(5)(k). Insufficiency of Facts to Constitute Cause of Action. Most Cited Cases

> Headnotes— published by West, used in legal research. Never quote.

(other headnotes omitted)

**673 *148 Jack A. Wintner, Carson & Wintner, McKeesport, for appellant.

Mark K. McNally, Pittsburgh, for appellee

NIX, Justice.

At issue in this appeal is the vexing and complex question of when a plaintiff should be allowed to recover damages for negligently caused mental trauma. The specific question presented for our review is whether the trial court properly sustained appellee's demurrer to the fourth count of appellant's complaint in which she sought to recover damages for physical and mental injuries incurred when she saw her minor daughter struck and killed by an automobile, although the plaintiff herself was not within any zone of personal physical danger and had no reason to fear for her own safety. For the reasons set forth below, we believe the demurrer was improperly sustained and therefore reverse the trial court and order the parties to proceed to trial on the fourth count of the complaint.

[4][5] The averred facts are as follows. Appellant JoAnne Marie Sinn lived with her husband and two minor children in Elizabeth Township, Allegheny County. On June 12, 1975, at approximately 5:53 p. m., the deceased, Lisa Sinn, and her sister, Deborah, were standing by the Sinn's mail box located along side the Greenock-Buena Vista Road . . . An automobile operated by the appellee struck Lisa and hurled her through the air, causing injuries which resulted in her death. Deborah was not struck by the vehicle, although it narrowly missed her. Appellant witnessed the accident from a position near the front door of her home. The Sinns filed a four-count trespass complaint against appellee on June 3, 1976. The first and second counts were brought under the Wrongful Death and Survival acts, respectively. The third count was brought for Deborah for psychological damages she sustained as a result of watching her sister die. The fourth count was brought by appellant for damages she sustained from the emotional stress of witnessing her daughter's death.

*152 Appellee filed preliminary objections in the nature of a demurrer to the third and fourth counts claiming that the complaint failed to aver that Deborah and appellant were in personal danger of physical impact, that they feared such physical impact, or that they suffered physical injury as a result of the emotional distress caused by the accident. The Allegheny County Court of Common Pleas, overruled the demurrer as to the third count but sustained it as to the fourth. Based on its reading of Niederman v. Brodsky, 436 Pa. 401, 261 A.2d 84 (1970), and subsequent Superior Court decisions, that court ruled that while Deborah was within the zone of danger and hence could proceed with her action, appellant was not within the zone of danger. Appellant appealed to the Superior Court which affirmed without opinion. Sinn v. Burd, 253 Pa.Super. 627, 384 A.2d 1003 (1978). We granted allocatur.

I.

Prior to the beginning of this decade, this state was a firm adherent to the "impact rule" regulating recovery for damages in tort. See, e.g., Knaub v. Gotwalt, 422 Pa. 267, 270, 220 A.2d 646, 647 (1966) and cases cited therein. . . . This rule prevented the complaining party from recovering damages for injuries resulting from fright, nervous shock, or mental or emotional disturbances, unless this distress was accompanied by physical impact, i.e., physical injury upon the person of the complaining party. Our cases applied this rule with obstinate rigidity in that recovery was denied not only when the complaining party was a nearby witness, but also to the actual victim of the tortfeasor's negligent or frightening conduct. See, e.g., Bosley v. Andrews, 393 Pa. 161, 142 A.2d 263 (1958).

In the first month of this decade, this Court joined the ranks of forward-looking jurisdictions and abandoned the impact rule in Niederman v. Brodsky, 436 Pa. 401, 261 A.2d 84 (1970) (Niederman). The trial court dismissed plaintiff's complaint for its failure to allege any physical impact. In an opinion by Mr. Justice Roberts, this Court reversed the dismissal, abandoned the impact rule, and adopted the zone of danger

Reasoning—Analysis of precedent on bystander recovery

theory. That is, "where the plaintiff was in personal danger of the direction force."

In so doing, we recognized that our decision was compelled by the "inherent humanitarianism of our judicial process." Id at 404, 261 A.2d at 85. Furthermore, the three basic arguments supporting the impact rule had been eroded away by societal and technological advancements.

The zone of danger concept was our attempt to provide meaningful redress for damages caused by mental distress.

Policy problems with zone of danger rule

Since the Niederman decision, experience has taught us that the zone of danger requirement can be unnecessarily restrictive and prevent recovery in instances where there is no sound policy basis supporting such a result. The restrictiveness of the zone of danger test is glaringly apparent where it is allowed to deny recovery to a parent who has suffered emotional harm from witnessing a tortious assault upon the person of his or her minor child.

Applications of the zone of danger test to situations where the death or serious injury of a child is witnessed by a parent creates the very evil that the test was designed to eliminate, i. e., arbitrariness. It would bar recovery depending upon the position of the plaintiff at the time of the event, and ignores that the emotional impact was most probably influenced by the event witnessed: serious injury to or death of the child rather than the plaintiff's awareness of personal exposure to danger.

Our cases have recognized five policy arguments relevant to bystander recovery. They are medical science's supposed difficulty in proving causation between the claimed damages and the alleged fright, the fear of fraudulent or exaggerated claims, the concern that to allow such a recovery will precipitate a veritable flood of litigation, the problem of unlimited and unduly burdensome liability, and the difficulty of reasonably circumscribing the area of liability. We will discuss them seriatim.

Five policy arguments against bystander recovery. Court rebuts each in turn.

Medical science is able to supply a causal link between the psychic damage suffered by the

#1—Medical science difficulty in

bystander and the shock or fright attendant to having witnessed the accident.

The growing competence of medical science in the field of psychic injuries has diminished the problems of proof in mental distress cases. The development of psychiatric tests and the refinement of diagnostic techniques has led some authorities to conclude that science can establish with reasonable medical certainty the existence and severity of psychic harm. In cases involving negligently inflicted mental distress, however, changes in the law have not kept pace with the increased sophistication of psychiatry. . . .

[Moreover], There is no reason to believe that the causal connection involved here is any more difficult for lawyers to prove or for judges and jurors to comprehend than many others which occur elsewhere in the law. . . [I]n any event, difficulty of proof should not bar the plaintiff from the opportunity of attempting to convince the trier of fact of the truth of her claim.

Niederman at 408, 261 A.2d at 87.

Bystander recovery will not open the courthouse door to fictitious injuries and fraudulent claims.

Courts upholding and those courts denying bystander recovery agree that concern over fraud is without justification. [citations omitted]

The reasons that compelled us to reject this argument in Niederman are equally valid today:

[W]e are unable to accept the proposition that our courts and the judicial system in general cannot deal with fraudulent claims when they arise. Factual, legal, and medical charlatans are unlikely to emerge from a trial unmasked. "Public policy requires the courts, with the aid of the legal and medical professions, to find ways and means to solve satisfactorily the problems thus presented not expedient ways to avoid them." (citation omitted)

The fear of a flood of similar litigation is an insufficient reason to deny bystander recovery.

This consideration focuses upon the belief that to grant recovery in the instant case would cause our courts to "be swamped by a virtual avalanche of cases." Knaub v. Gotwalt, 422 Pa. at 271, 220

A.2d at 647. Again, commentators and courts on both sides of the recovery issue agree that this fear is specious. As we stated in <u>Niederman</u>:

**681 *163 [The] fundamental concept of our judicial system [is] that any [caseload] increase should not be determinative or relevant to the availability of a judicial forum for the adjudication of impartial individual rights. "It is the business of the law to remedy wrongs that deserve it, even at the expense of a 'flood of litigation'; and it is a pitiful confession of incompetence on the part of any court of justice to deny relief upon the ground that it will give the courts too much work to do." Prosser, *Intentional Infliction of Mental Suffering: A New Tort*, 37 Mich. L. Rev. 874 (1939). We obviously do not accept the "too much work to do" rationale. We place the responsibility exactly where it should be: not in denying relief to those who have been injured, but on the judicial machinery of the Commonwealth to fulfill its obligation to make itself available to litigants.

Bystander recovery would not present a problem of unlimited or unduly burdensome liability.

#4—Unlimited and unduly burdensome liability

This is the heart of the controversy raised by the instant appeal. Under either the impact theory, which required a "battery" to the plaintiff, or the later developed zone of danger concept which required an "assault" upon the plaintiff, the courts remained securely ensconced within traditionally recognized areas of tort responsibility. Here the appellant is seeking recovery for injuries sustained as a result of witnessing a "battery" upon another. In considering the wisdom of extending civil liability for tortious conduct, courts have been inclined to impose a duty where public policy demands that "as between the tortfeasor who started the chain of circumstances resulting in the injury and the entirely innocent plaintiff, the tortfeasor should suffer the consequences." *Bystander Recovery for Mental Distress*, 37 Fordham L.Rev. 429, 449 (1969).

The leading decision espousing denial of recovery in these instances is that of <u>Tobin v. Grossman</u>, 24 N.Y.2d 609, 301 N.Y.S.2d 554 (1969).[FN15] The New York Court in <u>Tobin</u> argued that the

Opposing case from another jurisdiction: Tobin

extension of liability for damages sustained by third parties beyond the zone of danger would represent the creation of a new duty and that "there are no new technological, economic, or social developments" which would warrant the recognition of a new cause of action. Id. at 615, 301 N.Y.S.2d at 558. First, we suggest that the Tobin court overstates the nature of the request for recovery in these cases. The conduct which is offered as supporting the liability, i.e., in this case the negligent operation of the vehicle, is of the kind which has traditionally been held to have been actionable by plaintiffs who had sustained provable damages. The departure that is being urged is as to the scope of damages that will be recognized as flowing from that conduct. In this context, we are satisfied that the developments in the fields of medical science and psychiatry do provide the impetus for expanding our legal recognition of the consequences of the negligent act. . . .

The issue before the Tobin court was whether a mother could recover for her own mental and physical injuries caused by shock and fear for her two-year-old struck by a negligently operated automobile. The accident did not occur in the mother's presence; she was inside a neighbor's home, and the mother did not see the accident.

Distinguishes facts in Tobin

It should be noted that the facts of the case presently before us are markedly different in that Mrs. Sinn actually saw the defendant's vehicle strike and kill her daughter. . . . Our decision today is limited solely to those cases in which the plaintiff alleges psychic injury as a result of actually witnessing the defendant's negligent act. . . .

In an attempt to still the concerns of those troubled by "the fear of unlimited liability" the Supreme Court of Hawaii suggested the limiting of recovery "to claims of serious mental distress." Leong v. Takasaki, 520 P.2d at 764. We believe this is a reasonable response to the concern. We agree that it would be unreasonable to hold the defendant responsible for the mental distress that may be experienced by the most timid or sensitive members of the community. . . .

Another jurisdiction's method of limiting recovery

It is [also] possible to reasonably circumscribe the area of liability.

This issue raises the question of the extent to which bystander recovery will be permitted. We are confident that the application of the traditional tort concept of foreseeability will reasonably circumscribe the tortfeasor's liability in such cases. Foreseeability enters into the determination of liability in determining whether the emotional injuries sustained by the plaintiff were reasonably foreseeable to the defendant.

In the seminal <u>Dillon</u> case, the California Supreme Court identified three factors determinative of whether the injury to the Plaintiff was reasonably foreseeable:

(1) Whether plaintiff was located near the scene of the accident as contrasted with one who was a distance away from it. (2) Whether the shock resulted from a direct *171 emotional impact upon plaintiff from the sensory and contemporaneous observance of the accident, as contrasted with learning of the accident from others after its occurrence. (3) Whether plaintiff and the victim were closely related, as contrasted with an absence of any relationship or the presence of only a distant relationship.

<u>Dillon v. Legg</u>, 69 Cal.Rptr. at 80, 441 P.2d at 920

. . .

Applying this standard to the case before it, the California court reversed the summary judgment awarded the defendants on facts almost identical with those now before us.

In summary, we conclude that we cannot accept the callous view of the <u>Tobin</u> court that the possibility of a sudden and violent termination of a young life is a risk assumed in child rearing and does not require recovery where mental distress results from the witnessing of such an event. We are satisfied that public policy demands that we not permit the application of the zone of danger concept to deny recovery merely because of the nature of the damage. We are also satisfied that by the proper application of the tort concept of foreseeability the area of liability may be reasonably circumscribed.

#5—Difficulty of circumscribing liability—met by application of foreseeability

Reference to seminal California case which changed zone of danger law

In applying the preceding discussion to the facts presented in the instant appeal, it is apparent that the trial court prematurely sustained preliminary objections to the fourth count of the complaint on the basis that it did not state a cause of action. Since we have determined that a tortfeasor's liability for mental distress is not to be denied solely because the plaintiff was beyond the zone of physical danger, we must examine whether the injuries sustained by appellant were reasonably foreseeable. It is clear that appellant's injuries were of a nature reasonably foreseeable under the circumstances alleged. Where the bystander is a mother who witnessed the violent death of her small child and the emotional shock emanated directly from personal observation of the event, we hold as a matter of law that the mental distress and its effects is a foreseeable injury.	**Application of reasoning to facts of this case** **Holding**
Regardless of whether Mrs. Sinn will be ultimately successful in recovering the damages she sustained, we believe:	
the gravity of appellant's injury and the inherent humanitarianism of our judicial process and its responsiveness to the current needs of justice dictate that appellant be afforded a chance to present [her] case to a jury and perhaps be compensated for the injury [she] has incurred.	
The order of the Court of Common Pleas sustaining the appellee's demurrer to Court IV of the complaint is hereby reversed. The case is remanded to the Court of Common Pleas for proceedings consistent with this opinion.	**Disposition**

B. Contextualizing the Case

Once you are familiar with the structure of a published decision, begin your reading by putting the case in context.

- Note the date of the case and the court;

- Skim the decision, identifying the key issues and the holding and thinking about which parts are critical to your purpose in reading the case. Are all the issues relevant? If you are reading a case for its discussion of a question of law, then its facts and the factual discussion may not be critical. If you hope to use the case for factual analogy, however, these parts are crucial.

- Finally, determine what you know about the area of law. Have you read about this topic in a doctrinal class or in a treatise or hornbook? Does the law in your jurisdiction comport with or depart from what you know? Is this the first case you have read for a legal writing assignment or the fifth? If the topic is new, read the case especially carefully because there may be many unfamiliar principles you need to master. If you have already researched and read other cases, you may have a better sense of the big picture, but you still need to think about how the cases fit together, that is, you must synthesize them. Ask yourself the following types of questions.

1. Do all the courts in your jurisdiction apply the same rule or do the courts differ?

   How are the rules different?

2. If the highest court has not resolved the conflict, can you reconcile the holdings?

   Is one rule an extension or exception to the general rule?

   Do later cases seem to adopt one rule rather than another, i.e., is a trend emerging?

   What policies seem to drive the trend?

3. What are the consequences of the decision?

C. Reading as a Creative Activity

Reading law is an active rather than a passive activity. The most successful law students are those who acknowledge confusion and attempt to work through it. When they encounter unfamiliar terms and cannot infer the meaning, they use a legal dictionary. When they make inferences, after they finish reading the case, they check whether the inferences were correct. They reread sections that seem unclear, or read ahead to see if later discussions help to clarify earlier confusion. In short, they read, reread, paraphrase, and question the text to achieve understanding.[3]

When you read the fact statement in an opinion, pay attention to the facts that caused the underlying dispute as well as the

---

[3] Leah Christensen, *Legal Reading and Success in Law School: An Empirical Study*, 30 Seattle L. Rev. 603, 609 (2007).

procedural history of the case. Often this inquiry requires you to notice how the case came up through the courts, what arguments the parties made below, and what the lower court decided and why.

Once you are clear about this, the truly creative task of reading begins. Reading the analysis section is a multi-dimensional task that requires you to do the following:

- understand the case in and of itself;

- evaluate the soundness of the court's reasoning;

- determine how the case fits in with the jurisdiction's previous cases on this issue and

- determine how the case applies to your client's situation.

Your understanding of a case will improve if you annotate the parts, issues, and types of arguments in the same manner as the annotated case in the previous section. But you should engage with the text as well, try to work at what is confusing, predict the court's analysis and conclusions, identify the rule that the court applies, and hypothesize about its possible interpretations.[4] As you read, consciously monitor your predictions and hypotheses, refining or modifying them as necessary.

In addition think about the impact the case will have on your client. Does it support the outcome the client desires because your case is either factually similar or comes within its legal principles? If not, do you need to minimize the importance of the case, and if so, can you do so because of factual differences, weaknesses in the court's reasoning, or changes in society?

Evaluating cases may require you to evaluate the soundness of the court's reasoning. Ask yourself whether the court overlooked parties who might be affected by its decision, minimized or ignored important policies or facts, or failed to do justice. Look for unfounded assumptions or gaps in reasoning. These weaknesses are important because you may, if necessary, be able to use them to persuade a later court that an unfavorable precedent should not control.

D. Case Briefing: Finding the Parts of a Judicial Decision

Once you have read a case using the strategies described in the previous section, it is a good idea to brief it. A case brief gives you a framework for organizing and summarizing the elements of the

---

4   Ruth Ann McKinney, *supra* n. 2 at 212.

opinion. Although there is no one format for briefing cases, the typical components of a case brief are explained below.

1. Facts

The fact section describes the events between the parties that led to the litigation and tells how the case came before the court that is now deciding it. Be specific about the facts.

- First, include who the plaintiff and the defendant are, the basis for the plaintiff's suit, and the relief the plaintiff is seeking.

- Second, include the procedural history, although you may put the procedural facts under a separate heading. Procedural facts should include any dispositive motions, such as a motion to dismiss for failure to state a claim or a motion for summary judgment. If the case is an appeal, state the lower court's decision, the grounds for that decision, and the party who appealed. Often you have to understand the procedural posture of a case in order to understand the court's decision. For example, if the appeal is from a successful motion to dismiss, then the appellate court will decide whether the plaintiff's pleadings stated a claim and whether the plaintiff should be permitted to continue the lawsuit. The appellate court will not decide who should win the lawsuit if it continues.

- Third, include those facts that are relevant to the issue the court must decide and to the reasons for its decision. You will not know which facts are relevant until you know what the issue or issues are. For example, in the *Sinn* case, the issue is whether a mother can recover damages for negligent infliction of emotional distress caused when she saw her minor daughter struck and killed by an automobile, though she was not within the zone of danger. Relevant facts include the plaintiff's relation to the victim, the plaintiff's actually viewing the accident at the time it happened, and the plaintiff's acute distress as a result.

- Fourth, include relevant background information for the case. This might include significant facts about the parties' employment, economic bracket, recreational activities, or state of mind.

2.   Issue(s)

The issue is the question that the court must decide to resolve the dispute between the parties in the case before it. To find the issue, you have to identify the rule of law that governs the dispute and ask how it should apply to those facts. You usually write the issue for your case brief as a question that combines the rule of law with the material facts of the case, that is, those facts that raise the dispute.

3.   Holding(s)

The holding, as was explained in Chapter 1, is the court's decision on the question that was actually before it. The court may make a number of legal statements, but if they do not relate to the question actually before it, they are dicta. The holding provides the answer to the question asked in the issue statement. If there is more than one issue, there may be more than one holding.

4.   Legal Rule and Reasoning

State the rule and the court's explanations of it. Also supply the court's reasoning for its decision, i.e., why it applied the controlling rule as it did. Sometimes the issue in the case may involve the validity of the rule itself, and the court may have looked at two lines of authority and decided the case was more like one group of cases than another. Or the court may have decided that the policy justifying a rule was no longer valid, or may have concluded that the facts of this particular case required an exception to the rule. In any event, isolate the court's reasoning from the facts and the holding of the case.

5.   Policy

Underlying legal decisions are the social policies or goals that the decision-maker wishes to further. When a court explicitly refers to those policies in a case, include that information in your case brief, since it will probably help you understand the court's decision. If the court does not explain the policies on which it based its decision, then try to identify them for yourself.

6.   Reflection

After you identify these important parts of a court's opinion, spend some time evaluating what you are reading. This is the best preparation for your classes and for your writing. For example, think about the appropriateness of the legal rule that the jurisdiction has adopted and that the court applies. Consider the court's application of the rule to the facts of the case and the logic of the court's opinion.

- Are there relevant issues that the court did not address?

- Is there a dissenting opinion that gives a different perspective on the law or the facts?

- Is there a gap in the court's reasoning?

- Are there alternative policies not considered?

Finally, to prepare for class, think of how changes in the facts might change the court's decision. To prepare for your legal writing assignment, think about the impact this case will have on your client and how you can most effectively use it to your client's advantage.

Sinn v. Burd: Sample Case Brief

1.   Facts

The plaintiff Joanne Sinn sued the defendant Brad Burd for negligent infliction of emotional distress. She sought damages for physical and mental injuries caused when she saw the defendant's car hit and kill her minor daughter. She was not within any zone of personal danger at the time. Her daughter was standing by their mail box on the side of the road. Burd's car hit her daughter and hurled her through the air, causing injuries which resulted in her death. Sinn saw the accident while standing near the front door of her house. She became hysterical and emotionally shattered, suffering severe mental pain, severe depression, and an acute nervous condition. She has had to spend money for medication, including tranquilizers, and will have to spend money on present and future medical care.

The trial court sustained Burd's demurrer to her complaint on the grounds that she was not in a zone of danger from physical injury and so under the Pennsylvania bystander law was not entitled to recovery. The County and Superior Courts affirmed.

2.   Issue

Can a parent recover for negligent infliction of emotional distress when she viewed her child killed as a result of the defendant's negligence, but was not herself in the zone of danger, and when she suffered extreme distress as a result?

3.   Holding

Where the plaintiff is not within the zone of danger, the traditional tort concept of foreseeability determines the defendant's liability. When the bystander is a mother who witnessed the violent death of her small child and the emotional shock emanated directly from her personal observation of the event, the mental distress and its effects are foreseeable injuries.

4. Legal Rule and Reasoning

Under the original law in Pennsylvania denying bystander recovery, a plaintiff could not recover unless the plaintiff had suffered a physical "impact" along with emotional distress. This was changed ten years previously by the Pa. Supreme Court's decision in *Niederman v. Brodsky*, which permitted recovery if the plaintiff was in the "zone of danger," that is, in personal danger of physical impact. The Court in *Sinn* reasoned that experience showed that rule was unnecessarily restrictive.

The Court identified five policy arguments against expanding the rule beyond the zone of danger, and rejected them in order.

1. Medical science difficulty in proving causation (growing competence of medical science in the field of psychological injuries).

2. Fear of fraudulent claims (courts agree concern over fraud is without justification).

3. Floodgates of litigation (a fundamental concept of the judicial system is that caseload increase should not determine or be relevant to the availability of a forum).

4. Unlimited or burdensome liability (liability limited to situations where the parent actually saw the child killed and where the distress is severe).

5. Difficulty of circumscribing liability (liability can be circumscribed by the doctrine of foreseeability).

The Court's reasoning was based on its own prior decision in *Niederman* and cases from other jurisdictions that have considered this issue.

5. Policy

As the Supreme Court of Pennsylvania, the court was able to change the law on a question of state law. The court concluded that the policies against extending recovery were no longer valid, and given the "inherent humanitarianism of our judicial process" and the needs of justice, the plaintiff should at least be able to present her case to a jury.

6. Reflections

Where do you draw the line regarding family members? Could the child's sister bring a claim if she were outside the zone of danger? The child's best friend? How extreme does the emotional distress have to be?

III. ANALYZING COMMON LAW CAUSES OF ACTION[5]

MANY COMMON LAW CAUSES OF ACTION, such as intentional torts, are defined by elements, and the plaintiff must prove each element of the cause of action in order to succeed against the defendant. To prove the tort of assault, for example, the plaintiff must prove that the defendant (1) intentionally acted (2) to place him in apprehension of (3) a harmful or offensive (4) physical contact. These are the elements of that tort. If the plaintiff cannot prove that the defendant acted intentionally, for example, the plaintiff loses the lawsuit. Notice that the third element is disjunctive and can be proven in alternative ways—the plaintiff must prove that he apprehended either a harmful or an offensive contact. If the element was conjunctive, using "and," the plaintiff must prove both.

The rule could be broken down further to show its structure. For example, the defendant

1. intentionally (or with intent)

2. acted to place the plaintiff in apprehension

3. of a harmful or offensive

4. unconsented and unprivileged physical contact.

Several legal definitions, such as the definition of an intentional tort or of contract, have evolved over many years and the elements are now standard law. Some, however, have evolved from newer litigation, such as the tort of negligent infliction of emotional distress, which was at issue in the sample case, <u>Sinn v. Burd</u>, on p. 38. In <u>Sinn</u>, the court adopted the new tort using the decision in an earlier California case that it cited to limit recovery to cases in which the plaintiff's injury was reasonably foreseeable. Look again at <u>Sinn</u>. The court also adopted the California court's three requirements to determine whether the injury to the plaintiff was foreseeable.

1. The plaintiff was located near the scene of the accident,

2. The impact on the plaintiff came from the sensory and contemporaneous observations of the accident, and

3. the plaintiff and the victim were closely related.

---

[5] We use this term to mean a legal claim, that is, the ground for a plaintiff's lawsuit. In this chapter, we refer to claims from the common law. Chapter 3 discusses statutes and statutory claims.

The court remanded the case to the trial court for the plaintiff to prove her case to a jury.

We return to this topic of elements of a cause of action in Section IV, and in Chapter Four.

IV. USING THE PARTS OF A JUDICIAL DECISION

A. Reasoning by Analogy

UNDER THE DOCTRINE OF PRECEDENT, judges decide cases and attorneys argue cases according to principles laid down in earlier similar cases, that is, the precedents. Lawyers (and law students) who are working on a legal problem must find those earlier cases and analyze the impact that those cases will have on the decision in their own problem. By comparing their problem to decided cases, drawing analogies and distinctions, lawyers decide how the decisions of previous cases apply to the new problem. If the cases resemble each other in important ways, such as by their relevant facts, then they are analogous and should also resemble each other in their outcome. Cases are analogous if they are alike in ways that are important to their outcome and if the differences between them are not enough to destroy that analogy.

The first precedents to look for are those that are binding authority on the court in which the case will be litigated. If that court, or a higher court in that jurisdiction, decided a case or cases on the issue before the present court, those cases become the precedents to which the present controversy will be compared. If there are no cases in that jurisdiction on that exact issue, cases on similar issues will be important if the reasoning and the underlying policies in these cases also apply to the facts of the present case.

If you decide, however, that the cases are different and that the decision in the precedent case should not control the outcome of your problem, you are "distinguishing" the cases. If you distinguish a prior case, you avoid its impact on your case. You may distinguish a case by establishing that the differences in the facts require that the court apply a different rule. Or you may decide that the same rule should be applied, but that the facts in your case require a different outcome.

Be careful not to distinguish cases too easily. Each case will have some differences from other cases. The distinguishing facts you select must be legally significant, that is, they should tend to prove or disprove a rule.

In a recent case, a plaintiff answered a car dealer's online advertisement for a new Toyota for $19,900. The plaintiff went to the dealer's lot, test drove the car and said he would purchase the car. However, the dealer informed him that the price was $36,900, and that the ad had erroneously listed the lower price. The plaintiff sued for breach of contract.

In an earlier case in that state the court held that a car dealer's newspaper ad that included an incorrect price was not an offer to sell the car at the incorrect price, but an invitation to deal on the ad's terms, and a contract required that the parties agree to the terms. This case was a difficult precedent for the plaintiff, who attempted to distinguish that case. The plaintiff argued that in the first case, the dealer's advertisement did not include important terms such as equipment and warranties, and so it was too incomplete to be an offer. In this case, the ad furnished important information. In the first case, the plaintiff never promised to pay the dealer the advertised price. In this case, the plaintiff explicitly insisted on and offered the lower price.

The court, however, did not accept plaintiff's distinctions as important, but identified the fact that both ads contained wrong information about an essential term as the key to following the precedent case.

By comparing and contrasting your problem with the precedents, you will be able to show how well the rules of those cases fit your case. This in turn should enable you to predict the probable outcome of your own case. When you reason by analogy, though, you can offer only probable proof for your conclusions, not certainty. Your task is to assess all the possible applications of the relevant rules and to offer the best prediction of the outcome.

B. Applying Precedent

1. Issues

To determine whether a case is controlling as precedent, the issue in the precedent should be essentially the same as the one in the new problem. However, sometimes you can define the issue in the precedent more broadly in order to reveal its significance for your problem case by describing the key facts more broadly. For example, if your claim for negligent infliction of emotional distress is brought by a grandmother who did not live with the victim, you might characterize the relation between the plaintiff and the victim as "close family member."

The most relevant cases are those in which the issue is the same. However, sometimes you will not find a case in the jurisdiction with the same issue, but you will find a case or cases on similar issues. You may use those cases to draw analogies, but it is important that the reasoning and policies supporting those decisions are relevant to the current issue.

> A federal district court (a trial court) sitting in Pennsylvania had to determine whether it had diversity jurisdiction[6] in a personal injury suit (personal injury suits are typically litigated in state court under state law). The plaintiff, Ms. Last, sued a residential school for the developmentally disabled located in Pennsylvania. Ms. Last sued on behalf of her legally incompetent adult son who was injured when he was a resident of the school. Ms. Last was a domiciliary of New York. She argued that her son's domicile was also New York and not Pennsylvania, the defendant's domicile. (If Pennsylvania, the parties' domiciles would not be diverse.) A child's domicile is deemed to be that of the parents and an incompetent adult is deemed unable to form the intent to change domicile from that of the parents. The school's burden was to prove that the son had changed his domicile to Pennsylvania as a resident of the school so that the court lacked jurisdiction.
>
> The district court relied on an earlier case from its circuit, *Juvelis v. Snider. Juvelis* also involved the domicile of an incompetent adult, but the issue was different from that in *Last. Juvelis* raised the issue of domicile not to determine jurisdiction, but to determine whether the plaintiff qualified for benefits under a federal statute. Nevertheless, the court in *Last* used the rule developed in *Juvelis* to determine whether an adult incompetent had changed domicile from that of his parents. The *Last* court said the difference in the issue (domicile for benefits under a statute and domicile for purposes of diversity jurisdiction) should not change the inquiry into whether an incompetent adult changed domicile.

2. Facts

After you find cases on the same issue, or on issues that are sufficiently analogous, you compare the facts of those cases. When you brief a case, you concentrate on how the facts of that case are relevant to the issue in the case and the reasons for the court's holding. However, when you are considering the relationship between a precedent and your problem case, you view the facts

---

[6]   See Chapter 1. Where parties are domiciled in different states, a party may file suit to be heard in federal court, but the federal court must apply state law.

somewhat differently. Now, you also try to determine if the facts in the two cases are basically analogous or distinguishable.

The facts of one case need not be identical to the facts of another case for the cases to be analogous. Indeed, the facts will never be identical. A case can be a precedent for your problem, however, when the facts can be classified similarly.

> The relative bargaining strength of a party to a contract is one factor the courts will consider in deciding whether a contract is unconscionable (so unfair as to be unenforceable). Thus, an analogy could be drawn between a case in which the owner of a small gas station dealing with Exxon Mobil claimed a contract was unconscionable and a previous case in which a consumer dealing with General Motors successfully claimed a contract was unconscionable. Although the station owner is a business person, both the station owner and the consumer are vulnerable buyers in a weak bargaining position relative to the defendant. On the other hand, if these plaintiffs were described at a higher level of abstraction, as a consumer and a commercial enterprise, then the case about the consumer contract might not apply to the gas station. Similarly, a rule for automobiles may apply equally to snowmobiles or even to mopeds if all are classified as motorized vehicles.

In applying precedent, as when briefing a case, you must first determine which facts are relevant to the issue that a court must decide and to the reasons for its decision.

Exercise 2-A

False imprisonment litigation often involves employment situations. The plaintiff's employer wants to question the plaintiff about some aspect of the plaintiff's job performance, and often does so in the employer's office with the door closed. The plaintiff claims that he was involuntarily confined, one of the elements of false imprisonment.

Suppose that Mr. Brown claims he was involuntarily confined in his employer's office for five hours. During this time, he was questioned about his methods of billing his time, and then fired. The door to the room was closed but not locked, and Brown was sometimes left alone in the room, where there was a telephone. He never tried to leave.

The defendant employer relied on Towls v. McGann, in which the court held that the plaintiff was not involuntarily confined when she was called to her employer's office and questioned for three hours about money shortages. Though the door had been locked, she was not prevented from leaving the room when she became upset and wanted to leave. Before that time, she had not been left alone in the room.

Are these differences in the facts so relevant they will change the outcome? Evaluate the merits of Brown's claim.

a. The previous plaintiff walked out of the room, but Brown remained inside.

b. The previous defendant had locked the door.

c. Brown had been left alone in the office where there was a telephone. The previous plaintiff was never alone in the room.

d. Brown was in the defendant's office for five hours; the previous plaintiff was in the defendant's office for three hours.

Exercise 2-B

Analogize or distinguish the following facts and those in Sinn v. Burd and decide if the factual differences change the outcome of whether the plaintiff would succeed in a claim for negligent infliction of emotional distress. Explain why. Which elements of the claim must the court analyze?

a. The plaintiff, the mother of a child killed by a car, received a telephone call telling her that her daughter had been killed in an accident. She was four blocks away and arrived at the scene a few moments later. *won't succeed.*

b. The plaintiff looked through the window and saw her husband's car arriving at their house. She also saw a car speeding on the road behind his. She looked away for a moment and then heard a loud crash. The speeding car had hit her husband's car and killed him. *Might succeed*

c. The plaintiff was a kindergarten teacher who saw one of the children in her class get hit by a car in front of the school. The child died from his injuries. *Won't succeed*

Exercise 2-C

Read the following case. Identify the issue in the case and make a list of the facts that are relevant to a court's decision on that issue.

In re Estate of Winter

The heirs of Robert Winter seek to void a contract for the sale of land Mr. Winter made three weeks before his death. They allege that Winter was mentally incompetent to make a contract at that time. In this state, a contract may be voidable on grounds of mental incompetence if, because of a person's mental illness, he was unable to reasonably understand the nature and consequences of the transaction in question. Since Winter was incompetent under this standard, the contract he made for the sale of land is voidable and will not be enforced.

Mr. Winter, a widower, had a stroke in 2002. He suffered from a vascular disease which resulted in partial amputation of his foot. As a result of this amputation, he became unable to continue to operate his farm himself. Since he was unable to take care of himself, he moved in with one of his daughters, Sandra Bright. Another daughter testified that from that point on, Winter seemed to lose interest in everything. He stopped managing his own affairs. Ms. Bright handled all of his finances. She balanced his checkbook, deposited his social security checks, and managed the farm.

As time went on, Mr. Winter became easily confused and lethargic, spending much of his time sitting in a chair, staring out of the window. A family friend testified that when Winter described the farm, he sometimes said it was 200 acres and sometimes said it was 2,000 acres. (The farm is 2,000 acres.) Dr. Crabtree, Winter's longtime physician, said that in his opinion, from March 2004 until he died, Winter was totally incompetent to handle any of his own affairs, including taking care of his own body.

In May, 2004, while Ms. Bright was out for the afternoon, Herbert Spencer paid Winter a visit. Mr. Spencer offered to buy the farm from Winter. Winter agreed and signed a contract for the sale of the farm to Spencer for what a local real estate agent said was far below its actual value. In addition, Winter did not reserve a right of way for himself and his family, creating a problem of access from the road to their other piece of property. Mr. Winter died three weeks after the sale of the farm.

The evidence suggests that at the time of the contract, Winter was unable to understand the nature and consequences of the transaction of the sale of land. He did not appear to have a clear idea of the number of acres in question. The price he received was below the fair market value of the property. He failed to reserve an important right of access for himself. His physician testified that he was incompetent to handle his own affairs. His daughter had, in fact, been taking care of his personal and business affairs before the sale took place, as Winter had lost interest in these matters. Under these circumstances, I hold that Winter was unable to understand the nature and consequences of the transaction, and, therefore, the contract for the sale of land is voidable.

Exercise 2-D

Using Winter as the only precedent, identify the issue and make a list of the relevant facts in the following case:

Richard Bower wants to void the contract his uncle Joseph Black made for the purchase of a car shortly before Mr. Black's death on the grounds that Black was mentally incompetent at the time he made the contract. Excerpts from the following depositions, taken in the case, will provide the factual background.

DEPOSITION: DR. MARTIN DREW

(By Ms. Jones, attorney for plaintiff, Richard Bower)

Q: Was Joseph Black a patient of yours?

A: Yes, he was my patient for six years until he died on April 10, 2015, of cerebral apoplexy, what you would call a stroke.

Q: What had you been treating Mr. Black for?

A: Mr. Black had cerebral arteriosclerosis. He suffered from a hardening and shrinkage of the arteries, which reduced the amount of blood that gets to the brain.

Q: What are the symptoms of cerebral arteriosclerosis?

A: Well, since this disease develops gradually, the symptoms develop gradually as well, becoming more and more intense. The most common early signs are memory loss, irritability, anger, confusion, and forgetfulness. In Mr. Black's case, the symptoms were becoming more and more severe. You see, as the amount of blood that got to his brain diminished because the arteries continued to shrink, the amount of his confusion and forgetfulness increased. He also became more stubborn as his memory became more uncertain.

Q: When did you last see Mr. Black?

A: I last saw him on January 31, 2015.

Q: How would you describe his condition?

A: I would say that his arteriosclerosis had become quite severe—not enough that he needed to be hospitalized, but enough so that he needed home nursing care. He would talk to me and then he would forget what he said and tell me the same things again and again. And he thought I was my father, who had been his physician 30 years ago. I asked him to tell me his name and where he lived. He remembered his name, but couldn't tell me where he lived.

Q: Doctor, in your opinion, was Mr. Black able to understand ordinary business transactions?

A: Sometimes he was lucid, other times less so.

DEPOSITION: RICHARD BOWER

(By Ms. Jones)

Q: Mr. Bower, what is your relationship to Joseph Black?

A: He was my uncle, my mother's brother.

Q: Did you accompany your uncle to Miller Motors on February 12, 2015?

A: Yes I did. He came next door, where I live, and asked me to go with him to Miller Motors, which is around the corner. I couldn't understand why, but I humored him and went with him. When we got there, a salesman came out and said, "Your car is ready, Mr. Black." My uncle had gone to a car dealership with Rose Brown the day before and bought a red Kia. He wanted me to drive him home in it. I couldn't believe it because he hasn't driven in three years. I don't think he even has a valid license anymore. I asked him how he could do such a thing, because he only had $15,000 left to live on, except for Social Security, and the car cost around $19,000. He wouldn't even be able to make his mortgage payments and eat on what he had left. When I reminded him of that he said it was not a problem because he had only borrowed the car and it only cost a few hundred dollars. Then he said that he could give the car back in a few days. When I told him again that he had spent $19,000 on a car, he started yelling at me and making a terrible scene so I drove him home and put it in the garage beside his house. He never went near it. I started it once a week so that the engine wouldn't rot.

Q: What did you do after your uncle died?

A: I called Miller Motors and said I was my uncle's executor and that I wanted to give the car back. I said I would be willing to pay them for the two months' use of the car, even though we never even drove it. But they refused.

DEPOSITION: ROSE BROWN

(By Ms. Jones)

Q: Ms. Brown, were you employed by Joseph Black?

A: I took care of Mr. Black, though Mr. Bower actually paid me out of a joint checking account he had with Mr. Black.

Q: How long did you take care of Mr. Black?

A: I took care of him from February 3, 2015, until he died on April 10.

Q: What did your work consist of?

A: I did the shopping, cooked, cleaned, helped Mr. Black get dressed if he needed help.

Q: How did Mr. Black occupy his time?

> A: He sat around, sometimes watched TV. He didn't read the paper anymore. I had to watch him very carefully because he would wander off. But you had to be very careful how you talked to him, because he would get angry and use terrible language. He hated to hear that he had forgotten something and would just get more stubborn.

Exercise 2-E

Compare the facts in the Winter *case and in the problem case to determine whether the cases are analogous or distinguishable. Under what general classifications would you compare the facts?*

3. Holding

When you are considering the relationship between a precedent and your problem case, you might formulate a court's holding differently from the way you would if you were simply briefing the case. The holding of a mandatory precedent becomes a rule to apply in the next similar case. Nonetheless, as explained in Chapter 1, you have some flexibility in formulating the holding in that you can choose how many facts to include as essential, and how to characterize those facts. If you describe the facts exactly as they were in the case, then the holding you state will be very narrow. This is sometimes called limiting a case to its facts, because the case cannot be used as a precedent for many other cases. If, however, you describe the facts more broadly, then the holding will apply to a larger number of future cases whose facts come within that broader description. The holding in the *Last* diversity case could be stated in terms of the plaintiff in particular, in terms of incompetent adults, or more broadly, in terms of any category of persons incapable of choosing a domicile.

The way you formulate the holding may depend on the result you want the court to reach in applying that case, the purpose of the document you are writing, and its intended audience. For example, if you are writing to a court and the decision in the precedent case is one that is favorable to your client, then you will try to formulate the holding broadly enough to encompass the facts of your client's case. Or, if the decision in the precedent is unfavorable, you will try to state the holding more narrowly so that it will not encompass the facts of your client's case. If you were representing a defendant who had injured the plaintiff's granddaughter in a claim for negligent infliction of emotional distress, you would state the holding of *Sinn* so that it applies only to a parent who saw her child killed. Of course, there are limits to formulating the holding broadly or narrowly. If you manipulate the facts to violate the sense of the case, you will be engaging in unethical behavior and faulty analysis.

Exercise 2-F

Reread Miller v. Adam *in Chapter 1, page 21. Suppose you represented the plaintiff in each of the following two false imprisonment cases. How would you formulate the holding of* Miller v. Adam *to be most advantageous to your client?*

Case 1:

Same facts as in the Miller *case in Chapter 1, but your client's pocketbook contains only a handkerchief, a comb, and makeup. Your client stays five minutes and leaves.*

Which of these two statements would you use as the holding in Miller v. Adam?

a.   In *Miller v. Adam*, the owner of a restaurant confined the plaintiff when he took her pocketbook and told her she could not leave the restaurant until he determined that she had paid her bill.

or

b.   In *Miller v. Adam*, the owner of a restaurant confined the plaintiff when he took property of value from her in order to detain the plaintiff and detained her for twenty minutes.

Case 2:

Same facts as above but the restaurant owner tells your client that he does not believe that she left the money to pay her bill, and asks your client to wait while he gets someone to see if she left the money on her table. The owner does not take anything from her, but asks the restaurant hostess to keep an eye on your client. Your client waits for twenty minutes.

Which of these two statements would you use as the holding in Miller v. Adam?

a.   In *Miller v. Adam*, the defendant confined the plaintiff by duress even though he did not engage in threatening behavior.

or

b.   In *Miller v. Adam*, the defendant confined the plaintiff by duress by implied threats that if she left the premises she would lose her property.

---

4.   Reasoning

The court's reasoning in the precedent case must apply equally well to the facts in your problem case. This would certainly happen when the facts are quite similar, for example in applying *Last*, a case dealing with the domicile of an incompetent offspring for diversity purposes, to another case involving the same issue and similar facts. However, the court's reasoning may also apply in a different context. The *Last* court found the reasoning of *Juvelis* applicable to the issue of domicile to establish jurisdiction even though that case involved establishing domicile to receive federal benefits.

5. Policy

The court in the precedent may be basing its decision on an articulated (or unarticulated) policy. If the same policy would apply in your problem case, the result should be the same.

For example, suppose a state court has a well-established rule upholding releases from liability in litigation involving race car drivers and bicycle racers. One policy behind that rule is the public interest in participating in and watching competitive racing. A rule invalidating the release would decrease the number of racing events because the operators would fear potential liability from injuries. Another reason for the rule is that the participants in the races are usually experienced racers who can calculate their risks.

This rule upholding releases for competitive racing is invoked by the operator of a cave exploration tour for tourists. He requires participants to sign a release. The tour operator is sued by an inexperienced participant who was hurt in the cave because of the guide's negligence.

In this situation, a court may not enforce the release. Neither policy for upholding releases in competitive racing would apply: cave exploration is not a competitive spectator sport that involves the public, and the participants in these cave tours are not experienced spelunkers.

Exercise 2-G
A customer of a rafting outfitter company drowned in a white water rafting excursion in a Colorado river when her raft capsized because of the guide's negligence. Before the excursion she had signed a release of the outfitter's liability. This trip was her second rafting trip. The first one on a tamer river had been uneventful.
Should the release be enforced?

Exercise 2-H

Consider whether a court would decide that the plaintiff in the following case could succeed in the described lawsuit. Use these five questions as a guide.

  a. *Is the issue the same or analogous to the issue in* Sinn?

  b. *Are the relevant facts analogous or distinguishable?*

  c. *Would the court's reasoning in* Sinn *lead to the same or a different result?*

  d. *What impact, if any, would the policies behind the decision in* Sinn *have on this case?*

  e. *In light of the answers to these questions, is it likely that a court will follow the holding in* Sinn?

Bobby Jones' parents brought a claim for negligent infliction of emotional distress on behalf of their child. They allege that the harm was occasioned when Bobby witnessed his first cousin Stuart drown on the property of Steven Bain, as a result of Bain's negligence in not erecting a fence around his lake. Bain is a landowner in Brockton, Pennsylvania.

Both boys are eight years old. Bobby and Stuart grew up literally in the same house; Bobby's parents lived on the first floor and Stuart's parents lived on the second floor. Their mothers were sisters. Bobby and Stuart were born within six weeks of each other. Their mothers describe them as "inseparable," practically since birth. Stuart's mother said Bobby was "like a brother" to Stuart. Bobby and Stuart played together as toddlers, were in the same pre-school class, and stayed in the same class from kindergarten through grade four. They were cub scouts in the same troupe, members of the same little league team, and played together after school and on the weekends.

One afternoon, the boys were playing not that far from their home. They walked over to the lake on Bain's property and skipped a few stones. Then Stuart waded in because he saw something shiny in the water. He swam towards it, not realizing how quickly the lake deepened. When Stuart realized he could not stand, he panicked. He started flailing about and calling for help, but Bobby, a poor swimmer, could not help him. Bobby ran for help, but by the time they returned ten minutes later, Stuart had drowned.

Since the incident, Bobby has had panic attacks, vomiting episodes, weight loss, and nightmares where he wakes screaming Stuart's name. His parents have taken him to see a therapist because of his acute distress.

Fits well

"Closely Related"

Exercise 2-I

1. *Read* Smith v. Allen. *Then write an answer applying* Smith *to the problem in the* Peterson *case which follows* Smith. *In an action for negligence, is David's _father_ liable for injuries to Phil?* Peterson *would be litigated in the same jurisdiction as* Allen.

Smith v. Allen

Judith Smith alleges that James Allen owned a golf club which he left lying on the ground in the backyard of his home. On April 12, 2015, his son, the eleven-year-old co-defendant Jimmy Allen, was playing in the yard with the plaintiff, Judith Smith, age nine years. Jimmy picked up the golf club and proceeded to swing at a stone lying on the ground. In swinging the golf club, Jimmy caused the club to strike the plaintiff about the jaw and chin.

Smith alleges that Jimmy Allen was negligent since he failed to warn her of his intention to swing the club and he swung the club when he knew she was in a position of danger.

Smith also alleges that James Allen was negligent and that he is liable for his son's actions. She alleges that although Allen knew the golf club was on the ground in his backyard and that his child would play with it, and that although he knew or "should have known" that the negligent use of the golf club by children would cause injury to a child, he neglected to remove the golf club from the backyard or to caution Jimmy against the use of the golf club.

James Allen demurred, challenging the sufficiency of the complaint to state a cause of action or to support a judgment against him.

The demurrer is sustained. A person has a duty to protect others against unreasonable risks. A person who breaches this duty is negligent and liable for injuries resulting from his negligence. No person, however, can be expected to guard against harm from events that are not reasonably to be anticipated at all, or are so unlikely to occur that the risk, although recognizable, would commonly be disregarded. A golf club is not so obviously and intrinsically dangerous that it is negligence to leave it lying on the ground in the yard. Unlike a knife, for example, it is not commonly used as a weapon. Thus, the father cannot be held liable on the allegations of this complaint.[7]

Aarons v. Peterson

David Peterson stored a tool chest on the floor in the basement of his suburban home. In it he kept three screwdrivers, two wrenches, a hammer and several boxes of nails. Last Tuesday afternoon, his eleven-year-old son, David, Jr., and a nine-year-old neighbor, Phil Aarons, were playing knock hockey in the basement. Their exertions

---

[7] This example is based on and uses language from *Lubitz v. Wells*, 113 A.2d 147 (Conn. Super. Ct. 1955).

were so strenuous they knocked the side rail loose from the baseboard. Phil, who was losing, was glad. He was tired of playing knock hockey and wanted to play with David's trains. David, however, wanted to continue the match. Spotting his father's tool chest lying on the floor in the corner, he decided to fix the board. He took a hammer and a large nail out of the chest and, while Phil was playing with the train set, quietly set about repairing the damage. At first the work went well. He placed the nail at the joint and hit it firmly on the head. It pierced the wood and held firm. Then disaster struck. On the next hammer blow, the nail flew out from the wood and struck Phil in the face, chipping his two front teeth, bloodying his nose, and gashing his cheek.

2.   *Read the following case summary of* Green v. Kendall. *This case was decided by a court in the same jurisdiction as* Smith v. Allen. *Does this decision change your analysis of* Smith *and* Aarons v. Peterson?

Green v. Kendall

The plaintiff Lucy Green is suing for injuries she received on the Muni Golf course when she was struck on the knee by the defendant, John Kendall, who is eleven-years-old. Green was walking over a foot bridge about 150 yards from the eighth tee, when Kendall, who was playing in a foursome with his parents and sister, teed off the eighth tee without yelling "fore." The plaintiff was in clear view of the tee at the time Kendall teed off and hit her with the golf ball. The issue is the standard of care that the eleven-year-old defendant should be held to when he played golf.

A golfer should be required to use reasonable care. But whether John should be held to use the reasonable care of a reasonably prudent child or of a reasonably prudent adult depends on whether he used a dangerous instrument. Minors will be held to an adult standard of care if they used a dangerous instrument. A golf ball is a dangerous missile that can cause injury if it hits someone during its flight. Indeed, in some ways, hitting a golf ball is more dangerous than firing a gun or throwing a stone, because a person can have more control over the direction of a gunshot or a stone than over a golf ball.

Golf has become a very popular sport, and as golf courses have become more crowded, more accidents have occurred, especially accidents involving golf balls. Yet golf is an adult activity involving dangerous instruments. Since a child is, for practical purposes, on the course as an adult, he should be held to an adult standard. John could see the plaintiff, he did not yell fore, and he teed off with the plaintiff in sight. The judgment for the plaintiff is affirmed.

V. SYNTHESIZING CASES

YOU WILL RARELY WORK ON A PROBLEM for which there is only one case precedent. More likely, your research will turn up many cases relevant to the problem. To use the principles those cases offer to resolve your problem, you have to relate the cases to each other, that is, synthesize them. That way, you can consider how the law as a whole applies to your case.

The courts will frequently have done some synthesis for you. Often, when you read cases, you will see definitions of a claim for relief, like the definition of battery by a court or in the Restatement of Torts. Usually these definitions or rules have evolved as courts over the years have put together the decisions of many related cases. The judges who have formulated those definitions have worked inductively, that is, from the specific to the general. They have analyzed the outcome of each case and then combined those separate cases into a coherent rule. The rule summarizes, or synthesizes, the particular holdings of all of the individual cases.

When you analyze a legal problem, such as one of your class memo assignments, you will do further synthesis of your own. Synthesizing is the step between your research and your writing. You do research by reading one case at a time. If in your writing you merely report each case, one at a time, then you have compiled a list of case briefs, but you have not analyzed a topic.

To analyze and write about a topic, you will engage in one of three types of case synthesis, or in a combination of the following three types:

1) Grouping cases according to the rule they follow. This is necessary if you are analyzing a case of first impression in the jurisdiction of your assignment, and you need to argue why one rule is better than the other.

2) Defining the elements of a claim or defense.

3) Identifying the factors (the general categories of facts) that courts use to determine how to prove a particular cause of action.

A. Grouping Cases

The first type, which is perhaps the least difficult, essentially requires you to group cases. For example, if you read several cases from different states on the issue of whether to adopt the attractive nuisance rule, you will find that several states have adopted the rule, but that some have not.

In writing about your research, group the cases by which rule they apply, rather than list the cases one by one. Work deductively, starting with the general proposition that unites the cases.

The majority of the states have adopted the traditional rule that a landowner is liable for injuries to trespassing children if the landowner maintains an attractive nuisance on the property. See [cases applying this rule]. The reasons for this rule are that [explanation of reasons].

A number of states, however, have rejected the rule and instead apply the traditional rule that a landowner has no duty to trespassers. See [cases rejecting the rule and explanation of these cases].

This writer has identified two lines of decisions and described the basic characteristic of each in clear topic sentences. The two categories in this example were based on a legal rule that was explicit in the cases themselves.

B.   Defining Elements from Evolving Case Law

A second type of synthesis is required when courts have not yet clearly or fully articulated the elements of a cause of action. This type of synthesis involves putting together a general principle of law that is evolving in the case law.

Suppose you are analyzing some cases on the question of whether parents are immune from tort suits brought by their children. You know part of the rule, that parents may be immune from suit. Read the four case summaries to synthesize the rest of the rule. All suits are in the jurisdiction where the age of majority is 18. (Full citations are omitted.)

Case 1:

Jack Abbott sued his father Joseph for negligently pouring hot liquids in the Abbott kitchen so that he burned Jack in the process. Jack is twelve-years-old. Held: Mr. Abbott is immune from suit. *Abbott v. Abbott* (1999).

Case 2:

James White sued his father Walter for battery, an intentional tort. Walter knocked James's baseball cap off his head because James struck out in the last inning of a Little League game. James is ten-years-old. Held: Mr. White is not immune from suit. *White* v. *White* (2000).

Case 3:

Joan Brown sued her father Matt for assault, an intentional tort, for brandishing a tennis racket at her after she lost her serve in the final set of the women's 25 and under local tennis tournament. Joan is twenty-four-years-old and lives at home. Held: Mr. Brown is not immune from suit. *Brown v. Brown* (2001).

> **Case 4:**
>
> George Black sued his father Paul for negligently burning him in Mr. Black's kitchen by handing him a large hot pot. George is a twenty-four-year-old business man and is married. Held: Paul Black is not immune from suit. *Black v. Black* (2008).

These cases identify two requirements of whether the parent is immune from suit. To analyze the topic, you should identify them and consider how they determine immunity. Look at the facts that evidently led the courts to decide that the parent is immune, and at the facts that evidently led the courts to decide that the parent is not immune.

In each case, the court mentions the child's age. In **Case 1**, the child was a minor and the parent was immune from suit. In **Case 2**, however, the child was a minor but the parent was not immune from suit. In seeking an explanation for this difference, you notice that a second requirement is involved, the type of tort, whether an intentional tort or negligence. In **Case 3**, the daughter was not a minor and the case involved the parent's intentional tort. The parent was not immune. In **Case 4**, the parent was negligent, but the child was not a minor and the parent was not immune from the suit. These two requirements now become part of the rule: 1) the child must be a minor, and 2) the child must sue for negligence.

You may find a chart helpful.

Number of Case	Type of Tort	Age of Child	Result
1	negligence	12	immunity
2	intentional	10	no immunity
3	intentional	24	no immunity
4	negligence	24	no immunity

When you can characterize these facts in a way that explains the results, the full parental immunity rule, you are ready to begin writing. Start your written discussion of these cases with a topic sentence that identifies the elements of the parental immunity rule.

Notice the difference between the following two discussions of the immunity topic. Which is more effective and why?

1. A parent is immune from a tort suit brought by his child if the suit is for negligence and the child is a minor. First, parents are not immune from suits for intentional torts. The Lake Supreme Court has held that a parent is not immune from his child's suit for assault, *Brown v. Brown*, and for battery, *White v. White*. But the court has held that a parent is immune from a negligence suit brought by his child. *Abbott v. Abbott*. Second, in *Abbott*, the court held that the parent was immune from suit brought by a minor child for negligence. But in *Black v. Black* the parent was not immune from the negligence suit brought by his twenty-four-year-old son.

2. The Lake Supreme Court has decided four cases on parental immunity from tort suits by their children. In the first case in 1999, the court decided that a parent was immune from suit for negligence brought by his twelve-year-old son. *Abbott v. Abbott* (1999). However, in the next suit, in 2000, the court held that a parent was not immune from a suit for battery brought by a ten-year-old son. *White v. White* (2000). Only a year later in *Brown v. Brown* (2001), the court affirmed that a parent is not immune from suit for assault brought by a twenty-four-year-old daughter. The most recent case on this topic is *Black v. Black*, decided in 2008. In *Black*, the court decided another suit by a twenty-four-year-old against his parent, this time for negligence. The court still decided that the parent is not immune.

In the first discussion, the writer synthesizes the four cases and explains the two requirements for immunity. In thinking through the problem, the writer proceeded inductively by analyzing individual cases and then generalizing about these cases, i.e., by identifying two requirements that appear crucial on the issue of parental immunity. For the written product, however, the writer followed a deductive pattern. The writer put together a general rule to explain the law and started the discussion with that rule. Then she developed it, using the cases as authorities for her conclusion.

However, the writer of the second discussion has not analyzed the problem. She has written no more than a historical narrative of the four cases. The paragraph's only organizing principle is one of chronological order. The writer has recreated her research process, but has left the job of making sense of the cases to the reader.

Exercise 2-J

Consider these cases along with the preceding cases about parental immunity.

Case 5:

Bob Peepe sued his father Larry for negligence for driving his car into Bob while Bob was riding his bicycle. Bob is nineteen and a senior in high school. He lives at home and is not self-supporting. Held: Mr. Peepe is immune from suit. *Peepe v. Peepe* (1999).

Case 6:

Marilyn Smith sued her father Richard for negligence for riding his bicycle into Marilyn while she was gardening. Marilyn is nineteen-years-old, unmarried, and a part-time college student who does not live at home. She is self-supporting. Held: Mr. Smith is not immune from suit. *Smith v. Smith* (2004).

Case 7:

Gretel Andersen sued her father Hans Andersen for negligence for stumbling against Gretel and pushing her against the hot pottery she had just removed from her kiln. Gretel is twenty, married and lives in another city. Held: Mr. Andersen is not immune from suit. *Andersen v. Andersen* (2005).

How might you synthesize these three cases and add them to the preceding four? How do these cases change the rule?

C. Identifying Relevant Factors

The third type of synthesis is the kind you will be doing most often. It requires you to identify factors important to the application of a rule. To do this, read the precedents you found, and identify the types of facts that courts consider significant in proving or disproving the cause of action. Then articulate a general category for each type of fact. These categories of facts are called factors.

For example, in cases dealing with the domicile of students, the courts determined the students' domiciles by looking at a number of facts. One plaintiff had lived in the state for eighteen years, the other plaintiff for twenty years. The factor involved here can be described as length of time living in the state of the alleged domicile. In addition, one plaintiff received tuition payments from the state; the other received tutoring help. This factor can be described as benefits received from the state of alleged domicile. And, if one plaintiff returned to visit his parents in the alleged domicile at least once a month and the other plaintiff had friends and family living in that state, we can describe this as the factor of retaining personal commitments to the state of alleged domicile.

When you analyze an issue that requires you to determine a student's domicile, you analyze the facts under those categories, that is, you organize according to those factors.

You will find that the term "factors" is sometimes used in different ways, however. For example, in *Sinn v. Burd*, the court adopted the California rule to prove negligent infliction of emotional distress: that the plaintiff's injury must be reasonably foreseeable. The court also adopted what it called the court's "factors" to determine whether the injury to the plaintiff was foreseeable. In doing so, the court used the factors as requirements that the plaintiff must prove. Judicial use of factors, however, may occur in a different way. In the example of student domicile above, the term identifies types of facts the court considers in order to identify a student's domicile, but does not require a particular result (for example, that the plaintiff live in the jurisdiction for a required number of years), rather, the court evaluates whether the factors push the decision in one direction or another.

We return to explaining factors in Chapter Four.

Exercise 2-K

The question is whether at the time one defendant committed a murder, the other defendant was "in immediate flight" from a robbery they had both committed, and therefore was also chargeable with the murder under the state felony murder law.[8] The murder was of a third felon of their group. Synthesize the holdings in these five cases in order to formulate the relevant factors in determining whether a defendant was "in immediate flight."

Case 1:

The murder was committed by Alfred one day after Alfred and Bob robbed a store together. Bob was in another county 50 miles away. Held: Bob was not in immediate flight from the robbery.

Case 2:

The murder was committed by Delia as she and Gene were being chased by the police moments after they had robbed a store. Held: Gene was in immediate flight from the robbery.

Case 3:

The murder was committed by Adam one hour after he and Keith had robbed a store. Keith had gone to buy the two of them bus tickets to Atlantic City. They had agreed to divide the proceeds when Adam

---

[8]   Under the criminal law, one whose conduct brought about an unintended death during the commission of a felony is guilty of murder.

joined Keith at the bus terminal. Held: Keith was in immediate flight from the robbery.

Case 4:

The murder was committed by Barbara two hours after she and Dan had committed a robbery. One hour after the robbery, Dan had surrendered to the police and was in police custody. Held: Dan was not in immediate flight from the robbery.

Case 5:

The murder was committed by George at 10 p.m. At 5 p.m. George and Bert had divided the proceeds from the robbery that they had committed at 4 p.m. Held: Bert was not in immediate flight from the robbery.

Exercise 2-L

You represent Larry Kemp in his divorce from Mary, his wife of seven years. An issue still before the court is the financial winding up of the marriage, for example whether the court will award Mary what her attorney calls "restitutionary alimony," to compensate her for the marital money that they paid to Kemp's first wife for child support. Mary knew about and agreed to those payments, which came from both their earnings. There are two precedents in that jurisdiction regarding restitutionary alimony:

- *Haas v. Haas* in which the couple divorced one year after the husband finished medical school and his medical residency. The court awarded Ms. Haas repayment for her years of financing his education and training, and had delayed finishing her own higher education.

- *Johns v. Johns* in which the couple divorced fifteen years after Dr. Johns completed her medical degree and began her own, now lucrative medical practice. Phil Johns already had his accountant's license and job in an accounting practice. The court did not award him restitutionary alimony for the support he provided during her education and training.

As Larry Kemp's attorney, how do you argue this issue of the relevant factors for an award of restitutionary alimony?

Exercise 2-M

A husband and wife who are childless provided sperm and ova to create four embryos by in vitro fertilization at an assisted reproduction clinic where the embryos were kept frozen. The couple signed a consent document with the clinic, but did not fill in the part that instructs the clinic as to the disposition of the embryos in case the couple separated or divorced.

The couple later divorced. Each claims the right to the embryos, the husband to destroy them, the wife to use them to bear children. The wife has since been diagnosed with cancer and has undergone treatments that leave her unable to become pregnant.

The clinic has asked the court to decide to whom it should give the embryos. If the court awards the embryos to the husband, he will destroy them. If the court awards them to the wife, she will have them implanted in order to become pregnant.

Synthesize these three court decisions in that jurisdiction on the issue of how these courts awarded possession of frozen embryos when the couple disagreed as to their disposition.

1. *The husband's claim of a constitutional right not to become a parent outweighs the wife's right to parent her biological child. The couple has two children. The court awarded the embryos to the husband.*

2. *Where the parties agreed in the clinic's informed consent document as to the distribution of the embryos, the court will uphold that agreement although the couple no longer agrees to it. The couple had agreed to destroy the embryos if they divorced. The court awarded the embryos to the husband to destroy them.*

3. *The parties' consent form with the clinic is ambiguous. The wife has since undergone chemotherapy and can no longer become pregnant. The couple has no children. The court awarded the frozen embryos to the wife.*

Chapter 3

Analyzing Legal Authority: Statutes

I. INTRODUCTION TO READING STATUTES

JUST AS YOU SHOULD KNOW HOW TO READ and analyze a judicial opinion, so should you know how to read and analyze a statute. And just as there are layers of analysis involved in analyzing case law, from briefing a single opinion to synthesizing a group of related cases, there are layers of understanding involved in statutory analysis.

First, you need to understand the structure of the statute, which requires understanding its parts, their relationships, and the elements of individual sections. Second, you must understand the language of the statute. This includes words of authority—which tell the reader whether the provision is imposing a duty, like "shall" or providing discretion, like "may,"—and words that have special meaning because they are defined in the statute itself or by courts interpreting the statute. Lawyers read statutes either online or in a commercial publisher's unofficial print edition of each jurisdiction's code. These publications arrange statutes by subject matter, organize them in numbered chapters or titles, provide citations to the cases that interpret the statute, and give other information, such as legislative history. Finally, you need to determine whether and how the statute applies to your case and what the precise statutory issues are.

II. THE STRUCTURE OF A STATUTE

A. The Structure of a Whole Statute

ALTHOUGH MANY ASSIGNMENTS INVOLVE only one section of a larger statute, you should look at that section within the context of the statute as a whole.

1. Title and Preamble

Start by reading the title of the statute, which can help you understand its area of application. For the same reason, read the preamble or statement of purpose that follows the title. The statement may tell you, for example, whether the statute was written to codify the existing common law. If so, then the case law decided prior to the enactment of the statute should still be authoritative. If the statute was written to change the common law, then case law prior to it will no longer be controlling, although cases decided after its enactment will be. The statement may also include the underlying purpose of the statute in order to provide guidance to administrators and courts: for example, as with certain civil rights statutes, it may declare the statute is remedial, intended to provide broad relief, and meant therefore to be interpreted broadly.

2. Body

Also skim other sections of the statute to see if any of them affects your problem. Statutes have substantive provisions that set out rights, duties, powers, privileges, and exceptions. You would not want to overlook an exception that might pertain to your client's situation. They might also have administrative sections that either create or identify an agency responsible for the statute's enforcement and that outline procedures that entity must follow. For example, the Civil Rights Act of 1964 establishes the Equal Employment Opportunity Commission to prevent unlawful employment practices and enforce the prohibition against discrimination. If a statute gives an agency the power to draft regulations implementing its provisions, you will need to read those regulations also. It may be that your client has both a substantive and procedural claim under the statute.

3. Miscellaneous Provisions

Frequently overlooked, but important to know, is the date that the statute took effect. This is called the effective date provision, usually found at the end of the statute. It may be crucial: for example, the statute may not have been in effect at the time of the conduct at issue in your problem. Other provisions at the end of the statute may include sunset provisions, which suspend the operation of a statute on a given date; savings clauses, which ensure the statute applies prospectively only; and severability clauses, which declare that if one part of the statute is held invalid, the rest remains in effect. One of these miscellaneous clauses might also raise an issue in your case.

B. The Structure of a Provision

Statutory provisions are often hard to read. The sentences are frequently so long that is hard to identify the relationship between clauses or the elements that must be proven. Sometimes the drafter helps a reader parse the sentence by using tabulated sentence structure, which shows the relationship between parts of the sentence graphically.

'Severe Physical Injury' means:

1. brain injury or bleeding within the skull;

2. starvation;

3. physical injury that creates a substantial risk of death; or

4. physical injury that causes permanent or protracted serious

    a. disfigurement,

    b. loss of the function of any bodily member or organ, or

    c. impairment of the function of any bodily member or organ.

The tabulation aids in seeing that there are four main ways to establish a severe physical injury, and three ways to establish a serious permanent or protracted physical injury. Tabulated sentences also help to clarify the alternative ('or') or cumulative ('and') nature of the tabulated items. If the parts are connected by the disjunctive 'or,' only one of the parts needs to be proven. If the parts of a provision are connected by the conjunctive 'and,' then all parts must be proven. Moreover here the prosecutor need prove only one type of severe physical injury because the definitions are connected with 'or.' For the same reason, the prosecutor must prove only one type of permanent or protracted injury if the case depends on the fourth type of injury. The statutory requirements that must be proven are the elements of the statute.

Sometimes, a statutory provision is written in paragraph form and it is helpful to tabulate the sentence in your head or on paper to see how all the parts fit together.

Burglary in the Third Degree

§ 1. A person is guilty of burglary in the third degree if he knowingly and unlawfully either enters or remains in a building, and does so with the intent to commit a crime.

To determine the elements that the prosecutor must prove for burglary, break the statute into its constitutive parts.

> § 1. A person is guilty of burglary in the third degree if he
>
>   a.   knowingly **and** unlawfully,
>
>   b.   enters **or** remains in a building, **and**
>
>   c.   does so with the intent to commit a crime.

Under the language of § 1, a person needs either to have entered a building or remained in a building in order to be guilty (the disjunctive establishes that only one is required). In addition, the person must have done so knowingly and unlawfully (the conjunction requires proving both). Finally, the person must have intended to commit a crime. The final 'and' after item (b) makes it clear that the prosecutor needs to prove all three parts to determine whether a defendant has violated the statute.

Sometimes an exception to the rule is included in the basic provision.

> **Regulations Concerning Dogs on Private Property:** A person who owns or has custody of a dog shall not allow it to go on private property without permission of the occupant, or if the property is vacant, the owner of the property, unless the private property is open to the public.

This rule breaks down as follows.

> **Regulations Concerning Dogs on Private Property:**
>
> **Rule:**
>
> A person who
>
>   1.   owns a dog, or
>
>   2.   has custody of a dog shall not allow it to go on private property without permission of
>
>   3.   the occupant, or
>
>   4.   if the property is vacant, the owner of the property.
>
> **Exception:**
>
> unless the private property is open to the public.

This statute may be redrafted as

    1.   A person who

        a.   owns or

        b.   has custody of a dog

    2.   shall not allow the dog on private property that is not open to the public without permission of

        c.   the occupant or

        d.   if the property is vacant, the owner

    3.   unless the property is open to the public

Exercise 3-A

Animal Control Act

If a dog or other animal, without provocation, damages another's property or injures any person who is peaceably conducting himself in any place where the person may lawfully be, the owner of the dog or other animal is liable for the damages or injury caused.

---

    1.   *What are the alternatives within the Animal Control Act?*

    2.   *What are the required elements?*

III. THE LANGUAGE OF THE STATUTE

A. Specially Defined Words

ONCE YOU ARE CLEAR ABOUT THE ELEMENTS OF THE STATUTE and the relation of the parts, then make sure you understand the legal meanings of the words in the provision. Words in a statute do not always have the same meaning as they do in conversation. So check to see if there is a definition section of the statute and determine whether any of the terms in the sections that apply to your case are defined there.

For example, you may have a client who believes he was discriminated against because he was formerly a cancer patient. He is now in good health. After doing some research, you learn that the Americans with Disabilities Act defines the term "disability" broadly. *See* 42 U.S.C. § 12102 (1) (2012). It includes not only those currently suffering from an impairment, but also those who have "a record of . . .an impairment" or who are "regarded of having . . .an impairment." Therefore, your client may have a successful claim if he meets the other requirements of the Act.

Sometimes the courts need to define statutory terms because the language in the statute is ambiguous, general, or vague. You need to know the courts' definitions because they are binding. Thus, for example, a federal rule that allows a party to intervene in litigation requires timely intervention. Courts have said an application is "timely" if it is "reasonable" within the circumstances. "Reasonableness," a vague term, requires looking at (a) the stage of the proceedings, (b) the prejudice that delay by intervention may cause the parties, and (c) the reason the party delayed the application to intervene. This then becomes the test for determining "timely application." The tools courts use to interpret statutes are discussed at greater length in Part V of this chapter.

B. Words of Authority

When you read a statute, pay attention to words of authority. Words of authority are verbs that inform the reader whether a provision is mandatory, prohibitory, discretionary, or declaratory.

- Statutes commonly use 'shall' when they are imposing a mandatory duty upon a person or entity, as in "an agency shall keep records of all financial transactions."

- If a statute is prohibiting conduct, it will say 'shall not' as in "a parent shall not abuse a minor."

- If an action is discretionary, that is, permissible but not required, statutes use 'may,' as in "a person may intervene as of right if. . . ."

- If a statute states a rule, it uses 'is,' as in "a person is guilty of burglary in the third degree if. . . ."

- If a statute sets out a condition precedent, it will use "must," as in "For a successful appeal, the notice must be filed within 30 days of the entry of the order."

IV. FINDING THE STATUTORY ISSUES

WHEN YOU READ A STATUTE in light of the facts of your assignment, you determine first if the statute applies to your case at all. For example, one of the parties to litigation may rely on Article 2 of the state's Commercial Code, which applies to sales of goods. If the case concerns the leasing, rather than the sale, of goods then one issue is whether the requirements of Article 2 apply at all to a contract for the lease of goods.

When you brief a case or write any legal analysis in which there is a statutory issue, your writing should reflect the statutory nature of the case. You should state the issue to reflect the exact question that the statute raised, and you usually should include verbatim the operative language of the statute. Your statement of the holding of the case should answer that question, also in terms of the statute and its exact language.

The following are examples of issues written for a case brief.

1. Is a person's claim to land "hostile to the record owner" under the state's adverse possession statute if he occupied the disputed land by mistake?

2. Does a person enter a "building" within the meaning of the burglary statute if she without authority goes into a tent pitched in a park?

3. Is a signed writing that says only "I revoke my will," a "subsequent will which revokes the prior will" as required by the Probate Code?

Exercise 3-B

Do the following statutes apply to the sets of facts that follow them?

1. Statute: Deceptive Collection Practices Act

A collection agency or any employee of a collection agency commits a deceptive collection practice when, while attempting to collect an alleged debt, he adds to the debt any service charge, interest, or penalty, which he is not entitled to by law.

Facts 1:

John Brown, an interior decorator, loaned $3000 to his employee. When the employee had made no efforts to return the loan, Brown began harassing him for repayment and also claimed a usurious interest rate. The employee threatens to sue Brown under the Deceptive Collection Practices Act.

Facts 2:

Oscar Green, a secretary for Acme Collection Agency, plays poker with five friends every Tuesday evening after work. One night his friend Felix ran up a $500 debt that he couldn't pay, and Oscar loaned him the $500. Two weeks later, when he asked Felix to repay him, Oscar added a $25 charge.

What information about the statute's coverage might you want to know besides the section above?

2. Statute: The Animal Control Act includes the following paragraph from the definitions section:

Owner means any person who has a right of property in an animal, keeps or harbors an animal, has an animal that person's care, or acts as custodian of an animal.

Facts:

John Anderson, a home care provider, was injured when he walked his employer's dogs. One of the dogs nipped Anderson's leg, without provocation. Anderson wants to sue his employer.

Once you have determined that a statute applies to your client's case, you need to identify the elements of the statute that were violated.

What conduct does the statute require, permit, or not permit? Does your client's or the other party's conduct come within the statutory description?

Exercise 3-C

Identify the statutory issues in these problems.

1. **Statute: Distribution of Damages in Wrongful Death Action:**[1]

The jury in any wrongful death action may award such damages as may seem fair and may direct how the damages are to be distributed among the surviving spouse, the children, and the grandchildren of the decedent.

Facts:

Martha Smith, for whose death a wrongful death action was brought, was survived by her husband, by a natural born child of the marriage, by an adopted child, and by her non-marital child.

2. **Statute: Worker's Compensation**

If an employee suffers personal injury by an accident arising out of and in the course of the employment, the worker is entitled to recover under this Act.

Facts:

Nathan Hail was employed by a university's tennis facility as a teacher at its tennis camp for children. The facility sold summer passes and also solicited people to contribute as subscribers. The director of the facility made clear that the teachers should be friendly to the subscribers. Sam Hardy, a subscriber, asked Nathan to play one afternoon after Nathan got off work teaching tennis classes. During the match, Nathan twisted his ankle and had to stop working for the rest of the season.

3. **Statute: Parental Support**

It is the duty of every parent to support his or her minor child.

Facts:

Martha Smith and Joan Robinson lived together in a same-sex relationship. After three years together, they decided to have a child. To conceive the child, Martha used sperm donated by Joan's cousin Joe. Martha's pregnancy was successful, and Martha and Joan both raised the child. But four years after the child was born, Martha and

---

[1]   A wrongful death statute provides a civil recovery against a person who caused the death of another.

Joan ended their relationship. Martha plans to sue both Joan and Joe for child support.

Exercise 3-D

Write the issues for the three exercises above as you would write them for a case brief.

Exercise 3-E

For the following exercise, read the statute and the facts to which you will apply the statute.

Statute: Theft of Lost or Mislaid Property

A person who obtains control over lost or mislaid property commits theft if that person

(1) knows or learns the identity of the owner or knows of a reasonable method of identifying the owner,

(2) fails to take reasonable measures to restore the property to the owner, and

(3) intends to deprive the owner permanently of the use of the property.

110 Kent Rev. Stat. § 20 (2016).

Facts

Bill Smith saw a 14k gold locket on the ground of the park softball diamond at 1:30 p.m., just after a team from the YWCA had been practicing there. The diamond is located just west of a residential area of Kent and is in a large park that also contains children's playground facilities and tennis courts. The locket was engraved with three initials. Although he did not know the people on the team, Smith knew the name of the team because of the YWCA uniforms they wore. Smith was making deliveries for a nearby supermarket, where he worked a 10 a.m. to 4 p.m. shift. He also worked evenings for a newspaper.

Smith picked up the locket, looked it over, saw it was stamped 14k gold and saw that the initials were the same as those of his sister, who was in school 300 miles away. The locket needed polishing and had two pictures inside it. One was of a movie star. Smith pocketed the locket. He walked toward the street for his next delivery, in the opposite direction from the YWCA. About a block from the place where he picked up the locket, John Lyons robbed Smith of the groceries, Smith's own money, and the locket.

Someone who knows Smith saw him pick up the locket and gave his name to the police, who claim he violated the statute.

a.   *What does the prosecutor have to prove in order to convict Smith of Theft of Lost or Mislaid Property?*

b.   *What are the statutory issues?*

c.   *What are the legally relevant facts?*

d.   *Write an analysis of whether Smith violated the statute.*

V.   TECHNIQUES OF STATUTORY INTERPRETATION

ONCE YOU IDENTIFY THE EXACT DISPUTE about the application of the statute, you then analyze what the statute means in order to resolve how the statutory language applies to the facts of the case. A legislature enacts a statute to apply to future conduct, some of which is unforeseen at the time of enactment, rather than to a particular situation that has already occurred. Thus, legislative language is often more general than the language in a judicial opinion. General language, like vague and ambiguous language, may require judges to interpret the terms.

- In statutory litigation, the judge must often decide how the relatively general language of legislation, such as language that refers to a class of things, applies to a particular case. For example, a statute may require registration of motor vehicles. A court may have to determine which specific types of vehicles are included in that category, such as whether the requirement applies to a person's private airplane.

- Besides being general, statutory language may also be vague, sometimes purposely so. The statute may use terms like "fair use" or "reasonable efforts." The court must then determine the content of those vague terms within the framework of specific litigation.

- Statutory language, like all language, may also be ambiguous; it may have more than one meaning and the court may have to decide which meaning to apply. For example, a municipal ordinance revokes the license of a cab driver if he is convicted for a "second time of any offense under the Motor Vehicle Act." This statute may mean that the driver must be convicted twice of the same offense, but may also mean that the license will be revoked upon a conviction for a second but different offense.

In all of these situations, a judge may be called upon to interpret what the text means.

A. Legislative Intent

The court determines what statutory language means by asking what the legislature intended it to mean. The first source of the legislature's intended meaning is the language of the statute itself, its plain meaning. Often, however, the court must examine other evidence about the statutory language. Moreover, a court may seek to determine what policy the legislature intended to pursue through the statute by determining the purpose of the statute. Then the court interprets the statute in a way that furthers that policy.

1. Plain Meaning

Courts employ a variety of approaches to determine what the legislature intended the statute to mean. The first step for most courts is to determine whether the statute has a single plain meaning. This process determines whether the parties may submit evidence besides the statute itself to support their interpretations of the language. If the court can interpret the statutory language according to a plain meaning, then it often will decide not to permit the parties to submit other evidence to explain the statute's meaning; it will use only the statute itself to determine what the legislature meant. But even Supreme Court Justices can differ on whether the plain meaning of the statute resolves the question.

For example, Title VII of the Civil Rights Act of 1964 prohibits discrimination "because of . . . sex." Some federal courts of appeal have held that under the plain meaning of the statute, transgender persons are not members of a class protected by Title VII. They reasoned that Congress intended Title VII to apply to the traditional definition of sex, that is male or female. Therefore discrimination on the grounds of sex means discrimination against women because they are women and men because they are men.

"Plain meaning" is often the ordinary meaning, sometimes the dictionary meaning, rather than a technical meaning of the statutory words. However, words in some statutes, such as statutes that regulate a particular industry, may be interpreted according to their technical meanings in that industry. Some words may be interpreted according to their technical legal meaning. For example, if a lawyer drafts a document and uses the word "heir," that word will most likely be given its technical meaning (a person who inherits if the decedent died without a will). If a layman uses the word, it may be given its more colloquial meaning (a person's children).

Besides the "plain meaning" of the particular statutory language at issue, other internal aids to interpreting the scope of the disputed language can come from similar language in other parts of the same statute. If the exact language is used elsewhere in the statute, that use may provide the intended meaning of the words. If similar words are used, the difference in the wording may aid you in interpreting the disputed language. For example, if a statute refers to a person's "residence premises" in one section, but refers to "place of actual residence" in another section, a comparison of the terms indicates that the term "residence premises" is not restricted to the place at which the person is actually residing. Where the legislature intended that restriction, it used different wording. Of course, if the statute includes a definition section, that section should be the first place to look.

Exercise 3-F

Does the plain meaning rule help you decide the following cases?

1. Elena and Steven were married for 15 years. Three years ago, Elena suffered a stroke and became permanently partially paralyzed. Thereafter, she kept the thermostat at 85–90 degrees and always locked and bolted the door to the house when Steven was away, so that he had to wait 15 minutes for her to come downstairs and let him in. As a result, he moved out of the house and into their travel van parked at the back of the lot behind the house. He has lived there for the last 30 months. However, he continues to help his wife with household chores. Steven has filed for divorce. The grounds for divorce in that state include "when the spouses have, without interruption for two years lived separate and apart without cohabitation. . . ." Will Steven's petition succeed?

2. Travis and Melissa had two children of their marriage. Melissa died when the younger child was one-year-old. Travis re-married two years later, after which his relationship with Marion, his mother, cooled significantly and he refused to let Marion see the children. Marion has petitioned the court for visitation with her two grandchildren. The visitation statute provides, "If either the father or mother of a minor child is deceased, the court may grant the parents and other relatives of the deceased parent reasonable visitation rights . . . if the court determines that visitation is in the child's best interests."

Does the court have jurisdiction to grant Marion's petition?

3. A federal statute subjects defendants convicted of a violent felony to mandatory minimum sentences. The statute defines a violent felony as "burglary, arson, and other conduct that presents a serious potential risk of physical injury to another."

Has a suspect who flees at high speed from the police in a car committed a violent felony?

Exercise 3-G

A mental health patient killed his stepfather. The executor of the stepfather's estate sued the patient's psychiatrist and social worker alleging their negligence in not warning the stepfather of the patient's dangerous propensities. The patient had a long history of mental health problems and had been hospitalized several times. His former girlfriend had gotten an abuse prevention order against him after he threatened to stab her. The patient violated the order and spent time in jail. He was also later hospitalized and the staff took a knife from him. He was seen by the psychiatrist and social worker during that time and after he was discharged.

The state's statute provides: "A licensed mental health professional does not owe a duty to take reasonable precautions to warn or in any way protect a potential victim of the professional's patient unless the patient has a history of physical violence that is known to the mental health professional and the professional has a reasonable basis to believe that the patient imposes a clear and present danger that he will attempt to kill. . . a reasonably identified victim and fails to take reasonable precautions."

1. *What are the elements of his cause of action?*

2. *Under the plain meaning of the statute, must the patient's history of violence be connected with the victim?*

3. *Does the statutory language support the argument that the professional must investigate fully for information about the patient and the victim?*

---

2. Extrinsic Evidence

If the court cannot determine a plain meaning from the statutory language itself, but decides that the language is "ambiguous," meaning that the language may have more than one interpretation, then it will permit the parties to introduce other evidence to show what the legislature intended the statute to mean. Sometimes, a court uses other evidence as aids in construing the statutory language even if it can ascribe a plain meaning to the words. For instance, even if a plain meaning is discernible, a court will permit the parties to submit evidence explaining what the legislature intended in order to show that an ambiguity exists, or to show that enforcing the plain meaning would lead to absurd or to unintended results. To arrive at this conclusion, a court might examine the purpose of, or policy for, the statute.

For example, a federal statute prohibits importing aliens "under contract to perform labor or service of any kind in the United States." Has a church violated this statute by contracting and bringing from England an English minister to perform services as minister for the church? If it seems absurd to construe this statute to impose a monetary penalty on a church because it employed a minister from England, then the court will admit evidence to show that Congress did not intend the statute to prohibit that type of employment.[2]

a. Legislative History

The most favored evidence that parties employ to determine the legislature's intended meaning is the legislative history of the statute. A legislative history consists of different elements. One part of a legislative history is the predecessor statutes to the one at issue. More importantly, legislative history consists of the documents that were produced during the statute's legislative journey from its beginning as a bill introduced in the legislature, through proceedings in the committee or committees to which it was assigned, and to its passage into law. You use this type of legislative history to find legislators' statements about what they meant by the disputed language. In the case of the statute that prohibits importing aliens, for example, the transcripts of committee hearings, the committee report, and the Congressional Record account of the debate on the floor of Congress all show that Congress intended to prohibit importation of contract labor crews to perform unskilled labor, not to prohibit hiring an individual from abroad to perform professional services.

If, however, the documents do not reveal the legislators' intended meaning or if they show that the legislators never thought about the application of the statute to the particular problem posed by the case, then you read the documents to try to find the more general purpose of the statute and you interpret the language in a way that promotes that purpose or policy.

b. Example

For federal statutes, the legislative history can be extensive, the most favored source being committee reports. For example,

---

[2] At a recent Senate hearing a senator criticized a judicial candidate's vote in a decision that upheld firing a truck driver who abandoned his malfunctioning truck, because he was freezing in the truck. The judicial candidate testified that the plain meaning of a relevant statute required that result. However, the senator pointed out that the court need not follow the plain meaning rule if it led to an absurd result.

committee reports played a considerable role in one court's interpretation of Exemption 6 to the Freedom of Information Act. This section exempts from mandatory disclosure "personnel and medical files and similar files the disclosure of which would constitute a clearly unwarranted invasion of personal privacy." The section required judicial interpretation because of an ambiguous modifier. It is unclear which terms are modified by the phrase "the disclosure of which would constitute a clearly unwarranted invasion of personal privacy." The restriction could apply only to similar files or it could modify personnel files, medical files, and similar files.

If the restriction applies only to "similar files," then personnel and medical files are under a blanket exemption from disclosure regardless of whether their disclosure would constitute an invasion of privacy. A person requesting disclosure of personnel files would interpret the modifier to apply to all three descriptions of files. The government agency would interpret the modifier to apply only to "similar files."

Because of the ambiguous syntax of Exemption 6, the statute's plain language is unhelpful. Thus, the court facing this issue of statutory interpretation used the following information and reasoning to decide that the "invasion of privacy" language applied to all three types of files.

1. That court had already interpreted the policy behind the entire FOIA statute as one of disclosure, not secrecy.

2. The Congressional committee reports included language that applied to all of Exemption 6. That language requires a court to engage in a balance of the two policies of protecting an individual's private affairs from unnecessary public scrutiny and of preserving the public's right to governmental information. A court would not engage in that balance for medical and personnel files if those files were under a blanket exemption from disclosure.

3. The committee reports had no language about blanket exemptions in Exemption 6.

Thus, although the legislative history contains no explicit information, the court used these sources to decide that the limiting language modified the three types of files listed so that none was under a blanket exemption from the Act.[3] By doing so,

---

[3]   Based on *Department of Air Force v. Rose*, 425 U.S. 352 (1976).

the court interpreted the statutory language to promote the statute's policy of disclosure.

Unlike the materials available for federal statutes, the legislative materials available for state statutes may be meager. Even if considerable state or federal materials exist, however, they may be inconclusive as to what the legislature intended the litigated language to mean, or how the purposes of the statute bear on the application of the particular language to the facts of the case. The lawyer must assemble all the relevant pieces to form a coherent interpretation of legislative intent.

Exercise 3-H

Some of the relevant legislative history of the Freedom of Information Act § 7 exemption is set out below. Based on this legislative history, did the court interpret the § 7 exemption correctly? Was the statute intended to mean only human sources?

1. Original version of statute:

The original version of § 7 exempted records that would "disclose the identity of an informer." The committee to which the bill was referred amended the term "informer" to "confidential source."

2. Committee Report:

The Committee Report contains the following statements:

a. "The substitution of the term 'confidential source' in § 7 is to make clear that the identity of a person other than a paid informer may be protected if the person provided information under an express assurance of confidentiality."

b. "The bill in the form now presented to the Senate . . . has been changed from protecting the identity of an 'informer' to protecting the identity of a person other than a paid informer. . . . Not only is the identity of a confidential source protected but also protected from disclosure is all the information furnished by that source to a law enforcement agency. . . ."

3. Congressional debate:

The debate on the floor of the Senate recorded in the Congressional Record contains the statement by a senator on the committee, "we also provided that there be no requirement to reveal not only the identity of a confidential source, but also any information obtained from him in a criminal investigation."

How do you evaluate the following arguments in support of the court's plain meaning interpretation that § 7 applies to all sources including other law enforcement agencies and not human sources only?

1. The use of the word "person" in the Committee Report is similar to the use of any collective noun and refers to a variety of entities in addition to human beings.

2. The singular masculine pronoun, such as the "him" used by the senator, is often used where the sex of the referent is unknown or where it refers to a collective noun consisting of entities of more than one sex. A person using a pronoun during debates is not grammatically precise.

3. Congress was concerned that it not impair the ability of federal law enforcement agencies to collect information. The plaintiff's interpretation of § 7 would make other law enforcement agencies or other entities reluctant to share information with federal agencies.

4. The legislative history materials are themselves ambiguous and should not control the customary meaning of words in the statute.

Exercise 3-I

For the following exercise, read the facts of the problem. The case following the facts will provide some arguments relevant to the issue in the problem.

Facts:

The Kent Licensed Nursing Home Act § 15 provides a hearing for any licensee that has been charged with abusing a patient. The section provides "The Department shall commence a hearing within thirty days of the receipt of a nursing home's request for a hearing."

On April 10, 2016, the Department determined that TranQuil Nursing Home had abused a patient. TranQuil then requested a hearing on May 1, 2016. The Department, however, overlooked the request and did not schedule a hearing until December 1, 2016. At the hearing, the Department again determined that TranQuil was guilty of abuse. The Home now seeks judicial review of that determination and has moved to dismiss the Department's proceedings for lack of timeliness because it was held after the thirty day period.

Adam v. Personnel Board

The Personnel Code of Kent § 20 requires that the Personnel Board provide a review for all state personnel protesting their discharge. Section 20 provides that the review "shall be held within 60 days of a discharged employee's request for review." Donald Adam requested review on September 1, 2010. The Personnel Board hearing, which confirmed his discharge, was held January 15, 2011. Adam has asked this court to void the Board's decision on the grounds that it was not timely.

The plain meaning of the word "shall" is that of a mandatory verb. The dictionary so defines it. The word has sometimes been construed as directory, however. That is, it has been interpreted as "may." If the statute states the time for performance but does not deny performance after a specified time, then "shall" is usually considered directory. If the time period safeguards someone's rights, it is mandatory.

Section 20 is designed to protect the rights of government employees who protest their discharge. A delay in their hearing could prejudice their rights. We therefore interpret the section as mandatory.

1. *Which statutory argument will the plaintiff TranQuil Nursing Home make?*

2. *Which arguments will the state make?*

3. *Which arguments are better?*

Exercise 3-J

Anderson, Brown & Childress, P.C., a law firm whose primary business is bill collection, sent a collection letter to plaintiff Jane Bass. The letter did not meet the requirements of the Fair Debt Collection Practices Act (FDCPA), and Bass wants to sue the firm under that statute for civil damages. Bass owns a condominium, and received a one-time assessment from the condo board for her share of the cost of routine maintenance to the condo's roof. Bass disagreed with the board's decision and never paid the assessment. The only issue is whether the assessment is "a debt" as defined in the FDCPA, thus mandating the firm's compliance with its statutory protections.

The Act defines "debt" as "any obligation. . . of a consumer to pay money arising out of a transaction in which the money, property. . . or services which are the subject of the transaction are primarily for personal, family, or household purposes. . . ."

The defendant law firm argues that the debt must flow specifically from a credit-based consumer transaction, and that the FDCPA does not apply to condo or homeowner's association assessments because there was no extension of credit.

1. *Look first to the statutory language. Does the definition of debt have a plain meaning, and if so, does the definition include this transaction?*

2. *Is there any ambiguity in the definition because it does not define "transaction"?*

3. *How much should it matter that a draft of the FDCPA included a requirement that the transaction involve an*

> extension of credit, but that requirement was omitted in the final version of the Act?
>
> 4. Should the court consider the FDCPA's statutory structure? The FDCPA was passed as an amendment adding a subchapter to the Consumer Credit Protection Act. This Act, as its name suggests, applies to credit transactions only.
>
> 5. Should the court defer to another federal appellate court that concluded, on a different issue, that the word "transaction" in the above definition does not include tort liability (the case involved a person sued for conversion[4] because he pirated microwave television signals). However, this court went on to say that "transaction" involves the offer or extension of credit to a consumer.

B. The Canons of Construction

Another long-standing—and frequently criticized—method of determining statutory meaning is to apply what are called "canons of construction." These canons are maxims or guides that suggest possible interpretations of certain verbal patterns in statutes and certain types of statutes. The canons, however, may yield inconclusive results.

A well-known canon used to interpret verbal patterns is the canon known as **ejusdem generis**. Ejusdem generis is applied to mean that whenever a statute contains specific enumeration followed by a general catchall phrase, the general words should be construed to mean only things of the same kind or same characteristics as the specific words (ejusdem generis means "of the same genus or class"). For example, in the language "no one may transport vegetables, dairy, fruit, or other products without a certificate of conveyance," the catchall words "or other products" could be interpreted to mean food products but not manufactured goods. It can also mean non-manufactured goods that are not foods, such as fresh flowers.

Some canons are used to help interpret types of statutes by the presumed policy behind those statutes. An example is "**A penal statute should be strictly construed.**" This means that if it is not clear whether the language of a criminal statute (or a civil statute that imposes a penalty) applies to a particular defendant's conduct, the statute will be interpreted narrowly in favor of the defendant, that is, it will be interpreted not to apply. This type of

---

[4] Conversion is a taking of property that completely deprives the owner of its value.

construction is based on a policy that people should have fair warning of conduct that is punishable.

Canons do not explain what the legislature meant in enacting the particular statute being analyzed. Rather, they suggest how legal professionals usually interpret that kind of rule. A canon such as "A penal statute should be strictly construed" supplies a presumption about how any legislature enacting that type of statute would intend the statute to be interpreted. Thus, because the canons do not analyze the reasons for the particular statutory language being applied, a canon need not by itself compel a particular interpretation.

Moreover, just as there are arguments and counter-arguments, so are there canons and, so to speak, "counter-canons." Thus, if one canon says courts must give effect to unambiguous statutory language, another says plain language need not be given effect when doing so would defeat legislative intent or have absurd or unjust results.[5] See Chapter 11 for more explanation of the canons.

Statutory interpretation often can be a difficult process of analyzing the language of

- the text, the pre-enactment legislative history materials related to that text,

- other materials related to the statute, such as proposed amendments, and

- the canons of construction.

But just as you apply case law to further the policies behind legal precedents, you use the techniques of statutory analysis to determine the legislative policy in enacting the statute and to interpret the text to further that policy.

C. Stare Decisis and Statutes

Once a court interprets a statute, the principle of stare decisis applies and the court will then follow the interpretation it or a higher court has previously adopted. For each new case with the same statutory issue, the court then reasons by analogy to the facts of the prior cases in order to apply the statute to the new case.

When you write about a problem that involves statutory analysis and arguments, you should include these analytic steps in your written analysis. Focus on the exact statutory language and

---

[5] Many canons point to opposite conclusions. *See* Karl Llewellyn, "Remarks on the Theory of Appellate Decision and the Rules or Canons About How Statutes Are To Be Construed," 3 Vand. L. Rev. 395 (1950).

its possible interpretations. Summarize the relevant legislative history, if any, and its interpretations. If the canons of construction are relevant, explain how they apply to the language. If the statute has been interpreted by the courts, discuss the case law. If there is binding precedent interpreting the statute, explain how that interpretation applies to the facts of your problem. You will find that after a statute has been interpreted by the courts, its history becomes less important to its interpretation.

Exercise 3-K

Carol Thomas has filed a law suit against the owner-operator of a roller skating rink. Ms. Thomas alleges that she fell and was injured because the skating surface was wet. The defendant has answered that he did not know about any defect and had no reason to suspect it.

The Roller Skating Rink Safety Act requires a rink operator to have a floor supervisor on duty, to maintain a reasonably safe skating surface, and to inspect the surface before each skating session. The Act says nothing about notice. The defendant has moved for summary judgment, and his motion will be successful if the Act requires that the operator have notice of a defective surface.

The operator's memorandum in support of the motion makes the following arguments. Should the motion be successful? (There are no disputed material facts.)

1. *The statute's preamble says that "the purposes of the Act are to make it "more economically feasible for insurance companies to provide coverage for roller skating rinks," to ensure that occurrences that result in liability should be more predictable, and to encourage rink operators to implement risk reduction procedures.*

2. *The common law of premises liability subjects a possessor of land to liability for injury to invitees caused by a defect or danger on the premises only if the possessor knows or should have known of the defect or danger.*

3. *The state's Premises Liability Act, which imposes liability on landowners, has a notice requirement. Landowners have no duty to warn of dangers that are not known to them.*

CHAPTER 4

ORGANIZATION OF A LEGAL DISCUSSION: LARGE-SCALE ORGANIZATION

I. INTRODUCTION

IN THIS CHAPTER, YOU WILL LEARN how to identify the legal issues that are necessary for analyzing a problem and to use these issues to organize your written analysis of a legal problem. An analysis like this might appear, for example, in the Discussion section of that memorandum. See Chapter 7. In Chapter 2, we described how to brief a case. There we used the word "issue" to describe the basic question that the court has to answer to resolve the dispute between the parties. Here we use the word "issue" in a different way—to describe the points you must discuss to analyze a claim.

To write any analysis, you break a subject into its component parts. Using this format to analyze a legal subject.

- First, identify the claims or defenses (which we will call the claims) in your problem.

- Then break each claim down into its parts.

- Then where needed, break each part down into its sub-parts.

- Once you have identified the parts and sub-parts, arrange them in a logical order.

This logical order forms the organizational structure of your discussion.

II. ORGANIZING A DISCUSSION

A. Organize by Claim

THE ORGANIZATION OF AN ENTIRE DISCUSSION begins with the client's claims. If your problem contains only one claim, like battery, then your entire discussion will be an analysis of just that one claim. If your problem contains more than one claim, then you discuss each separately. For example, if your client has two claims, one for assault and one for battery, you should divide the discussion into two main sections, one for assault, and one for battery.

> **Order of Claims: Threshold Questions.** The order in which you discuss the claims depends upon the particular problem. If the problem requires resolution of a threshold question, then you should analyze it first. A threshold question is one that the court will answer first because its decision on that issue will determine whether the litigation will continue and whether the court must then decide the other issues.

Procedural questions are often threshold questions, for example, whether the plaintiff waited too long to file a complaint because the period for filing that type of complaint (governed by a statute of limitations) has expired. A court will resolve this first, because if the plaintiff has waited too long to file, the court will dismiss the complaint. Therefore, you should discuss it first in your analysis.

Some threshold questions go to the merits of the case, for example, whether a landowner has a duty to protect trespassers from dangerous conditions on the property. If there is no duty, the court will not discuss the other elements of the claim, such as whether the conditions were dangerous.

However, your resolution of the threshold question should not end the discussion. The judge may disagree with your conclusion on the threshold question, or your reader may want an analysis of the entire subject.

> **Order of Claims: Complexity.** If there are no threshold questions, you may want to organize the claims by degree of difficulty. You may decide to analyze the simpler claim first to dispose of it quickly and then work toward the more difficult one. Or you may decide to attack the most complex claim first while you have the reader's attention, and then follow with the claim that you think is easier to establish.

> **Order of Claims: Different Causes of Action.** Your discussion may require analysis of two or more different types of claims, for example, a statutory claim and constitutional one. You may decide to first analyze the statutory claim because if your client didn't violate the statute, the court need not reach the question of whether the statute is unconstitutional. For example, suppose your assignment involves a defendant charged under a local disturbance of the peace ordinance for loud and annoying comments he made on the street. You would first analyze whether the client violated the ordinance, and then

if he had, whether the ordinance is unconstitutional as applied to your
client because it violates his freedom of speech.

Other assignments may involve a common law claim and a
statutory one. For example, in the newspaper advertisement litigation
on page 56, the court first analyzed whether the defendant car dealer
had entered in a contract with the plaintiff, and next, whether the
defendant's newspaper advertisement violated the state's Consumer
Fraud Act.

B. Organization Within One Claim— Identifying the Issues

After you identify the claims in your assignment and decide the
order in which you will discuss them, then break down each claim
into its constituent parts. What are the elements of that claim or
the factors courts consider in analyzing it? These issues may come
from an established definition, such as the elements of a tort or
crime. When a claim has elements, the plaintiff must prove each
one. Or the court may have previously considered different factors
in determining how to decide particular cases, not all of which
must be proven. To decide the claim, the court balances the factors
that establish the claim against those that do not. The elements or
factors will form the organizational framework for your analysis.
But remember—when you analyze a claim, you organize your
analysis around the issues that the claim raises, not around
individual cases.

There are several different ways of finding these issues.

1. A common law claim has been defined by elements.

2. The terms of a statute identify the elements.

3. The elements of a rule evolve over a series of opinions.

4. The court identifies and balances factors: the totality
   of circumstances approach.

1. A Common Law Claim Has Been Defined by Elements

Sometimes, a court opinion will define for you the elements of the
claim, for example, the elements of a tort. Read the following
opinion to find out the elements of the tort of intentional infliction
of emotional distress. These elements will provide the
organizational framework for your analysis.

Davis v. Finance Co.

Sofia Davis (Davis) sued Finance Company (Finance) seeking to recover on the theory of intentional infliction of emotional distress.

In this jurisdiction, the courts have adopted the definition of intentional infliction of emotional distress provided in the Restatement (Second) of Torts. First, the defendant's conduct must be extreme and outrageous. The defendant will be liable only when his conduct has been so outrageous in character, and so extreme in degree, as to go beyond all possible bounds of decency.

Second, the plaintiff's emotional distress must be severe. Mental conditions such as fright, horror, grief, shame, humiliation, or worry are not actionable. The distress inflicted must be so severe that no reasonable person could be expected to endure it.

Third, the defendant's conduct must be intentional, or at least reckless. If the defendant acted recklessly, the defendant's conduct must be such that there is a high degree of probability that the plaintiff will suffer severe emotional distress and the defendant goes ahead in disregard of it.

In this case, Finance's conduct was not so extreme and outrageous as to constitute a basis for recovery under this tort. Davis claims that agents of Finance called and e-mailed her every day, several times weekly, that they went to her home one or more times a week, and that they twice called her at a hospital where she was visiting her sick daughter. She alleges that Finance continued its practices even after she told them she was on disability assistance and was unable to make any additional payments.

Davis, however, was legally obligated to Finance and had defaulted in her payments. A creditor must have latitude to pursue reasonable methods of collecting debts. Finance was attempting to collect a legal obligation from Davis in a permissible though persistent and possibly annoying manner. Such conduct is not outrageous, and therefore, Davis does not state a cause of action for intentional infliction of emotional distress.[1]

In the *Davis* case, the court identifies three elements to the tort.

- The defendant's conduct must be outrageous.

- The plaintiff must suffer severe distress.

- The defendant's conduct must have been intentional or, at least, reckless.

---

[1]   This example is based on and uses language from the case of *Public Finance Corp. v. Davis*, 360 N.E.2d 765 (Ill. 1976).

The plaintiff must prove each of these in order to succeed. Therefore, you would organize an analysis of a problem dealing with intentional infliction of emotional distress around the three elements of the tort. They become the issues you discuss.

You may find that some issues will require extensive analysis, and others need be discussed only briefly. For example, in *Davis*, the most difficult issue to resolve was whether the company's conduct was extreme and outrageous. Finding that it was not, the court did not need to discuss the other two issues, since the plaintiff must prove all of the elements of the tort for the claim to succeed. However, in writing a memorandum on this subject, you would discuss all of the elements but devote more space to whether the defendant acted outrageously because it was the most complex.

Although you usually analyze the elements in the order the court or statute sets them out, sometimes you may want to discuss the elements out of order. One of them may be more important than the other, or, you may want to discuss the least controversial issues first in order to dismiss them quickly. Then you would go into detail on the most problematic one. For example, in another case dealing with intentional infliction of emotional distress, the real controversy might be over whether the plaintiff's distress was severe. This time, the analysis of whether the defendant acted outrageously and intentionally may be so clear-cut that it could be disposed of quickly. You would then discuss extensively the more complex issue of whether the plaintiff's distress was severe. The discussion might run several paragraphs and be organized this way:

> Paragraph 1—The defendant's conduct was both outrageous and intentional.
>
> Paragraph 2—The plaintiff's distress was not severe because X.
>
> Paragraph 3—The plaintiff's distress was not severe because Y.
>
> Paragraph 4—The plaintiff's distress was not severe because Z.

If you analyze the elements out of order, include a brief explanation of why you are doing so.

A variant on this pattern may occur when you work with a rule that is followed by an exception. In this situation, your client may come within the rule, but the important analysis is whether your client comes within an exception to that rule.

Exercise 4-A

Read the following case and identify the three elements of the tort of false imprisonment. Each element will be an issue in the analysis of a false imprisonment claim. Here, the court also breaks down some of these issues into sub-issues.

East v. West

Carol West appeals from a judgment that she falsely imprisoned the three plaintiffs.

The plaintiffs were comparing voter registration lists with names on mailboxes in multi-unit dwellings. They intended to challenge the registration of people whose names were not on the mailboxes. Plaintiffs testified that they entered the building that West owned through the outer door into a vestibule area that lies between the inner and outer doors to West's building. They were checking the names on the mailboxes when West entered and asked what they were doing. They replied that they were checking the voter lists. She first told them to leave and then changed her mind and asked if they would be willing to identify themselves to the police. Plaintiffs said they would. West then asked her husband to call the police. While they waited, she stood by the door, but neither threatened nor intimidated the plaintiffs. In addition, the plaintiffs did not try to get her to move out of the way. When the police came, they said the plaintiffs were not doing anything wrong and could continue to check the lists. Plaintiffs later sued West for false imprisonment.

An actor is liable for false imprisonment if he acts intending to confine the other or a third person within boundaries fixed by the actor; if his act directly or indirectly results in such a confinement of the other; and if the other is conscious of the confinement or is harmed by it.

The evidence here is not sufficient to support the conclusion that West directly or indirectly confined the plaintiffs. The defendant may confine the plaintiff by actual physical barriers, by physical force, or by threat of physical force. The question in this case is whether West threatened to use confinement by threat of physical force. We think she did not. Plaintiffs acknowledge that West did not verbally threaten them. Since none of the plaintiffs asked her to step aside, they could no more than speculate whether she would have refused their request, much less physically resisted. Moreover, the three of them are claiming confinement by a single person. Accordingly, the judgment below is reversed.[2]

---

[2] This example is based on and uses language from the case of *Herbst v. Wuennenberg*, 266 N.W.2d 391 (Wis. 1978).

> *According to the East case, what are the three elements of the tort of false imprisonment? These provide the organizational structure for your discussion. Of the three elements, on which does the court focus its discussion? As to this element, what are the different ways by which the plaintiff can meet this requirement? These different ways provide sub-issues to include in organizing your analysis of a false imprisonment problem.*
>
> *Make an outline of how you would organize a false imprisonment problem. First, list the three elements of the tort—the basic issues that you must consider. Then look at the opinion and see how each of these elements is met. If any element can be met in different ways, list those ways beside the element. These are the sub-issues in the problem. This list provides the basic organizational structure for your analysis. Remember that sub-issues also merit different degrees of analysis, depending on their applicability to the facts of your case, their intrinsic complexity, and the other sub-issues involved.*

Sometimes the court defines the claim, but does not clearly outline the elements. Then you must identify and outline them yourself. Suppose your client, Mr. Smith, wishes to hire a new employee. He wants the employee to sign a restrictive covenant that he will not compete with him if the employee decides to leave Smith's employment in the future. In a restrictive covenant, the employee agrees not to engage in certain conduct that competes with the employer after he leaves employment with the employer. Read the following case. What does the court in this case consider necessary to determine whether to enforce a covenant not to compete?

Columbia Ribbon v. Trecker

We are required to determine whether a covenant made by a salesman not to compete with his employer after the termination of employment is enforceable in whole or in part.

Defendant Trecker was employed by Columbia Ribbon as a salesman for several years. He signed an employment contract with the following restrictive covenant:

1. The employee will not disclose to any person or firm the names or addresses of any customers or prospective customers of the company.

2. The employee will not, for a period of twenty-four months after the termination of his employment, sell or deliver any goods of the kind sold by the company within any territory to which he was assigned during the last twenty-four months prior to termination.

> After Trecker was demoted, he terminated his employment with Columbia Ribbon and took a job with a competitor, A-1-A Corporation. Columbia then sued to enforce the terms of the covenant.
>
> Restrictive covenants are disfavored in the law. On the other hand, courts must also recognize the employer's legitimate interest in safeguarding its business. Enforceability, therefore, depends on the reasonableness of the terms of the covenant. In this case, the terms of the covenant are broad and sweeping. The affidavits do not suggest that Trecker was privy to any trade secrets which he would use or disclose. Nor are there any confidential customer lists; the employer's past or prospective customer names are readily ascertainable from sources outside its business. Finally, Trecker was a good salesman, but he did not possess any unique or extraordinary abilities or skills.
>
> Since no facts indicating unfair competition, we need not consider whether the time and geographic restrictions are reasonable.
>
> Accordingly, Columbia's motion for summary judgment is dismissed.[3]

In the *Columbia Ribbon* case, the court tells you it will enforce covenants that protect the employer's interests only under certain circumstances. A court will enforce a covenant if the employee had access to trade secrets or confidential customer lists or that the employee provided unique services. The court, however, tells you at the end of the decision that it considers these factors only to prevent the employee from engaging in unfair competition. And then, even if the circumstances indicate unfair competition, the covenant's time and geographic restrictions must be reasonable. These elements, like those of a tort or crime, provide the organizational structure for the analysis of the problem.

An analysis of whether a covenant not to compete is enforceable could use this organizational structure:

> 1. The contract does not involve unfair competition
>
>   a. no trade secrets
>
>   or
>
>   b. no confidential customer lists
>
>   or
>
>   c. no unique employee's services
>
>   and

---

[3] This example is based on and uses language from the case of *Columbia Ribbon & Carbon Manufacturing Co. v. A-1-A Corp.*, 369 N.E.2d 4 (N.Y. 1977).

> 2.   The contract terms are reasonable
>
>   a.   reasonable time restrictions
>
>   and
>
>   b.   reasonable geographic limitations

Notice the order of the issues in this problem. Reasonable terms are relevant only if the employee engages in unfair competition. Thus section 1 must be discussed before section 2.

2.   The Terms of a Statute Identify the Elements

If you are analyzing a problem that is governed by a statute, the terms of the statute itself will identify the major issues you must analyze. These are the elements for the statutory claim. The language will tell you to whom the statute applies and the kind of conduct it governs.

Consider the following statute (elements are in bold.)

> **§ 140.20 Burglary in the third degree.**
>
> 1.   A **person** is guilty of burglary in the third degree if he **knowingly and unlawfully either enters or remains** in a **building, and**
>
> 2.   Does so with the **intent to commit** a **crime.**

Most criminal statutes are composed of elements of a crime, each of which the prosecution must prove at trial. As with the elements of a tort, the elements of a statute become the issues that you will discuss. The elements in this statute provide the organizational structure for an analysis of the crime of burglary in the third degree. There are two steps in determining those elements.

- First consider the overall structure of the statute. If any parts of the statute are given in the alternative, connected by the word "or," you need to prove only one element, but you may have to analyze each. If parts of a statute are connected by the word "and," you must prove all parts.

- Second, once you have a sense of the overall structure of a statute, you can go on to identify its elements. You identify the elements of the crime by looking at the terms of the statute. Each term may be significant and require some discussion. However, as with a tort, some elements will require detailed analysis, while others need be analyzed only briefly.

The statute defining burglary in the third degree is short and fairly simple. However, even this short statute includes a number of terms that identify the elements of the crime.

According to the statute, a prosecutor proves burglary in the third degree if:

1. [a] person

2. knowingly and unlawfully

   a. enters

                                              or

   b. remains

3. in a building

4. [with] intent

5. [to commit a] crime

You might organize your analysis by disposing of some elements, such as whether the defendant entered a "building" in a sentence or two, and analyzing others in a paragraph or series of paragraphs. Some elements may be so obvious, i.e., that the defendant is a person, that they need not be mentioned at all. As with the elements of a tort, your treatment of each statutory element depends on its complexity in relation to the facts of your case.

Some statutes however, are not easily outlined, and then the courts must pull out the requirements for themselves. For example, the Illinois Consumer Fraud Act reads in part:

> Unfair methods of competition and unfair deceptive acts or practices, including but not limited to the use or employment of any deception, fraud, false pretense, false promise, misrepresentation or the concealment, suppression or omission of any material fact, . . . in the conduct of any trade or commerce are hereby declared unlawful whether any person has in fact been misled, deceived or damaged thereby . . ."

How would you diagram this frequently litigated statute?

Illinois courts have boiled this unwieldy act down to its elements: (1) the defendant's deceptive act or practice, (2) the defendant's intent that the plaintiff rely on the deception, (3) the defendant's deception occurred in a course of conduct involving trade or commerce, and (4) the plaintiff suffered actual damage as (5) a result of the deception.

Exercise 4-B

Consider what issues are raised by the following statute, a section of the Uniform Commercial Code.

§ 2–315. Implied Warranty: Fitness for Particular Purpose

Where the seller at the time of contracting has reason to know any particular purpose for which the goods are required and that the buyer is relying on the seller's skill or judgment to select or furnish suitable goods, there is, unless excluded or modified under the next section, an implied warranty that the goods shall be fit for such purpose.

According to the statute, to whom does the statute apply?

What time period is relevant?

What must the seller know for the warranty to arise?

What type of warranty is created?

How may the warranty be excluded or modified?

Make an outline showing the organizational structure of an analysis of implied warranty of fitness for a particular purpose.

Exercise 4-C

According to the following statute, what are the elements of burglary in the second degree, a more complex statute than burglary in the third degree?

§ 140.25 Burglary in the second degree

A person is guilty of burglary in the second degree when he knowingly enters or remains unlawfully in a building with intent to commit a crime therein, and when:

1. In effecting entry or while in the building or in immediate flight therefrom, he or another participant in the crime:

   a) is armed with explosives or a deadly weapon; or

   b) causes physical injury to any person who is not a participant in the crime; or

   c) uses or threatens the immediate use of a dangerous instrument; or

   d) displays what appears to be a pistol, revolver, rifle, shotgun, machine gun or other firearm; or

2. The building is a dwelling.

> *To identify the elements of this crime, first examine the overall structure of the statute. Look for the relationships among the words connected by "and" and "or." Notice that the statute contains two sections that follow the introductory section. You need to determine how sections 1 and 2 relate to each other and to the introductory section.*
>
> *In a discussion analyzing whether someone had committed burglary in the second degree, you would have to decide which, if any, of the subsections of section 1 you could prove. You might decide that of the subsections of the statute, subsection (b) was totally irrelevant to your case, and that three subsections (a), (c), and (d) might be relevant. You might decide to briefly dispose of the irrelevant section, and then fully discuss those subsections that seem to be relevant to your case.*
>
> *Make an outline showing the organizational structure of an analysis of burglary in the second degree.*

3.   The Elements of a Rule Evolve over a Series of Cases

Organizing an analysis is more difficult when the elements of a claim are not found in a single case, but emerge from a series of cases. One case may provide the basic standard without identifying all of the elements eventually required. Thus you must read all the relevant cases on the general topic to identify the elements of the claim and the ways those elements can be proven.

Read the following summaries of cases about the tort of negligent infliction of emotional distress. All of them are from the same jurisdiction and all are relevant to this topic.[4]

> ### *Sinn v. Burd*
>
> The plaintiff, Robert Sinn, sued to recover damages for the emotional injuries he suffered when he saw his minor daughter struck and killed by a car. Mr. Sinn became hysterical and then lapsed into a depression, sustaining severe emotional distress and repeated nightmares. He has had to spend considerable amounts of money for medical care. Mr. Sinn was not in any personal danger of physical impact when he saw the accident from the front door of his home.
>
> Under the traditional rule, bystanders could not recover for mental injury unless they also suffered physical injury or were within the zone of danger, that is, they were in personal danger of physical impact. This rule, however, is unreasonably restrictive in cases where a parent views the death of a child, a situation which would cause at least as much emotional distress as being within the zone of danger. Here the injury was foreseeable since the plaintiff was the child's

---

   [4]   Case summaries in this example are based on *Sinn v. Burd*, 404 A.2d 672 (Pa. 1979); *Kratzer v. Unger*, 17 Pa. D. & C.3d 771 (Bucks Co. 1981); *Cathcart v. Keene Indus. Insulation*, 471 A.2d 493 (Pa. Super. 1984); and *Brooks v. Decker*, 495 A.2d 575 (Pa. Super. 1985).

father, the plaintiff was near the scene of the accident, and the shock resulted from his sensory and contemporaneous observance of the accident. Therefore, the court below incorrectly dismissed the claim.

Kratzer v. Unger

The plaintiff sued the driver of a car, which struck and seriously injured her foster child, for negligent infliction of emotional distress. The child had lived with the plaintiff for over eight years. The plaintiff may bring a claim for negligent infliction of emotional distress.

Cathcart v. Keene

Ms. Cathcart sued her husband's employer for negligent infliction of emotional distress. She alleged that her husband had contracted asbestosis on the job and that she suffered emotional distress in witnessing his continual deterioration and death. Although the plaintiff did have a close relationship with the victim, this court must dismiss her claim since her injuries did not arise from the shock of viewing a single, identifiable traumatic event.

Long v. Tobin

Ms. Long sued the driver of a car for negligent infliction of emotional distress caused by her viewing her neighbor's child being struck by a negligently driven automobile. She alleged that she became nervous and upset as a result of seeing the accident, since she has a child of the same age.

This court will grant the defendant's motion to dismiss the claim. Ms. Long does not have the requisite close personal relationship with the victim. Moreover, the mental distress she alleges is not sufficiently severe to warrant recovery. The type of stress required is that which no normally constituted reasonable person could endure.

Brooks v. Decker

Mr. Brooks' son, Bobby, was hit by an automobile while riding his bicycle on the street and died as a result of his injuries. Mr. Brooks did not witness the accident. Mr. Brooks arrived on the scene a few minutes later, after he heard the sound of an ambulance on his street. He then saw the broken body of his son.

Mr. Brooks' shock was not from the sensory and contemporaneous observance of the accident itself. Accordingly, he may not recover.

These case summaries show that the most extensive discussion of this tort is given in *Sinn v. Burd* a case decided by the highest court in the state. *Sinn* is the leading case in the jurisdiction on the claim of negligent infliction of emotional distress, setting out the basic standard for recovery.

To synthesize these cases, you would come up with this list of elements.

- A person may recover for negligent infliction of emotional distress if the emotional distress is foreseeable.

- Distress is foreseeable when
  - the plaintiff was the parent of the victim,
  - the plaintiff was near the scene of the accident, and the distress resulted from a sensory and contemporaneous observance of the accident.
  - the emotional distress was severe.

The other cases either elaborate on the elements raised in *Sinn* or introduce new elements. For example, the decision in *Kratzer* indicates that relationships other than parent and child can qualify, and thus elaborates on this part of the test. Ms. Kratzer was not a parent, but a foster parent of eight years. The *Cathcart* decision elaborates on the relationship between plaintiff and victim by suggesting that the tort may include spouses. In addition, the court in *Cathcart* establishes a new element. To be actionable, the distress must arise from a single, identifiable traumatic event. The court in *Long* offers a standard for the severity of the distress. Finally, in *Brooks*, the court required the plaintiff to be at the scene at the time of the accident and observe it as it happened.

If you had identified all of the elements the courts address in determining whether a plaintiff states a claim for negligent infliction of emotional distress and made a list, the list would look something like this:

1. whether the plaintiff was a family member of the victim

2. whether the plaintiff was near to the scene of the accident and whether the plaintiff's shock resulted from a sensory and contemporaneous observance of the accident

3. whether the shock resulted from a single, identifiable traumatic event

4. whether the plaintiff's distress was severe.

Exercise 4-D

Read the following case summaries and determine which factors a court will consider in analyzing whether to grant a motion to quash service of process on a nonresident.

Finch v. Crusco

The question before this court is whether a Delaware resident who brought a contract claim in Pennsylvania is immune from service of process in an unrelated action, if he was served in Pennsylvania while attending court proceedings in his contract claim. Philip Crusco was in Pennsylvania to testify in his breach of contract claim. When he came out of the courthouse, he was served in an unrelated tort action.

The courts in this state have long provided that non-resident parties and witnesses in civil actions are immune from service of process. The purpose of this grant of immunity is not to protect the individual, but to assure that the courts' business is expedited and that justice is duly administered. The rule provides an incentive to those who might not otherwise appear whose attendance is necessary to a full and fair trial.

However, courts should deny immunity where it is not necessary to provide this incentive. Where both cases arise out of the same transaction, the courts should not grant immunity. Under this circumstance, the reason for granting immunity would be outweighed by the importance of fairly resolving the full dispute between the parties. Nor will the courts grant immunity to a party or witness who is in the jurisdiction to serve his own interest, since he does not need an incentive to appear.

Mr. Crusco falls into the second category. He did not require an incentive to appear in the state court since he had brought the suit himself and was personally benefitting from the court hearing. Therefore, his motion to quash service of process is denied.

Dulles v. Dulles

Mr. Dulles was given a grant of immunity as a condition of his appearing and giving testimony in a matter relating to the Girard Trust Company. He remained in the jurisdiction for nineteen days after the matter regarding the Trust Company was resolved. On the nineteenth day, he was served with process in an action for support by his former wife.

Mr. Dulles had immunity for a reasonable time before and after his testimony. But there was no need for him to remain in the jurisdiction for such a lengthy period of time after the testimony. Therefore, at the time he was served, he was no longer immune from service of process.

Cowperthwait v. Lamb

Mr. Lamb a resident of Ohio was served with process in a tort action in Iowa as he was leaving a proceeding before the Secretary of Revenue regarding the suspension of his motor vehicle license. He argues that he was immune from process because he was summoned to testify before this administrative tribunal.

The rule granting immunity should be applied when a party is testifying before a tribunal which is judicial in nature, whether the hearing takes place in a court or not. This proceeding was judicial in nature. The Secretary may suspend the license only after a finding of sufficient evidence. He passes on the credibility of witnesses and applies law to the facts. The purpose of the rule, to have a full and fair hearing unhampered by the deterrence of the important witnesses, is just as important in proceedings of an administrative nature as before a court.

State v. Johnson

The defendant a resident of Ohio was charged in Iowa with the criminal acts of fraud and obtaining money by false pretenses. Moments after appearing before a magistrate and being freed on bail, Johnson was served with process in a civil matter. His motion to dismiss the complaint on grounds that he was immune from service of process is denied. Immunity from service of process is granted to a defendant in a civil action as an inducement to appear and defend. But a criminal defendant has no choice but to appear. Therefore, there is no need to extend the rule to provide such inducement.[5]

---

4. The Court Identifies and Balances Factors: The Totality of Circumstances Approach

When a court explicitly identifies the elements of a common law claim, or when the language of a statute supplies the elements, identifying and organizing the issues is not so difficult. Often, however, a particular common law or statutory claim is not so explicitly defined. There the courts will frequently focus on facts that are particularly relevant to deciding whether the plaintiff has proven her claims. Then you need to consider the facts a court deems important, generalize from these facts what factors are identified as important, organize around those factors, and balance them. This is sometimes called a totality of circumstances approach.

The Federal Copyright Act, for example, includes a defense known as the fair use defense. The statute includes four factors

---

[5] Case summaries in this example are based on, and use language from, *Cowperthwait v. Lamb*, 95 A.2d 510 (Pa. 1953); *Crusco v. Strunk Steel Co.*, 74 A.2d 142 (Pa. 1950); *Commonwealth v. Dulles*, 124 A.2d 128 (Pa. Super. 1956).

that courts should consider and balance to determine whether a defendant's use of another's copyrighted work was fair use (and did not violate the plaintiff's copyright). The statute also says that those four factors are not exclusive and the court may consider other facts that it considers important to that case (that is, a totality of the circumstances).

Suppose you want to bring a negligence suit in federal court but there is a question about whether the plaintiff, a minor, could survive a motion to dismiss for lack of diversity jurisdiction. The child's mother is a widow who has been in a one-year job training program in Massachusetts, where she intends to accept a job. While the mother was in this program, the child lived with her grandparents in New York, where both had always lived.

Read the following case to determine what factors the court considers relevant in deciding whether the child has the domicile of the mother in Massachusetts, or the domicile of the grandparents in New York. These factors will form the organizational structure of your analysis.

Elliott v. Kross

It is alleged that on May 1, 2006, the defendant, 9-year-old Michael Kross, approached 10-year-old Keith Michael Elliott in a backyard in Virginia and, with a slingshot, shot a gumball at Keith causing a serious eye injury. Plaintiff's complaint alleges diversity jurisdiction under 28 U.S.C. § 1332 (2006). There is no question about the Virginia citizenship of the defendants. On the eve of trial, however, the court became aware that the plaintiff, too, may have been a citizen of the Commonwealth of Virginia on the day this suit was filed. If so, there would be no diversity jurisdiction.

The court finds the facts to be as follows. Plaintiff is the son of divorced parents. His mother has custody. After the divorce, plaintiff continued to live in Virginia with his mother until early 2006, when his mother went to California to study law. The plaintiff was left in the custody of his maternal grandparents, who were citizens of Virginia. While in California, the plaintiff's mother formed an intent to remain indefinitely in California. The plaintiff's mother was residing in California when the gumball incident occurred. Though the incident occurred in May, the plaintiff's grandparents, who were caring for the plaintiff and paying for all of his support, did not inform plaintiff's mother of the incident until she returned to Virginia at Christmas time, 2006. The grandparents sought and obtained complete medical treatment and legal advice without reference to plaintiff's mother. In the spring of 2007, the plaintiff went to California to live with his mother. In the summer of 2008, the plaintiff moved back to Virginia. In the fall of 2008, the plaintiff's mother decided to return to Virginia.

The applicable date for determining the citizenship of the plaintiff is the day on which the law suit was filed, September 21, 2008. The elements necessary to establish citizenship are the same as those to establish domicile: residence combined with an intention to remain indefinitely. An infant's citizenship must be determined by reference to the citizenship of some other person, because an unemancipated infant is not capable of forming the requisite intent to establish independent citizenship.

The domicile of an infant whose parents are divorced is, for federal diversity jurisdictional purposes, the domicile of the parent to whom custody has been given. However, strict adherence to this rule is appropriate only if the result obtained comports with the underlying policies.

The principal purpose of diversity jurisdiction was to give a citizen of one state access to an unbiased court to protect him from parochialism if he was forced into litigation in another state in which he was a stranger and of which his opponent was a citizen. Strict adherence in the present case does not comport with this policy.

Neither the plaintiff in this case, his grandparents, nor his mother is a stranger to Virginia. Plaintiff was born in Virginia and has spent all of his life in this Commonwealth except for a one-year stay in California. Plaintiff's mother has returned to Virginia. Moreover, although plaintiff's mother was apparently awarded custody of plaintiff, plaintiff's mother was not exercising control and did not have actual custody of the plaintiff at the time this suit was filed. Plaintiff's grandparents were and had been acting in loco parentis in providing for plaintiff's support, maintenance, protection and guidance at the time this suit was filed. They made all the important decisions affecting plaintiff's medical care, legal services, and education.

These considerations lead us to hold that the courts of Virginia would not view plaintiff in this matter or view any person who could conceivably be considered his custodian as a stranger. Thus, the policy that underlies diversity jurisdiction will not support jurisdiction in this case. Accordingly, the court holds that plaintiff had the citizenship of his grandparents when suit was filed and there is no diversity of citizenship between the parties to this law suit. Thus the court lacks subject-matter jurisdiction over this action.[6]

In *Elliot v. Kross*, the court states that an adult's citizenship is determined by residence and intent to remain in a state for an indefinite time, but that a child's citizenship must be determined by reference to the citizenship of an adult because an unemancipated child is not capable of forming the requisite intent to establish independent citizenship.

---

[6] This example is based on and uses language from *Elliott v. Krear*, 466 F. Supp. 444 (E.D. Va. 1979).

Generally, a child has the citizenship of the parents or of the divorced parent who is the child's custodial parent. Sometimes, however, the child has the citizenship of the adult acting in loco parentis. To determine whether a child has the citizenship of the parent or of the adult acting in loco parentis, the court considers a number of factors.

- duration in a state

- intent of the adult to stay in a state

- actual custody and control of child

  o who supports the child?

  o who provides guidance?

  o who protects the child?

  o who is the decision-maker about medical treatment, education, legal advice?

When courts consider and balance a series of factors like these, they are engaged in what is called a totality of circumstances analysis. In a totality of circumstances analysis, you typically do not have to prove or disprove each factor. Instead you identify the most important factors in your case and decide, for example, whether on balance they establish citizenship in Virginia or in California.

Sometimes the factors of a rule are clarified in a series of opinions. For example, all states have adopted the Uniform Commercial Code § 2–302, which permits a court to refuse to enforce an unconscionable contract. The statute does not define unconscionable. The courts, however, typically require two types of unconscionability—procedural and substantive. Moreover, over time, courts have identified factors that can show that a contract is substantively or procedurally unconscionable. For example, one court held that a contract was procedurally unconscionable because of unequal bargaining power. Another court held a contract was procedurally unconscionable because one party had no meaningful choice. Finally, a third court held that hidden terms rendered the contract unconscionable. These factors form an organizational structure for procedural unconscionability.

You would start with the statutory language of § 2–302: "If the court as a matter of law finds the contract. . .to have been unconscionable at the time it was made, the court may refuse to enforce the contract. . . ." Then analyze procedural and substantive unconscionability separately, breaking each type of unconscionability into the factors that courts have identified. For example, because procedural unconscionability can result from unequal bargaining power, absence of meaningful choice, or hidden terms, you would analyze each relevant factor in relation to the contract in your case.

To prove this claim, like many totalities of circumstances claims, you usually do not have to prove each of the factors you have identified, although the more factors you can prove, the stronger the claim. Thus, a contract may be procedurally unconscionable although it does not have hidden terms, if the parties were in unequal bargaining positions and the plaintiff lacked meaningful choice of terms. These factors could weigh strongly in the plaintiff's favor.

You may organize a totality of circumstances discussion in several ways.

> • You may decide to analyze each factor separately. Then you balance the factors that weigh in plaintiff's favor against those that do not to come to a determination
>
> • You may organize around the principles a court has articulated for weighing the factors. In other words, instead of taking each factor separately, use the court's guidelines for assessing the factors to organize your discussion. For example, suppose the court has said, as it did in *Elliott*, that diversity jurisdiction is most appropriate to give a stranger to the state access to an unbiased court. A good way to organize your assessment of the factors is to group those that show plaintiff is not a stranger to Virginia, and then to weigh those against factors that show plaintiff is a stranger. You then determine which set of facts is stronger.
>
> • Alternatively you may organize by the parties. Group the factors that favor one party, then the factors that favor another party. Then evaluate the strength of each party's case.

Organization by parties might be the best way to analyze a statute that requires the courts to consider seven factors to determine the best interests of a child in a custody dispute:

1. the wishes of the child's parent or parents as to custody;

2. the wishes of the child as to his custodian;

3. the interaction and interrelationship of the child with his parent or parents, his siblings, and any other

person who may significantly affect the child's best
interest;

4. the child's adjustment to his home, school, and
   community;

5. the mental and physical health of all individuals
   involved;

6. the physical violence or threat of physical violence by
   the child's potential custodian, whether directed
   against the child or directed against another person;
   and

7. the willingness and ability of each parent to facilitate
   and encourage a close and continuing relationship
   between the other parent and the child.

In one custody dispute, for example, each parent may be
requesting custody of the child, and the court will evaluate the
strength of their requests. The child may wish to remain with her
mother, but may interact well with both parents and both sets of
grandparents; the child would remain in her current school if she
lived with her mother, but not with her father; the fifth and sixth
factors may not be relevant; and the mother may be less willing
than the father to encourage the child to retain a close relationship
with the other parent. The court will then have to weigh the child's
wish to stay with her mother and the importance of remaining in
the same school against the father's greater willingness to
continue the child's relationship with the other parent.

Exercise 4-E

Karen and Drew are divorcing after a one-year separation and
each is asking custody of their two children, Eli, age 11, and Missy, age
9. The children now live with Karen. These are the facts from the trial
for the court to weigh.

Karen's testimony:

- She is the children's primary care taker.

- She cooks, cleans, and cares for the children.

- She takes them to their activities and attends their
  functions at school.

- She works weekdays from 8:00 A.M. to 4:30 P.M. The
  children are at home alone from the time they return
  from school until Karen gets home. Several neighbors
  come by each day to check on them.

- She will raise the children as Catholics, which is Drew's religious faith, although not hers.

- The children told her that they want to stay with her.

Drew's testimony:

- During the time he and Karen were separated, he went to their house every morning to wake, feed, and dress them, prepare them for school, and walk them to the school bus. He stopped this practice after Karen told him she did not want him to come to the house anymore.

- When he and Karen lived together, he took charge of the children in the evenings, bathing them, putting them to bed, and leading them in prayer.

- He has been and is involved in their activities. He takes them fishing and swimming, coaches Eli's baseball team, goes to Missy's gymnastics meets, and attends parent-teacher conferences.

- He lives near Karen and the children.

- The children told him that they want to stay with him.

Drew's brother and Karen's sister and mother testified that Drew had an excellent relationship with his children and was a wonderful father. Karen testified in rebuttal that she and her mother and sister never got along well.

Write a short analysis of how you would decide this case.

CHAPTER 5

ORGANIZATION OF A LEGAL DISCUSSION: SMALL-SCALE ORGANIZATION

I. INTRODUCTION

IN CHAPTER 4, WE DISCUSSED the need to organize a legal analysis around the legal issues of each claim for relief. In this chapter, we focus on the organization of a single legal issue and suggest a structure that will enable you to write a clear analysis of that issue. The structure presented here is a fairly standard format for fact-based legal problems because it logically orders the steps necessary for this type of legal reasoning. We focus here on fact-based problems because these are common assignments in both legal practice and first-year legal writing courses. However, a different kind of legal problem—one involving the meaning or the validity of a law, for example—will require you to adapt this pattern. There your focus is on statutory construction, weight of authority, judicial reasoning, or underlying policies rather than on factual comparison (see Chapter 11).

With this caveat in mind, a useful pattern for analyzing a single legal issue often has the following structure:[1]

1. Identify and explain the applicable rule of law

2. Examine how the rule is applied in the relevant precedents

3. Apply the law to the facts of your case and compare to the precedents

4. Present counterarguments

5. Evaluate the parties' arguments and conclude on the issue.

This structure ensures that the reader gets necessary information in a logical order. For example, if you begin the discussion with a summary of the facts of your case, the reader cannot assess the legal significance of those facts because you haven't explained the controlling rules, the relevant case law, and the kinds of facts courts have previously decided were legally

---

[1] Various professors use anagrams like IRAC, TRAC, CRAC, CREAC as easy ways of remembering the pattern of small-scale organization.

significant. Similarly, you should raise and answer counterarguments on an issue before you reach a conclusion because the success with which you handle a counterargument should be reflected in your final conclusion.

Sometimes the analysis of an issue is so clear cut that you can include all five analytic steps in a single paragraph. For example, if the case law in your jurisdiction on false imprisonment requires that a plaintiff be confined involuntarily and your client was clearly confined involuntarily, you can treat that requirement quickly, as in the example below.

Topic sentence on issue **Rules** **Precedents**	A plaintiff has not been confined if she remains voluntarily. *Watts v. West.* However, if a defendant takes or threatens to take something of value from the plaintiff, the confinement is involuntary. *Goodhart v. Bowley's Restaurant.* In *Goodhart*, the restaurant owner took the plaintiff's wallet to ensure he remained while the owner determined whether the patron had paid his bill. Since a wallet is something of value, the court held the plaintiff remained involuntarily. However, in *Lopez v. Winchell*, the court held there was no confinement because the plaintiff, who was accused of stealing money from her employer, voluntarily remained in the store with her employers so that she could clear her name. However, Kingsford's situation is more akin to that in *Goodhart* than that in *Lopez*. Although she agreed to remain in Peterson's office to discuss the conditions of her severance from the firm, she stayed only because Peterson told her that if she left, he would refuse to give her a reference. Kingsford's professional reputation is not a tangible object like a wallet, but it is a thing of value, one vulnerable to the defendant's threat. This threat distinguishes Kingsford's situation from that of the plaintiff in *Lopez*. Although the plaintiff there was also concerned about her reputation, the defendant in that case did not threaten her. Thus *Goodhart* is the controlling case here, and Kingsford should be able to show she was confined against her will.
Application & Comparison	
Conclusion	

For most issues, however, you will need to break your analysis into paragraphs. Sometimes you may need a paragraph or more on each of the five analytic steps. Sometimes you can combine steps, especially if you can do this in a paragraph that is not more than half or a third of a page. For example, you can explain the rule and summarize its application in precedent in one paragraph, or present both an argument and counter-argument in another. You should also use topic and transition sentences to remind the reader what you have covered and to indicate where the discussion is going.

II. ORGANIZATION OF A LEGAL ANALYSIS ON A SINGLE LEGAL ISSUE USING A SINGLE CASE

THE FOLLOWING PAGES ILLUSTRATE the development of one element in an action for negligent failure to provide police protection. Although a municipality has a general duty to protect the public, it is not usually liable for failure to protect individuals. Nonetheless, there is a narrow exception that arises when there is a "special relationship" between the municipality and the claimant based on the following elements:

(1) an assumption by the municipality, through promises or actions, of an affirmative duty to act on behalf of the person who was injured;

(2) knowledge on the part of the municipality's agents that inaction could lead to harm;

(3) some form of direct contact between the municipality's agents and the injured party; and

(4) that party's justifiable reliance on the municipality's affirmative undertaking.

In the hypothetical, Ms. Stella Moran, Lily Moran's mother, went to the local precinct to report to the Captain, Jeff Malloy, that a drug dealer in one of Lily's neighboring buildings had threatened her daughter. This dealer, with the street name "Psycho," had told Lily that he had seen her talking to cops and that if she ever said anything about his business, he would "personally shut her mouth forever." Stella reported that Lily was so terrified she was afraid to be seen entering the stationhouse, so Stella agreed to go on her behalf. Captain Malloy himself acknowledged that Psycho was a tough customer and agreed to provide a patrolman to escort Lily from the subway to her home when she returned from work. Starting on October third and for the next three evenings, an officer was waiting for Lily at the subway and walked her home. On the seventh of October, he was not there. When Lily told her mother, Stella was angry. She called the Captain to find out why. He told Stella there had been a robbery that the officer had to investigate, but assured her someone would be there for Lily that evening. As promised, a patrolman was there. However, no one appeared on the eighth or ninth of October. On the ninth, Lily

Moran raced home in terror. As she was unlocking her door, Psycho pushed her into her apartment and severely beat her. Lily Moran is suing the city for injuries suffered when the police failed to escort her home.

A.   Step One: The Rule of Law

The discussion of a particular legal issue should begin by explaining the governing rule of law. When the rule of law is both widely accepted and clearly articulated, a complete paragraph explaining it may be unnecessary. In these instances, you would still need to begin with a topic sentence informing the reader of the governing rule, but you could follow with a discussion of its application in decided cases. When the intent and the scope of the law are more complicated, however, you may need to write a much longer explanation clarifying its meaning or components. These explanations may require you either to

- analyze the language of a constitution or a statute,

- set out the tests governing a law's application, or

- summarize a court's discussion of that rule or a pertinent discussion in a secondary authority, which has, perhaps, been adopted in that jurisdiction.

The discussion below focuses on **the last element of a special relationship claim: the party's justifiable reliance on the municipality's affirmative undertaking.** The first paragraph explains what is meant by justifiable reliance, using just one case. The marginal comments identify the paragraph's mode of construction. Full citations are omitted.

Topic Sentence on Element **Discussion of Rule**	The last element of a "special relationship" claim requires plaintiff to prove she relied on the municipality's affirmative undertaking to protect her. Reliance is critical in establishing a special relationship because it provides the causal link between the municipality's assumption of duty and the plaintiff's injury. *Cowl v. City of New Devon*. It would be unfair to preclude claims when the city's voluntary undertaking lulls an individual into a false sense of security that causes her to forego other means of protection. *Id*. However, a city cannot be liable every time a citizen is injured and the city is notified. *Id*. Only the legislature can determine if there are the resources to extend municipal responsibility. *Id*.

B. Step Two: Case Law

After you analyze the governing rule of law, your next step is to examine the relevant case law from which that rule came or in which it has been applied. In a fact-based problem, you should give the relevant facts of the precedents because you give the rules meaning by identifying how they were applied to the facts of those cases and what facts were considered significant. Then by identifying similarities and differences between the facts of the precedents and those of your client's case, you predict the outcome of your case. Include the court's holding as well since, under stare decisis, the holding tells us how to interpret the facts. Finally, you should summarize the reasons and policies behind a court's decision.

This analysis provides a basis for generating arguments about whether the client's claim will be successful. We illustrate this step with one paragraph because this discussion is based on only one precedent. A more complex discussion may require more than one paragraph.

Remember that you are examining these cases to shed light on the rule of law you introduced in the opening paragraph. Therefore, connect the case discussion to that rule. Show how the precedent illustrates, limits, expands, or explains the law. One suggestion is to avoid beginning this paragraph with a sentence giving the facts of a case, as in "In Cowl *v. City of New Devon*, the plaintiff relied on the city's assurances it would deal with the threats made by Ted Adams in the morning." Rather, start either with a topic sentence that states the legal principle that case shows or with a transition sentence that makes it clear you are continuing the same topic.

Topic Sentence on Legal Principle Case Establishes	If a plaintiff knows that the police had never fulfilled its assurances of protection, then the plaintiffs cannot claim she justifiably relied on assurances. *Id.* In *Cowl*, landlords Ella and John Cowl had had repeated disputes with their downstairs tenants, the Adamses. On July 27th, Ted Adams physically attacked and injured Ella Cowl, whereupon Mr. Cowl went to the local precinct to ask for protection. Mr. Cowl told the desk officer that the Adamses had threatened
Precedent Facts	their safety and that unless they received protection, they were going to leave home that night. The officer told Cowl not to worry because the police would deal with Ted Adams in the morning. As a result, the Cowls unpacked their

	suitcases and remained in the house. In the morning, a nervous Mrs. Cowl repeatedly looked out the window to see if the police had arrived. By midday, it was clear they were not coming. Nonetheless, the Cowls remained in the house. In the late afternoon, however, they decided to do some shopping. As they were leaving the building, Ted Adams again confronted them. John Cowl and his adult son, who had just arrived for a visit, were seriously hurt. *Id.* The court held that when it was clear the police were not coming, the Cowls could no longer justifiably rely on police protection and could not reasonably contend they were lulled into a false sense of security. They should have taken other steps to protect themselves. Thus, there was no causal link between the police department's assumption of duty and the plaintiff's injury. *Id.*
Holding **Reasoning**	

C. Step Three: Application of Precedents to Your Own Case

The next step in a legal analysis involves applying the facts, policies, and reasoning of relevant cases to your case. The central job here is to compare the relevant facts in the precedents to those in your own case and to evaluate the strength of the claim you wish to make in light of these comparisons. You also apply the reasoning or policies from the precedent to your own case.

It is helpful to begin this step with a transition sentence that weighs the merits of the client's case in light of established precedent.

Transition **Distinguishing** **Case** **Distinguishing** **Facts**	Lily Moran more justifiably relied on police assurances of protection than did the Cowls. The police in *Cowl* never followed up on their promise to visit the Adamses in the morning, but an officer met Lily Moran and escorted her home from the third to the sixth of October. Even when the patrolman failed to appear on the seventh, Stella Moran's phone call to Captain Malloy brought renewed promises of protection, and indeed, a patrolman was there that evening. Thus, the Morans justifiably believed that an officer would continue to appear. Captain Malloy never phoned Ms. Moran to tell her that the department could no longer afford to escort her.

When you believe your adversary has no authentic counterargument on this issue, do not create one. Instead, end your discussion with a conclusory sentence, for example, "Because Ms. Moran acted upon the assurances of the department, it had a duty to notify Ms. Moran when it was no longer able to protect her. Its failure to do so meant Ms. Moran was justified in relying on the police." Usually, however, the other party will have a valid argument that you must assess before coming to a conclusion, as discussed below.

D & E. Steps Four and Five: Counterarguments, Evaluation and Legal Conclusion

A thorough discussion requires you to present and evaluate significant counterarguments. Evaluation of a counterargument is usually the last step before the conclusion and may require an extended analysis.

Discuss those precedents and those facts from your problem upon which your opponent is going to rely. Opposing counsel will highlight facts and cases that are clearly unfavorable to your client or that the parties can interpret differently. In an objective analysis, it is important to raise all reasonable interpretations of the facts and issue, including counterarguments, and to evaluate their strength. It may help to ask the following questions.

- Is the counterargument based on legally insignificant or incomplete facts?

- Does the counterargument fail to work with facts favorable to you client?

- Does it misapply the law to the facts?

- Does an opposing argument rest on a misinterpretation of the court's reasoning in a precedent?

- Does an opposing argument rely on inapplicable policy arguments?

Although policy arguments are more traditionally raised in appellate briefs than in office memoranda,[2] some might be relevant in an objective analysis. Some examples follow.

- The rule does not extend to this situation

- The rule needs to be amended because social changes render it obsolete

---

[2] Appellate courts are more likely to amend or make law than trial courts. One function of appellate courts is to ensure consistency of application and within the jurisdiction. They also are more willing to make law based on changes in society.

- The rule is ambiguous

- The rule results in inefficient allocation of resources and is unworkable

If opposing counsel presents arguments like these, you should try to rebut them. Sometimes one type of factual or policy argument can be met by another type, as illustrated in the examples below.

- The adversary's theory of the case is based on legally insignificant or incomplete facts or on a misapplication of the law to the facts

- Even if the rule is ambiguous, to comport with legislative intent it cannot be interpreted as opposing counsel suggests

If your analysis of the opposing argument convinces you that your client cannot prevail on this issue, or that you cannot definitively determine the outcome, you should say so, since an office memorandum is an objective exploration of your client's legal situation and the basis for legal advice. (See Chapter 7.) However, you do not want to be misleading even if the client will be unhappy with your conclusion.

The final sentence of your analysis is often a legal conclusion, a conclusion grounded in the prior analysis of the law, precedent, and facts. This conclusion differs from the one given in the thesis paragraph that begins the Discussion section of the memorandum. (See Chapter 6.) That conclusion offers an assessment of a client's overall chance of winning a suit or defending himself against a charge. Here, the conclusion refers only to the issue that you have discussed.

Transition Introducing Counter-Argument	On the other hand, when the Captain told Stella Moran that the officer who was to escort Lily had to leave to investigate another urgent crime, both Morans should have known that other police responsibilities could call officers away from their escort duty and that Lily might need to take other
Opponent's Facts & Reasoning	precautions to ensure her safety. This is particularly true when no officer appeared on the eighth and ninth. Like the Cowls, Lily Moran no longer could justifiably rely on police assurances. Moreover, she had no false sense of security. Indeed, she admitted she was terrified each time she raced home alone.
Conclusion	Thus she will have trouble proving there was a causal link between the department's promises and her injuries and may be unable to establish the element of justifiable reliance.

Although you can handle counterarguments in separate paragraphs, you may also be able to weave rebuttal into your analysis and application of the case law. When the counterargument or the rebuttal is complex, however, or when the counterargument is based on policy or reasoning rather than facts, it may be preferable to handle the rebuttal separately, as in the paragraphs above.

Exercise 5-A

In order to win a suit against New Devon for failure to provide police protection, the municipality's agents must have some form of direct contact with the injured party. Read the following summary of Keech v. New Devon. *Using that case and Cowl, write a discussion on whether Stella Moran's contact with the police for the benefit of her daughter (previously summarized in Section II) satisfies the direct contact element.*

Keech v. New Devon

On June 23rd, plaintiff Julia Keech was accosted by Ty Little as she was approaching her car. Little began pulling Keech, who was kicking and yelling, into the car. Before he had succeeded, Julia screamed to two witnesses, Kristen and Kevin Stewart, to call the police. As the car sped off, the Stewarts noted the license plate number and ran back into the mall to find a police officer. They found Officer Sonia Watson and reported the abduction and plate number. Officer Watson said she would call the incident in, but apparently never did. Julia was found in the trunk of her car twelve hours later, raped and beaten. She began an action charging the City as vicariously liable for Watson's negligent conduct. We affirm the Appellate Division's holding that failure to respond to a report of possible criminal activity is within the scope of governmental immunity.

Liability depends on there being a special relationship between the municipality and the individual. Although we sympathize with the plaintiff's ordeal, plaintiff cannot prove she justifiably relied on police protection or had direct contact with the police. Given her circumstances, plaintiff obviously could not contact the police herself or receive assurances. Admittedly, this court has relaxed the rule of direct contact in some cases. In *Sorenson*, for example, we recognized that a mother's contact with police on behalf of her threatened infant was a reasonable substitute for direct contact between the infant and police. Because the child was helpless, only the mother could contact the police to obtain protection. In addition, in *Cowl*, a husband's request for protection extended to his wife, with whom he resided. It did not, however, cover his adult son who lived elsewhere.

Unlike in those cases, the witnesses in this case were strangers to the plaintiff. She could not be sure they would contact the police. More importantly, the purpose of the special relationship rule is to limit the scope of liability. Without direct contact, the police had no way of knowing whether their inaction could lead to harm. The Stewarts admitted they could have been witnessing a domestic scene rather than abduction. Thus, we hold the city immune from liability for its agent's failure to call in the witnesses' report because there was no special relationship between the plaintiff and the police department.

III. RULE AND CASE SYNTHESIS IN A LEGAL ANALYSIS OF A SINGLE ISSUE

OCCASIONALLY, ONE CASE will provide all the authority you need to resolve a legal question. More frequently, however, you will need to use several cases to analyze that question. The following example is an analysis of one of the issues in a child abuse case requiring both rule and case synthesis.

David Leroy has been indicted for child abuse in the death of his fourteen-year-old daughter, Dawn Leroy. Leroy admits that in the early hours of September 17, 20___, while in a drunken rage, he beat the child at the home he shares with Celia Shaw, his fiancé. Dawn suffered injuries that resulted in fatal brain damage. She died three weeks later. Shaw was present during the second half of the beating but did not intervene or summon help. She knew Leroy was a recovering alcoholic who had been in brawls in the past, but had hoped that a quarrel between father and daughter earlier in the day would not lead to a relapse. The legal question is whether Celia Shaw's relationship exposes her under the child abuse statute, and if so, whether Shaw's failure to remove Dawn from her father's home or intervene in the beating constituted cruel and inhumane treatment that caused injuries additional to those inflicted by her father.

Second Degree Child Abuse, s. 3–601, states as follows:

    i)   A parent or other person who has permanent or temporary custody or responsibility for the supervision of a minor may not cause abuse to the minor.

    ii) A household or family member may not cause abuse to a minor.

There are two relevant definitions

"Abuse" means physical injury sustained as a result of cruel or inhumane treatment . . . under circumstances that indicate that the minor's health or welfare is threatened by the treatment . . . .

"Household member" means a person who lives with or is
a regular presence in a home of a minor at the time of
abuse."

It is clear Shaw did not have permanent or temporary custody
as she and David are not yet married. She was responsible for
Dawn's supervision while her father was out. Nonetheless, a
person's responsibility ends when the parent returns. Moreover,
although Shaw was a member of David's household, David's home
was arguably not Dawn's. Although children of divorced parents
often have homes in the households of both parents, Dawn lived
with her mother and had few belongings at her father's home. She
had run away from her mother's house, but was staying with her
father only until he could arrange for her return. Thus, the
remaining issue is whether Shaw caused the child abuse by cruel
and inhumane treatment, the issue discussed below.

When you synthesize rules and cases in your discussion, do not
feel compelled to give all cases equal treatment.

- If it is a statutory problem, begin with the statute and
  then with precedents from the jurisdiction of your
  problem since they have more weight than do
  precedents from other jurisdictions.

- Then let your treatment of a case depend on its
  relevance to your client's situation. Some cases may
  not provide useful facts for comparison, for example,
  but may provide a helpful explanation of a rule of law
  or relevant policy. Then, a short summary of the rule
  or policy may be all you need to use. Where, however,
  a case is especially relevant to your problem—either
  for the facts or for its discussion of the rule—discuss
  the precedent more extensively.

In reading through the sample discussion that follows, notice
when a short summary is used to state a rule or to characterize a
set of facts and when a case is more thoroughly treated. The cases
you select and emphasize are one way you show your mastery of
the problem.

The rest of the discussion demonstrates how the basic
technique for organizing a discussion of an issue when working
with a group of cases is similar to that used when working with
one case. First, you explain the rule, you discuss and synthesize
the precedents. Then compare them with the facts of your case.
Raise and evaluate the strengths and weaknesses of your case and
the opposing arguments. Finally, you conclude.

When a requirement can be easily established, all the analytic steps described above may be covered in a single paragraph. When the discussion is complex or case law abundant, however, you need to divide the discussion into paragraphs following the steps in a legal analysis, as discussed in this chapter. Finally in the example that follows, all cases are from the jurisdiction of the problem, but full citations have been omitted.

Topic Sentence **Rule Synthesis**	A person who falls within one of the categories in the child abuse statute is guilty of child abuse by a malicious act or by cruel or inhumane treatment. Cruel and inhumane treatment need not be an action, but could be omission as well, where failure to act exposed the child to abuse beyond the injury caused by another. *Fabritz.* Thus, failure to intervene to stop a beating could constitute abuse. *Pope.* One caveat, however, is that a person is guilty of abuse by failing to prevent it only when it is reasonably foreseeable and reasonably possible to act. *DeGren.*
Topic Sentence on Precedent **Precedent Facts**	When a person responsible for a child can reasonably foresee that failure to intervene in a beating could lead to the child's deterioration or death, that person is guilty of child abuse. In *Fabritz,* the defendant mother, Virginia Fabritz, left Windy, her 3 ½ year-old daughter, with her housemates, Thomas and Anne Crocket, for two days. *Id.* at ___ When she returned, Windy complained of feeling sick. While bathing her, Fabritz noticed bruises over her body, indicating she had been badly beaten. *Id. at* ___. Nonetheless, she sought no medical treatment, fearing trouble were Windy to be examined. Instead, she put the child in bed and spent the afternoon watching Thomas fix his motorcycle. *Id.* Later, Windy awoke, vomiting, before falling unconscious. *Id.* at ___. At ten p.m., Mrs. Crocket took her to the hospital, where she died of contusions, peritonitis, and over seventy bruises. The physician said Windy had a good chance of survival up to an hour before her death if she had had surgery. *Id.* at ___. The court held that Fabritz' s failure to act when she was aware of Windy's physical deterioration was "cruel and inhumane" and caused Windy injuries beyond those inflicted by Thomas. *Id.* at ___.
Transition Relating Cases	Similarly, in Palmer, although a manslaughter case, the mother was found to have subjected her daughter to cruel and inhuman treatment by failing to remove her child from a situation in which her

lover beat, whipped, dragged, and spanked her infant over a period of 10 months. *Palmer* at ___. On the day of the baby's death, doctors found bite marks on both buttocks, her liver ripped in half and the tissue connecting the colon to the abdomen wall torn. *Id.* at ___. Although the mother said there was nothing she could do about the beatings, the court disagreed, stating that she could have removed the child but, instead, "affirmatively" begged a concerned neighbor not to remove the baby. The consequences of failing to protect this "little defenseless urchin" from "merciless . . . brutality of a protracted nature" established a causal connection between the mother's negligence and the child's death. *Id.* at ___. The court said it is not essential that she foresaw the danger; rather, the test was whether a reasonable person would have seen the defendant's acts as cruel and inhumane. *Id.* The courts have extended this to the child abuse statute. *Fabritz* at ___.

Transition Sentence to Contrasting Cases

However, a person is not guilty of child abuse if she does not intervene to stop an abusive parent who has returned and resumed responsibility for the child. *Pope* at ___. There, the mother was staying overnight with the defendant Pope, a woman who failed to intervene when the mother started shaking and beating the child to rid it of evil. *Pope.* The court held that Pope did not fall within the class of persons to whom the statute applies since the mother was present and responsible for the child. Thus while Pope "may have had a strong moral obligation to help the child," she was "under no legal obligation to do so." *Id.* at ___.

Application & Case Comparison

Here, as a person "responsible for the supervision" of Dawn, Shaw had a duty to prevent abuse, although—like Pope—not after Leroy had returned home because responsibility for a child ceases when a parent is present. Thus her only possible culpable omission was her failure to remove the child after her quarrel with her father and before the father's return. Although Shaw's failure to remove Dawn then was the but-for cause of the child's beating, it was not the proximate cause. It was not foreseeable that Leroy would return home, see a sex text message on Dawn's phone, and beat her in a drunken rage, especially since he had never struck the child before and was a reformed alcoholic. These circumstances are unlike the months of abuse in Palmer.

1st Counter- Argument

On the other hand, Shaw's failure to remove the child from harm's way may be the proximate cause of the child's injuries. Shaw knew Leroy and Dawn had quarreled before he left for work, knew Leroy was a recovering alcoholic, and knew the stress of Dawn's unexpected arrival might have sent him back to the bottle. She "hoped" the situation would blow over, but concedes she may have been in "denial." Yet instead of removing the child from the house, she drank some wine and fell asleep, leaving Dawn vulnerable. Thus, a reasonable person could have foreseen harm if the child was not removed.

Rebuttal

Nevertheless, given that Leroy's behavior had been exemplary for five years, a trier of fact would probably not find that Shaw's failure to remove Dawn from the house was reasonably related to the fatal abuse Dawn sustained at the hands of her father.

2nd Counter- Argument

Only if Shaw was a "household member" within the meaning of s. 3–601(ii) in "a home" of Dawn could her failure to intervene in Dawn's beating be abuse by omission. In that event, however, it would be necessary to prove both that it was reasonably possible to intervene and stop a large and very drunk man from striking the child and that Shaw's failure to intervene caused further or worsened injuries, like the mother in *Fabritz*. Moreover, although David beat Dawn brutally, he stopped quickly and took Dawn to the hospital soon after it was over.

Rebuttal

Thus it would be difficult to prove both that it was reasonably possible to intervene and that her omission caused injury beyond those caused by Dawn's father. It is unlikely Shaw will be found guilty of child abuse.

IV. RULE AND CASE SYNTHESIS WHEN THE ISSUE HAS FACTORS

SOMETIMES AN ISSUE OR ELEMENT has subissues or factors. When there are subissues, you may need to take each individually and go through all the analytic steps in small-scale organization for each. Factors come into play when there is a variety of ways to establish the issue or element. Sometimes a single factor is enough to satisfy the element and you can analyze the factors individually. Sometimes a combination of factors is required to establish the element. If so, you may want to group factors to illustrate when there are sufficient number to satisfy the rule. The following example illustrates the discussion of an issue involving factors.

It is an analysis of one part of a false imprisonment case brought by Anna Kingsford against her former employers. Anna Kingsford claims that her employers summoned her to an office where one of them, Susan Smith, blocked the exit by standing in front of the door. They then threatened and shouted at her in an effort to force her to resign from their firm and forego severance pay. The tort has three requirements:

1. the defendant must actually have confined the plaintiff,

2. the defendant must have intended to confine the plaintiff, and

3. the plaintiff must have been aware of or harmed by the confinement.

This part of the discussion is an analysis of the **first element: actual confinement**. Thus, only those cases that discuss actual confinement are relevant.

A plaintiff can prove that a defendant confined her in several different ways. Kingsford's argument is that the defendants confined her in a room to question her by threatening to use physical force if she left the room. Your focus should therefore be on those cases that show the defendant confined the plaintiff by threat of physical force. These are the cases to synthesize by articulating the factors that make analytic sense of decisions involving diverse fact patterns. In this false imprisonment problem, your case synthesis will reveal that plaintiff can prove a threat of physical force by a defendant's actions or size advantage. In addition, the defendant must be able to carry out the threat and must confine the plaintiff against her will. You should discuss each of these factors separately and begin each discussion with a topic sentence that states how those factors can be established.

When you synthesize cases in your discussion, do not feel compelled to give all cases equal treatment.

- Begin first with precedents from the jurisdiction of your problem since they have more weight than do precedents from other jurisdictions.

- Then let your treatment of a case depend on its relevance to your client's situation. Some cases may not provide useful facts for comparison, for example, but may provide a rule of law or relevant policy. Then, a one sentence summary of the rule or policy may be all you need to use. Where, however, a case is especially relevant to your problem—either for the facts or for its discussion of the rule—discuss the precedent more extensively.

In reading through the sample discussion that follows, notice when a one-sentence summary is used to state a rule or to characterize a set of facts and when a case is more thoroughly treated.

The sample discussion begins with an introductory paragraph, the first sentence of which introduces the element of whether the plaintiff had actually been confined. The paragraph then identifies the factors that prove confinement and concludes with a statement about whether the plaintiff can prove the element.

The rest of the discussion demonstrates how the basic technique for organizing a discussion of an issue when working with a group of cases is similar to that used when working with one case—you explain the rule, you discuss the precedents and compare them with the facts of your case, you raise and evaluate the strengths and weaknesses of your case and the opposing arguments, and you conclude.

When a requirement can be easily established, all the analytic steps described above may be covered in a single paragraph. When the discussion is complex or case law abundant, however, you need to divide the discussion into paragraphs following the steps in a legal analysis. In the following example, notice that the writer did not always raise counterarguments. When counterarguments seem insubstantial, this step can be omitted or incorporated into the fact application paragraph. Finally, all cases are from the jurisdiction of the problem, but full citations have been omitted.

	Pattern of an Analysis Involving Case Synthesis
Topic Sentence: The Element of Confinement	The first element of false imprisonment requires that the defendant confine the plaintiff. In Kent, a defendant can confine a plaintiff by physical barriers, overpowering physical force,
Case Gives General Rules	threats to apply physical force if the victim goes outside the boundary fixed by the defendants, or submission to other types of duress, like
Issues Narrowed to Threat of Physical Force	submission to an asserted legal authority. *Johnson v. White* (adopting Restatement Second of Torts). Kingsford's chances of establishing she was confined depend on her showing that the
1st Factor: Conduct	defendants threatened physical force. A defendant's actions may establish a threat of physical force if the defendant is able to apply

**2nd Factor:
Ability**

**3rd Factor:
Involuntariness**

**Legal
Conclusion**

force. *See Atkins v. Barton*. Under any of these circumstances, the defendant must also be able to apply force. *Watts v. West*. Finally, the restraint must be against the plaintiff's will. *Id*. If the plaintiff voluntarily agrees to stay, he or she has not been falsely imprisoned. *Lopez v. Winchell*. Kingsford was confined because Peterson and Smith were able to carry out their threat to use force and she submitted to them against her will.

**Topic Sentence
on 1st Factor**

Precedent

A defendant's movements, gestures and gender may be so intimidating that its effect is to confine the plaintiff by threat of physical force, especially if the plaintiff perceives the defendant to have a size advantage. *Atkins v. Barton*. In *Atkins*, the plaintiff successfully sued a deprogrammer, Barton, for false imprisonment. Barton was 6'2" and 225 pounds. When he stepped in front of the door to the plaintiff's bedroom and held out his arms as if to stop her, she reasonably believed that she was confined by threat of physical force even though he did not say a word. *Id*.

**Comparison
with Problem
Case**

**First
Counter-
Argument**

Rebuttal

Similarly, Ms. Kingsford may have believed she was confined by her supervisors' threatening movements and size advantage. Smith moved to the door and leaned against it when Kingsford rose from her chair as if to leave. Smith, however, is only 5'6", significantly smaller and less physically intimidating than the defendant in *Atkins*. Nonetheless, Smith is five inches taller than Ms. Kingsford. She is also athletic and works out at a health club several times a week.

**Second
Counter-
Argument**

Rebuttal

**Legal
Conclusion**

Moreover, the female plaintiff in *Atkins* perceived the male defendant as having an unfair physical advantage because of his gender, while here there is no gender disparity between Kingsford and Smith. Yet this difference is probably not determinative. Courts have consistently regarded the comparative sizes of the parties as more important for establishing intimidation than gender alone. *See Cane v. Downs* (defendant was six inches taller and fifty pounds heavier than plaintiff); *Carey v. Robier* (defendant at 5'5" was four inches taller); *Mussel v. Winston* (defendant was a 5'11" male, plaintiff a 5'6" male). Thus, based on their gestures and size advantage, the defendants threatened physical force.

2nd Factor: Ability

Cases Comparison & Conclusion

Another factor is whether a defendant is actually able to carry out the threat. In addition to size advantage, courts look at whether the defendants outnumber the plaintiff. *See Appley v. Owens & Norton* (two defendants confined plaintiff); *Atkins* (parents and deprogrammer confined a single woman). Here too, Peterson and Smith outnumbered the plaintiff. As Kingsford said, "there were two against one."

3rd Subissue: Involuntariness

Cases

Finally, the plaintiff is not confined if she remains voluntarily. *Watts v. West*. The plaintiffs in *Watts* remained voluntarily when told the police had been called. *Id.* Similarly, in *Lopez v. Winchell*, the plaintiff, who was accused of stealing money from her employer, remained voluntarily. She decided to remain in the store with her employers so that she could clear her name.

Transition Suggesting Counter-Argument

Like Lopez, Kingsford agreed to remain in Peterson's office. Peterson and Smith had initially summoned Kingsford to the office to fire her. They also wanted her to agree to leave their firm without receiving severance pay. When Kingsford said that she would never agree to such a condition and that she would not hang around to be bullied into submission, Peterson told her that if she left, he would not only refuse to give her a reference, but would actively spread the word that she was a sullen and incompetent employee. Threatened by the prospect of both present and future unemployment if Peterson did as he said, Kingsford agreed to remain in the office to discuss the matter further, as Lopez did to clear her good name.

Distinguishing Unfavorable Case

Favorable Case

Yet Kingsford, unlike Lopez, stayed because she was threatened. A plaintiff does not submit voluntarily if the defendant threatens to take something of value from her. *Goodhart v. Butcher Restaurant*. In *Goodhart*, a restaurant owner took and held onto a patron's wallet until he could determine if the patron had paid his bill. During this time, the patron remained because he did not want to lose the wallet's valuable contents. The court held that when a defendant takes something of value from the plaintiff in order to ensure the plaintiff remained, the plaintiff has not acted voluntarily. *Id.* Although Peterson did not take a tangible object like a wallet, he did have control

Evaluation & Conclusion	over Kingsford's professional reputation, which is a thing of value. In contrast, although the plaintiff in *Lopez* was worried about her "good name," her employer did not threaten to give Lopez a bad reference if she left. Like the plaintiff in *Goodhart*, Kingsford should be able to show that she was confined against her will. Thus, she should be able to prove all three requirements for confinement by threat of physical force.

Two important writing techniques for handling case synthesis have been used in this discussion. First, the paragraphs often begin with topic sentences that state in general terms the principles that have been extracted from the precedents. For example, the defendants' overbearing size and movements in *Atkins v. Barton*, *Cane v. Downs*, and *Carey v. Robier* give rise to the topic sentence in paragraph two that "an action so intimidating that its effect is to confine by threat of physical force may result from the defendant's movements and gestures and from the plaintiff's perception of the defendant's size advantage." Constructing such general statements is one important way of bringing to your reader the results of your analysis. The topic sentences also promote clear organization by orienting the reader to the paragraph's place in the analysis.

The second important writing technique used in this discussion is the writer's use of parenthetical discussion. Because the deprogrammer Barton is such a clear and dramatic example of size advantage, the author discusses *Atkins* thoroughly in order to establish the main point. *Cane v. Downs* and *Carey v. Robier* are necessary because they refine the point that size advantage can be relative, but the facts can be parenthetical because these cases are only used to supply details and general support of *Atkins*. By using these parentheticals, the author keeps the text free from the specific factual details of these cases.

Exercise 5-B

The District Attorney has asked you to assess the success of defense counsel's motion to suppress his client's confession for failure to give timely Miranda *warnings. Read Detective Donald's account of the facts and the following summaries of precedent. Then write the discussion section.*

Facts

Joseph Bolton is on trial for the murder of an off-duty police officer, Tom Jones, during a subway robbery. During the investigation of the murder, the detectives received a tip that Bolton was one of the participants in the crime. The detectives drove to Bolton's house in an unmarked police car at 7:00 p.m. on a Saturday night. A woman let them into the house, Bolton was told that the police "wanted to take him to the police station for questioning" about a recent incident, Bolton hesitantly agreed, and the detectives waited for about 15 minutes to take him to the station. They did not draw their weapons, although their guns were in plain view in their holsters. They walked Bolton to the police car; there was no physical force or contact. Bolton sat in the back seat, while the detectives sat in the front. The car had a door locking device which could be controlled only by the driver. Detective Douglas said he locked the doors as he always does, although he did not think Bolton would attempt to escape.

Because the precinct was busy, Bolton was placed in a small interrogation room in the back of the precinct for approximately four hours. The door to the room was not locked. He was told he could use the bathroom across the hall, and he was given food and reading material. Before midnight, the two detectives and a sergeant came to question Bolton. All of the participants were seated except Detective Donald who stood in front of the closed door allegedly because there was not room for another chair. After a few minutes of questioning, Detective Donald falsely told Bolton that an eyewitness had seen Bolton and another man kill an off-duty police officer. Donald said things would go easier on Bolton if he cooperated. Bolton broke down and said, "I didn't shoot him, Bert Terrence did." Only then did the police read Bolton his *Miranda* rights.

Defense counsel is planning to move to suppress the confession for failure to give timely *Miranda* warnings.

People v. Parker

A suspect is not entitled to *Miranda* warnings unless he is in police custody. Whether a suspect is in custody depends upon whether a reasonable person in the suspect's position, innocent of a crime, would believe he was free to leave. We balance a number of factors in deciding this, including the amount of time defendant spends with police, the degree to which he is restricted, the location and atmosphere of the questioning, and the administration of his constitutional rights.

In only two instances since 1993 have we reversed a trial court's finding that a defendant was not in custody. In both cases, the circumstances were quite egregious—as they were here. In this case, the defendant was awakened at gun point, ordered out of bed, and searched. The police officer then put away his gun and claimed that the suspect voluntarily accompanied the four officers to the precinct in an unmarked police car with a locking device. The detective could not recall whether he had handcuffed the defendant or the defendant offered any resistance. The defendant then waited for four hours before being questioned at the precinct.

We hold that the coercive and intimidating atmosphere, which necessarily resulted from the defendant being awakened and ordered out of bed at gunpoint, would have led a reasonable person innocent of any crime to have concluded that he was in custody and was not free to decline the request by the detectives to accompany them to the precinct.

The presence of four officers in the apartment, and the fact that the defendant was locked in the police vehicle and waited for four hours in the precinct before being questioned, also counseled against a finding that the defendant was not in custody. Thus the police should have given him a *Miranda* warning.

People v. Matthews

The defendant initially agreed to accompany a State Trooper to the barracks for questioning around 11:00 p.m. He was continuously questioned by several different troopers for six hours before being apprised of his rights at 5:30 a.m. His statements were met with skepticism. He was told that he fit the description of someone they were looking for and that they were attempting to verify his alibi. We hold that a reasonable person innocent of any crime would not have believed he was free to leave.

People v. Tinker

We uphold the lower court's refusal to suppress a confession where the defendant was questioned at the police precinct for two hours about his father's murder despite the officer's false statement that the victim had identified the defendant as the perpetrator before he died. Although the detective used a ruse to cause the defendant to believe that there was inculpatory evidence against him, that ruse had nothing to do with whether the defendant was in custody for the purposes of the *Miranda* rule. *See Wynn* (police officer's groundless accusation that the defendant had been implicated in 15 or 20 robberies during investigation of a robbery would not cause an innocent person to think he was under arrest).

People v. Ross

Although the suspect was with the police for four hours, that amount of time is insufficient for a finding of custody. This is particularly true when, as here, the suspect was not searched or handcuffed getting into the car, came to the station upon request, was free to visit the restroom on his own, and was given food and a TV set.

CHAPTER 6

THE THESIS PARAGRAPH

I. INTRODUCTION

THE DISCUSSION SECTION OF AN office memorandum should begin with a paragraph that introduces the reader to your client's claim for relief, to the legal issues it involves, and to your conclusions about their probable resolution. This paragraph is frequently called a thesis paragraph because it states your thesis, that is, your position on the outcome of a client's prospective case. One benefit of providing this kind of introduction early in the discussion is that it makes it easier for your reader to evaluate the analysis as you build it. Another benefit is that it sets out the organization of the discussion.

One logical way of arranging relevant introductory material in a thesis paragraph is to:

1. identify the claim or defense in your problem;

2. set out the general rules that govern that claim in the order you intend to discuss them and explain how those rules relate to each other;

3. if length permits, or complexity requires, briefly apply those rules to your facts; and

4. state the thesis (your legal conclusion).

If your memo is fairly simple, however, or if your professor or law firm requires a Conclusion section rather than a Short Answer section, you may want to shorten your thesis paragraph by eliminating or abbreviating some of the steps outlined above. One thing you can do is to eliminate step 3, the application of the law to the facts. You can also combine steps 1 and 4 and begin with a thesis sentence that both introduces the topic of the discussion and gives your conclusion as to the claim or defense in your problem. After this, you could still indicate the organization of your discussion by introducing the rules that govern that claim. A simple thesis paragraph should be no more than a half to two-thirds of a page.

A. Thesis Paragraph with One Claim

Assume that you are working in a law firm that has a new client who has suffered physical injuries and wants to know if she can recover damages. After doing some research, you have written the following thesis paragraph.

Topic Sentence on Claim	Mary Bennett was attacked in the lobby of her apartment building by an intruder and we are considering a negligence action against Fulton Apartments, her landlord. A plaintiff alleging negligence must show that the defendant owed the plaintiff a duty of care, that the defendant breached
Applicable Rules	the duty, that the plaintiff was injured, and that the breach of the duty was the proximate cause of the plaintiff's injuries. [cite.] A landlord's legal duty to avoid harm is limited to harm that is foreseeable. [cite.] Since there were no previous acts of violence in
Application	the building itself or in the immediate neighborhood, it is unlikely that Ms. Bennett will be able to show that the attack was foreseeable. Moreover, since her attacker was inadvertently let into the building by
Conclusion	another tenant, Ms. Bennett will not be able to show a causal link between the landlord's refusal to hire security guards and her injuries. Thus, a suit would likely be unsuccessful.

This paragraph is an effective introduction in that it clearly states the legal question, the relevant legal test, and the author's reasoned conclusion. Thus, it clearly orients your reader. Be careful, however, that the length of the thesis paragraph is proportionate to the length of the discussion. If your problem involves many rules of law, remember that the thesis paragraph is not the place to offer an elaborate explanation of them. It is not the place to give precedent facts or make case comparisons. In addition, if your problem presents intricate facts, you may shorten or eliminate your application of the rules to the facts of your case. After stating the elements of negligence, for example, you could conclude, "As Ms. Bennett cannot show duty or causation, she will not succeed in her claim."

A thesis paragraph is supposed to be a helpful roadmap for the reader. Thus, you need to delineate the legal claims, rules, and conclusions carefully. An introductory paragraph that leaves the reader unclear about which issues you will discuss, how they relate, or how they will be resolved will make it harder for the reader to follow the analysis. It is, however, an *introduction* to the discussion, not the discussion itself.

B. Thesis Paragraph with Multiple Claims

The Bennett problem involved only one claim and thus it was possible to announce and apply all the legal requirements. When your case involves more than one claim, however, each of which has several elements requiring discussion, you may need to rethink your strategy in order to prevent your thesis paragraph from becoming too long. One helpful tactic is to write a thesis paragraph that sets out all the legal claims and explains how they relate to each other. Then write a second paragraph in which you apply the law to your facts and then conclude.

Topic Sentence on Claim	Joan Bell, a psychiatrist, has been sued for failure to warn the plaintiff against a patient's violent behavior. A psychotherapist has a duty to warn of a patient's threatened violent behavior where the patient has communicated "a serious threat of physical violence against a reasonably identifiable victim." Cal. Civ. Code § 43.92(a)(West 2006). If brief
First Issue	reflection would reveal a victim's identity, then the victim is reasonably identifiable. *Tarasoff v. The Regents of the University of California*, 17 Cal. 3d 425, 439 (1976). This duty also extends to persons are
Second Issue	so close to the victim that they would likely be harmed when the patient acts against the intended victim.
	Since Joan Bell is a psychiatrist, she qualifies as a "psychotherapist." Bell had been treating Susan Lacey for ten months, during which time, Lacey had expressed animosity towards the seven leaders of a college sorority that had rejected her. However, Lacey
Application	never made an explicit threat against the sorority leaders. In addition, they were not reasonably identifiable since Lacey never identified them by
Conclusion on First Issue	name and only said they were juniors and seniors at the college when they rejected her years before. Accordingly, although Lacey did, in fact, attack one of the sorority leaders, Bell had no duty to warn her.
Conclusion on Second Issue	Finally, Bell had no duty to the victim's recent boyfriend who was with her at the time of the attack and was also injured, since he, too, was not reasonably identifiable.

Of course, not all problems involving multiple issues or claims are necessarily complex. When you have a problem involving simple issues or claims, you may still use one thesis paragraph to introduce all the issues, their relation to each other, their governing rules and their disposition. This is the situation in the following problem.

Topic Sentence on Claim **First Issue** **Application & Conclusion on First Issue** **Second Issue** **Conclusion**	The issue is whether George Ferguson can bring a successful motion to quash service of process on the grounds that he was enticed to enter the jurisdiction by John Young's fraud and trickery. Personal service of a defendant who is induced to come into the jurisdiction of Ohio by fraud or trickery is "an abuse of process and will be set aside upon proper application." [cite]. The inviter must have intended to trick at the time of the invitation. [cite] John Young intended to serve George Ferguson with process when he invited him into the jurisdiction, so that Young enticed him. Nevertheless, service may be valid if the defendant stays within the jurisdiction for more than a "reasonable time." [cite] Ferguson remained for three extra hours to have dinner with his sister, which was reasonable. Therefore, Ferguson's motion to quash service should be successful.

After this introduction, you would discuss each ground separately.

Exercise 6-A

1.   *Your client, John Wheeler, wants to sue Donald Lindhorst in a federal district court in Connecticut for negligence. There is a threshold question, however, as to whether the district court has diversity jurisdiction to hear this case. Lindhorst is a citizen of Arkansas. Wheeler lived in Arkansas until he was sent to serve a prison sentence in Connecticut, where he is still an inmate. If Wheeler is still a citizen of Arkansas, the federal court will lack diversity jurisdiction. Which thesis paragraph for this problem is better and why?*

Thesis A

Wheeler is a citizen of Connecticut based on the decision in *Ferrara v. Ibach*. In *Ferrara*, the court ruled that serviceman Ibach was a citizen of South Carolina because of his physical presence there and his intention not to return to his former domicile in Pennsylvania. He established domicile by moving his family to South Carolina, renting a house there, enrolling his children in public school there, and maintaining a bank account there.

Thesis B

John Wheeler, a domiciliary of Arkansas before his incarceration in a Connecticut prison, wants to sue Donald Lindhorst, an Arkansas domiciliary, for negligence. In order to sue in federal court, however, Wheeler must be a domiciliary of Connecticut for the purposes of establishing diversity jurisdiction under 28 U.S.C. § 1332 (2012). In cases involving a person's involuntary relocation, a presumption favors the original domicile over an acquired one. Nonetheless, this presumption can be overcome by showing that the person clearly and unequivocally intended to make the new domicile home. *Jones v. Hadican.* The Wheeler family's move to Connecticut and Wheeler's statements demonstrate they intended to make Connecticut their new home and diversity jurisdiction can be satisfied.

2. *Read the following facts and rules of law and then write a thesis paragraph on whether John Starr and Alice Doe can recover for negligent infliction of emotional distress as a result of Pennsylvania Deluxe Hotel's negligence in hiring and supervising the security guard who fired at Jane Starr. (You can assume the negligence for the purpose of this exercise.)*

———————

On Election Day, John Starr, the husband of candidate Jane Starr, and Alice Doe, Jane's great aunt and former guardian, decided to watch the television election coverage at campaign headquarters at Pennsylvania Deluxe Hotel. They were waiting for Jane to return to the hotel after visiting her supporters at local campaign offices. The campaign had been marred by numerous threats of violence against the candidate and her family.

At 9:30 p.m., Jane and several staff members arrived at the hotel, and Jane began walking to the hotel's entrance. Halfway there, a psychotic hotel security guard pulled out a pistol and shot at Jane. The television cameras picked up the guard pointing and shooting his pistol in Jane's direction. The shot was heard on the T.V. The cameras did not actually show Jane being hit and falling, but they did immediately show her lying on the sidewalk, unconscious, in a pool of blood.

John and Alice were watching the T.V. as the entire scene unfolded. They say they realized immediately after the shot was fired that Jane was seriously hurt. John immediately collapsed, and Alice became hysterical.

Although Jane's injuries were not fatal, both John and Alice were extremely depressed in the months following the incident. Alice was put into a sanitarium to recover from a breakdown. John was too shaken to work for three months. John and Jane's marriage suffered as John insisted that Jane resign the post she had just recently won. Neither John nor Alice has any physical ailment associated with their emotional problems.

———————

As you may recall from Chapter 4, negligent infliction of emotional distress has four elements.

1. *The plaintiff must be closely related to the victim, as opposed to being distantly related or unrelated.*

2. *The plaintiff must have been near enough to the scene of the accident that the ensuing shock was the direct result of the impact of a sensory and contemporaneous observance of the accident, as opposed to shock which results from learning about the accident from others after its occurrence.*

3. *The shock must have resulted from a single, identifiable traumatic event; it cannot be the result of a condition that occurs over time.*

4. *The plaintiff's distress must be severe, although there need not be a physical manifestation of a psychic injury.*

CHAPTER 7

WRITING A LEGAL DOCUMENT: THE LEGAL MEMORANDUM

I. PURPOSE OF A MEMORANDUM

ONE OF THE MOST COMMON FORMS of legal writing is the legal memorandum, in which you analyze a legal problem and write up the results of your analysis. A legal memorandum is a document written to convey information within a law firm or other organization. It is usually prepared by a junior attorney or by a law clerk for a more senior attorney early in the firm's handling of a legal dispute. The writer analyzes the legal rules that govern the issues raised by that problem and applies those rules to the facts of the dispute. The attorneys will then use the memo to understand the issues that the case raises, to advise the client, and to prepare later documents for the case.

The memorandum is an objective, exploratory document. It explores the law, evaluates the strengths and weaknesses of each party's arguments, and reaches a conclusion based on that analysis. It is not an advocacy paper in which you argue only for your client's side of the case. The memorandum should be persuasive in the sense that you convince your reader that your analysis of the problem is correct. However, in practice, you will find that the assigning attorney does not want you to give up easily on the firm's client's case.

We recommend that you start to work on your assignment as soon as possible, preferably immediately after you receive it. Your writing assignments will take more time than you think. Even if you have a successful track record writing papers as an undergraduate or graduate student, or in a business or professional career, your legal writing assignments involve many new skills. Until you have had more practice and some of the work, such as citation form, becomes more automatic, even short assignments will take a lot of time.

A. Audience

When you write a memorandum, you should be aware of your reading audience and its needs and expectations. The hypothetical audience for a student memorandum assignment is usually an attorney who is not a specialist in the field. Most attorneys for whom you write are busy and have certain expectations that you must fulfill. For example, they will expect to receive a core of information about the controlling law and its application to the facts of the problem, but will not expect an explanation of the legal process steps of the sort that you have been learning the first weeks of law school. You need not explain, for example, "This case is from the highest court of this state and so is binding in this dispute." You may wish to give this information to a lay reader, but a lawyer knows that a case decided by the jurisdiction's highest court is binding. On the other hand, the lawyer probably does not know the facts, holding, and reasoning of that case and does expect you to supply that information.

B. Writing Techniques

Your reader will also have expectations about how the memorandum should be written. Although you may be unfamiliar with legal analysis and its presentation in a professional document, you are still writing English and you should continue to follow the principles of good written English. The general characteristics of good writing need to be cultivated because legal analysis can be complicated and involve difficult ideas. In order to communicate these ideas clearly to your reader, you need a firm control over language.

The memorandum is a formal document in that it is a professional piece of writing. Thus, you should use standard written English and avoid slang, other kinds of informal speech, and overuse of contractions. One problem of legal writing that deserves particular attention is the problem of legalese. Lawyers frequently are criticized for using archaic terms and incomprehensible sentence constructions in legal documents. This criticism is especially aimed at the form documents that many attorneys use. An example is a form that begins "whereas the party of the first part," and uses expressions like "herein" and "hereinbefore." This type of legalese usually does not afflict law students, and we hope it will not afflict you. In the end, you will sound more professional and more in control if you use a vocabulary and syntax with which you feel comfortable. Chapters 9 and 10 and Appendix A explain the principles for clear writing.

Some legal terms are substantive, however, and you should use them. For example, you should use the operative language of a statute or of a judge's formulation of a rule when that language controls the analysis of a problem on which you are working. Although that language may not strike you as well written, it supplies the general principle of law to which you must give meaning. Your reader should be told what that language is and will expect you to repeat those operative terms.

Terms of art aside, your language should also be responsive to your audience. You will be writing for several different audiences during your legal career and you will have to adjust your prose accordingly. Not all of your readers will be lawyers. For example, often you will write to your clients, to administrative personnel, and to other government officeholders. You may also write to lawyers and clients for whom English is not their first language. Although you should write accurately about the law, you should also explain your message in good written English, using terms that a non-lawyer can understand. When you write to lawyers, you should also use good written English, although you may use legal terms without as much explanation. Keep in mind that each audience has a different need, but that all audiences need and appreciate good writing.

Another aspect of presenting yourself as a legal professional is that you are writing as the client's attorney. Many students forget that role and, for example, write, "John Doe's attorney moved for a continuance." Remember that you are John Doe's attorney, or part of a team of attorneys, and instead should write, "we filed for a continuance." You should not, however, inject yourself into your legal analysis by using the first person pronoun. The purpose of the memorandum, and of many other legal documents, is to analyze the law and facts. You want to communicate that analysis persuasively and convincingly, not present it as your opinion only. For example, you should say "in Doe v. Doe the court held . . .," not "I believe [or I think] that in Doe v. Doe the court held. . . ."

As a law student you face the particular challenge of navigating between legalese and terms of art. In most respects, however, legal writing requires only what any thoughtfully written paper requires. As long as you keep your reader's needs in mind, and your prose adheres to the rules of standard written English and composition and respects legal terms, you will fulfill your reader's expectations for memorandum style.

II. THE TRADITIONAL OFFICE MEMO

IN THIS PART we explain the format for the traditional office memo. In Part III we discuss more informal memos, often sent as an e-mail message.

Although there is no required format that all lawyers use or that all law schools use for a legal memorandum, most memoranda are divided into three to six sections. Each section performs a particular function within the memo and conveys a necessary core of information:

- The Statement of Facts
- The Question Presented
- The Short Answer or Conclusion
- The Applicable Statutes
- The Discussion, and perhaps
- The final Conclusion

Under some formats, the Question Presented and Short Answer or Conclusion may come before the Statement of Facts.

You do not need to write the memorandum in the order you assemble it, however. Instead, you may first want to write tentative formulations of certain sections (such as the Question Presented) and then rewrite those sections when you have a final draft of the Discussion, the most pivotal section of a memorandum. Once you have written the Discussion, you may need to rewrite the sections you wrote earlier to ensure they comport with the finished section. This writing process requires drafts and revisions before you reach your final copy. (See Chapter 8.)

The memorandum usually begins with a heading with the following information:

To:	Name of the person for whom the memo is written
From:	Name of the writer
Re:	Short identification of the matter for which the memo was prepared, for example, "Sophia Ward: Claim of Gender Discrimination"
Date:	

Then the body of the memo may be divided into the sections described below.

A. Statement of Facts

Because the heart of legal analysis is in applying the law to the facts, the facts of the problem can be the most important determinant of the outcome of a case. Each case begins because something happened to someone or to some thing.[1] The Statement of Facts introduces the legal problem by telling what happened.

The purpose of this section is to state the facts and narrate what happened. Therefore, use only facts in this section; do not include conclusions, legal principles, or citations to authorities unless you are citing a statute. This section should include the following:

- all legally relevant facts,
- all facts that you mention in the other sections of the memo, and
- any other facts that give necessary background information.

If the problem for your memo is already in litigation, you should include its procedural history.

Facts are relevant or irrelevant in relation to the legal rules at issue. In order to know which facts are relevant, you will need to know what the issue in the problem is. If the issue is whether the client committed a crime, then you must know the elements of that crime from the statute. The relevant facts are those that are used to prove or disprove those elements.

Do not omit facts that are unfavorable to your client. The attorney for whom you are writing the memo may rely on the Statement of Facts to advise the client, for negotiations with other attorneys, and to prepare other documents for the case. Without the complete facts, the attorney for whom you are writing will be surprised and unprepared while handling the case.

Be careful to use objective language. The facts should not be slanted, subtly or not so subtly, toward either party. Sentence 1 of each of the following sets describes facts using partisan language inappropriate for a memorandum. Sentence 2 of each set uses language more appropriate for a memorandum.

1. John Smith endured three hours of his family's presence.

2. John Smith remained with his family for three hours.

3. Because Ms. Jones deserted her husband, he was left the unenviable task of raising three children.

4. After Ms. Jones left her husband, he raised his three children by himself.

---

[1] You may be assigned to write a memorandum that involves a legal issue only, such as how a new statute has changed the common law. Then, you may wish to omit a Statement of Facts, and perhaps substitute a short Introduction. See Part III of this chapter.

Whether you are given the facts with your assignment or you gather them yourself, you should sort and organize them rather than set them out in the order as the information came to you. Put the crucial information first. Generally, in the first paragraph, you should tell who your client is, what your client wants, where the information came from, and what the problem is about. By doing so, you provide a framework and the reader then can more easily evaluate the rest of the facts within that framework. For example, compare these two paragraphs, each of which was written as the first paragraph of a Statement of Facts for the same problem.

1. John Davis is a high school graduate who has been unable to keep a job. He first worked as a machinist's apprentice, but after two years he was asked to leave. Since then he has worked at various trades, including carpentry and plumbing, in retail stores, and at McDonald's. None of these jobs lasted more than a year.

2. Our client, William Mathews, has been sued by John Davis for fraud. The charge stems from statements that Mathews made to Davis in the course of a stock investment proposal.

Example 2 is better because it tells the reader the context of the problem. The reader of the first paragraph does not know what the problem is about. Is it an employment contract case? An unemployment compensation application problem? The reader of the second example knows that she should read the rest of the facts with an eye toward a fraud suit.

Use the rest of this section to develop the facts. Explain who the parties are and give any other descriptions that are necessary. Always group like facts together. For example, if your memo topic is a false imprisonment topic about a person confined in a room, you may want to present in one paragraph or series of paragraphs all the facts that describe the physical appearance of the room.

For many of the assignments you receive, the best and easiest way to develop the events is chronologically, that is, in the order in which the events occurred. For some problems, however, a topical organization in which you structure the facts in terms of the elements you need to establish or by the parties involved, if there are many parties, may work better.

You also may want to include what relief your client wants, or what you have been asked to analyze in the memo. This information often provides a natural ending to the section.

For example:

> Our client is Perry Moy, the executor of the Robert Jones estate. Jones was killed by his stepson Jason Farmer. On Moy's behalf we have filed suit against Dr. Zig Ernst, Farmer's psychiatrist, alleging negligence in failing to warn Mr. Jones of Farmer's dangerous condition.
>
> [Continue with facts of Farmer's violent propensities and Ernst's treatment of Farmer.]
>
> We will move for summary judgment against Ernst. You asked me for a memorandum analyzing Atlantis Rev. Stat. § 100; a Mental Health Professional's Duty to Warn or Protect a Patient's Potential Victim, to use as a basis for a memorandum in support of our motion.

The facts of this problem can be organized by topics: For example, Mr. Jones' family situation, Jason Farmer's health situation, Farmer's visit to Dr. Ernst, and Farmer's murder of Jones.

Exercise 7-A

Which Statement of Facts about a prisoner's domicile for a memo about a diversity jurisdiction issue is best? Why?

1. Mr. Fred Wheeler is a prisoner in the federal prison in Danbury, Connecticut. Wheeler was convicted of bank robbery in Arkansas, which was his domicile at the time of the robbery. He has asked us to sue his attorney in that case for malpractice. The attorney, Donald Lindhorst, is a domiciliary of Arkansas. We would like to sue in the United States District Court if we can establish diversity jurisdiction.

Wheeler is in the second year of a five-to-seven year prison term. His wife and son moved to Danbury four months ago, and his wife is now working here. His son is enrolled in the Danbury public school. Mrs. Wheeler has registered to vote in Danbury and has opened an account at a bank there. The Wheelers have no financial interests in Arkansas. His wife's sister, who is her only family member still alive, lives in nearby Bethel, Connecticut. Wheeler's brother-in-law has offered Wheeler a job there after Wheeler's release from prison. Wheeler has said he will not return to Arkansas, and that he wants to "start fresh in Connecticut."

This memo analyzes whether Wheeler is a citizen of Connecticut for purposes of federal diversity jurisdiction.

2. Donald Lindhorst is a lawyer in Little Rock who unsuccessfully defended Fred Wheeler against a bank robbery charge in Arkansas. Wheeler is now in federal prison here in Danbury and wants to sue Lindhorst for malpractice. Wheeler has called Lindhorst a "rotten lawyer" and "a crook," who was only interested in getting his legal fee from him.

Wheeler is serving his second year of a five-to-seven year prison term. He hates the prison because of the food and lack of recreational facilities. His wife has moved to Danbury with their son and visits him often. Wheeler wants to remain in Connecticut when he gets out of prison and take a job offered him by his brother-in-law in nearby Bethel. His wife is working in Danbury and his child is in school here.

Lindhorst had been recommended to Wheeler by a mutual friend in Arkansas, and now Wheeler is sorry he hired him. He says that Lindhorst spoke to him only once, and did not interview any witnesses before the trial. He has asked us to handle his malpractice case. We would like to sue in the United States District Court in Hartford if we can establish diversity jurisdiction.

3.   On March 4, 2015, Fred Wheeler was convicted of bank robbery in the federal district court in Arkansas. At his sentencing hearing in May he was sentenced to a five-to-seven year term in federal prison in Danbury, Connecticut. Wheeler was represented by a Mr. Donald Lindhorst, an Arkansas attorney, in the bank robbery case.

Wheeler now wants to sue Lindhorst for malpractice, and wrote us on March 10, asking us to represent him in this suit. We want to sue in the federal district court in Hartford. When I interviewed him last month, Wheeler told me that he does not intend to return to Arkansas and wants "to start fresh in Connecticut."

Mrs. Wheeler moved to Danbury in January, 2016. That month she enrolled their son in the public school and opened a bank account. In February, she started work in Danbury, and has remained with that job. Mrs. Wheeler visits her husband frequently. Her brother-in-law has offered Wheeler a job in Connecticut when he gets out of prison.

B.   Question Presented

The most important inquiry for the memo writer as it is for other legal inquiries is "what is the legal issue in this problem?" The Question Presented is a sentence that poses the precise legal issue in dispute. There are two ways to formulate the questions for a memorandum. The first, and easier way, is to be specific to the problem: identify people by name and refer specifically to relevant facts. This type of question works best if the reader already knows the facts of the case. For example, suppose you represent Waterview Condominium Association and the fact statement of your memo includes the facts that Ms. Jones, a condo owner, may have violated a regulation that forbids condo owners from displaying advertisements in their windows. If you write the question as "Did Jones violate Waterview's Regulation #15.05?" the reader who read the facts will understand what it refers to. If you write this kind of specific question, make sure that the reader knows the facts to which it refers.

The other way of formulating an issue is to write it so that it can be understood by a reader who does not know the facts of the case. It is usually necessary to write the question this way if the Question Presented precedes the Statement of Facts. Then you should write the question to include the legal principle at issue and the key facts that raise the issue. This type of question does not describe people or events specifically by name, because the reader does not know who or what they are. Instead, you write the question more generally to describe the people or events involved. So the question about the condo rule could be written,

> "Did a condominium owner violate a regulation that forbids unit owners from displaying advertisements in their windows if she displayed her election poster as a candidate for the school board?"

If the question involves people, then identify them in general terms, as in the example above, rather than by name, and identify the relationships among the people appropriate to the cause of action. For an adverse possession problem, this example identifies the parties as a claimant to land and a title holder:

> "Does a claimant to land take title by adverse possession against the titleholder if she planted a garden on the disputed strip beyond her property line and cultivated the garden for twenty-two years?"

You can write the question either in the form of an interrogative sentence as in the sentence above, beginning with a word such as "is" or "does" or beginning with the word "whether," as in this sentence:

> "Whether a claimant to land takes title by adverse possession against the titleholder if she planted a garden on the disputed strip beyond her property line and cultivated the garden for twenty-two years."

You may find it helpful at first when you begin research for the case to isolate the issue in specific terms (Does Jones take title by adverse possession?") ("Did Jones violate Waterview regulation 15.05?") But after you begin to write the rest of the memo, rewrite the question into more general terms that include important facts.

Typically, the question should identify the cause of action, either a common law cause of action or the statutory or constitutional provision that the plaintiff is suing under or the state is prosecuting, the relevant key facts, and the people involved described in general terms.

An exception to this pattern exists, however, if the problem involves a question of law only rather than a question of law applied to facts. For example, the issue may be whether a jurisdiction will adopt a new cause of action, or an element of an established cause of action. Then, the question may not require specific facts of the problem. In the following set of questions for a memo, the first issue is a question of law. The second issue asks how the law (assuming the new rule is adopted) applies to the facts. The second question thus includes specific facts of the problem, and is logically linked to the first question.

---

1. Under Illinois law, must a plaintiff in a false imprisonment claim be aware of the confinement?

2. If so, is a plaintiff aware of his confinement if he believes a door will not open because it is stuck, when in fact, it was locked by the defendant?

If the problem contains more than one issue, as in the example above, then set each out as a separately numbered question. If the problem has one issue, but two or more sub-issues, you may consider using an inclusive introduction and then sub-parts. For example, a wills issue could be written as follows:

Is a handwritten unwitnessed will valid under the Wills Act if

a. the will is dated with the month and year but not the day of the month, and

b. the will is written on stationery that contains a printed letterhead?

One important decision you must make is the level of generality to use for your description of facts. To identify parties, we have suggested that you not name the parties specifically, but, instead describe them more generally in relation to the claim at issue. Ms. Jones becomes a "condominium owner." But do not generalize the category so much that you obscure the issue in the problem. For example, if the case involves the duties of a school district to provide services, then "an arm of the county government" is not specific enough. The proper level of generality here is probably just "a local school district".

The facts other than the identities of the parties should be described specifically enough to be understood. The issue in a problem involves how the law applies to those particular facts. If a contract is at issue between Smith and Jones, call it a contract, not a business relationship. If the school district is being sued for not providing a sign language interpreter to a hearing impaired student, do not write "appropriate instructional aids" instead. If the defendant is sued for building a one-car garage that intrudes over a property line, do not write "a small structure." One benefit of using specific facts is that you will avoid inappropriately inserting judgments into the Questions. For example, if you called a garage a "small structure," you have made a judgment about the size of the structure that intrudes over the property line. If you said a "one-car garage," you avoided that judgment.

Some law firms and writing faculty also use Questions Presented of more than one sentence, although most court rules and law firms require a one-sentence question. The writer uses the first sentence to introduce the issue or explain the law and then asks the question in the next sentence. For example:

1. The Hawaii Statute of Frauds requires that, to be enforceable, a contract "not to be performed within one year of the making thereof" be in writing, signed by the party to be charged.

2. Does the Kingston-Jones employment agreement come within the statute if it is a five-year contract but either party may terminate after six months?

1. The Family and Medical Leave Act (FMLA) provides that an employee is eligible for leave "in order to care for" a family member. 29 U.S.C. § 2612(a)(1)(c).

2. Does an employee who takes her critically ill mother to Las Vegas to fulfill her mother's last wish, and while there took her mother's blood pressure daily, helped her to bathe, and filled her prescriptions "care for" her mother within the meaning of the FMLA?

Consider these other suggestions for a good Question Presented.

1. Isolate the specific issue. The issue should not be so broadly stated as to encompass many possible issues under the cause of action. For example, "Was Carey denied due process?" is an unhelpful question because due process refers to many different legal issues and the question does not specify the relevant one. A question that adequately isolates the issue is, "Is a juvenile denied due process because he is not represented by counsel at a delinquency hearing?"

2. Do not conclude. The Question should pose the inquiry of the memorandum, not answer it. You will avoid making conclusions if you use facts and legal principles. For example, if the case law in a jurisdiction establishes that a person can be guilty of criminal contempt if he disobeys a court order intentionally or recklessly, the following question contains a conclusion.

> Is a person guilty of criminal contempt if he recklessly does not read a court order and disobeys it?

The inquiry in this case is whether the person acted recklessly. By concluding that the defendant acted recklessly, the writer has concluded that the defendant is guilty. The writer should have asked whether the defendant is guilty under these facts, as in the following question.

> Is a person guilty of criminal contempt if he disobeys a court order because he did not listen to or read the order?

Where is the conclusion of law in this question presented?

> Was the appellant denied his constitutional right to raise his children when the agency removed the children from his custody without due process?

3. Keep the question to a readable length. You should not include all the relevant facts in the question, just the key ones that raise the issue. The following question includes too many facts.

> Is a person guilty of criminal contempt if he disobeys a court order that he never read because he left the country for several weeks, his attorney's letter was lost while he was gone, his seven-year-old daughter forgot to write down the telephone messages she took, and his cat shredded the messages from his wife?

4. Keep the question readable by moving from the general to the specific. One way of doing that is to first identify the claim and then move toward the specific facts, as in these examples.

> Did a person commit theft of lost or mislaid property when he pocketed a watch that he had found on a baseball field just after the conclusion

> of a YWCA team practice, and that watch was stolen from him as he walked away from the field?
>
> Whether a prisoner's domicile changes for purposes of federal diversity jurisdiction when he is incarcerated in another state, the prisoner's family moves to the state of incarceration, and the prisoner has secured employment there upon his release from the penitentiary.

5. Begin with a short concrete subject. Questions are less ambiguous and are easier to understand on a first reading if they begin with a short concrete subject that is quickly followed by an active verb, rather than if they begin with a long abstract subject. For example, for these questions, the writers have used abstract nouns (the failure, the entrance) as the subjects of their sentences.

> **a.** *Not:* Whether the failure to appear in court for a scheduled trial by an attorney is contempt of court if he was notified of the date of the trial but never wrote it in his calendar.
>
> **b.** *But:* Whether an attorney is in contempt of court when he fails . . .
>
> **a.** *Not:* Does entrance into a tent pitched in a park constitute entering a "building" for purposes of burglary?
>
> **b.** *But:* Does a person enter "a building" for purposes of burglary when he enters a tent that is pitched in a park?

The subjects of both questions (a) are nominalizations, that is, they are nouns or noun phrases that have been constructed from verbs. Sentences that begin with nominalizations are often difficult to understand because the subject is long and the reader has to unpack the event described in the nominalization (the failure to appear in court . . . by an attorney) and then fit that event into the question.

Another type of abstract subject that can be difficult to understand on first reading is a subject that is a gerund. A gerund is a present participle of a verb that is used as a noun. Because a gerund is a form of a verb, it may be ambiguous whether the word is the subject or the verb of the sentence. In the following question, "refusing" is a gerund.

> **a.** *Not:* Did refusing to give an entrapment instruction by the trial court because the defendant pleaded not guilty constitute error?
>
> **b.** *But:* Did the trial court commit error when the judge refused to give an entrapment instruction. . . .

In example (a), "refusing" is the subject. But the sentence is about the trial court. "Refusing" is what the trial judge did.

These questions have been rewritten so that they use short concrete subjects that name who the sentence is about, followed quickly by the verb.

See Chapter 10 for more information about nominalizations and concrete subjects.

C.   The Short Answer or Conclusion

The function of this section is to answer the Question Presented and to summarize the reasons for that answer. This section can be written in either of two ways: as a short answer or as a conclusion.

The Short Answer. A short answer is usually one or two sentences such as "Yes, a juvenile is denied due process if he is not represented at a delinquency hearing. Due process does not require that the juvenile be represented by an attorney, however." To write this form of Answer, you answer the Question Presented and add a sentence that summarizes the reason for your conclusion or adds a necessary qualification to the answer. Some lawyers write only one or two sentence answers to the Question. For your assignments, the Short Answer may be more appropriate for a short memorandum, such as one of three or four pages.

The Conclusion. A conclusion answers the Question and summarizes the reasons for that answer from the Discussion section of the memo. A Conclusion should be longer than the Short Answer, but it still should be a summary only, and it should answer the Question. Depending upon the complexity of the problem and the length of the memorandum, the Conclusion may be one or two paragraphs or, for a long memorandum, it may require a few paragraphs.

You should have a Short Answer or Conclusion for each Question Presented and number each to correspond to the number of the Question it answers.

Sometimes you cannot confidently reach a conclusion because the law is too uncertain or you need more facts. In that situation, explain briefly why your conclusions are tentative, or what the alternatives are, or which additional facts you need.

Especially when written as a Conclusion, this section can be very important to the attorney for whom you write your memo. It gives the attorney quickly attainable information that she will need to prepare for a phone call to a client or another attorney or for an upcoming conference. Sometimes this section is the first section the attorney reads.

Write the conclusion after you have completed the Discussion, and spend some time to write a careful and useful summary.

Suggestions for writing this section.

1.   **Be conclusory.** A Short Answer or Conclusion should be an assertion of your answer to the issue you have posed. But it is not a discussion of how you evaluated strengths and weaknesses of alternate arguments in order to reach that conclusion. That evaluation and a full discussion of your reasons for the conclusion belong in the Discussion. Which of these examples is conclusory?

---

a.   Jones was falsely imprisoned because he reasonably believed that he was confined by Smith's dog. Jones's belief was reasonable because the dog growled at him and Jones knew that the dog had bitten other people in the past.

b.   Jones may have been falsely imprisoned depending upon whether he reasonably believed that Smith's dog would bite him if he moved. Several facts show that Jones could have reasonably believed he was in danger because the dog had bitten other people before. But some facts do not. For instance, the dog had been sent to obedience school after those incidents. The issue depends on the importance of these latter facts.

Example a is appropriately conclusory. The writer has reached and explained an answer to the Question Presented. The writer of example b is discussing and weighing alternate arguments.

2.   **Do not include extensive discussions of authority.** Although your answer to the question will necessarily come from your analysis of the relevant primary and secondary authorities, your discussion of those authorities belongs in the Discussion section. In the Conclusion or Short Answer, you need not discuss or name particular cases or other authorities you rely on unless they are necessary to explain your answer.

Notice the difference in the following examples.

---

a.   The Popes adversely possessed the strip of land between their lot and Smith's. Although they occupied the land mistakenly believing it was theirs, their mistaken possession should be considered hostile as to Smith's ownership.

b.   Whether the Popes adversely possessed the strip of land between their lot and Smith's if they mistakenly believed that the strip is theirs depends upon whether the Atlantis court relies upon old

decisions that a claimant's mistaken possession cannot be hostile
to the title holder. Several courts in other jurisdictions recently
have decided that a person who possesses land mistakenly
thinking it is his own can still possess the land hostilely to the
true owner. The Atlantis court has strongly indicated that it may
adopt those rulings.

Example a is a short answer. Example b is a longer conclusion
and a discussion of authority explaining possible answers to the
adverse possession problem, but does not name or analyze the
cases.

One exception to this rule arises when the problem is a
statutory issue, in which case you should refer to the statute and
include the essential information about the statutory
requirements.

Smith did not violate the Theft of Lost or Mislaid Property Act, 12
Atlantis Rev. Stat. § 2 (2000). The statute applies only if a person
"obtains control over lost or mislaid property." Because Lyons robbed
Smith of the watch almost immediately after Smith found it, Smith
never obtained control over the property.

Another exception occurs if one case is so crucial to deciding
the issue that it controls the analysis and cannot be omitted. In
this situation, you should also include the citation.

The defendant attorney should be liable for malpractice even if the
plaintiff is not in privity of contract with him. The Atlantis Supreme
Court has held that a notary public who practiced law without a license
by writing a decedent's will was liable to the decedent's intended
beneficiary for his negligence. *Copper v. Brass*, 10 Atl. 200 (2005). This
decision should apply to attorneys as well as to notary publics. If so,
the defendant will be liable to Jones for negligently drafting the Jones
will.

Exercise 7-B

*Evaluate the following pairs of Question Presented and
Conclusion. Which pair is best? Why? What is wrong with the others?*

1.   **QP:** Whether an attorney should have been convicted of
criminal contempt of court for negligently failing to appear at a
scheduled trial and not representing his client if he was told the date,
had cases in other courts that same day, and had already failed to
appear in court once before.

Conclusion: The attorney should not have been convicted. Applying the precedents to this case, his failure to record the trial date and his failure to appear will not be criminal contempt.

2. QP: What shall determine if an attorney's failure to appear in court for his client's trial constitutes criminal contempt?

Conclusion: In Atlantis, whether an attorney is in criminal contempt for failure to appear at trial depends on the attorney's intent. If the attorney shows that the failure to appear was not willful disregard of duty, then there is no contempt. Mr. Bass should be able to show that.

3. QP: Is an attorney who does not appear in court for his client's trial guilty of criminal contempt if he was notified of the trial date but did not record it, and on the day of the trial, had the case file in his briefcase along with files of cases for which he did appear?

Conclusion: The attorney should not be held guilty of criminal contempt. In Atlantis, the attorney's failure to appear must have been willful, deliberate, or reckless. Mr. Bass did not act with the intent required. Instead, he inadvertently did not appear in court because he forgot to write down the court date and never took the case file from his briefcase in the rush of his other court appearances.

4. QP: Does an attorney who fails to appear at his client's trial commit criminal contempt of court under Atlantis law?

Conclusion: In Atlantis, an attorney is in criminal contempt of court if he acts willfully, deliberately, or recklessly in disregarding a court order. The court will have to decide. If the court can be persuaded that Mr. Bass did not so act when he did not appear for his client's trial, then Bass will not be in contempt.

D. Applicable Statutes

If your problem involves the application of a statute, a section of a constitution, or an administrative regulation, set out the exact language of the pertinent parts in block quote form. Include the citation.

A block quote is indented, single spaced, and does not include quotation marks.

E. Discussion

Up to this point, the memorandum contains the facts of your problem, poses the specific legal question that those facts raise, briefly answers that question, and sets out the relevant enacted law. In the Discussion, you will analyze the question by applying the relevant legal rules and their policies to the facts of the case. The process of analyzing is a process of breaking down a subject into its component parts. To analyze a legal subject, you break it down into its issues and then break each issue down into subissues. You give content to the legal rules you have found by examining the facts of the cases from which the rules came and in which the statutes were applied. You also examine the reasons for the rules and compare those cases to your problem. Only then can you determine what those rules mean. The purpose of this inquiry is to reach a conclusion and predict the outcome of the problem, that is, to determine whether the requirements for that claim are satisfied by the facts of your problem. This analysis provides the reasons for your conclusion about the outcome.

Because a memorandum is used to advise a client or prepare for further steps in litigation, the reader is looking in this section for a thorough analysis of the present state of the law. Thus, the Discussion should not be a historical narrative of the relevant case law and statutes or a general discussion of that area of the law. Instead, you should discuss the law specifically as it controls your problem.

The Discussion provides an objective evaluation of the issues. Thus, you should evaluate all the interpretations possible from applying the law to the facts, not just the interpretations that favor your client. Analyze as many arguments for your client that you can think of, but also analyze those arguments against your client. In addition, evaluate which ones are most persuasive. Do not predict an unrealistic outcome only because that outcome favors your client. If you will need more facts than you have been given in order to reach a conclusion, then explain which facts you need and why they are relevant.

A legal discussion is written according to certain patterns of analysis. These patterns were discussed in Chapters 4, 5, and 6.

F.   Conclusion

In some formats, where the memorandum includes a Short Answer of one or two sentences after the Question Presented, and the memo is long and complex, the memorandum ends with a Conclusion section that summarizes the Discussion. We have explained this type of Conclusion in Part C above.

III.   INFORMAL MEMORANDA/E-MAIL

ELECTRONIC COMMUNICATION, especially communication by e-mail, has significantly changed a lawyer's day-to-day practice. Clients e-mail questions to their lawyers and expect a quick answer. Senior attorneys e-mail questions and assignments to other attorneys in the firm and also expect a fast turnaround. Many attorneys spend a good part of their day writing and answering e-mails. Attorneys comment that their time is frequently interrupted—indeed constantly interrupted—by e-mails and faxes. Nevertheless, the attorney is expected to respond accurately and with well-written professional prose.

In many law firms, the traditional formal memorandum explained in the first part of this chapter has given way to a shorter, more informal document. These are less expensive in terms of billing time and they accommodate the recipient's need for a fast response. However, traditional memos are still often used—and sent as e-mail attachments—for complex issues, to show that the law firm has carefully researched and analyzed the issues, and to provide a complete more formal document for the client's case file. Nevertheless, for more discrete issues that do not require complicated analysis or long description of facts, informal memos, often generated electronically, have become more widely used.

There is no generally accepted format for an informal e-mail memo. They are usually written in response to a specific question, however, and should inform—or remind—the e-mail's recipient of the question she asked. The memo should include necessary facts and analyze the issue. So, the memo might have an introductory paragraph that would include the facts, the issue, and a conclusion, and continue with the analysis of the issue. It is good practice to begin with a salutation to the recipient and close with your name as the writer.

An informal memo may look like the examples below.

To: Sonia Partner

From: Tony Associate

Re: Gestational Surrogacy Agreement

Date: _____

Dear Sonia: (or Ms. Partner, depending on the firm's custom or whether Tony Associate is on a first-name basis with Ms. Partner)

You asked me for a short memo to respond to your clients, Mr. and Mrs. X, who are contemplating using a surrogate to gestate a child. The child will be conceived by in vitro fertilization (IVF) using sperm and eggs, each donated by the clients' relatives. The question is, under Atlantis law, who will be recognized as the child's parents:

- The egg donor (genetic mother)

- The gestational surrogate (gestational mother)

- The sperm donor (genetic father)

- The gestational surrogate's husband (presumed father under traditional law)

- The husband and wife who arranged for the IVF and the contract with the gestational surrogate (the intended mother and father)

Tony Associate would then continue:

The Atlantis Gestational Surrogacy Act, 750 Atl. Comp. Stat. 47/20 controls. The statute recognizes the intended mother and father as the child's legal parents if the surrogacy agreement complies with the statutory requirements.

As a preliminary matter, § 47/20(a)(1) requires that the surrogate be at least 21 years old, and that one or both of the intended parents have a medical need for a surrogate, § 47/20(b)(2). The other statutory requirements are:

[listing the requirements]

If you would like me to draw up the agreement, please let me know.

Tony

Whether you write to a client, to another attorney, to a judge, or any other recipient, use professional language and spell and punctuate accurately. Edit carefully. You are not tweeting or texting. Your memos are "informal" only in the sense that they do not follow all the steps of the traditional memorandum. For example, Tony Associate said "As a preliminary matter," not "For starters," or "First off." Be sure to edit for organization and content, and to proofread before you hit the send key. Remember that spellcheck is useful, but does not catch all spelling errors. If Tony had typed "feather" instead of "father," spellcheck will not highlight the error for him. He must proofread to find it. See Chapter 14 for information about proper e-mail use.

A last caveat: If § 47/20 had already generated considerable case interpretations and unresolved ambiguities, consider writing a longer fully researched more traditional memo instead and sending it as an attachment.

Here is an example of a slightly longer, but still informal, memo.

TO: Sonia Partner

FR: Tony Associate

DATE:

RE: X's Common Law Marriage to Ms. Y

Introduction:

Your client Mr. X is trying to collect spousal survivor benefits from his deceased spouse's employment plan. You asked me if Mr. X and Ms. Y will be recognized as married. They were not married in any religious or civil ceremony, nor do they have a marriage license. So they have no public ceremony or official record of a marriage.

However, as you know, this state is one of the few states that still recognizes common law marriage. If the couple has fulfilled the state's requirements, Mr. X was legally Ms. Y's surviving husband and he should qualify for survivor benefits.

Analysis:

The state's requirements for a common law marriage are fairly standard: The couple must have

- entered an express present agreement to marry,

- cohabited as husband and wife, and

- held themselves out to the public as husband and wife.

The state does not require that they cohabited for a specific period of time, but the longer their cohabitation, the stronger their proof of marriage.

From what you told me, X and Y lived together for seven years and were both parties to their lease. They each kept separate savings accounts but kept a joint checking account from which they paid their rent and certain expenses, such as groceries and utilities. They each owned a car registered in their own name and paid all car expenses separately. Neither had life insurance. They filed their taxes separately and had separate health insurance policies and charge cards.

This record is somewhat mixed. Except for their joint lease, and utilities and food payments, they individually maintained other aspects of their lives.

One important fact in the case law has been whether the couple parented and raised children together. Your clients have no children, although they began living together when she was 45 years old and he 48, so they were older than typical child-bearing years. Also, Ms. Y did not take Mr. X's surname, although that is no longer the norm, especially because she would want to maintain her professional name.

Conclusion:

Because this record is mixed, Mr. X's success will depend on other factors. We need to gather facts about the nature of their agreement, that is, whether they just agreed to live together, or agreed to live together as a married couple. We also need to speak to neighbors, tradespeople, colleagues at work, etc. as to whether they held themselves out as married.

I hope this memo helps and I am available to work on this with you if you need me.

Tony

Exercise 7-C

1. *Your client is Mr. Brown of Exercise 2-A on page 58. Your supervising attorney asks you to e-mail a short memo to him responding to the issue raised in that exercise.*

2. *Your client is Larry Kemp of Exercise 2-L on page 75. Write an e-mail memo to the supervising attorney answering the question of whether he will be required to pay restitutionary alimony.*

3. *Your firm represents Irving Pick, the trustee in bankruptcy for Bernard Nadoff. Nadoff is the infamous "entrepreneur" convicted of securities fraud for running a Ponzi scheme with the money that others invested with him. One of the investors, Bill Baird gave Nadoff a valuable sculpture as thanks for Nadoff "taking good care" of the money Baird invested with him. Baird's fifteen-year old daughter presented the sculpture to Nadoff who smiled at her and thanked her warmly.*

Nadoff declared bankruptcy and Pick is auctioning off many of Nadoff's personal possessions, including the sculpture. Baird has demanded its return, claiming that the gift was never completed, but was a conditional one.

Remember that a completed gift requires

- The donor's donative intent,

- delivery of the item of gift, and

- acceptance by the donee

Write an informal e-mail memo to the senior partner evaluating whether Baird can get the sculpture back.

Editing Checklist: Formal Memoranda

I. **Statement of Facts**

   A. Did you provide an introduction that sets out the context of the problem?

   B. Did you then arrange the facts in an organization that is easy to understand, such as chronologically, topically, or chronologically within a topical organization?

   C. Have you included all the facts that bear upon the analysis of the problem and are necessary to understand the problem?

   D. Have you omitted distracting and irrelevant facts?

   E. Does this section include only facts and not analysis or argument?

   F. Did you include procedural facts, if any?

II. **Question Presented**

   A. Have you identified the correct and the specific issue and referred to the common law, statutory, or constitutional claim?

   B. Unless the issue is solely a question of law, have you incorporated the facts that raise the issue?

   C. Have you identified the facts as specifically as appropriate, rather than use an overly generalized description?

   D. If there is more than one issue, have you organized the issues in a logical order, which you will adhere to through the memo?

   E. Is the Question readable?

III. **Conclusion or Short Answer**

   A. If you use a Short Answer, have you accurately and clearly answered the Question Presented?

   B. If you use a Conclusion,

      1. have you accurately and clearly answered the Question Presented, and

      2. have you summarized the analysis in the Discussion and briefly applied the controlling law to the facts of your problem?

IV. **Discussion (See Chapters 4–6)**

   A. Did you begin with a thesis paragraph, the length of which is appropriate to the length and complexity of the discussion?

B.   Have you organized your discussion logically?

1.   Is the discussion organized into separate claims that are presented in a logical order?

2.   Is each claim broken down into the issues and subissues by which the claim is analyzed?

C.   For each issue and sub-issue, do you

1.   analyze the controlling rules drawn from the jurisdiction's statutes and case law and then the persuasive authorities,

2.   examine the application of those rules in the precedents.

3.   apply the legal rules from those statutes and cases to the facts of your problem,

4.   draw analogies and distinctions to the precedents, and

5.   objectively evaluate and explore all credible interpretations?

D.   Does your analysis reflect an accurate synthesis of the authorities so that you explore all the ramifications of a topic as a related analysis?

E.   Have you kept firmly to what is relevant for the claim or defense you are analyzing?

F.   Have you explained and supported your conclusions with adequate reasons? Do you analyze all interpretations before coming to an unqualified conclusion?

G.   Are you creative in using facts and analogizing to similar issues?

H.   Have you supplied citations to authority and are they accurate?

Editing Checklist: Informal Memoranda

A.   Have you included the relevant background information to give context to your assignment?

B.   Have you isolated the issue, either in an introductory section or as a discrete line item?

C.   Have you taken the time you need to research the question and analyze accurately?

D.   Have you analyzed and organized your response as explained above?

E.   Do you adhere to proper e-mail etiquette?

Writing Style (See Chapters 9–10 and Appendix A): Formal and Informal Memos

A. Are your paragraphs unified around a topic and is that topic clear?

B. Do you use transitions to show the logical relationships between sentences and between paragraphs?

C. Do your sentences carry the reader forward rather than bog the reader down?

    1. Are your sentences a readable length without too many interrupting phrases and clauses?

    2. Do the verbs of your sentences carry the action or have you nominalized the verbs?

    3. Do you use concrete nouns as subjects rather than abstract ones?

    4. Are most of your sentences in the active voice?

    5. Did you edit out unnecessary throat clearing words and phrases?

D. Have you checked for correct grammar and punctuation?

E. Do you use past tense for events that already occurred?

F. Do you use quotations only when necessary, and do you fit them into your text?

CHAPTER 8

THE WRITING PROCESS

I. INTRODUCTION

THE FIRST TIME YOU ARE ASKED to prepare an inter-office memorandum is often the first time you have to integrate many of the concepts being taught in your legal writing course: issue organization, identification of rules and holdings, case summaries, application of law to fact, citation, and memorandum format. This chapter focuses on the process of writing that memo and breaks the process down into steps that can then put together. The chapter assumes that your research is complete or, as is common in many first memorandum assignments, that your teacher provided relevant cases and statutes. It also focuses only on memos that require you to apply established rules to facts, rather than to predict new rules of law. (For more complex issues of law, see Chapter 11.)

The suggestions offered here help many people to break through writers' block. If you have a process that works well in organizing your thoughts and putting them on paper, you may want to continue to use that process. But if you have difficulty getting started or find the transition from writing in other fields to writing legal documents difficult, these suggestions may smooth the way and help you avoid hours of staring at blank sheets of paper or empty computer screens.

Writing is often a four-step process:

- Transform your notes into an issue outline

- Write a first draft

- Revise for organization and analysis

- Revise for fluidity, clarity, and error

The suggestions below are linear in that they suggest a series of steps from beginning to end. The writing process, however, is recursive, and at any point along the way, you may find you have to go back, either to reassess some of your primary authorities to take account of new insights, or to add or omit something from an earlier discussion.

II. FROM RESEARCH TO OUTLINE

ONCE YOU HAVE BRIEFED YOUR CASES and thought about how they apply to your problem, you need to organize your notes into an outline. Rewrite your case summaries so that they are organized around the elements of the rule or the factors that govern your problem. This outline of the rule is the large-scale organization of your memorandum discussion. Then flesh out that outline using the analytic steps that comprise the small-scale organization of a memorandum discussion.

A. Issue Organization

The next pages use several examples to illustrate how to organize your notes into an outline. Start by taking your case briefs or summaries and rewriting them so they are organized by issues. Whether you take notes on a word processor, on index cards, or on a legal pad, identify each issue. Write the information from each case relevant to that issue. Include citation and page numbers so that you do not have to go back later. The important point is to organize your analysis by issues, not by cases. As explained in Chapter 4, your outline is dictated by the structure of the claim.

Assume, for example, your assignment involves an attempted bank robbery. Under 18 U.S.C.A. § 2113(a), this crime occurs when a person takes or attempts to take by force or violence, or by intimidation any property from a bank.

In the jurisdiction of your assignment, the courts have interpreted the statute as requiring two elements for attempted bank robbery:

1.   whether the defendant had culpable intent, and

2.   whether the defendant's conduct constituted a substantial step toward the commission of the crime.

United States v. Mott. The court in *Mott* said there are two parts to the culpable intent element. First, whether the defendant intended to take the bank's property, and second, whether he intended to do so by force or violence or by intimidation. In an attempted bank robbery, there is no need to show force, just the intent to act this way. *Id.* Thus, the first element of this crime has two subissues, while the second has only one issue. These then are the issues and sub issues for your outline's large-scale organization.

B. Small-Scale Organization

Once you have outlined the requirements for each issue, you are ready to analyze what each requirement means. For this step, you must first find the types of facts that satisfy or do not satisfy the requirements.

For example, if you are outlining the issue of requisite intent for attempted bank robbery, you will find that the prosecution must prove specific intent to rob, as opposed to a general intent required for the completed crime. *United States v. Dart.* Such intent may be proven by the defendant's own statements, *United States v. Stine*, by the statements of informants or co-conspirators, *United States v. Shell*, or by the defendant's conduct. *United States v. Buffer.* These factors can be grouped under the requisite intent heading, as in the outline that follows.

I. **Culpable Intent: Intent to take property by force or violence, or intimidation.**

   A. **Intent to take Property**

      1. **Specific Intent**

         a. *United States v. Stine*: When a friend phoned defendant, defendant's statement that "you caught me five minutes before robbing a bank with a gun" held sufficient to show intent.

         b. *United States v. Buffer*: Driving by a bank twice and standing by car staring at bank does not show requisite intent b/c actions do not show intent to rob a specific bank when no defendant came within 50 yards of bank.

         c. *United States v. Odell*: Informer who wore wire provided sufficient evidence of defendant's intent to rob a specific bank.

         d. *United States v. Hart*: Requisite intent could be inferred by Defendant's jamming of ATM machine with money to cause technicians to come to location.

      2. **Intent to take using force or violence or intimidation**

         a. *United States v. Stine*: Defendant's plan to bring a gun shows intent to use force or violence, or intimidation.

         b. *United States v. Brigham*: Defendant's mask and knife enough to infer intent to use force or intimidation.

After outlining this element, you would next outline conduct constituting a substantial step toward the commission of the crime, the second element.

To get an overall picture and to help you synthesize cases, you may find it helpful to make a case chart before you create an outline like the preceding one. Write the issues across the top, list the cases down the left side, and then fill in the boxes. You can use this chart to develop the kind of outline that has been illustrated in this section.

ATTEMPTED BANK ROBBERY				
Case	**Requisite Intent**		**Substantial Step**	**Proven**
	Specific Intent	**Force, etc.**		
U.S. v. Buffer	No—driving by insufficient	—	No—casing the bank insufficient	No
U.S. v. Hart	Yes—jamming ATM to get tech to come sufficient	—	No—ATM ruse only future robbery	No
U.S. v. Odell	Yes—informer's wire proved intent	Yes—were to be armed	No—in future	No
U.S. v. Shell	Yes—bank named	—	No—had mask, demand note, but didn't enter	No
U.S. v. Mott	—	Yes—gun, mask	No—never entered bank	No
U.S. v. Homer	Yes—entered bank w/demand note	Yes—threatened	Yes—in bank w/ demand note	Yes

You can use the case chart to help you develop your case outline into a more detailed outline that reflects the five-step analysis discussed in Chapter 5 on small-scale organization. To fill in your outline of each element or factor, supply both information from the cases about that point, and information about how the law and precedents apply to your case. In this outline, you should be thinking about the cases' relevance to your problem. You will probably be listing cases in different sections. Remember to include cites and specific page numbers.

It is especially important to be open-minded and thoughtful about different ways to interpret the facts and to draw inferences from them. Usually not all the factors you identify for your small-scale organization are present in any one case. Thus, you must evaluate their importance to each issue or element. Remember also that in writing a memorandum, you want not only to analyze the reasons that lead to one set of conclusions, but also the reasons for the opposite conclusions. The cases should give you ideas about what kinds of arguments to raise for both sides of the issue. For example, if, in the precedents, the defendants who had incurred liability all acted in bad faith, can you discern any facts by which to characterize the defendant's conduct as bad faith in your case, or to characterize the conduct as good faith? Is there any way that the facts you characterize as showing bad faith can be explained differently? The last entry on your outline for each issue should summarize how the point applies to your assignment. You may want to use two columns here: one for cases and analysis that lead to one conclusion, the second column for those that lead to the opposite conclusion.

What follows is an example of a more complete outline for the attempted bank robbery assignment. The facts of the problem case are as follows.

At 3 p.m. on a Friday, bank teller Sophia Bellman was waiting for the armored truck to make its pick up when the phone rang. When she answered, the caller said there was a bomb in the bank and everyone should leave immediately. Sophia called the police. Then everyone left. While Sophia was waiting for the police, she realized the voice sounded like her boyfriend, Don Gold, who was supposed to pick her up. Don is a jack of all trades who does some carpentry and plumbing. Sophia reported her suspicions to the police, who started canvassing the area. They found Don in his truck, which was parked near the bank. In the truck were a surgical mask, latex gloves, and some tools. The last phone call on his cell was to the bank. The police arrested him. Don admitted he had had a few beers and began thinking about the bills piling up at his home and all the money in the bank. So he called in the bomb threat to make it easier to take the money, but he never tried to enter the bank.

The outline below is of the second element: whether the defendant attempted to take property, that is, made a substantial step toward the completion of the crime. A complete issue outline would have begun with the two sub issues of culpable intent. Note that the problem is set in a fictitious jurisdiction.

II. Substantial Step

    A. Rule:

Defendant's conduct is a substantial step if it "constitutes that requisite 'appreciable fragment' of a bank robbery. . . [or] a step toward the commission of the crime of such substantiality that, unless frustrated, the crime would have occurred." *U.S. v. Buffer*, 35 F.9d 70 (17th Cir. 2001). A substantial step is "conduct that is strongly corroborative of the firmness of defendant's criminal intent"; mere preparation is not enough. *Id.* at 73.

    B. Cases:

- *U.S. v. Hart*, 40 F.9d 105 (17th Cir. 2004): Defendants left money in ATM, causing a bill trap that would bring repair technicians to the ATM w/i 60 minutes. *Id.* Court found conduct was not a substantial step b/c a bill trap was an equivocal act that would have allowed for robbery in the future, not a move that necessarily would result in robbery unless frustrated. *Id.* at 110.

- *U.S. v. Buffer*, 35 F.9d 70 (17th Cir. 2001): Conviction reversed where, although armed, all the defendant did was drive by and then stand outside the car watching the bank. *Id.* at 171. No substantial step b/c never displayed weapons, moved toward bank, or entered. *Id.* at 172.

- *U.S. v. Shell*, 48 F.9d 170 (17th Cir. 2006): No substantial step where defendant—although in possession of fake bomb, blond wig, note demanding money—was merely sitting in car when police approached.

- *U.S. v. Mott*, 36 F.9d 223 (17th Cir. 2002): Substantial step found where defendant was almost at door of bank wearing a ski mask and gloves, and carrying a pillowcase and a concealed, loaded gun.

- *U.S. v. Homer*, 38 F.9d 51 (17th Cir. 2003): Substantial step where defendant entered bank and gave teller note demanding money and threatening injury.

C. Application to Problem:

Gold's conduct probably does not rise to level of substantial step. Unlike the *Shell* defendant, he did more than wait in the car, and his phone call is similar to the creation of the bill trap in *Hart*. Like the defendant in *Buffer*, he did not walk towards, enter, or give any indication of entering the bank.

D. Counter-Argument:

The prosecution could argue that the phone call, which was designed to empty the bank of people, was more than mere preparation. Once the bank was empty, all that remained for Gold was to take the mask, gloves, and tools from the car and enter the bank.

E. Evaluation and Conclusion:

Defendant could rebut this argument by saying the phone call was too removed from the accomplishment of the crime to constitute a substantial step. *Shell, Mott,* and *Homer* seem to require defendant to physically move toward the bank with paraphernalia needed to effectuate the robbery. No such movement here. Thus, the prosecution probably cannot prove the element of substantial step.

III. THE FIRST DRAFT: PUTTING IT DOWN ON PAPER

A. Getting Started

AFTER DEVELOPING AN OUTLINE, you are ready to begin writing your first draft of the memo. Before actually putting pen to paper, however, remember that a legal memorandum has several sections; you need to decide where to start. Each part of the memo has its own purpose, and each part should be written with that purpose in mind. The purpose of the Question Presented, for example, is to raise the issue in the case, not to conclude on the issue. Answering the Question Presented is the purpose of the Conclusion section. The Conclusion also summarizes your analysis, so it should not include material that is not in the Discussion section. The Facts section is supposed to include the "relevant" facts. To determine the relevant facts, you must know how you are going to analyze the issues in the Discussion section.

Thus, you may not want to write the memorandum in the order you present the sections. Instead, you may want to write a rough statement of the Question and either an outline or a rough draft of the relevant facts. Then concentrate on writing the

Discussion. When you complete your Discussion, you will be able
to cross-check that your Question isolates the issue you wrote
about, and that you selected facts for the Question and the Fact
section that actually are relevant to the issue. Similarly, once you
have completed the Discussion, you can ask yourself what the
essential elements are and summarize each for the Conclusion.

The important point in approaching each section is to
remember its purpose and the type of information it includes.

B. Writer's Block

Sometimes, despite all the advice on how to get started that you
may have gotten over the years, you may experience a paralyzing
uncertainty about where and how to begin your memorandum.
Almost all authors confront writers' block at one time or another.
Fortunately, there are a couple of techniques that may help you
break through.

1. Write in Order of Ease

Writers frequently have trouble getting started because they find
introductory or thesis paragraphs hard to write. Until the analysis
has been completed, for example, you may be unsure of your
conclusion. Thus, it may come as a relief to know that you do not
need to write your thesis paragraph first. In fact, you do not need
to write up your issues in the order you finally present them. If one
issue is easier to analyze than other issues, write the easier one
first. Then go on to the next easiest. Not only does your confidence
grow as the document grows, but the sorting and thinking that
occurs as you write the easier sections may equip you to handle the
difficult issues. You then have to rearrange the sections in the
right order.

Although writing in the order-of-ease often makes a lot of
sense, you must be careful to review your organization once you
have put all the sections together. Do you address threshold issues
first? Does your thesis paragraph reflect your final structure? Do
you provide transition sentences? It is important to make sure your
final draft is consistent and has smooth logical connections.

2. Freewrite

If you are the kind of writer who finds it either difficult to outline
or difficult to flesh out an outline, you might find "freewriting" is a
helpful technique to get started or to break a writer's block.
Freewriting is stream-of-consciousness writing. When you
freewrite, you dump every idea you have about your topic on paper
without regard for logical sequence, grammar, or spelling. You

simply put your pen on the pad, or fingers on the keyboard, and record all your passing thoughts. If you are unable to think of anything to say, that is what you type until you have a breakthrough.

> I can't think of anything to say. I still can't think of anything. Still not. Not. Not. Still no thoughts. This is boring . . . it's also making me feel silly. Guess I'd better focus harder on covenants not to compete. What should I say? Did I mention geography seems to be a big factor? It comes up in quite a few cases. Let's see. One case says. . . .

As the example suggests, freewriting often begins as a rambling, even banal, muttering. But after a paragraph or page of private inanity, valuable thoughts usually begin to emerge. For a while, therefore, just go with the flow. Then, when some useful thoughts have been committed to paper, stop writing and reread your musings to determine what they amount to. Do certain points crop up more than others? Why? Do some facts loom large? Why? Do some points seem related? Try some provisional re-ordering: group related paragraphs and points, separate primary and secondary ideas, try to articulate headings or categories that encompass details.

This sorting, grouping, and categorizing may enable you to undertake a more focused type of freewriting. Summarize in a sentence or two one of the main ideas in your initial freewriting. Then embark on further free association just on that topic. Make lists of every aspect of that topic, focus on what confuses you, role play—explore your case as if you were your opponent. Once some profitable thoughts emerge, stop and assess your work again. Perhaps your role-playing has led to a viable counter-analysis. Perhaps your confusion stems from an ambiguity or gap in the facts or the law. Does this ambiguity or gap help you or harm you? As your freewritings become more directed you may find that you are able to work some of these more focused meditations into your actual first draft with only minor revision.

3. Take a Break

Sometimes writers get bogged down in the middle rather than at the beginning of a draft. You may find you have gotten stuck on a particular point and keep writing and rewriting that section. If this rewriting is unproductive, generating more frustration than insight, abandon that section temporarily. Some distance on the topic may help you gain perspective. You may have gotten so bogged down in detail that you lose the forest for the trees or the facts do not seem to favor either the plaintiff or the defendant very clearly, or the law seems hopelessly mysterious. During a break, your subconscious is often working on the problem and the solution may come to you hours later in a flash or when you return to the text.

IV. REWRITING

EVEN THOUGH YOUR FIRST TASK is to get your ideas down, most people will do some revision from the very beginning. This is especially true using a word processor. In the process of writing a first draft, you may find yourself moving whole sections, omitting paragraphs, and even altering your conclusion. This happens because the first draft is typically the place where you clarify your ideas as you struggle through the analysis. The process of writing is a means for thinking through the problem, learning where you need more information, and arriving at a conclusion that you may not even have been aware of when you started the writing process.

Once you have written the first draft, however, it is very important to put the work aside for a day, or at least a few hours, so that when you come back to it, you can view it from a different perspective. (Few people have any perspective on their writing at three a.m., let alone a different perspective.) To revise your draft, you need to think about your work in a somewhat different way. You need to consider whether the document answers the question that you have been asked, and whether the reader, who does not have your familiarity with the issues, can understand your analysis. The first is easier to determine. Go back to the original question in your assignment and make sure that your analysis responds to that question. It is more difficult, however, to take a hard look at your own work to see whether you have presented your analysis to the reader in a logical, coherent manner.

You will probably find it easier to revise your work if you do the revision in stages instead of trying to do everything at once. The most important and most difficult revision is in checking the organization and analysis (see Chapters 4, 5, and 6). Start by printing out your first draft. For most people, editing hard copy is much more effective than trying to edit on the screen. (When reviewing copy in print, you are much more likely to notice, for example, that one paragraph is two pages long.) When you are reasonably satisfied that your overall organization and analysis follows an issue and IRAC type organization (with all steps included and developed), you can next focus on paragraph unity and coherence (see Chapter 9) and sentence level changes (see Chapter 10 and Appendix). The final step is proofreading. You do not want to create a bad impression and detract from the substance of your work with spelling errors, typos, and incorrect citation form.

A. Revising Your Organization and Analysis

The most important part of a legal document is the section in which you present your analysis of the problem. Throughout the writing of the first draft, you have attempted to identify the issues, put them in logical order, and analyze them fully, relating the law to your particular problem. But it is hard to assess your work from a reader's perspective. You, unlike your reader, usually know what you mean. A number of different techniques are available to help you do this.

- First, try to put yourself in the position of the person for whom you are writing the document. Ask yourself whether a person who does not have your familiarity with the research and analysis that you have just done would be able to follow your analysis.

- A second technique is to use the Editing Checklist for Memoranda at the end of Chapter Seven.

- A third method is to use the thesis paragraphs as a check. See if you have started each major topic with a thesis paragraph that states the issues, identifies the basic rules, and concludes, applying the law to the facts of your case. If so, then check to see whether you in fact have analyzed the issues that you identified in the thesis paragraph, generally in the order in which you raised them.

- Another technique is to make a topic sentence outline. On your word processor, you can block and then print all of the headings, sub-headings, and topic sentences in your analysis. Or you can take a print copy of your draft and, with a colored marker, either underline or highlight the headings, sub-headings, and topic sentences.

As you read this outline, ask yourself whether the topic sentences accurately identify the material in the paragraph, whether the topic sentences in the outline seem to be in logical order, and whether each step in the analysis is included.

- Where there is ambiguity, the idea in the paragraph may be appropriate but the topic sentence may not identify the idea. So write a new topic sentence.

- Or the topic sentence may be the correct next step, but the paragraph is about something else. Then revise the paragraph.

- Or the problem may be that you omitted a step in the analysis. You have gone from A to D assuming the reader understood B and C. In this case, supply B and C. Or the problem may be that the issues are not in the logical order. In this case, revise the order.

- Finally, after you make these changes, make sure that you have included transitions that clarify the relation between paragraphs.

B.   Revising Sentences

Some sentence level problems will disappear once your analysis is effectively organized. However, you still need to look at the sentences you have written and make sure that you have presented your ideas grammatically, clearly, and concisely (See Chapter 10 and Appendix A).

- Avoid long, complicated sentences. A sentence that runs more than four lines in the text should be scrutinized.

- Omit wordy, unnecessary phrases ("It is established that," "It is clear that," "It must be shown that").

- Omit legalese.

- Put the action of the sentence into the verb.

- In general, use the active voice.

- Keep your language simple and straightforward.

- If you have been told that you have a particular sentence level problem—like faulty parallelism or misplaced modifiers—try editing your work just looking for that one thing.

- Read the document aloud. A sentence that does not work when you read it aloud probably does not work in writing either.

- Finally, check and correct your punctuation.

C.   Proofreading

Nothing detracts as much from a document as spelling errors, typos, or omitted words or phrases. If you have a program on your computer which checks spelling, use that first. Do not, however, rely solely on spell-check. Such programs do not pick up on errors like typing "statue" for "statute" or "the" for "they," nor do they detect omitted words, or an incorrect homonym like "their" for "there." Thus you must read the document aloud to yourself, or even better, read it line by line, using a ruler to help your eye focus on one sentence at a time. Then, proofread your citation form. Finally, make sure that you have not exceeded the word or page limitation of the assignment, and that your pages are in the right order and numbered.

CHAPTER 9

EFFECTIVE PARAGRAPHS

I. INTRODUCTION

A PARAGRAPH IS OFTEN DESCRIBED as a group of sentences developing a dominant idea that is usually expressed in a topic sentence. A paragraph should have both unity and coherence. It has unity when every sentence relates to the topic. It has coherence when sentences flow smoothly and there is a clear and explicit connection between each sentence and the topic of the paragraph.

While unity and coherence are essential for any effective paragraph, well written paragraphs in a lengthy discussion have an additional function. They must not only be understandable internally, but they must also indicate their place in the overall argument. Clear writing depends on providing the reader with signals so that the direction and point of an analysis are always apparent. The most common way of achieving continuity and logical progression is to begin paragraphs with topic and transition sentences. Topic sentences introduce new issues and sub-issues and show their connection with the thesis presented in the thesis paragraph. Transitional sentences bridge subjects or connect the steps within an analysis.

II. TOPIC SENTENCES AND PARAGRAPH UNITY

A PARAGRAPH IS A SUBDIVISION OF A TEXT that develops one idea. That idea is usually expressed in a topic sentence that pulls the lines of a paragraph together by summarizing the paragraph's basic idea. Without this summarizing sentence, the reader may have difficulty understanding the paragraph and its place in the analysis. Thus, the topic sentence expresses the writer's intention for the paragraph the way a thesis paragraph expresses the writer's intention for a paper. And just as a thesis paragraph ought to be the first paragraph in your discussion, so a topic sentence should generally be the first sentence of a paragraph.

A. Topic Sentences Establish Context

Topic sentences can unify ideas that might appear unrelated by establishing a context which makes their relation and the point of a paragraph clear. Consider this paragraph.

> In *Red v. Black*, five-year-old Johnny Black broke a windshield while throwing rocks. The court held him to the standard of conduct of a reasonable person of like age, intelligence, and experience under like circumstances. *Id.* Similarly, a twelve-year-old was held to a child's standard of care for his negligence in swinging a badminton racquet and hitting a teammate. *Nickelby v. Pauling.* However, the same court held an eight-year-old to an adult standard of care when the child defendant injured a spectator while driving a go cart on a golf course. *Delican v. Cane.* That decision was affirmed two years later when an adult standard was applied to an eleven-year-old girl who shot another child with an arrow during archery practice. *Marion v. Hood.*

Although each sentence seems vaguely connected to the others, the reader does not understand their precise relation. The discussion suffers from the vagueness that often occurs when a paragraph begins with the facts of a case rather than with a topic sentence. A topic sentence eliminates this vagueness or confusion by establishing a context for understanding the cases. For example,

> Young children are held to a child's standard of care for damages occasioned by their tortious acts, except when those infants engage in adult activities involving dangerous instruments for which adult skills are required. *Delican v. Cane.*

Thus, topic sentences play a key role in ensuring paragraph unity by forcing the writer to articulate the point and the function of the paragraph. If the topic sentence given above was added to the sample paragraph, the author would have at least presented the principle explaining how these cases fit together instead of having offered a mere summary of her research. In fact, if the author had written that topic sentence, the substance of the rest of the paragraph might have improved. The writer would probably have realized the relevance of the courts' explanations of why archery and go cart driving are adult activities, and would have included those discussions in her paragraph.

Because the first sentence in a paragraph plays a crucial role in informing the reader of the point of the paragraph, it should not be wasted on a citation. Citations often distract the reader from the point you mean to stress. The following sentence should have introduced the claim, not the facts behind a precedent which recognized that claim.

> In *Apple v. Baker*, 688 N.E.2d 600 (2001), the plaintiff brought an action for breach of warranty based on the blighted quality of 20% of the wheat delivered to him.

It would have been preferable to use the first sentence to introduce the basic idea of the paragraph. Then, if appropriate, follow with a citation that shows your authority. After this, you can use the case as an illustration of the basic idea.

> A seller breaches an implied warranty of merchantability when the goods are not fit for their ordinary purposes. *See Apple v. Baker*, 688 N.E.2d 600 (2001). In *Apple*, the plaintiff brought an action for breach of warranty based on the blighted quality of 20% of the wheat delivered to him.

In addition, you do not want to waste your opening statement on a sentence that merely "treads water," that is, one that does not go anywhere and that immediately needs to be explained.

> The court has had to deal with the issue of a child's suit for loss of parental consortium. In a recent case, the court has held that the child has no cause of action.

The paragraph should immediately say that the court has held against the claim, not that the court "dealt" with it.

B. Topic Sentences Introduce Issues and Subissues

Not only do you need topic sentences to present your analysis of a case or group of cases, but you need topic sentences to introduce legal issues and subissues. In a problem involving the admissibility of expert testimony on the Battered Wife Syndrome, for example, you would need a topic sentence to introduce each prong of a test that is often used to determine admissibility. For example,

> To determine the admissibility of expert testimony, many courts first decide if the subject matter is so distinctly related to some science, profession, or occupation that it is beyond the ken of the average juror.

C. Topic Sentences Aid Paragraph Unity

After you have written a first draft, you can focus on your topic sentences as a method of editing your work. Topic sentences, or the lack of them, can help you to assess paragraph unity. You can check the body of a paragraph against the topic sentence to see if the paragraph contains more than one topic, wanders into an irrelevant digression, or lacks development. If so, you should divide, edit, or develop the paragraph to achieve unity. If you find yourself unable to state the topic in a sentence, your paragraph needs to be sharpened, focused, or omitted.

Evaluate the following two paragraphs for unity.

Example 1:	Courts have held an infant will be held to an adult standard of care if their activity involves a dangerous instrument that requires adult skills. In *Marion v. Hood*, archery was considered an adult activity because of the intrinsic danger of arrows and the skill required in operating a bow and arrow. See also *Delican v. Cane* (go carts are intrinsically dangerous and require skill in handling). In contrast, in *Nickelby v. Pauling*, the court held a badminton racquet is so lightweight it is not an intrinsically dangerous instrument.
Example 2:	An infant will be held to an adult standard of care if the infant was engaged in an activity involving a dangerous instrument for which adult skills are required. *Marion v. Hood*. Because of the intrinsic danger of arrows and the skill required in using a bow and arrow, the court held that archery was an adult activity in *Marion v. Hood*. In *Delican v. Cane*, an infant driving a go cart was held to an adult standard of care because of the intrinsic danger of go carts and the skill required in their handling. Although the court in *Ashley v. Connor* did not scrutinize a squash racquet for its intrinsic danger, it found squash to be an adult activity because the player should know the game's traditions and customs in order to mitigate the potential risks of the game. In squash, it is customary for a player to yell "clear" before taking a shot directed at the partner in order to avoid striking that player.

Example 1: This paragraph has a clear topic sentence supported by the succeeding sentences. The paragraph exhibits direction and unity. Each sentence develops the general principle articulated in the topic sentence by providing authority for that principle.

Example 2: This paragraph lacks unity because it introduces a factor not announced in the topic sentence. The paragraph begins well. It initially focuses on one factor the courts examine to determine whether a game is an adult activity: whether the instrument used in the activity is so inherently dangerous as to require adult skill. Yet the writer gets sidetracked in the last two sentences. The Ashley court's silence on the first factor leads the author to a second: whether traditions and customs have evolved to mitigate the risks of the game. This is an important factor and deserves discussion. But the discussion should begin in the next paragraph and should be announced in a separate topic sentence. Having written a topic sentence that refers to the first factor only, the author should be guided by it.

D. Topic Sentences Help You Assess Paragraph Length

Attention to paragraph unity and topic sentences may help with paragraph length also. Long paragraphs—paragraphs the length of a page or more than 250 words—should send you looking for logical subdivisions, which are often natural places for paragraph division. In contrast, a very short paragraph, when used other than for emphasis, is often part of a larger discussion and should, therefore, be combined with another paragraph. A one sentence paragraph, for example, is frequently the conclusion of a prior paragraph or an introduction to the next. If it is not, you should examine a short paragraph for lack of development.

Examine the following paragraph for a logical subdivision.

A landlord's duty to maintain the premises in safe and sanitary condition does not require the landlord to provide protection from criminal activities directed against persons lawfully on the premises. *Pippin v. Chicago Housing Authority. Pippin* was a wrongful death action against the landlord concerning not so much the conditions, but the policing, of the premises. Pippin had been an acquaintance of one of the tenants in the building. During an argument with the tenant, Pippin was fatally stabbed. The *Pippin* decision was a simple restatement of the common law in Illinois: a landlord does not have the duty to protect a tenant from criminal acts, nor does it have a duty to protect a third party lawfully on the premises from criminal activities. Nonetheless, a landlord who has provided part-time guard service may have a duty to make security provisions for the hours when the guards are not on duty. In *Cross v. Wells Fargo Alarm Services*, the court held the landlord responsible for the safety of the building during those hours for which it had not provided guard

> service. The court relied on the theory that the provision of part-time guard service had the effect of increasing the incidence of crime when the guards were not there. The plaintiff had been injured by several unknown men at a time when the guards were not on duty.

The paragraph breaks naturally after the fifth sentence when the writer begins explaining an exception to the common law rule that a landlord has no duty to provide protection from criminal activity. The writer should indent and begin a new paragraph there.

Decide which of the following paragraphs can be logically combined with another.

> In *Holley*, the plaintiff paid $5.00 a month as a security fee, aside from the regular rent. The court stated that this fee created a contractual duty on the landlord to provide protection to the tenants. Ms. Parsons was charged a $10.00 a year security fee. This fee, like the one in *Holley*, was for the purpose of maintaining a security system. Although Ms. Parsons paid $50 a year less than the plaintiff in *Holley*, the $10 fee could establish a contractual duty for Fly-by-Night to provide the plaintiff with protection against third party crimes occurring on the defendant's premises.
>
> If the duty is not contractually established, Fly-by-Night may still be under a duty to protect the tenant from the results of reasonably foreseeable criminal conduct. *See Ten Associates v. McCutchen*.
>
> For example, in *Stribling v. Chicago Housing Authority*, the plaintiff was a tenant whose apartment was burglarized on three separate occasions. On each occasion, the thief entered the plaintiff's apartment through a wall shared with a vacant adjacent apartment. The landlord negligently failed to secure the apartment after the first burglary, despite many demands by the plaintiff. The court held that the landlord was liable because the second and third burglaries were reasonably foreseeable.

The second paragraph should be combined with the third. That sentence provides a transition from the first paragraph and introduces the issue illustrated by the third.

III. PARAGRAPH TRANSITIONS

ALTHOUGH TOPIC SENTENCES PLAY A MAJOR ROLE in orienting your reader to your organization, not every paragraph requires a topic sentence. A complicated topic will require several paragraphs to explain, and thus a new paragraph may just be continuing the topic of the preceding paragraph. For this series of paragraphs, you would use a topic sentence in the first paragraph, and then use transitional words or sentences to begin the next paragraphs.

Transitional phrases or sentences are often used to show the relationships between an individual paragraph and the preceding and succeeding ones. They tend to appear either at the end or at the beginning of paragraphs and are used to summarize what has been covered and introduce what is to come. They are particularly important in long or complex discussions to prevent a reader from feeling lost. Although you can expect your reader to read carefully, you should not expect that reader to do your work, to provide the clarity, structure and development which are not in the paper itself. You can avoid overreliance on your reader if you use transitional phrases or words to show how a paragraph advances your discussion.

Sometimes transitions announce a change in subject. Thus they can underscore a shift in topic that might otherwise be announced in a heading or topic sentence. Sometimes transitions track the steps in an argument, informing the reader, for example, that a case just described is now going to be distinguished or that a rule just discussed will now be applied. There are numerous ways to effect these transitions.

1.   You may want to raise a new point with a sentence that summarizes a completed discussion while relating it to the upcoming issue.

> Although the prosecution will have little difficulty showing assault, it may have trouble proving battery.

2.   You may want to keep track of the issues with enumeration.

> The second exception to the employee-at-will rule arises when there are implied contractual provisions such as terms in an employee handbook.

3.   You may want to show the relation between paragraphs by showing a substantive connection.

> The defendant offered no causal connection linking Joan's prior passivity with her present aggressive activity.
>
> A similar causal element was missing in the expert testimony on the battered wife syndrome offered in *Buhrle v. Wyoming*.
>
> **or**
>
> The *Tarasoff* holding has been applied in this jurisdiction.

4. You may want to link paragraphs with a simple transitional word or phrase showing the logical connection one paragraph has with another.

Therefore, although a court will not enforce that part of the contract which is unconscionable, it will generally refuse to award punitive damages.

In *Frostifresh*, however, the court awarded the seller not only the net cost but also a reasonable profit.

Since transitions play so central a role in showing the reader how you are building the argument, it is especially important that your transitions be thoughtful. You should not mechanically insert transitional words or phrases between your paragraphs without thinking about the relationship you wish to establish. Imprecise, erroneous, or ambiguous transitions can be misleading because they point the reader in the wrong rather than the right direction. The list of transitional expressions provided below, therefore, should be used cautiously. Although it supplies some of the phrases that establish particular kinds of logical relationships, you must still check that the transition you have selected is the one most appropriate for the connection you wish to establish. You should also be sure that you are entitled to use the transition. For example, the word "therefore" signifies a conclusion. Yet, before you can persuasively signal your conclusion with "therefore," you must be sure that you have provided supporting reasons.

Transitional Expressions

1. **To signal an amplification or addition:**

   and, also, moreover, in other words, furthermore, in addition, equally important, next, finally, besides, similarly, another reason, likewise.

2. **To signal an analogy:**

   similarly, analogously, likewise, again, also.

3. **To signal an alternative:**

   in contrast, but, still, however, contrary to, though, although, yet, nevertheless, conversely, alternatively, on the other hand.

4. **To signal a conclusion:**

   therefore, thus, hence, as a result, accordingly, in short, consequently, finally, to summarize.

5.   To establish a causal consequence or result:

because, since, therefore, thus, consequently, then, as a result, it follows, so.

6.   To introduce an example:

for example, for instance, specifically, as an illustration, namely, that is, particularly, in particular.

7.   To establish temporal relationships:

next, then, as soon as, until, last, later, earlier, before, afterward, after, when, recently, eventually, subsequently, simultaneously, at the same time, thereafter, since.

8.   To signal a concession:

granted that, no doubt, to be sure, it is true, although.

Exercise 9-A

1.   *Reread Exercise 5-B. Write a topic sentence synthesizing the holdings in Keech and Cowl on the direct contact element.*

2.   *Reread Exercise 2-I. Write a topic sentence synthesizing the holdings in cases 5, 6 and 7.*

3.   *Read the following discussion. Then provide topic and transition sentences where appropriate.*

Ellen Warren must show that Diethylstilbestrol (DES) was more than a merely possible cause of her various injuries in order to present her negligence claim against the manufacturers to the jury. Since statistics show that DES is a probable cause of adenosis, distortion of the uterus, and cervical cancer, the question of the defendant's liability for Ellen Warren's injuries should be presented to the jury. However, Ellen Warren will have a harder time showing that DES is more than a merely possible cause of her infertility, although she can probably establish this also.

In *Kramer Service Inc. v. Wilkins*, the defendant negligently cut the plaintiff's skin. Two years later a skin cancer developed at the spot. Two medical experts testified. One said the cancer was not caused by the cut; the other said it was possible that the cut caused the cancer, but the chances were only one out of one hundred. The court ruled that this evidence was not sufficient to permit the jury to find the defendant liable for the cancer. The court held that a plaintiff must show more than a merely possible connection between the defendant's negligence and the plaintiff's injury to permit a jury to consider whether the negligence caused the injury.

Ellen Warren's evidence includes the FDA decision to ban DES for use during pregnancy; the statistics that a substantial percentage of women exposed to DES develop cancer; and her doctors' diagnoses that adenosis, distortion of the uterus, and cervical cancer are characteristic of DES exposure. These facts demonstrate that DES is more than merely a possible cause of those injuries.

Ellen Warren's family has a hereditary history of cancer. Because heredity does not seem a more likely cause than DES, particularly in light of Warren's combination of DES-related disorders, this argument does not negate the evidence that DES is a probable cause of her cancer.

While DES causes or contributes to infertility in a substantial percentage of exposed women, many women are infertile without exposure. Indeed, Warren has suffered some other reproductive disorders that may be to blame. Nevertheless, given her combination of DES-related symptoms and the statistical evidence the DES contributes to infertility, Warren still has more evidence of causation than Wilkins did and should be able to present the issue to the jury.

IV. PARAGRAPH COHERENCE

A PARAGRAPH HAS COHERENCE if it promotes continuity of thought. Even a unified paragraph—that is, a paragraph with a single topic—can seem choppy and disconnected if the sentences are not in a logical order or are not clearly related to each other.

Paragraph coherence depends in part on clear paragraph organization; you must arrange your sentences in a logical order. If the final sentence of a paragraph contains information that the reader needs in order to understand the first sentence, then the paragraph will be hard to understand, regardless of the clarity of these sentences.

Although logical sequence promotes easy comprehension, it alone does not ensure paragraph coherence. Smooth progression from one sentence to the next often requires you to use connectors or transitions, just as you use transition sentences to get from one paragraph to the next. Sometimes, of course, you can juxtapose two ideas and feel confident the reader can infer their logical connection. For example, a reader can probably infer the connection between the following sentences: "You said you put the check in the mail a week ago. I have not received it." The discrepancy between these two events alerts the reader to the writer's skepticism about the first assertion, even without a connector like "but." Sometimes, however, the specific relation of one sentence to the next is not obvious. In this situation, part of your second sentence must be devoted to giving directions which enable your reader to perceive an otherwise buried connection. One way writers do this is by repeating key words or by using transition words and connectors. Another way writers promote continuity of thought is to overlap their sentences so that a new sentence begins with a brief summary of an idea in the prior sentence. By moving from old, known information to new information, the writer links the sentences together and moves the reader forward.

Of course, coherence on the paragraph level cannot be achieved without sentence coherence, that is, there must be clear and logical connections between the parts, even the words, of a single sentence. See Chapter Ten for suggestions on how to achieve sentence coherence.

A. Paragraph Coherence: Organization

The sense of a paragraph becomes clearer when you put ideas in a logical order. What is logical depends, of course, on the purpose of a paragraph. If, for example, you are trying to narrate events, such as in a Statement of Facts, you would probably use a chronological order. If you are developing an analysis, however, the order of ideas will probably follow either a deductive or inductive pattern of reasoning. Although thought processes are frequently inductive— that is, an examination of particulars enables you to formulate a generalization—most written arguments benefit from a deductive presentation—that is, the argument opens with a generalization which is then supported by particulars.

When ideas are not in a logical order, as in the following paragraph, the sense of that paragraph is hard to understand.

> A mental hospital has a duty to provide its patients with such care as would be reasonable to prevent self-injury given their individual mental problems. *Stallman.* Ms. Brown was a nonviolent patient diagnosed with major depression whose cure had been progressing steadily during her sixteen month hospital stay. The standard of care is based upon the reasonable anticipation of the probability of self-inflicted harm. *Gregory.* In *Stallman*, the court held the duty breached when a violently suicidal woman was left unattended for 30 minutes. Based on Ms. Brown's progress, the doctors would not have reasonably anticipated her suicide.

If the writer had discussed the test defining a hospital's duty of care before launching into the facts of Brown, i.e., if the ideas had been organized deductively, this paragraph would have been easier to understand.

A mental hospital has a duty to provide its patients with such care as would be reasonable to prevent self-injury given their individual mental problems. *Stallman.* The standard of care is based upon the reasonable anticipation of the probability of self-inflicted harm. *Gregory.* In *Stallman*, the court held the hospital breached its duty when a violently suicidal woman was left unattended for thirty minutes. Ms. Brown, however, was a nonviolent patient diagnosed with major depression whose cure had been progressing steadily during her sixteen month hospital stay. Based on Ms. Brown's progress, the doctors would not have reasonably anticipated her suicide.

B. Paragraph Coherence: Sentence Transitions

1. Transition Words and Coherence

For a reader to follow your thought processes, you must provide transitions that signal where you are taking your analysis next. After finishing a discussion of a general rule, clearly indicate to the reader that you now want to explain an exception. If you have just described two requirements for a cause of action, announce that you are now going on to the third. Transitions (perhaps "nevertheless" in the first instance, "in addition" or just "third" in the second) will tell the reader what you are doing.

The following passage is an example of a paragraph that lacks coherence because the sentences are not explicitly connected to each other.

Express oral contracts between unmarried, cohabiting couples are enforceable. Implied contracts in these situations are unenforceable. Vague terms render a contract unenforceable. Jessica Stone and Michael Asch expressly agreed that Mr. Asch would repay his share of their living expenses once he began practicing law in exchange for Ms. Stone's support for three years. They entered into an enforceable contract. Ms. Stone may bring an action for its breach. Ms. Stone's understanding that Mr. Asch would support her during graduate school is unenforceable since it is an implied agreement. Mr. Asch's boast to "take care of" Ms. Stone forever is too vague to be enforced.

The sense of this passage would be clearer if more transitional expressions were used to establish the logical relationship one sentence has with another.

Although express oral contracts between unmarried, cohabiting couples are enforceable, implied contracts in these situations are unenforceable. Vague terms **also** render a contract unenforceable.

> **Because** Jessica Stone and Michael Asch expressly agreed that Mr. Asch would repay his share of their living expenses once he began practicing law in exchange for Ms. Stone's support for three years, they entered into an enforceable contract. Ms. Stone may, **therefore**, bring an action for its breach. Ms. Stone's understanding that Mr. Asch would support her during graduate school is unenforceable, **however**, since it is an implied agreement. **Similarly**, Mr. Asch's boast to "take care of" Ms. Stone forever is too vague to be enforced.

2.   Other Connectors

Transition words are used to show the reader the logical connection between sentences. Other kinds of connectors orient your reader in time or place or inform your reader that you are looking at the material from a particular point of view or perspective. The phrases in bold in the following passages illustrate the use of these kinds of connectors.

> **During Mardi Gras week 2004**, Jeffrey Bond boarded a trolley in New Orleans and sat down in the rear of the car. **One stop later**, three teenage boys, Joseph Claiborne, Robert Landry, and Thomas Vallee, boarded the trolley. The three boys wore stockings over their heads and streamers around their necks. They were obnoxiously loud and drunk. **At one point**, Claiborne, who was 6′7″ tall, turned to Bond and demanded, "What are you looking at?" The two other boys gathered behind Claiborne, blocking Bond's exit through the aisle. **Given these circumstances**, Bond thought it best not to antagonize this group of teenagers; thus he averted his eyes and kept quiet. **From a tactical point of view**, however, this proved to be a mistake. Claiborne started screaming, "Answer me when I speak to you!" **Then** he stood up, drew a gun, and shot Bond in the leg.

3.   Overlapping Sentences

Cohesion is often achieved when a new sentence opens with a brief reference to all or part of the prior sentence. In other words, you begin a sentence with old information and then move on to new information. This overlapping of sentences leads your reader gently into the new idea. The phrases in bold in the following passage illustrate overlapping.

> Ms. Moultry has been addicted to crack for the past two years. **During this time**, she gave birth to a son, a baby born with a positive toxicology. **After his birth**, Ms. Moultry placed her child into temporary foster care so that she could enter an inpatient drug rehabilitation program. **While there**, she repeatedly said that her resolve to come "clean" would weaken if she was denied visitation with

her infant. **To prevent such a relapse**, Ms. Moultry's foster care worker sanctioned visitation. **The initial visits** went smoothly; the foster parents were supportive of Ms. Moultry and Ms. Moultry felt good about the care her baby was receiving. **Then** Ms. Moultry learned she tested positive for the AIDS virus. **When the foster parents learned she was HIV positive**, they refused to admit her into their home. Ms. Moultry disappeared three days later.

4.   Coherence and Complex Sentences

Complex sentences—sentences with a dependent and independent clause—often establish relationships more economically than do compound sentences—sentences consisting of two independent clauses joined by a coordinating conjunction. Dependent clauses begin with subordinating conjunctions that establish that clause's temporal or logical connection with the main sentence. Therefore, complex sentences clarify relationships between ideas within a sentence. There are many subordinating conjunctions, but some key ones are *because, since, if, when, while, although.*

In contrast, independent clauses joined by the coordinating conjunction "and" are clauses which are juxtaposed but not related. "And" is a vague connector; it joins sentences without establishing a logical connection between them.

Example:	Richard began suffering from arthritis in 2001, **and** he stopped working.
Rewrite:	**Because** Richard began suffering from arthritis in 2001, he stopped working.

5.   Coherence and the Repetition of Key Words

Continuity is better served by the repetition of key words than by elegant variation. For example, transitions and key words effectively bridge these paragraphs.

Thus the only factual distinction between *Hughes* and this case seems to be the **emotional nature** of Mr. Jackson's response.

> **Emotions, however**, are at the core of many family matters, especially those involving finances.

It is also important to use consistent terminology when referring to the parties to a suit. In the following sentence, it is unclear whether the court is referring to one person or two persons. It is also unclear whether the court is referring to the particular defendant before it or is stating a principle of law:

> In *Windley*, the court stated that if **a person** has any personal or financial interest in bringing trade to the seller, then **the defendant** was not acting solely as an agent for the buyer.

Some of the ambiguity in this sentence also comes from the change in verb tense. Propositions of law should be stated in the present tense while the facts of a case should be described in the past tense. Thus, the sentence should be rewritten in one of the following two ways.

> In *Windley*, the court stated that if **a person has** any personal or financial interest in bringing trade to the seller, then that person is not acting solely as an agent for the buyer.
>
> or
>
> In *Windley*, the court stated that if **the defendant had** any personal or financial interest in bringing trade to the seller, then **the defendant was** not acting solely as an agent for the buyer.

Exercise 9-B

1. *Reorder the sentences in the following paragraph to improve organization.*

In *Kelly*, the court found that the defendant, who had demonstrated a long and broad experience with the legal process, had knowingly and intelligently waived counsel, although the trial judge made no detailed inquiry. *Kelly v. State*, 663 P.2d 967, 969 (Alaska Ct. App. 1983). In some cases, a defendant may be permitted to waive his right without detailed inquiry. *Id.* Furthermore, unlike Miller, Kelly availed himself of some of the services of court appointed counsel while defending himself. *Id.* Here, although Miller stated that his mother had married an attorney after his father's death, this cannot be construed as meaningful legal experience. Because a waiver of the right to counsel may not be lightly inferred, *Ledbetter v. State*, 581 P.2d 1129, 1131 (Alaska 1978), the degree of the court's inquiry must be tailored to the particular characteristics of the accused. *O'Dell v. Anchorage*, 576 P.2d 104, 108 (Alaska 1978).

2. *Add transition words to improve the coherence of the following passage.*

The degree of judicial inquiry will also depend on the complexities and gravity of the legal issues raised by the charge against the defendant. *O'Dell v. Anchorage*, 576 P.2d 104, 108 (Alaska 1978). Traffic misdemeanor cases are easily

for example

However *Therefore* *Here*

understood by lay persons and the consequences are usually not severe. *Id.* The inquiry in such cases need not be extensive. *Id.* Miller, if convicted, faces a mandatory jail term and not a simple parking fine. The severity of the charges mandated a more extensive inquiry by the judge. *These*

3. *Rewrite to improve the coherence of this paragraph. Use transition words, connectors, subordinate clauses, and sentence overlapping.*

The state's suppression of evidence in a criminal prosecution may constitute a violation of the defendant's due process rights. Whether the defendant's rights were in fact violated depends on four conditions. The state must be responsible for the loss of the evidence. The evidence must have had exculpatory value that was apparent before it was lost. Then the defendant must show that he would be unable to obtain comparable evidence by any other reasonable means. If the evidence was only potentially exculpatory, the defendant must demonstrate that it was lost due to bad faith on the part of the state. Roger Keith can prove that the state was responsible for the loss of the alleged murder weapon, the car. The car disappeared from the police garage before it was examined. Its exculpatory value was never demonstrated. It would be difficult to determine what comparable evidence might consist of. The record offers little to prove that the loss of the potentially exculpatory car was due to bad faith on the part of the police. Keith cannot meet the conditions for determining violation of his due process rights because of state suppression. The court will most likely deny the motion for dismissal.

4. *Rewrite the following paragraph to improve its organization and coherence.*

The parties agree that First Sergeant Valiant of C. Company first picked up the phone to learn who was being called. During the first few seconds after picking up the phone, Valiant overheard a conversation between members of his Company that began "Do you have any of the good stuff?" He recognized the speakers, who were later court martialed on drug charges. Valiant had not "intercepted" the conversation. The sergeant's act in picking up the phone must be considered in the ordinary course of business. When the use of an extension comes within the ordinary course of business, no unlawful interception of the defendants' communication occurs. When there are several extension phones, as there are in the orderly room, it is not unusual that when a call comes in, a person will pick up the receiver to see who the call is for.

Exercise 9-C

The following exercise is a review exercise of some of the principles covered in earlier chapters and in Appendix A. Reread Exercise 2-H(1); then read and edit the following sample answer to the Peterson exercise in Chapter 2. Consider the following questions:

1. *Does the statement of the issue include enough information about the rule of law and relevant facts?*

2. *Does the "thesis" or introductory paragraph end with a conclusion that relates the law to the facts of the case? If not, write one.*

3. *Can you eliminate wordiness and improve sentence coherence?*

4. *Do the topic sentences effectively introduce the point of each paragraph?*

5. *Does the writer include the relevant law and facts from the precedent in the second paragraph?*

6. *What problems with paragraph unity does the third paragraph have?*

The issue that we must explore in this case is the question whether the father is responsible for the injuries resulting from his son's misuse of a hammer. The applicable rule would be that a person has a duty to protect another against *unreasonable* risks. A person who breaches this duty is negligent and liable for injuries resulting from his negligence. It must be shown that leaving the tools in the basement was an unreasonable risk.

In the present case, the father left his tools in the basement. Tools are not "obviously and intrinsically dangerous." The case must be discussed in light of relevant precedent. The *Smith* case clearly applies to the case herein. In *Smith*, the court sustained defendant's demurrer to the complaint, challenging the sufficiency of the complaint. In *Smith*, the children were playing with a golf club. Many similarities obviously can be pointed out between Smith and the present case. The children were identical in age. The instruments were left in an area played in by children; the accidents occurred without warning the victims.

Plaintiff herein may claim that the tools should not have been left where children could reach them. Defendant may state that in *Smith*, the golf club was left in the backyard, also a play area for children. The golf club was not held to be intrinsically dangerous. We must also be concerned with whether tools, although not inherently dangerous, can be considered more dangerous in the hands of a child than a golf club. Tools are like a golf club because they are not weapons; however, they may be misused by a child.

CHAPTER 10

SENTENCE STRUCTURE

CHAPTER 9 ON PARAGRAPHS EMPHASIZES that the flow of a discussion depends on the effective use of topic and transition sentences, paragraph organization, and transition words. But coherence on the paragraph level needs coherence on the sentence level as well. Poor diction, punctuation, and sentence construction slow down your readers by forcing them to stop to decipher the meaning of a particular sentence. Thus, even if law students and lawyers do everything else right (display deft organization and incisive analogies), they cannot communicate effectively if their sentences need translation.

It is surprising—but true—how many lawyers have sentence level problems, a phenomenon caused in part by the abstract and complex ideas that are the core of many legal documents. To write about these complex matters clearly, to communicate effectively with such diverse audiences as law professors, clients, colleagues, judges, witnesses, and juries, law students and lawyers need to pay special attention to syntax (the structure of sentences). They must make clear and logical connections between the parts, even the words, of a single sentence. This chapter, therefore, gives you specific suggestions that will help you avoid common sentence level problems. Before enumerating these "do's and don'ts," however, it might be useful to consider what a sentence actually is.

A sentence is traditionally defined as a set of words that expresses a complete thought and that contains, at the very least, a subject (a noun) and a predicate (a verb). Yet this is a somewhat bloodless definition that directs a writer to grammatical requirements of a sentence at the expense of giving a writer a "feel" for readable sentence structures.

Many sentences are narratives about real characters who perform real acts. This realization should have an impact on sentence structure. Since many sentences are narratives about characters and their actions, you should write sentences that follow the action of the narrative rather than sentences that bury the characters and their actions in passive voice constructions or that begin with abstract nouns. Sentences are clearest when the character in the sentence is the subject of the sentence and when the verb in the sentence describes what the character did, does, or should do.[1]

Even sentences about abstract ideas—principles of law, for example—are nonetheless also sentences with characters who perform actions. Sometimes these characters are mistakenly concealed. For example,

> Contractual choice-of-forum clauses are "prima facie valid" and should be enforced unless their enforcement would be unreasonable or the clause was procured through fraud or overreaching.

The characters in this sentence go unidentified, although a reader could guess at their identities. The character who should enforce a choice of forum clause is the court, and the character who must show unreasonableness or fraud is the resisting party to the suit.

Because your reader probably needs information about each party's responsibilities, the sentence should chart those parties and their obligations, as in the following rewrite:

> Because a contractual choice-of-forum clause is "prima facie valid," a court will enforce it unless the resisting party can show that enforcement would be unreasonable or that the other party to the suit procured the clause through fraud or overreaching.

Of course, not all sentences are about actions. Some describe people, things or conditions. Others are about ideas and concepts. Sentences about ideas often have abstract nouns as their subjects and frequently define or comment on that subject, as in, "Truth is Beauty," or "The necessity of protecting the First Amendment rights of the press from the chilling effects of defamation actions makes summary judgment an appropriate procedure." In most analytic writing, some sentences will inevitably begin with abstract subjects. Yet abstract subjects, or long subjects that present a lot of new and complex information, tend to strain the reader's concentration. To alleviate that strain, begin as many of these sentences as possible with easily comprehensible, short, and specific subjects: "Summary judgment is an appropriate procedure for protecting the first amendment rights of the press from the chilling effects of defamation actions."

As first-year law students, you might worry that short, specific subjects and simple active voice sentences are unimpressive. Yet legal writing is often a lawyer's single opportunity to tell a client's

---

[1]   *See* Joseph M. Williams, *Style: Ten Lessons in Clarity and Grace* (9th ed. 2006), for a fuller discussion of some of the ideas in this chapter.

story and to reveal its legal significance to audiences that are pressed for time and unwilling to translate archaic diction and contorted sentence constructions. Thus, simple and direct sentences are more effective than convoluted sentences. In fact, the ability to write about complicated matters in a straightforward manner is the art of lawyering.

The following suggestions will help you write clear and persuasive sentences.

1. WHENEVER POSSIBLE, USE SHORT, CONCRETE SUBJECTS

A subject is that part of a sentence about which something is being said. It may consist of a single word or of many words (a simple subject and all its attendant modifiers). The easiest sentences to read, however, have short subjects that use concrete rather than abstract nouns. No reader wants to wade through a fifteen word subject, comprised in the following sentence of "use" and its modifiers.

> Defense counsel's use of racially discriminatory peremptory challenges arising out of a state-created statutory privilege deprives excluded jurors of their equal protection rights.

Your reader would much prefer you to start with a short, concrete noun.

> Defense counsel deprives jurors of their equal protection rights when counsel uses racially discriminatory peremptory challenges arising out of a state-created statutory privilege.

2. USE SHORT, ACTIVE PREDICATES— NOT NOMINALIZATIONS

The predicate is that part of a sentence that says something about what the subject is or is doing. Sentences are more dynamic and more concise when you use short verbs that express actions rather than states of existence.

> **Not:** The actions of the transit authority in firing appellants for criticizing fare increases were a violation of the appellants' first and fourteenth amendment rights.
>
> **But:** The transit authority violated the appellants' first and fourteenth amendment rights when it fired them for criticizing fare increases.

Sentences are more forceful if they focus on a verb rather than on a noun. Yet many writers convert verbs into cumbersome nouns called nominalizations. They write "the judge made a decision to continue the trial," instead of writing "the judge decided to continue the trial." They write "the defendant had knowledge that injury could result from his negligence," instead of writing "the defendant knew injury could result from his negligence." The former sentence, with the nominalization "had knowledge," dissipates the energy of the verb.

3. TO PROMOTE THE MAIN IDEA OF THE SENTENCE, DO NOT SEPARATE THE SUBJECT FROM THE VERB WITH INTRUDING PHRASES AND CLAUSES

A sentence does not begin to become understandable until the reader knows its subject and verb. When you separate the subject and the verb with a series of interrupting phrases and clauses, you leave the reader in limbo. To be reader-friendly, keep the subject of the sentence near the verb and the verb near the object. You can move interrupting phrases and clauses either to the beginning or the end of a sentence. You can also break the sentence in two.

Example: In 2017, the patients of Kent Family Planning Center, 50,000 in number, 35% of whom were adolescents, 50% of whom were at or below the poverty level, received in the mail a sex education manual published by the Center.

Rewrite: In 2017, Kent Family Planning Center published and mailed a sex education manual to its 50,000 patients, 35% of whom were adolescents, 50% of whom were at or below the poverty level.

Or

In 2017, Kent Family Planning Center published and mailed a sex education manual to its 50,000 patients. Thirty-five percent of these patients were adolescents, and fifty percent were at or below the poverty level.

Example: Officer Miller, who at the preliminary hearing on August 8 had said the car did not look like it had been in an accident, fell ill just before the trial was due to begin and never testified.

Rewrite: Although Officer Miller had said at the preliminary hearing on August 8 that the car did not look as if it had been in an accident, he fell ill just before the trial was due to begin and never testified.

---

4. KEEP YOUR SENTENCES RELATIVELY SHORT (UNDER 25 WORDS)

Although varying the length of your sentences makes your writing less monotonous and more interesting, it is not a good idea to pack several ideas into one unreadably long sentence. If you have written a long and involved sentence, consider dividing it into shorter ones.

It is easy to split apart a compound sentence (two independent sentences joined by a coordinating conjunction). Instead of joining those sentences with a coordinating conjunction (and, but, or, nor, for, so, yet), put a period between them. You can also divide a long complex sentence (a sentence that has a dependent and independent clause). To do so, you must make the dependent clause independent by deleting the word that makes the clause dependent. These words are called subordinating conjunctions and include, among others, such often used words as because, since, while, when, and although.

Example: Although the Kent statute authorizes a court to sentence a defendant for criminal contempt, the statute does not define contempt.

Rewrite: The Kent statute authorizes a court to sentence a defendant for criminal contempt. However, the statute does not define contempt.

You can also shorten a sentence that ends with a long modifier tacked on to the end by converting that modifier into an independent sentence.

When you break long sentences into shorter ones, link your ideas with transition words that carry a preceding idea into the next sentence. Put these transition words early in the sentence so that the relation between the sentences is quickly apparent.

Example: *Although* a city cannot be liable every time a citizen is injured and the city is notified, it would be unfair to preclude claims when the city's voluntary undertaking lulls an individual into a false sense of security that causes her to forego other means of protection.

Example: A city cannot be liable every time a citizen is injured and the city is notified. *However,* it would be unfair to preclude claims when the city's voluntary undertaking lulls an individual into a false sense of security that causes her to forego other means of protection.

---

5. WHENEVER POSSIBLE, USE ACTIVE RATHER THAN PASSIVE VOICE

In the introduction to this chapter, we suggested that sentences focus on characters and actions. To achieve such a focus, you should write most of your sentences in the active voice, that is, you should follow a subject-verb-object sequence (actor—action—object of action). Active voice sentences are easier to read because they begin with a short specific subject, an actor, who then explicitly does something to someone or something. They have the additional virtue of being somewhat shorter than passive voice sentences.

A passive construction follows an object-verb-subject sequence (object of action-action-actor). The verb is constructed from forms of the verb "be" and the past participle of the main verb. In passive construction, you do not have to include the actor to have a grammatical sentence, although you risk obscuring the narrative if you end the sentence without identifying the actor.

Passive voice may be appropriate, however, if you do not know or do not want to emphasize the actor or subject, if the object of the sentence is more important than the actor, or if the actor is obvious, as in "a new mayor was elected." Finally, passive voice sentences are appropriate when they promote paragraph coherence. Beginning a new sentence with the object of the prior sentence is one way of overlapping and connecting sentences.

---

a.   Unclear Use of Passive Voice

Example: In balancing the interests, full factual development is needed in order to ensure the fair administration of justice. (Who needs full factual development? Who is balancing?)

Rewrite: To balance the interests, the court needs full factual development in order to ensure the fair administration of justice.

Or

Rewrite: In order for the courts to balance the interests, the parties should fully develop the facts.

b.   Wordy Passive Voice

Example: A duty of care to the plaintiff was breached by the defendant when the slippery floor was left unmopped by the defendant.

Rewrite: When the defendant failed to mop the slippery floor, he breached his duty of care to the plaintiff.

> **c.** Appropriate Use of Passive Voice
>
> **Example:** Under Rule 11 of the Federal Rules of Procedure, factual errors alone are not enough to justify sanctions. Sanctions would be granted, however, if the attorney knew there was no factual basis for the complaint. (Here, passive voice promotes paragraph coherence in that the second sentence picks up where the first left off and focuses the reader on what is really at issue: grounds for sanctions.)

6. MAINTAIN PARALLEL SENTENCE STRUCTURE (PARALLELISM)

Repeating a grammatical pattern is a good way of coordinating ideas in a sentence and maintaining control over complicated sentences. By making phrases or clauses syntactically similar, you are emphasizing that each element in a series is expressing a relation similar to that of the other elements in the series. Such coordination promotes clarity and continuity.

To maintain parallelism, nouns should be paired with nouns, infinitives with infinitives, noun clauses with noun clauses, etc. Faulty parallelism results when the second or third element breaks the anticipated pattern. "Hypocritical and a fraud" shows faulty parallelism, for instance, because an adjective is paired with a noun. Parallelism can be restored either by changing "hypocritical" to the noun "hypocrite" or "fraud" to the adjective "fraudulent."

> **Example:** She also served on the Board of the Fresh Air Fund, as a participant in the YMCA programs, and she worked for Planned Parenthood.
>
> **Rewrite:** She also *served* on the Board of the Fresh Air Fund, *participated* in the YMCA programs, and *worked* for Planned Parenthood.
>
> **Example:** An agency defense depends upon whether the agent was acting as an extension of the buyer and not for himself, if the agent was motivated by compensation, and finally, was salesman-like behavior exhibited.
>
> **Rewrite:** An agency defense depends upon *whether the agent was* acting as an extension of the buyer and not for himself, *whether the agent was* motivated by compensation, and finally, *whether the agent acted* like a salesman.

When you are coordinating ideas in a sentence, you normally begin your coordination after the subject, that is, with the verb (as in the first example above) or with the complement (as in the second example). A complement is that part of the sentence that completes the meaning of the subject and predicate. For example, if you said only "They made," your sentence has a subject and verb, but the thought is unfinished. You need a complement to complete the idea: "They made a last effort to settle out of court." If you have a series of parallel complements or verbs and complements, a good idea is to build your sentences so that the shortest unit of the series comes first and the longest comes last, unless logic dictates otherwise.

> **Example:** Some of the factors a court considers in determining the reasonableness of enforcing a forum selection clause are the residence and citizenship of the parties, the proximity of the contractual forum to probable witnesses, and the comparative convenience for the parties of litigating in each forum.

Here, the parallelism begins with the complements and the complements are arranged in order of length.

7. AVOID MISPLACED AND DANGLING MODIFIERS

Aside from the primary parts of a sentence (the subject, predicate, and complement), sentences have secondary parts called modifiers. Modifiers are words, phrases, or clauses that describe or define one of the primary parts or that further describe or qualify one of the modifiers (as in, "a court may impose sanctions upon an **attorney** *who omits cases unfavorable to the client*").

If possible, place modifiers to avoid uncertainty about the word or phrase they modify. A modifier should, in general, stand as close as possible to the word it modifies.

> a. **A modifier is misplaced** if it modifies or refers to the wrong word or phrase. You can correct this situation by shifting the modifier closer to the word being modified. If this is not possible, rewrite the whole sentence.
>
> **Example:** The court reached these conclusions by applying the "general acceptance" test for the admission of evidence resulting from the use of novel scientific procedures first articulated over sixty years ago. (The test was first articulated over sixty years ago, not the use of novel scientific procedures.)
>
> **Rewrite:** The court reached these conclusions by applying the general acceptance **test, *which was first articulated***

over sixty years ago, for the admission of evidence resulting from the use of novel scientific procedures.

Or

The court reached these conclusions by applying the general acceptance test for the admission of evidence resulting from the use of novel scientific procedures. The test was first articulated over sixty years ago.

Example: Undercover agent Jones walked up to a group of teenagers standing in front of a store with the intention of buying some cocaine. (Did Jones intend to buy cocaine or did the teenagers?)

Rewrite: *Intending to buy cocaine,* **undercover agent Jones** walked up to a group of teenagers standing in front of a store.

b.   **A dangling modifier** points to a word that is not in the sentence. Revise by inserting the word which is being modified.

Example: In Kent, a plaintiff whose spouse has been wrongfully killed has no cause of action for loss of consortium, denying, in effect, recovery for the destruction of the marital relationship.

Rewrite: In Kent, a plaintiff whose spouse has been wrongfully killed has no cause of action for loss of consortium, **a ruling that** denies, in effect, recovery for the destruction of the marital relationship.

Example: After dismissing the claim, the attorney was chastised. (The attorney cannot dismiss a claim. The passive voice construction omitting the actor creates a dangling modifier).

Rewrite: After dismissing the claim, **the court** chastised the attorney. (The "dismisser" is inserted into the sentence.)

8.   IDENTIFY AND PUNCTUATE RESTRICTIVE AND NONRESTRICTIVE MODIFIERS CORRECTLY

There are two kinds of modifiers, restrictive and nonrestrictive. Restrictive modifiers are those that narrow the denotation of a word, that is, they narrow the class of things or persons covered and are best introduced with "that."

Example: Courts *that recognize loss of parental consortium as a cause of action* emphasize the child's best interest.

Here, the modifier—"that recognize loss of parental consortium as a cause of action"—is restrictive because it limits the number of courts under discussion.

Nonrestrictive modifiers add information about a primary element in the sentence but do not define that element and are often introduced with "which."

Example: Trial courts, *which are bound by precedent,* tend not to make policy decisions but rather follow precedent.

In punctuating your modifiers, notice that **nonrestrictive modifiers are surrounded by commas** while **restrictive modifiers are not**. It is important to recognize the difference between restrictive and nonrestrictive modifiers, and to punctuate accordingly, because of the impact they have on the meaning of a sentence.

If you write, "the court is opposed to loss of consortium damages that are speculative," you have limited the number of consortium damages to those that are speculative and to which the court is opposed.

If you write, "the court is opposed to loss of consortium damages, which are speculative," you imply the court opposes **all** consortium damages because they are all speculative in nature.

Far too often litigation arises because of disputes over whether a modifier is restrictive or nonrestrictive. Although "which" can be restrictive or non-restrictive, to avoid ambiguity in legal writing you should always use "that" for restrictive modifiers and "which" for non-restrictive. If you wrote, "I leave to my son all my stock certificates which are less than $10,000," the will provision could be litigated. Can the son recover only those certificates that are under $10,000, or is the modifier merely descriptive of the monetary value of the stock certificates at the time of drafting, but the testator intended the son to get all the stock certificates? If non-restrictive, put a comma before "which" to indicate the son gets all the certificates.

Besides using commas to indicate restrictive and nonrestrictive meaning, and using the relative pronoun "that" to introduce restrictive modifiers, you should know that "who," like "which," can also introduce both restrictive and nonrestrictive modifiers. Be clear about which you intend and punctuate accordingly.

Conventional usage also requires you to use

- "who" when referring to a specific individual,

- "that" when referring to a class composed of persons, and

- "which" or "that" when referring to things or ideas.

9. ELIMINATE UNNECESSARY WORDS

Aim for economy and simplicity of phrasing. Unnecessarily verbose or complex language will not impress a supervising attorney or judge. Instead, it simply makes your writing more difficult to understand. Avoid throat-clearing introductions, needless modifiers, redundant pairs, unnecessary prepositions, and unnecessary detail.

---

a. **Use a Word for a Phrase:**

Not: By reason of the fact that the witness was out of the country, the trial was postponed.

But: Because the witness was out of the country, the trial was postponed.

b. **Avoid "Throat-Clearing" Introductions to Sentences**

Start right away with an argument. If you make the argument well, you do not have to tell the reader that you are about to do so. Most "throat-clearing" introductions are padding. They frequently begin with expletives like "it is" or "there are." They can usually be replaced with a word or omitted entirely.

Not: There were few witnesses willing to come forward.

But: Few witnesses were willing to come forward.

Not: After discussing this question, it is important to consider the possibility that Michael's "acceptance" may have been a counter-offer.

But: A second question is whether Michael accepted the offer or, instead, made a counter-offer.

c. **Avoid Redundant Pairs.**

Not: each and every person

But: each person **OR** every person (not both)

Not: Read the terms and conditions carefully

But: Read the terms carefully

---

d. **Avoid Unnecessary Adjectives and Adverbs**

Demonstrate the clarity of an idea by supplying supporting arguments rather than insisting on it with adverbs like the intensifiers "clearly" or "certainly." Do not overuse adjectives and adverbs. One apt adverb is more effective than many.

Not: The officer clearly violated the Fourth Amendment.

But: The officer violated the Fourth Amendment.

e. **Avoid Unnecessary Use of Prepositions**

Not: Many think the sentences of first time offenders are exceedingly harsh.

But: Many think first time offenders are too harshly sentenced.

10. SELECT CONCRETE, FAMILIAR, AND SPECIFIC WORDS: AVOID VAGUENESS AND IMPRECISION

Use concrete facts in your descriptions rather than words that characterize. Instead of saying, "The defendant drove several miles over the speed limit," report that the defendant drove sixty miles per hour in a fifty mile zone. If you say, "After a period of time, Roche purchased the drugs," we do not know whether minutes elapsed or years.

Do not be afraid to use a familiar vocabulary, one you feel comfortable with. To sound professional, you do not need to inflate or strain your diction. You need not say, "The car accident victim expired." Simply tell us that he died.

11. AVOID JARGON, INFORMAL, AND ESOTERIC LANGUAGE

As an attorney, you will be writing mostly formal documents. Informal expressions in these documents jar the reader because of their inappropriate tone. Even your emails should have a professional tone. Do not say, "The car's rear end abutted the public road." Say, "The rear of the car abutted the public road."

You need not be a slave to or legalese, however. Delete expressions like "hereinafter" and "cease and desist" (unless the phrase describes the remedy that is being asked for). Moreover, although courts sometimes employ an esoteric vocabulary, you need not parrot that language. If a court says, "the statute does not pass constitutional muster," you can paraphrase that statement in a more contemporary idiom. For example, you could simply say that "the statute is unconstitutional."

On the other hand, you should use the wording of a court when applying a particular test that a court uses to evaluate claims and use the exact statutory language that you are applying.

12. USE QUOTATIONS SPARINGLY

> a. **In using quotations, be selective, grammatical, and accurate.** Quotations should be used selectively for two main reasons.
>
> - First, a heavy reliance on quotations frequently signals adequate research but inadequate analysis.
>
> - Second, a paper littered with quotations often lacks fluidity and is hard to read.

Before you use a quotation then, think about whether the quote is necessary or whether it can be eliminated from your paper. You may be able to put the idea into your own words more efficiently and effectively. Whether you quote or you paraphrase, make sure that you then cite to the source of the idea.

> b. **It is sometimes appropriate to quote the holding of a case, and you should quote language that supplies the controlling standard for a particular area of the law.** When you quote the controlling language of a statute, it is important to repeat the exact wording of the statute as you apply it to your problem. Besides using necessary quotes from the language of precedents, you might want to quote some judges for their particularly eloquent or apt language.
>
> c. **Generally, do not quote a court's description of the facts. However, you should quote, rather than paraphrase, the words of a party or a witness if they are important to your case.**
>
> **Example:** The witness said, "I killed him and I'm glad."
>
> **Not**
>
> The witness dramatically confessed.
>
> d. **A quotation that is embedded in a longer sentence must fit into that sentence grammatically and logically.** This sometimes takes some juggling. It is frequently easier to recast that part of the sentence that is not a quotation than to alter the quotation. The following sentence needs to be revised because the possessive pronoun "its" in the quotation wrongly refers to the parent company. "Its" is meant to refer to subsidiaries.
>
> **Example:** The court found it decisive that the parent company, through its American subsidiaries, had "continued

> to engage in the market penetration and expansion that are its raison d'etre. . . ."
>
> **Rewrite:** The court found it decisive that the American subsidiaries of the parent company had "continued to engage in the market penetration and expansion that are its raison d'etre. . . ."

Keep quotes short. But if you do use a long passage of fifty words or more, you must set out the quote in block form, that is, indented and single spaced. You do not use quotation marks when you set out a quote in block form. Put the citation as the first nonindented text after the quotation.

13. USE THE APPROPRIATE TENSE

English is a language that has many verb tenses. This characteristic shows the importance we place on accurately reporting the sequence of events and conveying the relation of one event to another. In legal writing, it is particularly important to pay attention to tenses when narrating facts and discussing case law. You should use the past tense to state all facts that have already occurred. Thus, you should use the past tense to discuss precedents. However, use the present tense to state a proposition of law.

> **Example:** The court held [past tense] that due process requires [present tense] court-appointed counsel.

When discussing two events both of which occurred in the past, use the past perfect tense ("had" plus the past participle) to describe the earlier of two past actions.

> **Example:** The defense objected, arguing that the court had already overruled that line of questioning.

14. MAKE YOUR COMPARISONS COMPLETE AND LOGICAL

A comparative sentence must have two terms. Do not say "Jones has a stronger case." Finish the comparison by adding the second term: "Jones has a stronger case than you."

In addition, make sure you are comparing like or comparable things. Do not compare, for example, your facts to a case. Compare your facts to the facts in a case. Do not say "Smith's fraudulent statements are like *John v. Doe*." The proper comparison is

"Smith's fraudulent statements are similar to those of the defendant in *John v. Doe*."

15. CHECK THAT THE WORDS IN YOUR SENTENCE HAVE A LOGICAL RELATIONSHIP

The subject of your sentence should be able to perform the action expressed by the verb; if the subject cannot, your sentence lacks coherence. A court, for example, does not contend or argue that a defendant is negligent. It "holds" the defendant negligent. A court is not an advocate in the litigation; the attorneys are. Nor do courts feel or believe; their decisions are presumably based on reasons, not emotions or beliefs. What then might a court do? The court may have said something, or decided, stated, concluded, held (for propositions of law), found [that] (for facts), weighed, reasoned, indicated, implied, considered, stressed, noted, compared, added, analyzed.

A court, for example, might "apply" a balancing test or might "balance" the state's interest against a private interest. It would be incorrect, however, to write that a "test" balances those interests. A "requirement" does not "show" a "foreseeable injury," although a test might "require" a plaintiff to "show" the defendant could have foreseen injury.

In other words, make sure the subject, predicate, and object of a sentence rationally relate to each other.

16. AVOID SEXIST LANGUAGE[2]

The legal profession has become increasingly sensitive to the use of sexist language. To avoid antagonizing colleagues and clients, it is important to use gender neutral language when you write.

a. Try to avoid the generic use of the pronoun "he".

— Use plural nouns and plural pronouns.

> **Example:** The attorney must represent his client to the best of his ability.
>
> **Rewrite:** Attorneys must use their best abilities in representing their clients.

---

2   The recommendations made in this section are adapted from the "Guidelines for the Nonsexist Use of Language" written for the American Philosophical Association by Virginia L. Warren. They were published in PROCEEDINGS AND ADDRESSES OF AMERICAN PHILOSOPHICAL ASSOCIATION, vol. 59, no. 3 (Feb. 1988), at 471–84. Copyright © 1988 by the American Philosophical Association; reprinted by permission.

— Substitute articles for pronouns or use "who" instead of he.

> **Example:** The judge handed down his opinion on June 1st.
>
> **Rewrite:** The judge handed down the opinion on June 1st.
>
> or
>
> **Example:** If an attorney solicits a client, he may be disciplined.
>
> **Rewrite:** An attorney who solicits a client may be disciplined.

— Substitute one, you or we for "he" or delete pronouns altogether.

> **Example:** The litigator must exercise his judgment in selecting issues.
>
> **Rewrite:** The litigator must exercise judgment in selecting issues.

— When all else fails, try the passive voice.

> **Example:** The judge handed down his opinion on June 1st.
>
> **Rewrite:** The opinion was handed down on June 1st.

— If you know that the judge is a man or a woman, use the correct pronoun.

b. The generic use of "man" and other gender specific nouns should be avoided.

— Use person, individual, human, people.

— Use spouse instead of wife or husband, sibling instead of sister or brother.

c. Address people by their titles whenever possible.

— Use Dr., Prof., Ms., Editor, Colleague, Chair or Chairperson.

17. DO NOT USE APOSTROPHES WITH POSSESSIVE PRONOUNS

Although apostrophes are used to indicate possession or contraction, there is an important exception: possessive pronouns are not formed with apostrophes.

Examples:	
"It's" is the contraction of "it is."	**Example:** It's time to deliberate.
The possessive form of "it" is "its."	**Example:** The jury made its decision.
"Who's" means "who is."	**Example:** Who's going?
"Whose" is the possessive form of who.	**Example:** Whose hat is this?
"You're" means "you are."	**Example:** You're so wrong.
"Your" is the possessive form of you.	**Example:** Have you made your decision yet?

18. MAKE SURE AN APPOSITIVE AGREES IN NUMBER, GENDER, CASE, AND PERSON WITH THE NOUN BESIDE IT

An appositive, a word that can substitute for the noun beside it, must agree in number gender, case, and person with its referent. You cannot follow a possessive noun with a noun.

Not: The court accepted the Plaintiff's, Gear Limited, argument.

But: The court accepted the argument of Plaintiff, Gear Limited.

Exercise 10-A: Sentence Structure

Diagnose errors and correct. / *missing subject*

1. In calculating damages, the salary of a full-time companion was considered to be the greatest expense.

2. The drug companies can either insure themselves against liability, absorb the damage awards, or the costs can be passed along to the consumer.

3. Canon 9, which prohibits both impropriety and the mere appearance of impropriety, and which alone is a basis for a disqualification motion, reflects the Bar's concern with protecting the integrity of the legal system.

4. Heated arguments had often occurred over technicalities in the middle of negotiation. *who is arguing*

5. A trial by jury was requested by defendant.

6. Keith Johnson's case is more *the* factually similar to *Ziady v. Curley*.

7. Almost non-existent in 19th century America, the use of a will has steadily increased.

8. A determination of the awarding of consequential damages is done largely on a case-by-case basis.

9. The state interest in setting a filing fee relates to revenue raising and arguably to act as a deterrent to unmeritorious use of judicial time.

10. Unlike *Elliot*, Keith's mother had never relinquished her custody.

11. In order for the plaintiff to state a claim, it must be shown that he suffered severe emotional distress.

12. Any instrument, article, or substance which, under the circumstances in which it was used, is capable of causing death or serious injury is a dangerous instrument.

13. The jury, knowing the prosecutor has the authority of the government behind her, and aware of her access to the files, gave her words great weight.

14. The proscription against a prosecutor expressing his personal opinion goes to the heart of a fair trial.

15. The McCarran-Ferguson Act makes an exemption for the business of insurance.

16. Breach of the implied warranty of habitability can occur even without a landlord's violation of city building and housing codes.

Turn the material below into a sentence with parallel structure.

The landlord agrees to

- Provide heat

- All utilities will be paid for

- Premises to be in good order

- He will keep the air-conditioning system maintained

Exercise 10-B: Sentence Structure

Diagnose errors and correct.

1. A social host may be liable for the consequences of a guest's drunken driving if the host directly serves the alcohol, continues serving after the guest is visibly drunk, and knowing that the guest will soon be driving home.

2. Her innovative programming drastically increased attendance at the youth programs.

3. The firm entered into a two year contract with Ms. Taylor, who introduced several new products which

increased sales and earned her an "employee of the year" award.

4. By silencing you, I believe your teacher violated your First Amendment rights.

5. The trial court, in dismissing Mann's complaint under Rule 12(b)(6) of the Federal Rules of Civil Procedure, stated that it was not necessary to decide the merits of defendant's argument.

6. The defendant's acting with deliberate indifference is the second requirement.

7. Robertson granted visitation rights to Ms. Cavallo after she had abandoned Julia, abused another child, and she had committed heinous acts of abuse against Julia.

8. Although settlement will probably not result in the compensation of your damages to the same extent as that which would occur if you prevail at a formal hearing, it is a much quicker and more flexible process.

9. Only when the court would be interfering in inherently ecclesiastical matters and the court would be excessively entangled in Church matters will a church be able to avoid state laws.

10. By firing you, your contract was violated.

11. Such neutrality on the part of Utopia's School District cannot be compared to cases such as *Lee*, *Engel*, and *Abington*.

12. Julia was born prematurely and shortly thereafter began suffering withdrawal symptoms associated with drug addiction on August 3.

13. Should these matters go to trial, the Board will be exposed to the possibility of having to pay compensatory and punitive damages.

CHAPTER 11

TYPES OF LEGAL ARGUMENTS IN RESOLVING QUESTIONS OF LAW

I. INTRODUCTION

THE FIRST HALF OF THIS BOOK FOCUSES on the relatively straightforward application of settled legal rules to the facts of a case. Not all legal disputes stem from disagreement about the appropriate application of a rule, however. Some disputes concern the rule itself. Disputes about rules, called doctrinal questions or "questions of law," arise in several situations: (1) it is unclear what a rule means; (2) there is a gap in the rules, perhaps because an issue has not been litigated in your jurisdiction; (3) there are conflicting rules because of a split among the courts; or (4) changes in law and society suggest a rule is no longer practical or equitable. In these situations, lawyers must either

- interpret the rule before applying it
- extend a rule or create a new rule to fill the gap,
- explain why one rule is better than another, or
- explain why a rule needs to be refined or overruled.

Only after you clarify the law can you apply it. Many disputes require both a decision about the law and its application to the facts.

The types of arguments lawyers make about questions of law can be helpfully catalogued, for many legal arguments are standard and therefore predictable. Indeed, not only are legal arguments often predictable, but so are their counter-arguments. Legal reasoning tends to fall into dualistic patterns that reflect law's adversarial nature. If there is a sound analogy, there is likely a sound distinction. If a flexible rule ensures equity, a fixed rule provides notice and stability. Thus, up to a point, arguments and responses can be matched. Finally, lawyers tend to support their conclusions with multiple arguments (including arguments in the alternative), and these arguments often appear in predictable sequences: arguments based on authority generally precede arguments based on policy; plain meaning analyses precede legislative history. Nonetheless, not all arguments are equally relevant or equally strong. The choice and order of legal arguments are strategic decisions, especially in persuasive documents, and they require thought.

This chapter looks first at the types of arguments lawyers make about legal authority—precedents and statutes. It then describes the kinds of policy arguments that are prominent in legal discourse.

II. AUTHORITY ARGUMENTS BASED ON PRECEDENT

STARE DECISIS MAKES precedent binding authority within a jurisdiction. Precedent functions in two ways: courts create common law rules and they also create binding interpretations of enacted law. Yet, under either of these two situations, stare decisis does not necessarily result in a rigid and mechanical application of law because there are often debates about what the precedent means. These debates tend to fall within four categories mentioned above and discussed in more detail here.

A. Broad and Narrow Interpretation

Arguments based on precedent state, in effect, that prior decisions compel a particular outcome because the precedents and the instant case are analogous or distinguishable. Yet courts and practitioners rarely find the matter so simple. First, it can be difficult to determine exactly what the precedents require. Then, courts' holdings are also influenced by fairness to the parties and social goals, requiring them to frame holdings either broadly or narrowly depending on the results they seek. Lawyers also frame holdings to support their position.

Assume a rent control law fails to define "family" (who are protected under the tenant's lease) and a court needs to decide if unmarried domestic partners are included in that term. One court might conclude that a domestic partner is not included in the term "family" because he or she is not a legal spouse by virtue of marriage, an institution supported by the state. In addition, this court might fear the difficult problem of defining unmarried domestic partners or of predicting the economic and social consequences of a broad definition. Yet, another court might define the term "family" in a noneviction provision to include adult partners unrelated by blood or law whose relationship is long-term and characterized by emotional and financial commitment and interdependence. The court might use this definition of family both because of the changing configuration of domestic nuclear units and to avoid the health and welfare problems that could result from evicting large numbers of people from their homes upon the death of the tenant-of-record.

A good practitioner will similarly interpret the scope of a holding to serve a client's interests. The decision to interpret law broadly or narrowly is shaped by an attorney's persuasive purposes. If a precedent is favorable, an attorney may seek to have it be interpreted broadly and analogized as similar to the instant case. A broad interpretation is one that characterizes facts, reasoning, and holding in general or abstract terms. Thus a lesbian ex-partner might argue that the changing notions of family that prompted one court to define that term broadly in the rent control case are equally applicable in a child visitation case and support her visitation rights as the non-biological parent of a child jointly reared.

Conversely, if the precedent is unfavorable, it is often easier to argue that it is inapplicable to your case, and thus distinguishable, than it is to convince a court to overrule it. To convince a court to overrule, you must convince the judges that the court's own precedent is wrong. Thus, the first tactic where unfavorable precedent is involved is usually to distinguish the cases by interpreting the decision narrowly. Thus the biological mother fighting visitation by her ex-partner might argue that the health and welfare concerns that come from evicting a large number of people do not apply in a visitation situation, and that visitation should therefore be awarded to biological or adoptive parents only.

B. Extending Precedents to Cover a Gap

Sometimes the facts of a precedent are significantly different from the facts in a case on which you are engaged, but the underlying rationale of the precedent seems applicable to your case. In this situation, you might want to argue that the precedent is sufficiently analogous that it should be extended to the new situation.

Assume, for example, that the courts in your jurisdiction recognize a discovery rule exception to the statute of limitations for negligence suits. The statute requires the plaintiff to file an action within two years of the accrual of the claim, unless it is unclear when a claim begins to accrue. Generally, claims have been held to accrue at the time of injury. However, where the plaintiff learns of the injury only after the two-year limit has expired—as is often the case in toxic torts, for instance—the claim accrues not at the time of injury, but at the time the injury is discovered. The courts recognized this discovery rule exception because of the unfairness to plaintiffs who, through no fault of their own, would be denied an opportunity to litigate if the claim began to accrue at the earlier time.

Suppose your case is somewhat different. Your client knew about her injury before the statute expired, but she did not know its cause. She had undergone radiation therapy for breast cancer. Her reaction to this course of therapy was poor. She suffered burns, nausea and pain. Within two years of the radiation therapy, necrotic ulcers appeared, requiring surgery. During a follow-up visit six months after the surgery, your client overheard her surgeon talking to colleagues about the radiologist in her case, "And there you see, my friends, what happens when the radiologist puts a patient on the table, and goes out and has a cup of coffee." Here the patient knew of radiation burns and ulcers within the two-year limitations period, but she did not know that the injury was caused by her radiologist's negligence until after the limitations period had expired and she overheard her surgeon's comments.

As plaintiff's attorney, you would argue that the situation is analogous to hidden injury, and as with hidden injury, so here justice demands the client be afforded a day in court. The discovery rule is a rule of equity, developed to mitigate the harsh and unjust results that flow from a rigid adherence to a strict rule of law. In this case, the strict rule should not apply because the passage of time does not make it unduly difficult to present a defense and the claim is not false, frivolous or speculative. Thus you would argue that the discovery rule should be extended to include the delayed discovery of negligence as well as the delayed discovery of injury because the rationale for each exception is the same.

C. Conflicting Lines of Authority

Sometimes there are two equally valid lines of authority that point in opposite directions. In cases of first impression, for example, a court may look to other jurisdictions for guidance and find that there are two or more dominant trends. These alternatives require courts and counsel to explain why one line of authority is preferable to another. Among the reasons an attorney might offer is that one line of authority is easier to apply than the other or that one trend reflects a sounder social policy. Often advocates make a "weight of authority" argument to support their positions, arguing that more courts have adopted one position than another. But numbers do not always prevail, and this type of argument must be supported by other reasons.

For instance, until resolved by the Supreme Court, there was a split among the federal courts about what the term "use" meant in a federal statute that enhanced the prison sentence for anyone who "uses" or "carries" a firearm during a drug transaction. One line of cases distinguished "active" from "passive or potential" employment of a firearm and held that active employment is required because such an interpretation is consistent with the ordinary meaning of "use." The other line of cases suggests that if a firearm in any way facilitates a drug transaction, it has been "used." Under this definition, a gun left on a table that is visible through a doorway may be "use" of a firearm. The Supreme Court eventually settled this split by adopting the narrow definition of use, requiring "active employment" of a weapon.[1]

D. Overruling Precedent

Sometimes precedents need to be overruled because they are outdated and no longer reflect good policy. An increase in teenage drunk driving, for example, has led some courts to overturn precedents prohibiting "social host" liability; the new rule renders hosts negligent when they serve liquor to teenage guests who then drive and injure a person. The old rule of nonliability simply did not work well under modern conditions.

Even if a rule is not an old one, another reason to overrule a precedent is that courts rendering important new decisions in other jurisdictions have come to different conclusions based on better reasoning. For example, many state courts have held that a defendant who raises an entrapment defense cannot also deny the crime by pleading not guilty.[2] Entrapment presupposes the defendant committed the crime. Thus many states do not permit a defendant who pleads not guilty to use an entrapment defense because the defenses of not guilty and entrapment are thought to be inconsistent.

The Supreme Court has held, however, that a criminal defendant could plead not guilty and still enter an entrapment defense if the defendant denies an element of the crime. In *Mathews v. United States*,[3] the defendant had pleaded not guilty because he denied the intent element of the crime. The Court acknowledged that inconsistent defenses ("I didn't do it; I did it but

---

[1]   *Bailey v. United States*, 516 U.S. 137 (1995).

[2]   Entrapment is a defense based on the claim that the government "set up" the defendant. In the Supreme Court case cited most often as authority for this defense, the Court explained that entrapment occurs "when the criminal design originates with the officials of the Government, and they implant in the mind of an innocent person the disposition to commit the alleged offense." *Sorrells v. United States*, 287 U.S. 435, 442 (1932). Entrapment is thus interpreted as a two-part test: The criminal design must originate with the government and the defendant must not be predisposed to commit the crime.

[3]   *Mathews v. United States*, 485 U.S. 58 (1988).

was entrapped") could be seen as encouraging perjury. Nonetheless, the Supreme Court said other more beneficial consequences outweighed the perjury concern. The legitimate purpose of entrapment in a sting operation is to take a dangerous criminal out of circulation. This purpose is thwarted if entrapment leads an otherwise law-abiding citizen into unintentionally committing a crime. Permitting the defense in this situation is a way to discourage the abusive use of sting operations. Moreover, the Court stated that the risk of perjury is actually minimal because a defendant who offered conflicting testimony would significantly reduce his credibility before the judge and jury, and thus reduce the chance of acquittal.

The *Mathews* case does not bind the states because it is based on federal criminal law, not on a state criminal statute. Thus, to state courts, it is only persuasive authority. Nonetheless, in a state criminal trial, defense counsel could argue that the superior reasoning in *Mathews* should persuade a state court to overrule precedents that held the defenses of not guilty and entrapment inconsistent.

III. AUTHORITY ARGUMENTS BASED ON STATUTES

ADDITIONAL LAYERS OF COMPLEXITY are added with statutory interpretation. As we mentioned in Chapter 3, statutory interpretation begins with the "plain meaning" rule. To determine legislative intent, you look first at the statutory language to determine whether the words have a commonly accepted meaning that render the statute unambiguous. If not (and many times, even if so), you then analyze what the legislature intended the statute to mean by using the materials that were generated during the legislative process leading to enactment of that the statute. You might also look at the larger legislative history—at predecessor statutes, amendments, and even similar statutes in other jurisdictions. Another technique of statutory interpretation is the use of canons of construction, which interpret statutory language according to types of statutes or general principles of grammar and usage.

Both courts and advocates use these interpretative techniques to explain and justify their positions. Advocates are, of course, bound by the interpretative analyses of the courts in their jurisdiction. However, since these techniques do not always yield clear answers, arguments about interpretation are the basis of many persuasive documents. And there, as with a case law analysis, you must marshal as many arguments as are relevant to support your conclusion about the statute's meaning.

A. Plain Meaning Analysis

The plain meaning rule dictates that where the language of a statute is clear, other evidence of legislative intent is inadmissible. Only when the meaning is vague or ambiguous should extrinsic sources be consulted. Frequently, the plain meaning of a rule can be inferred because language is governed by rules that help us to interpret it uniformly. The rules of grammar govern the structure of a sentence, that is, the order and relationship of words within a sentence. Thus, for example, when Section 12102(2) of the 1990 Americans with Disabilities Act [ADA] defines disability as "a physical or mental impairment that substantially limits one or more of the major life activities," we know from the rules governing adverb and adjective placement that "physical" and "mental" modify impairment, not activities, and "substantially" modifies "limits." Dictionaries, stipulative definitions,[4] and common and technical usage also govern the meanings of words. Thus, for example, when Congress defines "public entity" in the ADA as "any department, agency, . . . or other instrumentality of a state . . . or local government," an entity like a state department of welfare falls squarely within the plain meaning of the statutory definition.

Nonetheless, plain meaning analyses are often less definitive than they might first appear. The plain meaning of a statute is often threatened by syntactic ambiguity (uncertainty that results from the arrangement and relationship of words in a sentence) and semantic uncertainty (uncertainty that results from confusion about a word's meaning or its range of meanings).

1. Syntactic Ambiguity

Syntactic ambiguity is the ambiguity that results from confusion about how the parts of a sentence fit together. One of the most common syntactic problem results from the careless use of conjunctions and disjunctives: "It is a crime to solicit funds and to loiter while on public transit." Must a person both solicit and loiter to be guilty of a crime? Although the drafter probably wanted to forbid each activity independently, the use of "and" instead of "or" undermines this intention.

Another common problem is caused by the unclear placement of modifiers, especially modifiers that are positioned at the beginning or end of a series. Consider the provision, "Your insurance does not cover elective surgery and therapy without

---

4   Stipulative definitions are definitions created for use in just that one regulation.

prior authorization." It is syntactically unclear whether the modifier "elective" pertains only to "surgery" or whether it also applies to "therapy" since an adjective or adverb preceding a series can be interpreted to modify the first or all the elements of the series. Moreover, end modifiers can describe all the items in a list or only the item closest to it. Thus it is unclear whether "without prior authorization" is confined to therapy, or whether it also modifies surgery.

Dangling modifiers also create confusion. Dangling modifiers occur when the word being modified fails to get into the sentence. Consider the rule, "While preparing food, gloves must be worn." It is unclear who must wear gloves: restaurant workers? But restaurant workers never appear in the sentence. Thus, the modifier "while preparing food" dangles. When syntax is ambiguous, context should direct our interpretation.

Yet another ambiguity that bedevils legal prose is the common failure to distinguish between restrictive and nonrestrictive modifiers. If a provision requires "two day delivery of all produce which is quickly perishable," it is unclear whether all produce is being regulated or only that which is quickly perishable. If the clause said "two day delivery of all produce that is quickly perishable," the modifier would be restrictive. It would limit the kind of produce regulated to that which perishes quickly. If the drafter had written "two day delivery of all produce, which is quickly perishable," using a "which" and a comma, the modifier would be nonrestrictive and mean that all produce is regulated because all produce perishes quickly. Without the comma, however, it is unclear whether the modifier is restrictive or nonrestrictive, and thus the scope of the provision is ambiguous. (See Chapter 10, Section 8.)

Finally ambiguous pronoun reference causes syntactic ambiguity: "After a plaintiff makes a prima facie case and the defendant articulates a legitimate reason for the discharge, he resumes that burden of proof." It is unclear whether "he" refers to the plaintiff or the defendant. When syntactic ambiguity exists, you must seek clarification from other sources.

2.   Semantic Uncertainty

Semantic uncertainty occurs when the meaning of a word is unclear. One common semantic problem is atypical usage. Words have a range of meanings—some of which are more typical than others. When the Supreme Court in *Smith v. United States*, 508 U.S. 223 (1993), held that trading a machine gun for drugs is active employment of a firearm and thus one way of "using" a firearm in violation of a statute, it was not wrong. Nonetheless, it was not employing the ordinary meaning of "use" of a firearm either. When most people think about using firearms, they think about using them as weapons, not as commodities of exchange. Thus practitioners and courts sometimes stretch words in ways that generate heated debate about their meanings and that require looking at other sources to determine intent.

There are two other frequent causes of semantic uncertainty: ambiguity and vagueness. Semantic ambiguity exists when words have two or more meanings. The meaning of "no drinking in the pool room" is ambiguous because we cannot determine on the basis of the word alone whether a "pool room" is a room with billiard tables or a room with a swimming pool, or whether "drinking" refers to the consumption of any beverage or only alcoholic beverages. Although context could possibly remove some of our uncertainty, language alone cannot.

Vagueness is uncertainty that results when the boundaries of a word are fluid. Consider the ordinance "No Parking Near Hydrant." It is unclear whether "near" means 5 inches, 3 feet, or fifteen feet.

To cover unanticipated situations, legislatures sometimes purposely use vague or general language, as in "unfair competition." In these situations, the legislatures expect courts to decide on a case-by-case basis what conduct falls within the category and what falls outside it. However, some statutes are so hopelessly vague that courts hold them "void for vagueness." Yet again, sometimes legislatures find agency or judicial interpretation of a statute undercuts legislative intent and it will amend the statute to overturn those misreading. This is what happened with the Americans with Disabilities Act [the "ADA"].

The EEOC, the federal agency charged with enforcing Title III of the ADA, initially defined the vague term "substantially limits" by saying that a person is "substantially limited" if that person is "unable to perform" a major life activity or is "significantly restricted" in performing an activity. The Supreme Court followed suit, defining "substantially limited" in a "major life activity" to require an individual to have an impairment "that prevents or severely restricts the individual from doing activities that are of central importance to most people's daily lives."[5] However, Congress repudiated this interpretation of its statute.

In enacting the ADA Amendments Act of 2008 (Public Law 110–325, ADAAA), Congress repudiated the Supreme Court's and

---

5   *Toyota Motor Mfg, KY v. Williams*, 534 U.S. 184 (2002).

EEOC's narrow interpretation of the Act, reiterating the ADA's broad and inclusive scope. It expanded the EEOC's list of what is considered "major life activities." The EEOC's list was narrow and included only basic activities like caring for oneself, walking, seeing, hearing, speaking, breathing. The ADAAA's list is non-exclusive and added intellectual activities to the list, as well as "major bodily functions" like functions of the immune system and neurological, brain, respiratory, and reproductive functions.[6] Previously, many courts said procreation, for example, was as fundamental as the EEOC's listed activities of breathing and speaking. In amending the Act, Congress showed its disagreement by not leaving the phrase "major life activities" open to interpretation. It provided its own directions to government agencies and the courts.

B.   Other Sources of Legislative Intent

When there is no commonly accepted judicial interpretation of statutory language, as in the lower courts' split over the meaning of use of a firearm, you may need to consider other evidence of legislative intent. Sometimes an ambiguous term or provision can be clarified by examining the statutory context, since the language in one part of a statute may help in determining the meaning of ambiguous language in a different part of the same statute. Preambles, Findings, or Statements of Purpose are another important source. Evidence of legislative intent also comes from extrinsic evidence, especially from a bill's legislative history. Intent is often inferred from the paper trail that tracks a statute's process through the legislature—from its introduction as a bill, to its deliberation in committee, to the vote on the floor. Each stage produces documentation that provides evidence of intent. Committee reports are important sources of legislative intent. Legislative activity and inactivity is yet another useful type of analysis: a statute's relation to predecessor statutes as well as its history of amendment, whether the amendments are rejected or adopted, all provide clues to legislative intent. Sometimes lawyers go even further afield to determine intent: they examine similar statutes in other jurisdictions to see what light they may shed on the statute in question.

1.   Statutory Context

Sometimes statutory context can resolve questions about the meaning of terms within that statute. Statutes should be interpreted to promote coherence among the parts of the statute

---

[6]   ADAAA § 4(a), redefining § 3(2) of the ADA.

itself. If the exact language of one provision is used elsewhere in the statute, that initial use may give clues to the intended meaning of the words when they are used later. If similar but not identical language is used elsewhere in the statute, the difference in the wording may help you interpret the different meanings. It also follows that language should be interpreted in the spirit of a statute's preamble or statement of purpose.

For example, the introductory language of the ADA indicates its broad remedial purpose. The introduction states "the Nation's proper goals regarding individuals with disabilities are to assume equality of opportunity, full participation, independent living, and economic self-sufficiency for such individuals" 42 U.S.C. § 12101(a)(7). The Act aspires to give "people with disabilities the opportunity to compete on an equal basis and to pursue those opportunities for which our society is justifiably famous." 42 U.S.C. § 12101(a)(8). The ADAAA reiterates this purpose when it says the definition of disability "shall provide a broad scope of protection to be available under the ADA." § 2(b)(1).

2. Legislative History

When Congress enacted the Americans with Disabilities Act in 1990, it left a well documented record of its deliberations. The ADA is therefore a good illustration of the uses of legislative documents. Indeed, the United States Congress often produces a voluminous legislative history, whereas state legislatures tend to have insubstantial records. Where the record is insubstantial or where it reveals ambivalence and conflict, courts have to extrapolate purposes from evidence other than legislative documents.

In the case of the ADAAA, Congress was responding to the report of an independent government agency, the National Council on Disability, which discussed the Supreme Court's misinterpretation of congressional intent. The agency proposed language that would clarify the purpose of the ADA and prevent misreading. Also influential was a somewhat controversial draft bill prepared by the Consortium for Citizens with Disabilities that closely resembled early versions of the ADAAA, called the ADA Restoration Bill. Some of this language was sufficiently controversial that sponsors of that bill encouraged a coalition of interested members of the disability and business communities to find mutually agreeable language. The group agreed that once negotiated, it would support the amended Act as it proceeded through the legislative process. Their efforts resulted in the ADAAA.

3. Regulatory Agencies

If the administrative agency charged with enforcing a statute offers a construction that is reasonable and that does not conflict with the statute, courts usually defer to that agency's construction. Although a court is the final arbiter of statutory construction, it will not substitute a different reading for that of an agency interpretation unless that interpretation is capricious or manifestly contrary to the statute. In the context of the ADA, the EEOC definitions of "substantially limits" and "major life activity" had been, as we discussed earlier, essentially adopted by the Supreme Court. However, because Congress decided that the EEOC and Supreme Court construction of these terms was overly strict and contrary to the purpose of the statute, those regulations were ultimately overturned.

4. Predecessor and Similar Statutes

It is often helpful to look at predecessor statutes when interpreting a current statute, since continuity and change are both equally significant.

The ADA incorporated almost verbatim the definition of disability used in the Rehabilitation Act of 1973,[7] and Congress included within the Act a provision directing the courts to construe the ADA as granting at least as much protection as that provided by the regulations implementing the Rehabilitation Act. Thus the precedents that arose under the Rehabilitation Act applied to the ADA because statutes that adopt provisions of predecessor statutes should be interpreted consistently, as should other statutes relevant to the same area of law, in order to keep the body of the law coherent. This is the policy behind the in pari materia canon discussed later in this chapter. However, when the ADAAA was passed, it explicitly rejected Section 7 of the Rehabilitation Act and required the Rehabilitation Act to conform to the ADAAA. Thus, precedent applying Section 7 no longer applies.

5. Legislative Activity

A sometimes useful, but often inconclusive, type of analysis is one that examines related legislative action or inaction. If language was changed by amendment or changed in a related statute, the change may clarify and make explicit the legislature's intent. If it remains the same, the continuity may indicate that the language as currently interpreted comports with legislative intent. An illustration of the former is the ADAAA's changes to the definition

---

[7] The Rehabilitation Act applied to government employers and employees. The ADA extended the scope of the Rehabilitation Act.

of major life activity. An illustration of the latter occurred when the ADA adopted the Rehabilitation Act's definition of disability.

Regulatory action and inaction are also important. For example, the Justice Department originally took the position that decisions about whether asymptomatic HIV-positive persons were disabled should be made on a case-by-case basis rather than by a per se rule. It later reversed its position on the physiological impact of HIV infection, reasoning that the overwhelming majority of infected persons exhibit abnormalities of the immune system and are therefore disabled as a matter of law, an outcome affirmed by the ADAAA. Changes like these need to be tracked for your analysis to be complete and accurate.

C. Canons of Construction

The canons of constructions are another method of determining statutory meaning. These canons are guides to interpretation of the syntax, language, and policies behind certain kinds of statutes.

1. Ejusdem Generis

A well-known canon is the canon known as ejusdem generis (which means "of the same genus or class"). In other words, whenever a statute contains specific enumeration followed by a general term, the general term should be interpreted to mean the provision applies to other things of the same kind. Take, for example, the provision it is illegal to ship obscene "books, pamphlets, pictures, motion picture films, papers, letters, writings, prints or other matter of indecent character." In a prosecution under the statute for mailing obscene phonograph records, the defense will argue that, under the canon of ejusdem generis, obscene phonograph records fall outside of the provision because the enumerated list only regulates visual matter, not oral matter. The Supreme Court, however, did not construe the statute that way because to have done so would have defeated the obvious purpose of the statute, which was to make illegal the use of the mails to disseminate obscene matter. The Court read the entire statute, beyond the portion under which the defendant was charged, to construe the statute as a "comprehensive" one that should not be limited by a mechanical construction.

2. Expressio Unius, Exclusio Alterius

Another well-known canon, which is again always referred to in Latin, is expressio unius, exclusio alterius (expression of one thing excludes another), usually shortened to expressio unius. Expressio unius is applied to mean that if a statute expressly mentions what is intended to be within its coverage, then the statute excludes that which is not mentioned. For example, a statute that prohibits importing aliens to work in the United States contains a section that excludes actors, artists, lecturers, professional musicians, and domestic servants, but does not exclude ministers. A court applying expressio unius in litigation against a church that hired an English minister would interpret the list of exemptions as an exclusive one, yet the legislature may not have intended the enumerated exclusions to be exclusive or may not have thought about other categories of people who should also have been excluded from the statute's broad coverage.[8]

3.   In Pari Materia

A third well-known canon is "statutes in pari materia (on the same subject matter) should be read together," that is, they should be interpreted consistently with each other. For example, a section of the Family Law Code on the topic of adopted children provides, "the adopted child shall be treated for all purposes as the natural child of the adopting parents." A section of the Probate Code provides that the property of a person who dies without a will should be distributed "one-third to the surviving spouse and two-thirds to the surviving children." If this statute and the section of the Family Law Code are to be read in pari materia so as to be consistent with each other, then the word "children" in the Probate Code should be interpreted to include adopted children of the person who died.

Of course, the statutory language of one or both statutes may show that the statutes should not be interpreted together. For example, the Family Law Code may provide that the adopted child be "treated for all purposes, including relations with the kin of the adopting parents, as the natural child of the adopting parents." The Probate Code, however, may provide only that "the adopted child shall inherit from the adopting parents as would a natural child." If the issue is whether the adopted child inherits from an adopting parent's mother (where the adopting parent has died), the differences in language between the statutes now make a difference. The Probate Code does not employ the specific language about "kin of the adopting parents," nor does it define the child as a natural child "for all purposes." Because the drafters of the Probate Code did not use that language, they may not have intended that the statute apply to all the situations to which the Family Law Code applies. Of course, the drafters also may not

---

[8]   The definition of the ministerial exception was recently resolved by the Supreme Court in *Hosanna-Tabor Evangelical Lutheran Church and Sunday School v. EEOC*, 132 S. Ct. 694 (2012).

have read the Family Law Code, and had not thought about problems arising from interpreting the two statutes consistently. The court will have to decide if it should do so, or whether the more narrow language of the Probate Code should control because it is the statute that more specifically applies to this problem.

4.   Canons on a Statute's Policy

Some canons are used to help interpret types of statutes by the presumed policy behind those statutes. An example is "remedial statutes should be liberally construed." If the remedial statute is one that changes the common law, however, such as a worker's compensation act, then the canon might conflict with another that says "statutes in derogation of the common law should be strictly construed." These two canons' presumptions conflict.

Thus, you will find that just as there are arguments and counterarguments, so are there canons and, so to speak, "counter-canons."[9] If one canon says courts must give effect to unambiguous statutory language, another says plain language need not be given effect when doing so would defeat legislative intent or have absurd or unjust results. Opposing lawyers will often supply a conflicting interpretation based on another canon.

Canons do not explain what the legislature meant in a particular statute and thus do not by itself compel a particular interpretation. Nonetheless, even if they are inconclusive, you should become familiar with the canons because many courts employ them as aids in construing language, especially when legislative intent is unclear.

IV. POLICY ARGUMENTS

POLICY PLAYS AN IMPORTANT ROLE in cases of first impression and in statutory and constitutional interpretation. In these situations, a court may need guidance as to how to proceed and will look to social policies in attempt to identify core interests and values. It will then try to fashion rules that promoted those goals and benefit society. The identification of a desirable goal is, of course, a normative one, but non-legal information can help both courts and advocates support their normative judgments and inform their arguments about how a rule would work in practice. Thus, they may seek information about customary business practices, economic consequences of a rule, psychological reactions

---

[9]   For a more complete listing of opposing canons, *see* Carl Llewellyn, *Remarks on the Theory of Appellate Decisions and the Rules or Canons about How Statutes are to be Construed,* 3 Vand. L. Rev. 395, 401–06 (1950).

to a situation, or accuracy of a scientific test. This empirical research and policy analysis can be immensely helpful.

Of course, advocates and judges can misuse scientific and social science research. Misuse sometimes arises because lawyers lack the expertise to evaluate their sources of information. Moreover, not all research is equally reputable. Thus, good policy arguments require lawyers to gain some competence in the area of research. In addition, they must read not only the studies themselves, but professional appraisals of those studies if they are to assess the validity and sufficiency of the evidence. This is important when lawyers rely on policy arguments previously articulated and adopted by a court. It is even more important when they need to construct original policy arguments.

As a law student and lawyer, it is helpful to be familiar with different types of policy arguments and the types of authority that support them. Policy arguments can be categorized in many ways, but one useful system is to divide them into four basic groups:

- normative arguments, that is, arguments about shared values and goals that a law should promote;

- economic arguments, that is, arguments that look at the economic consequences of a rule;

- institutional competence arguments, that is, structural arguments about the proper relationship of courts to other courts and courts to other branches of government; and

- judicial administration arguments, that is, arguments about the practical effects of a ruling on the administration of justice.

These categories are not, of course, mutually exclusive.

A. Normative Arguments

Normative arguments fall into at least three types. There are

- moral arguments, which are arguments about whether a rule advances or offends moral principles;

- social policy arguments, which involve a discussion of whether a rule advances or harms a social goal; and

- corrective justice arguments, which involve a discussion of whether the application of a rule is just in a particular case.

Moral and social policy arguments are not always easily separable because they both debate the greater good. Some rules of equity are derived from moral principles and social policy, for example, a person may not profit from his own wrong, and a plaintiff must come into equity with "clean hands." Corrective justice arguments focus on the actual parties before the court and are traditionally both the basis of our legal system and the province, in particular, of every trial court.

Assume you are involved in a case that asks the court to recognize for the first time a claim for damages for loss of parental consortium. Your clients are children whose mother suffered injuries when an intoxicated driver went through a red light and struck her. The mother now suffers from permanent spinal paralysis, brain damage, and impaired speech. She is confined to bed and requires constant custodial care. She no longer recognizes her children.

Plaintiffs here can make corrective justice and social policy arguments. They can argue that a small but steadily increasing number of jurisdictions permit loss of parental consortium claims because compensation comports with notions of public policy and fairness. Between the two parties, corrective justice demands that the tortfeasor compensates the children for their tragic loss of parental guidance, services, love, and companionship. Providing them with the resources to obtain live-in help or to receive psychiatric assistance can help the children make a permanent adjustment to their loss. Recognition of the claim also serves two important social policies: it preserves the deterrent function of tort law and compensates for real losses.

Some normative arguments are vulnerable to the accusation that they are political. Judges may be therefore reluctant to base, or to admit basing, decisions upon their moral and political views. Yet, as one judge has written, cases that break new ground[10] are often decided on "moral, social, or economic, i.e., political reasons."[11]

B. Economic Arguments

Economic arguments have assumed an increasingly important role in legal decisionmaking. Economic arguments are concerned with efficient allocation of resources. One economic approach to the law asks, for example, whether a particular decision is preferable

---

[10] Consider, for example, *Brown v. Board of Educ.*, 347 U.S. 483 (1954); *Roe v. Wade*, 410 U.S. 113 (1973); *Meritor v. Vinson*, 477 U.S. 57 (1986).

[11] Robert A. Leflar, *Honest Judicial Opinions,* 74 Nw. U. L. Rev. 721, 741 (1979). *See also* Judith S. Kaye, "[A] court must resolve every dispute before it. The court has to go one way or another, and either result necessarily involves a judge's choice, sometimes a judge's social policy choice." *Things Judges Do: State Statutory Interpretation,* 13 Touro L. Rev. 595, 610–11 (1997).

because it spreads the losses among larger segments of the population. Other economic arguments focus on whether a rule ensures optimal efficiency.[12] For those who subscribe to this approach, an efficient outcome is the preferred outcome regardless of fairness between the parties.

The defendant in the loss of parental consortium problem may have trouble countering the plaintiffs' normative arguments, but he has some reasonable economic ones. First, he may argue that permitting these claims could effectively result in a double recovery since a jury may, as a practical matter, compensate a child by means of an award to the surviving parent, if there is one. Moreover, double recovery costs will ultimately be borne by the public generally through increased insurance costs.

C. Institutional Competence Arguments

Institutional competence involves an examination of the proper role of each branch of government. For example, courts may defer to the legislature to create or to repeal a cause of action if they believe that the legislature, as the popularly elected branch of government, is the more appropriate forum to change the law. Lower courts will defer to the binding power of higher appellate courts' rules. Another aspect of institutional competence that courts consider is whether a particular decision will interfere with the work of administrative agencies.

Both parties in the loss of parental consortium hypothetical have strong institutional competence arguments. The defendant will argue that any change in the law on an issue of public policy should be made by the elected members of the legislature and not the courts. As an institution, the legislature, unlike a court, can gather facts on a number of relevant questions, such as:

1. whether there is any practical necessity for creating a separate cause of action for a child whose parent has been negligently injured;

2. what limiting principles—for example, the age of the child—should circumscribe such a cause of action;

3. what impact such a cause of action would have on insurance rates and other costs to the general public;

4. what, if any, limit on allowable damages should be imposed as a matter of social policy.

---

[12] For an explanation of the application of basic economic analysis to law, *see* Helene Shapo and Marshall Shapo, *Law School Without Fear,* 123–147 (3rd ed. 2009).

Accordingly, the defendant will contend it is for the members of the legislature to debate and decide this issue.

Plaintiffs will respond that loss of consortium is an item of damages that was initially created by the courts. Changes in the law of consortium have been made by the courts, for example, in permitting wives as well as husbands damages for loss of consortium. Moreover, it is not a highly complex doctrine. Therefore, it is wholly appropriate for the courts to decide this issue and not defer to the legislature. In fact, the plaintiff will argue the courts would be abdicating their responsibility if they did not reform the common law to meet the evolving standards of justice.

D. Judicial Administration Arguments

Judicial administration arguments are arguments about the practicality or impracticality of applying a rule.

One typical administration of justice argument analyzes the merit of a **"bright line" rule versus a flexible rule.** Precise, narrow rules provide clear notice and consistency and are easy to administer. They leave little to judicial discretion. In contrast, flexible rules are more responsive to individual circumstances and more likely to promote fairness to the parties. Because flexible rules involve judicial discretion, however, they are less predictable and relatively prone to judicial abuse.

Other judicial administration arguments include **"slippery slope"** and **"floodgate"** arguments respectively, that the rule is so broad it will be applied in inappropriate circumstances or inundate the courts with suits. Such suits waste judicial resources, as do rules that open the door to speculative, frivolous, or false claims.

Finally, if a rule is so complex that it will be difficult to administer, practitioners might make arguments about **conserving judicial resources.**

The defendant in the loss of parental consortium suit will argue that since each injury would lead to an increased number of law suits, the liability of an individual tortfeasor to a single family based on a single event would become unreasonable and oppressive. Moreover, recognition of the claim will create a slippery slope. It could become unclear how to measure damages and whether to draw the line at children or to include grandparents, or aunts and uncles. Plaintiffs will counter that where children's welfare is at stake, administrative concerns, like the possibility of increased litigation, should be secondary.

Moreover, damages are no more uncertain in this type of claim than they are for pain and suffering in personal injury and wrongful death actions, or in the spouse's claim for loss of consortium. Thus this claim is no harder to handle than those, especially since the possibility of double recovery can be avoided by careful jury instructions.

As the issue of loss of parental consortium illustrates, policy arguments often compete against each other. Sometimes one party will directly refute the logic of another's argument: although children whose parents have suffered a severe injury have themselves suffered a severe loss, an action for loss of parental consortium is simply unnecessary since compensation for emotional loss and lost economic support can be factored into an uninjured parent's award. Sometimes, one policy argument is countered by shifting the context. If one party argues fairness to the individual, the other stresses the needs of the community or efficiency. If one party focuses on freedom of action (the right to drive), the other focuses on the right to be secure (the right to be protected from drunk drivers). In the consortium case, competing policies need to be balanced. The negative effects of an increased burden on judicial resources and increased insurance costs must be weighed against fair compensation for children and society's interest in deterring negligent conduct. A court might decide, for example, that, in the context of single-parent families, the possibility of parental injury compels recognition of the cause of action because a child of a single parent cannot receive compensation through an uninjured parent's cause of action. This interest outweighs concerns over economic and judicial resources. Thus you must assess competing policies by testing their logic or by deciding that although a number of policies have merit, some policy interests are weightier than others.

V. ORGANIZING LEVELS OF ARGUMENT IN QUESTIONS OF LAW

WHEN YOU WRITE ABOUT QUESTIONS OF LAW, there are four primary analytic strategies.

- Statutory interpretation focusing on the language of a statute.

- Statutory interpretation focusing on the legislative history of a statute.

- Case law analysis focusing on which common law rule applies, how to frame a common law rule, or how courts have interpreted statutory language.

- Policy analysis focusing on the underlying reasons why a statute or common law rule should or should not control or be interpreted in a particular way.

The extent of these analyses depends on the strength of the arguments you want to make, although in statutory analysis you would always start with plain meaning, even if you can only say there is none or that it is ambiguous. Then go to legislative history.

For example, the Lilly Ledbetter Fair Pay Act provides that an unlawful employment practice occurs when an "individual" becomes subject to or is affected by a discriminatory pay decision. Assume that an employer wants to know whether the spouse of a deceased employee can bring a claim as an "individual" who has been affected by a discriminatory pay practice. Since the plain meaning of "individual" may be unclear in this context—does it mean non-employees as well as employees—the employer's lawyer might focus on the legislative history, which favors a narrow construction. During the floor debate on this issue, the senator who managed the legislation on the Senate floor said the law was not intended to include anyone other than the affected employee, the EEOC, or the Department of Labor. A non-employee pursuing a claim, however, might focus on the plain meaning of "individual" rather than legislative history and then go on to discuss favorable case law.

In addition to making a variety of arguments in support of a contention, you will often need to make alternative arguments. Alternative arguments are a staple of legal analysis. To argue in the alternative, you must concede your first theory in order to raise additional ones. In an entrapment case, for example, you might be defending a client who denied the intent element of a state charge of drug possession: he did not know that the pipe an undercover government agent handed him contained cocaine, although he admitted committing the act itself that is, admitted smoking the pipe. As defense counsel, you would interpret the state precedents narrowly and try to distinguish them. Unlike your client, the defendants in the precedents had not denied intent; they denied committing the crime altogether. If the state court is not persuaded by this distinction, your alternative argument is that those precedents should be overruled. You would justify this argument by pointing to the important policy argument in *Mathews* (see page 252) that the government must be prevented from enticing innocents into a criminal act.

As the above example suggests, authority arguments often depend on or are supported by policy arguments. In assessing the merits of a broad versus a narrow interpretation of precedent or of one line of cases over another, policy plays a role. In deciding whether to extend a precedent or to overrule it, policy plays a role. Thus policy arguments are best often raised in context, interwoven into the discussion of other points, rather than separated out. Sometimes, however, policy concerns are raised in a separate section. Here you could organize either around the types of policy arguments being made, describing and evaluating each party's argument on one policy concern. After discussing all the relevant policy issues, you would assess which party had the stronger overall position. Alternatively, you could organize around parties—making all the arguments of one party before moving to the next. Here too, you would need to conclude by weighing the overall merits of each position.

Thus, complex legal analysis often involves strategic thinking and several levels of argument. You will need to examine a variety of sources and their interrelationships, and to develop analytic strategies that will enable you to resolve a question in a logical and persuasive manner. Persuasion is especially important when you write a persuasive document, but even in a memorandum you want to persuade your reader that your analysis is correct and complete.

Exercise 11-A

The defendant Smith was charged with burglary, which under the New York Penal Law § 140.20 requires the defendant to "enter . . . unlawfully in a building with intent to commit a crime." Smith had climbed on the roof of a one-story structure in order to pour oil on the building to set it on fire.

1. *Which statutory language is at issue in this prosecution?*

2. *Below are two columns of arguments that can be made in this case. The left column lists arguments the defendant can make; the right column lists the state's answering arguments. The arguments are not listed in matching order.*

    Match the defendant's and the state's arguments and characterize them as to the type of argument each is. Then write an outline of the order in which you would analyze this issue.

3. *How would you decide this case if this were before you on the defendant's motion to dismiss the indictment?*

Smith	State
a. The statute does not define "enter . . . in a building" and the plain meaning of the words requires some opening to the building large enough for the defendant's body to pass through.	**a.** The scope of the common law of burglary and its purpose was expanded by the concept of the curtilage, which is the area in close proximity to the dwelling house. Unlawful entry of an outbuilding within the curtilage is burglary. The crime is not restricted to maintaining security within the four walls.
b. In a recent case from the N.Y. Court of Appeals, *People v. King*, the court held that the defendant violated § 140.20 when he cut a small hole in a part of a metal security gate. Defendant attempted to get into a store on the ground floor of a building. The metal gate covered the display windows and the vestibule area that led past the display windows into the interior of the store. Defendant cut the hole in the gate directly in front of the vestibule. The court held that the vestibule was functionally indistinguishable from the display window and store because it could be closed off from the public by the security gate. *King* requires that a defendant must intrude into an enclosed space in or connected to a building.	**b.** Because the Penal Law does not define enter, the word retains its common law meaning which is that entry is accomplished when a person intrudes within a building no matter how slightly.
Smith	State
c. The purpose of burglary statutes is to preserve the internal security of a dwelling and the crime requires some breaking of the planes created by the threshold and walls of the structure.	**c.** *King* means that the element of entering is satisfied if the defendant goes into an area of a building or an area related to a building to which the public can be denied access.

Exercise 11-B

When John Trent was arrested for possession of a controlled substance, he was in Illinois and with his friend Timothy Lot, who had given him the cocaine-filled pipe. Suppose that Lot was not a police informer, and indeed did not know that it was an undercover police officer who supplied him with cocaine. Suppose also that the undercover officer urged Lot to provide the drugs to his "special friends in government positions," and Trent was a local government official.

An Illinois statute, § 7–12, provides the entrapment defense for a person whose conduct "is incited or induced by a public officer or employee, or agent of either." The statute does not define "agent."

The trial court denied Trent's request for an instruction on the ground that Lot was not an agent of a public officer because he did not knowingly act on the officer's behalf.

1.   *List the types of materials you would research to analyze whether an agent must be a knowing agent under the Illinois statute.*

2.   *Which types of arguments would you want to use? How would you organize your analysis?*

3.   *Read the arguments set out below. Which kinds of strategies are each of these writers using? Evaluate the strength of each. Which ones would you prefer to use? Which ones would you avoid? Organize the strategies you would use in a memorandum analysis as they pertain to 1) statutory arguments, 2) case analysis, and 3) policy analysis.*

Arguments:

a.   Section 7–12 does not define the term "agent." However, the Committee Comment suggests that the legislature did not intend to require a knowing agent. The Comment provides:

> The defense has been recognized as proper not only when the person alleged to have incited the offense was a government officer or agent, but also when he was an investigator privately hired and acting without contact with law enforcement authorities. One case sometimes cited as an entrapment case involved a burglary of a private office, planned and executed by a detective with the knowledge of the owner of the office, to cause the arrest and prosecution of several men who were suspected of having perpetrated a series of burglaries. Although the Illinois Supreme Court referred to the entrapment situation, the basis for the reversal of the judgment was that the "victim" consented to the conduct,

and since lack of consent is an element of the offense, no burglary was committed.

b. If the legislature intended to require a knowing agent, it would have said so. For example, § 4–3 of the Criminal code generally defines the mental state element for the entire Criminal code and says that "knowledge is not an element of an offense unless the statute clearly defines it as such."

c. Two Illinois appellate courts have reached opposite conclusions as to whether a defendant is entitled to an entrapment instruction where a private person unknowingly worked with an undercover policeman to buy drugs from the defendant.

   In one case, in which the appellate court held that the trial court correctly rejected the instruction, the private party had initiated the contact with the police officer. He also had initiated the contacts with the defendant, and urged the defendant to sell the drugs. In the other case, the private party's only role was to communicate the government's inducements to the defendant directly. The appellate court held that the trial court should have instructed the jury on entrapment.

d. The lower federal courts are split as to whether the middleman must know he is acting for the government.

e. Recognition of entrapment where the police use an unknowing middleman is necessary to prevent the police from engaging in unchecked abuses. Otherwise, police will avail themselves of this technique and unfairly induce people to commit crimes.

f. When the police instruct a middleman to target a particular person, all courts permit that person to raise the entrapment defense. In this case, the police did not name Trent as the target but described the target in a way that logically led Lot to Trent.

g. If the legislature were opposed to police using middlemen, it would have legislated against it.

h. Law enforcement agencies can best control abuses administratively by issuing clear guidelines to their personnel.

i. Section 7–12 defines the terms "public officer" and "public employee" as well as several other terms. In light of this specificity, the fact that the section does not define "agent" implies that the legislature intended not to restrict its meaning.

j.   Black's Law Dictionary defines agent as "one who represents and acts for another under the contract or relation of agency."

k.   If a police officer is not present during the transaction between a defendant and a middleman, an entrapment defense would present the danger of collusion between the defendant and middleman and would encourage false statements at trial.

Exercise 11-C

1. *Title 18 U.S.C. § 2511(1)(a) of the Omnibus Crime Control and Safe Streets Act makes it unlawful for "any person . . . [to] intentionally intercept . . . any wire . . . communication" without a court order. Edna Mack was charged with a violation of this section for installing a tape recording device on her home telephone and taping her husband John's conversations with a woman with whom he was having an extra-marital affair. Her husband had not consented to the wiretap and Ms. Mack had not gotten a court order. John Mack sued his wife (from whom he then separated) under the statute, which permits civil damages suits for violation of the statute.*

This suit raised two issues: Does the statute apply to Ms. Mack, and if so, was her husband entitled to damages?

For the first issue, organize the following into arguments for each party, and explain what type of argument each is.

a.   The statute apples to "any person." Section 2510 defines "person" to include "any individual." Therefore, Ms. Mack is a person within the meaning of the statute.

b.   The statute implicitly excepts from its coverage interspousal wiretapping. The purpose of the statute is to regulate the law enforcement personnel and prevent them from invasion of privacy of citizens by wiretapping without court order. Congress would not have intended to interfere with domestic relations and household use of the telephone.

c.   The legislative history concerns only law enforcement personnel and crime control. The only mention of other uses of wiretapping concerned testimony of matrimonial lawyers who used recording devices for divorcing spouses.

2. *If the court holds that this statute applies to interspousal wiretapping, is Mr. Mack entitled to damages?*

Section 2520(c)(2) provides that "the court may assess as damages" the plaintiff's actual damages, or statutory damages of $100 a day up to $10,000, whichever is greater. John Mack had no actual damages, and his wife violated the Act on two days.

At issue is whether the court has discretion to award damages or whether it must award Mr. Mack $200. Consider this information.

—   In 1986, Congress amended the damages section, increasing maximum statutory damages to $10,000 from $1,000. The amendment also changed the language from "the court shall assess as damages" to the current "the court may assess. . . ."

—   Section 2500(c)(1) assesses damages in cases involving interception of private satellite video communication. That section's language is "the court shall assess. . . ."

—   The legislative history does not contain an explanation of why Congress changed "shall" to "may," or whether Congress intended damages as discretionary or mandatory.

—   Besides increasing the maximum statutory damages and changing "shall" to "may" in § 2520(c)(2), the 1986 amendments changed the damages for intercepting private video satellites, and the legislative history documents contain information only about the penalty structure for this violation.

—   The only precedent on this issue held that the statute does not give a court discretion to withhold damages. The court said that to adopt a literal application of the word "may" would lead to results at odds with the purpose of the statute, which is to protect privacy.

Evaluate these possible conclusions. Which is best supported by the previous information?

—   Congress apparently intended to give the courts discretion in order to ameliorate the possible harshness of the increased statutory damages amount.

—   The wiretap provisions were designed to protect the privacy of wire and oral communication and to set out uniform standards for courts to authorize wiretaps. To accomplish these goals, the statute does not permit the court to exercise discretion, but requires the court to assess damages for violation of the Act.

—   In the absence of a legislative record explaining why Congress changed "shall" to "may," the court should hesitate to read a grant of discretion where none had been permitted in the past, especially when the language is somewhat ambiguous.

3. *If the court decides that the Crime Control Act applies to spousal wiretapping, in that jurisdiction does the statute give a cause of action to a minor child against his custodial mother, when the mother recorded the child's conversations with his father from their home telephone, and the parents are divorced?*

Exercise 11-D

Our client, Crombie Cyberware & Cellular Co., Inc., wants to know what practices and procedures it should implement to reduce the risk of employer liability under the Lilly Ledbetter Fair Pay Act of 2009. It also wants to be notified of potential grey areas and problems that might arise. After reading the summary of the Act below, come up with a list of helpful practices and potential pitfalls.

Under the Act, an employer commits an unlawful employment practice with regard to disparate pay when

1.   a discriminatory compensation decision or other practice is adopted;

2.   an individual becomes subject to a discriminatory compensation decision or other practice; or

3.   an individual is affected by application of a discriminatory compensation practice including each time wages, benefits, or other compensation is paid, resulting in whole or part from such a decision.

The Act overruled the Supreme Court's decision in *Ledbetter v. Goodyear Tire & Rubber Co.*, 550 U.S. 618 (2007), which held that unlawful discrimination occurs only when the employer first set the discriminatory rate, even if the employee does not learn of the discriminatory rate until years later. In her dissent, Justice Ginsburg said that under the Court's decision, "knowingly carrying past pay discrimination forward must be treated as lawful conduct. . . . The Court's approbation of these consequences is totally at odds with the robust protection against workplace discrimination Congress intended Title VII to secure."

The Ledbetter Act extended the time period for pursuing disparate pay claims under Title VII, The Age Discrimination in Employment Act, the ADA, and the Rehabilitation Act.

Exercise 11-E

John Hume is charged with violating a federal statute, 18 U.S.C. § 2114 (2006), which provides as follows:

> whoever assaults any person having lawful charge. . . or custody of any mail matter or of any money or other property of the United States with intent to rob or robs any such person of mail matter or of any money or other property of the United States shall be imprisoned. . . .

Hume assaulted an undercover Secret Service agent while attempting to rob him of $2000 of United States money entrusted to the agent to "purchase" counterfeit money from Hume.

Hume's defense is that the language in § 2114 "any money or other property" applies only to crimes involving robbery of postal money or postal property. The predecessor statutes to § 2114 all applied only to mail robbery and appeared in the section of the Criminal Code about offenses against the Post Office. The Postmaster General requested Congress to amend the statute to include robberies of money and other valuables as well as mail from a Post Office.

How would you evaluate the following arguments about the question of what the statutory language means? Which arguments would be used by the prosecutor and which by the defendant?

1. The statutory language is plain and unambiguous: the statute applies to any lawful custodian of three distinct classes of property. Nothing on the face of the statute limits its reach to offenses against custodians of postal money or postal property.

2. The principle of ejusdem generis demonstrates that the general terms "money" and "other property" should be limited by the specific term "mail matter" to postal money or postal property.

3. The bills introduced to amend the predecessor statute, which broadened its language, were referred to the Post Office Committees of both the Senate and the House of Representatives. A member of the House Post Office Committee said on the floor of the House that "the only purpose of the pending bill is to extend protection of the present law to property of the United States in the custody of its postal officials, the same as it now extends the protection to mail matter in the custody of its postal officials."

4. The Committee Reports of both the House and Senate Committees say that "the purpose of the bill is to bring within the provisions of the Penal Code the crime of

robbing or attempting to rob custodians of government moneys."

5.   The federal Criminal Code § 2112 contains a general statute penalizing thefts of government property with a much lesser sentence than the one imposed by § 2114.

6.   In an earlier case, the Solicitor General of the United States conceded that § 2114 covered only postal crimes.

CHAPTER 12

INTERVIEWING THE CLIENT

I. INTRODUCTION

IN YOUR FIRST FEW WEEKS OF LAW SCHOOL, you may have been assigned a legal office memorandum, a document containing a section called the Statement of Facts. But you may not have thought about the process by which a lawyer gathers the facts that appear in that section. You may have assumed that the client would provide all of the relevant facts and that the lawyer would easily know what facts are relevant to the client's problem. You may not have considered how often in describing a problem, people are likely to omit critical facts, to characterize facts in a way that puts them in the best light, to misstate facts, and to give facts in an idiosyncratic order. You may also have assumed that a lawyer would know which facts to probe. However, if a lawyer is not familiar with all of the issues relating to a legal theory, a lawyer is not likely to initially ask about all relevant facts. Moreover, a lawyer's ability to help the client may depend on whether the client trusts and has confidence in the lawyer. A client who does not trust a lawyer will probably not be forthcoming about providing facts or even revealing objectives.

Thus, effective interviewing involves skills in listening, in questioning, and in understanding the full dimensions of a client's problem. At your initial interview with the client, you will have your first opportunity of what will probably be an ongoing process of both gathering facts related to a client's problem and establishing a relationship of trust with the client.

Example

To understand how a client may feel when meeting a lawyer for the first time, imagine that you are a college senior on your way to see a doctor. You have had recurrent headaches and blurred vision for the previous two months and have decided to do something about the problem. Although you assume that nothing terrible is happening to you, you are uneasy about what the doctor may conclude. In fact, this has not been an easy year for you. You have done well academically, but have developed major doubts about a career in law, although this had been your goal since high school. Ultimately, you decided not to apply to law school. Your parents were surprised, then concerned, then anxious about why you changed your mind and about what you are going to do with your life. They have said that they cannot support you indefinitely. You do not want to cause them economic or personal anxiety, particularly since your father is not well. Moreover, the person you have been dating seems to have lost interest in you now that your career plans have changed.

How would you want the doctor to deal with your situation? First, you would want the doctor to be skilled in diagnosing and treating the medical issues relating to the headaches and blurred vision. But you might also want to doctor to be interested in some of the other problems that you have been having, both because they are troubling you and because they may be related to the medical issues. What would make you likely to discuss these other problems with the doctor? The doctor would have to be someone who listened carefully to what you are saying, who seemed both to understand what your concerns are and to care about them, and who believed you could decide better than anyone else what the right career choice was for you.

Like patients seeking medical advice, clients come to lawyers first for legal advice and help. Foremost, the client wants a competent lawyer. In fact, the first rule in the ABA Model Rules of Professional Conduct deals with competence.

> A lawyer shall provide competent representation to a client. Competent representation requires the legal knowledge, skill, thoroughness and preparation reasonably necessary for the representation. Rule 1.1.

But your ability to help your client also requires your understanding that the "legal" problem may not be the whole problem.[1] Thus your interpersonal skills can be as important as your research and analytic skills. Clients' legal problems often relate to other non-legal concerns that the client has, just as medical problems may relate to non-medical concerns. For example, the college senior who has decided not to go to law school might be wondering if the headaches are related to the other concerns which may be psychological (where do I go from here?), interpersonal (I am causing my parents a lot of worry by changing my mind about law school), economic (I have to go out and get a job now), or moral (I should not be a burden to my parents at their age).

---

[1] Throughout this chapter, the authors have drawn on material from the following very helpful texts: David A. Binder *et al., Lawyers as Counselors: A Client-Centered Approach* (3rd ed. 2011); Robert M. Bastress and Joseph Harbaugh, *Interviewing, Counseling and Negotiation: Skills for Effective Representation* (1990); Marilyn J. Berger *et al., Pretrial Advocacy: Planning, Analysis & Strategy* (2007); and Thomas L. Shaffer and James R. Elkins, *Legal Interviewing and Counseling in a Nutshell* (4th ed. 2004).

Finally, your ability to help your client may depend on your understanding the lawyer-client relationship. You may have thought that your role as a lawyer means that based on your legal expertise, you tell the client how to solve the client's legal problem. After all, what did you go to law school for if not to dispense legal advice?

Yet Rule 1.2(a) of the Model Rules of Professional Conduct on the Scope of Representation states:

> A lawyer shall abide by a client's decisions concerning the objectives of representation. . . .

Your role, then, is not simply that of the technical expert and adviser. Although you must be knowledgeable about the law (just as a doctor must be knowledgeable about medical issues), you also need to understand that the person in the best position to make the decision about a legal problem is the client. After all, the client, not you, is the person who must live with that decision. Your role is to help the client find the best solution to the client's problem. To do this, you need to understand the problem as the client perceives it, and to discover what is most important to the client.

Every client is different. So your approach to each client will vary depending on the client's basic situation. Is the client meeting with a lawyer for the first time? Does the client want to bring a lawsuit? Is the client a defendant in a civil lawsuit? Has the client been charged with a crime? Is the client a sophisticated business person who wants to set up a new company and who has had significant contact with lawyers? Is the client someone who has no knowledge of the law? Is the client dealing with painful personal issues like divorce or a relationship with estranged children? Is the client worried about the cost and stress of litigation? Just as you consider your audience when you write, you should consider each client individually when you meet with that client.

II. GOALS OF THE INTERVIEW

A CLIENT MAY COME TO DISCUSS a matter relating to litigation (suing a hotel for negligent infliction of emotional distress, defending an adverse possession claim, defending a charge of armed robbery) or relating to a transaction (buying a house, negotiating a commercial lease, signing an employment contract). Consider then what you want to achieve in an initial interview with the client. You may think it is obvious—you want to find out what the client's legal problem is. You can then research the problem to find out if the client has a good case, or if the client should renew the commercial lease under the terms offered, or if the client should sign the contract, and then tell the client what you know.

Certainly, one of the major goals of the interview is to get the facts that are relevant to the client's problem and to understand what the client's goals are. However, if you focus your efforts in the interview only on the facts relevant to the "legal" problem, you may discourage the client from providing other highly important information. For example, if a client describes a series of conflicts that have occurred between her and her spouse, you might assume that the client has come to get representation for a divorce. You may be tempted to tear yourself away from the interview so that you can immediately begin researching the state law on divorce. But the client may not consider divorce for religious or moral reasons. Rather, the client may be concerned about the escalating conflicts with her spouse and wants to know if there is a way in which she could get an order of protection or could force her spouse to vacate the premises. Or the client may ultimately want a referral to a marriage counselor. If you failed to elicit or develop this information, you would have completely misunderstood the client's objectives. So a more useful way of viewing the goals of the interview would be to try to gather facts that relate to what brought the client to see you, to what the client would like to happen, and to how the client feels about the situation.

Gathering facts is not your only goal. The interview is also the critical first stage of your developing a lawyer-client relationship based on trust and mutual respect. The client will be revealing information about issues of importance and concern. The client will want to feel that you are an understanding and trustworthy professional, capable of effectively representing the client's interests.

Finally, assuming that the client agrees to hire you and you agree to represent the client, you and the client will be establishing a contractual relationship. That relationship entails your assuming obligations to the client under the Model Rules of Professional Conduct. Moreover, you will probably discuss your fee arrangement with the client at the end of the initial interview and indicate what tasks you will probably need to undertake in order to achieve the client's objectives. Accordingly, bear in mind your goals for the initial interview:

- to establish a relationship of trust with the client,

- to gather as many of the relevant facts as you can,

- to establish a contractual relationship (you may have the client sign an agreement), and

- to assign tasks to yourself and to the client in preparation for the next meeting.

III. PREPARATION FOR THE INTERVIEW

PLANNING IS IMPORTANT AT EVERY STAGE of your relationship with your client. Interviewing is a skill. You cannot expect to "wing it" and assume that you will intuitively know how to conduct an initial interview, even after you have gained some experience.

Even before you have met the client, you may be able to begin considering the client's situation. Often the client making the appointment over the telephone will have provided you or your assistant with some information about the problem, or the client may have dropped off some documents before the interview. In these situations, you may have learned some of the facts relating to the client's problem and some idea of what to expect. Thus you can think about the client's situation in advance, and even do some preliminary research on what the legal problem seems to be. Consider, also, whether there are any documents you want to ask the client to bring (a notice from the landlord, a summons and complaint in a lawsuit filed against the client, a business contract which is about to expire).

For example, assume that a new client, John Starr, has made an appointment to meet with you in two days. Mr. Starr mentioned over the phone that his wife is Jane Starr, the newly elected city councilor. You remember that around three months ago, there was a terrible incident during the election in which Jane Starr was shot and wounded by a hotel security guard. Before meeting with John Starr, you looked up the newspaper account of the shooting. You consider whether Mr. Starr's visit relates to the shooting incident. Or since Mr. Starr, but not Mrs. Starr, is coming to talk with you, you wonder if the meeting deals with a totally different matter. So although you should consider the likely content of the interview and how you would generally like to structure it, you should keep an open mind and not prematurely diagnose the client's problem or prejudge the client personally.

IV. THE INTERVIEW

YOU WILL PROBABLY BEGIN YOUR INTERVIEW of the client by meeting the client in your waiting room, introducing yourself, and bringing your client into your office. Once you sit down, spend some time chatting with the client about non-legal issues to put the client at ease. This is not a waste of time. Remember, you are a stranger. The client has to feel comfortable about discussing all sorts of issues with you. In addition, the preliminary conversation may give you some insight into the client's personality and concerns.

> *Good morning Mr. Starr. My name is ____ ____, I'm pleased to meet you. Let's go into my office to talk. Would you like some coffee, or tea, or perhaps a cold drink? [Did you have any difficulty finding the office?] OR [I understand that Joe Black gave you my name. How is Joe doing? I haven't seen him in a while.]*

When you feel the time is right, begin with a general question to the client. [*Mr. Starr, what brings you here today?*] This will give you an idea of how the client characterizes the problem that brought him to see you. This is the best way to begin understanding the problem from the client's perspective. Asking an open-ended question and permitting the client an initial opportunity to talk without interruption will give you very important information and will also aid in putting the client at ease. If you take control of the conversation too early, you may inadvertently silence the client. You should also ask how the client would like to have the problem resolved. The client may have already considered some possible solutions or at least can give you a range of objectives. [*I want the hotel management to admit that they should never have hired that guard and to pay for the misery they caused.*] In telling the story, the client may also gradually feel unburdened and begin to feel a rapport with you. Finally, the client may reveal important non-legal concerns that may bear upon the client's situation. [*I have to tell you that my wife thinks this is a bad idea. We have had a lot of arguments about it, and I don't know if I am doing the right thing or if a lawsuit would just make things worse between us.*]

While listening to the client's story you will probably begin thinking of potential legal theories that relate to the client's case. But before prematurely diagnosing the client's problem, ask the client for a chronology of the events (often called a time-line) which led to the client's coming to see you. [*Mr. Starr, could you give me a step-by-step account of the events leading to the shooting of your wife, and of what has happened since.*] Remember that although you may ask the client to start at the beginning, do not expect a flawless narrative that proceeds from one legally relevant fact to another in perfect chronological order. Like all of us, clients are likely to include irrelevant facts, to omit important events assuming the other party is aware of them, to provide information out of order, and to be reluctant to provide certain information because it may be personal, embarrassing, or even incriminating.

To get a reasonably complete time-line, you will have to ask different types of questions (open-ended, specific, leading, follow-up, yes/no) to try to get a step-by-step sense of what happened.

A broad, open-ended question will encourage the client to respond at length, focusing on the material that seems most important to the client. [*Mr. Starr, would you tell me about what happened the day you and your aunt were watching television coverage of your wife's campaign?*] A narrow, specific question or a yes/no question will elicit detail. [*Where were you and your aunt sitting in relation to the television set?*] A leading question will clarify or verify information or enable the client to respond to a difficult question. [*And you and your wife continue to disagree about whether you should sue the Hotel?*] You will likely use a combination of these types of questions. A general approach is using a "funnel" technique; that is, beginning with open-ended questions and then moving on to narrower, more specific questions.

Your skill as an interviewer depends on your ability both to listen and to ask questions. Of course, you need to listen carefully to the client's account of the events in order to learn the details that relate to the client's case. This is particularly important at the beginning of the interview when you have asked the client a general question about why the client came to see you. However, you are listening not only for an understanding of the client's legal problem, but also for the client's concerns. You need to understand what the client wants, as well as what the client needs. You may sometimes become aware of the client's attitude and concerns by observing the client as he or she is telling the story. Non-verbal cues like facial expressions and hand gestures can help you understand the client's concerns. Finally, you want to establish a rapport with the client, and to do that you have to give your full attention.

You can encourage the client to talk using two different listening techniques (sometimes described as "passive" and "active" listening). When your client is responding to an open-ended question and you want to promote the free flow of information, you can encourage him or her by using short phrases [*I see. Really? And then what happened?*] and by nodding or maintaining eye contact. Even "passive" listening requires that you remain involved and attentive. A more difficult technique but one that demonstrates empathy with the client's situation, is to respond to a statement by summarizing the content of the statement and the client's feelings about it. [*So you are furious at how the Hotel's carelessness disrupted your life?*] If a client can respond to your summary by saying "Yes, that's what I meant", then you have been successful in using that technique.

As you listen to the client's account and record the events, you may at the same time be considering the legal theories that the account suggests. At some point, you need to consider elements of the potential legal theories and ask questions eliciting facts that relate to those elements. Here you are seeking detail, wanting to verify certain facts and clarify others. To get these details, you will probably have to ask specific questions and be a more active questioner than you were in the initial part of the interview when the client was doing more of the talking.

At the end of the interview, the client will probably ask you for a legal opinion. If you are sufficiently familiar with the law, you may want to give a tentative assessment of the client's situation. But as a new associate, it is likely that you would need to do some further research into the client's case before you can provide a final assessment. Moreover, you may not have gotten all of the relevant factual information in the initial interview. Accordingly, a useful way to end the interview is to tell the client what you are prepared to do and tell the client what you would like the client to do. [*Mr. Starr, I am going to . . . . I would like you to . . ..*] You should also indicate a future date at which you will meet again or at which some event will take place. Finally, if the client wishes your representation and you wish to represent the client, you need to formalize an attorney-client relationship. That means you have the authority to act on the client's behalf and have reached an understanding as to fees.

V. THE MEMO TO THE FILE

AFTER A CLIENT INTERVIEW, lawyers often write a Memo to the File. This is different from the legal office memo described in Chapter 7. The Memo to the File summarizes:

- who the client is
- the nature of the client's problem as the client perceives it
- the client's goals
- the factual information the client gave
- what the lawyer told the client
- how things were left:

  the lawyer's tasks

  the client's tasks

the next steps

- the lawyer's preliminary case theory assessment

Here is an example of a Memo to the File written by an attorney who just completed an initial interview of John Starr, a new client.

Memo to the File: First Interview of JOHN STARR

Attorney Work Product

July 1, 20___

I met a new client, JOHN STARR, this morning. John is a 38-year-old computer programmer who is married to Jane Starr, a newly-elected member of the city council. John has recently returned to work after a three-month absence. He said he was unable to work during that period because of depression and nerves stemming from an incident before the election involving the shooting of his wife by a Hotel security guard at the Pennsylvania Deluxe Hotel. John spoke at length about the problems he and his wife have been having, focusing on a major disagreement over her continuing as a city council member. John believes the position is too public and that Jane could be in more danger. I remembered the incident when he called to make an appointment, and re-read the newspaper account before our interview. I was not sure for the first half of the interview whether John was coming to me because he wanted to institute divorce proceedings. But he says he loves his wife and is just concerned about her safety.

John came to see me because he is furious at the managers of the Pennsylvania Deluxe Hotel. He wants to sue them because they hired the security guard who wounded Jane. Jane's campaign headquarters was at the Hotel. John believes the Hotel did not adequately check the references of the security guard, and if they had, they would have discovered that Raymond Acker, the security guard, had a history of violent behavior. John seems less interested in the money he would get from the Hotel if he succeeds than in holding them accountable for the injury to Jane, for his shock, and for the continuing disruption of their normal lives.

As John described the facts, on Election Day, April 2, 2012, he and Alice Doe, Jane's great-aunt and former guardian, were watching the television election coverage at campaign headquarters at the Hotel. They were waiting for Jane to return to the Hotel after visiting her supporters in local campaign offices. At 9:30 p.m., Jane and several staff members arrived at the Hotel and Jane began walking towards the Hotel's entrance. When she was halfway there, Acker pulled out a gun and shot at Jane. John and Alice heard the shot on the television. The cameras showed Jane lying on the sidewalk, unconscious, in a pool of blood. John said they realized immediately after the shot was fired that Jane was seriously hurt. John collapsed and Alice became hysterical.

Jane was elected, recovered from her injuries in a month, and according to John, wants to put the whole thing behind her. But both John and Alice became depressed and anxious after the incident; Alice is still under a doctor's care for her nerves. Neither of them has any physical problems resulting from the incident and its aftermath, but John has just now felt able to return to work.

John seems to be largely recovered from his depression. But he still seems agitated about the incident and it is not clear whether he will be able to resume his work without any psychological after-effects. John and Jane also have a number of issues that they need to work out between them. Jane personally does not want to sue the Hotel. Acker has been charged with aggravated assault and will either be incarcerated or committed to an institution. That seems to give Jane a sense of closure.

I told John that, depending on the results of my research, I would represent him on a claim against the Hotel if he decided to sue them and told him my customary fee in cases like this. Since he personally was not injured by Acker, I told him he would not be able to sue the Hotel under general negligence theories. But one possible theory of recovery would be negligent infliction of emotional distress. I told John we would have to prove certain things to recover, and that we would have difficulty with some of them. First, we would have to prove that the Hotel was indeed negligent in hiring Acker. Then we would have to convince the court that seeing an event on television was the same as seeing it in person. I forgot to ask John if he and Alice actually saw Jane getting shot on television. It could make a difference if they heard the shot, but did not actually see her being shot. And I need to make sure that they saw live coverage as the event occurred, rather than a later taped version. Finally, since he did not suffer any physical injury, we would have to prove that his emotional distress from the incident was nonetheless severe.

I also strongly suggested to John that he and Jane should discuss his desire to sue the Hotel even though she opposed the idea. This conflict could create a major source of tension between them in addition to their already serious dispute about whether Jane should keep her seat on the city council. Their entire relationship could be at risk. Moreover, as a practical matter, if Jane refuses to cooperate, the success of the lawsuit would be unlikely.

We set up a second interview for July 14th. I said I would do some research on the cases in this state dealing with negligent infliction, and, in particular, how strict the courts have been in requiring that the plaintiff actually be present at the time of the injury. I also need to do some research on whether the plaintiff has to see the injury at the exact moment that it occurred. In addition, I would check the cases dealing with the severity of the psychological injury when there was no physical injury. I asked John to bring in his medical bills containing a diagnosis from the psychiatrist he has been seeing over the past three months. I asked him for the psychiatrist's name and phone number and got John's written permission to call him at a later time. In addition, I asked John if I could speak with Alice to get some additional information from her. He was not sure that she was in a strong enough condition to review the events, and also thought that Jane might have strong feelings about my speaking to Alice. John said he would get me a list of other people who worked in Jane's campaign headquarters and their phone numbers to see if they had any information about Acker.

John has a chance to succeed in his claim, but I will have a better sense of that after I do some research. He will be a credible witness and remembers many details of the shooting. I also need to get a clearer sense of Acker's history, and will try to find out if he has a conviction record. Finally, I think that John and Jane have a number of issues to work out which will bear upon whether John decides to go ahead with his suit.

Exercise 12-A

In this exercise, your teacher or one of your fellow students is going to play the role of Anne Atkins who is coming to your law office to see you for the first time. You got very little information over the phone. You only know that it is about an incident in which her parents hired a "deprogrammer" in an effort to convince her not to live on a communal farm run by an organization called the "Family of Truth and Light."

The person acting as Ms. Atkins will be provided with the facts. Before you interview her, think about the likely content of the interview and how you would like to structure it. Consider what questions you would need to ask to determine her objectives and the facts of her case.

After the interview, write a Memo to the File on Ms. Atkins' case.

CHAPTER 13

COUNSELING THE CLIENT

A LAWYER OFTEN ENGAGES in an on-going relationship with a client that involves counseling, either in person or by letter. Because our focus in this text is on writing, we have concentrated on counseling by letter. (See Chapter 14.) However, more often than not, a lawyer would not simply write a letter to a client without also meeting the client in person. An interpersonal meeting provides an opportunity for dialogue, client involvement, and client decision-making not possible in a letter, which is solely under the lawyer's control.

This brief chapter is not intended to deal with counseling in all its complexity. Rather, the chapter is intended to give you an introduction to the process of counseling.

I.   ROLES OF THE LAWYER AND THE CLIENT

ALTHOUGH BOTH THE LAWYER AND THE CLIENT have significant roles in decision-making, we noted in Chapter 12 on Interviewing that the client is the ultimate decision-maker. The Model Rules of Professional Conduct are explicit. Rule 1.2(a) states:

> A lawyer shall abide by a client's decision whether to settle a matter. In a criminal case, the lawyer shall abide by the client's decision, after consultation with the lawyer, as to a plea to be entered, whether to waive jury trial and whether the client will testify.

Moreover, according to that same rule, the lawyer shall abide by the client's decisions concerning the objectives of the representation and consult with the client as to the means by which they are pursued. The final decision is appropriately the client's, since the client is the one who has to live with the decision.

Yet lawyers also have a very important role in the process of decision-making. Clinicians have characterized this role in two ways: counseling and advice giving.[1] Counseling is primarily guidance and is part of virtually every lawyer-client interaction. A

---

[1]   Throughout this chapter, the authors have drawn on material from the following very helpful texts: David A. Binder et al., *Lawyers as Counselors: A Client-Centered Approach* (3rd ed. 2011); Robert M. Bastress and Joseph Harbaugh, *Interviewing, Counseling and Negotiation: Skills for Effective Representation* (1990); Marilyn J. Berger et al., *Pretrial Advocacy: Planning, Analysis & Strategy* (2007).

lawyer is counseling when the lawyer discusses with the client the client's objectives in light of the facts of the situation, suggests alternatives, identifies the pros and cons of each, helps the client evaluate the pros and cons of the alternatives, and finally, helps the client come to a decision that provides the best solution to the client's problem.

But clients may sometimes ask their lawyers for more. The client may want the lawyer's opinion about what the client should do. The client may simply say, "What would you do if you were me?" This is a question you may have asked a doctor at some point in your life. In responding to this question, lawyers must be aware both of their professional obligations and of the client's objectives and values, so as not to suggest a result based on the lawyer's own values, which could yield an unsatisfactory result for the client. On the other hand, this situation requires the lawyer to be a more complete counselor than one who only provides information about the law. On the lawyer's role as counselor, Rule 2.1 of the Model Rules states

> In representing a client, a lawyer shall exercise independent professional judgment and render candid advice. In rendering advice, a lawyer may refer not only to law but to other considerations such as moral, economic, social and political factors that may be relevant to the client's situation.

The Comment to Rule 2.1 goes even further:

> [2] Advice couched in narrowly legal terms may be of little value to a client, especially where practical considerations, such as cost or effects on other people, are predominant. Purely technical legal advice, therefore, can sometimes be inadequate.

Since nonlegal factors may be as important to the client's decision as legal factors, the lawyer must also make them a part of the counseling process and help the client give them appropriate weight in the client's decision-making. And to encourage frankness, the lawyer must be both objective and nonjudgmental. In all of these ways, the lawyer can help the client make a decision, while giving the client a sense of support and confidence.

II. PREPARATION FOR COUNSELING

A LAWYER MAY COUNSEL A CLIENT at various points in their relationship. Certainly, the lawyer is likely to counsel the client soon after the initial interview. But since the lawyer-client relationship may be an ongoing one, a lawyer and client may discuss strategy many times during the course of litigation or a transaction, or the lawyer may be asked to deal with a legal question tangential to, or completely unrelated to, the original problem.

In a transactional context. Preparing for and conducting a counseling session will be different where the matter deals not with litigation, but with a transaction, such as an employment contract. For that, the initial interview will likely focus on the client's objectives, any contractual terms upon which the parties may already have agreed, other potential terms of the contract, and any conflicts between the parties on the terms. The lawyer must become familiar with business practices in that area and the client's business situation in particular. The lawyer may then prepare a draft agreement, send it to the client for review, and discuss it more fully with the client at their next meeting. When the lawyer and the client have come up with a satisfactory revised draft, they will send that draft to the other party. Or the client may receive a draft agreement from the other party that would be the basis of a counseling session. Then the lawyer would negotiate with the other party, which may lead to further discussions with the client, further revisions, and, one hopes, a deal which meets the client's objectives.

In a litigation context. To get a sense of how to prepare for a counseling meeting with a client in a litigation context, however, assume that you are representing John Starr whose problem was discussed in Chapter 12 on Interviewing the Client. He saw his wife being shot by a security guard while watching the news on TV. At the end of your interview with him, you indicated that you were going to research certain issues relating to negligent infliction of emotional distress. You were also going to speak with John's psychiatrist as soon as John gave you permission. Finally, you were going to speak with Alice Doe if you got John's written permission, and to try to learn more about Raymond Acker's history. John, in turn, was going to provide you with copies of medical bills, his written consent to speak with his psychiatrist, and a list of people involved in the election campaign of John's wife, Jane Starr. John also said he would discuss the whole question of a lawsuit against the Hotel with Jane. You and John agreed to meet in two weeks.

To be prepared, you should plan the counseling meeting in advance. This means focusing again on the client's problem, researching the law as it relates to the problem, and investigating the facts as much as you can. Begin by thinking about what the client said in the interview that relates to the problem as the client sees it, and what the client would like to happen. Then consider the results of your research. In researching John Starr's problem, you have come upon the question of whether the plaintiff has to be physically present to satisfy the requirement that the shock results from a sensory and contemporaneous observance of the act. You are not sure whether watching the shooting on television is enough. If Pennsylvania courts strictly enforce the requirement of physical presence, you then need to decide if there is a Rule 11 problem in bringing a suit on Starr's behalf. You may conclude from reading the precedents that extending the law to cover Starr's situation would not be frivolous and that there would be no impediments to suit on that account.

As to the facts, John told you over the telephone that he spoke to Alice Doe, Jane Starr's great aunt and former guardian. Alice said she does not want to talk about the incident anymore and refuses to meet with you. You did speak, however, with John's psychiatrist. She said that John was seriously depressed following the shooting. He was unable to work for more than three months, had difficulty sleeping, and when he did sleep, often had nightmares about the shooting. He lost weight and became withdrawn. The psychiatrist also said that she believes he has fully recovered. His spirits are good, he is looking forward to returning to work, and he has regained his equilibrium. Finally, you checked the Hall of Records, which contains records of criminal convictions for the city and surrounding counties. You learned there that Raymond Acker was convicted of assault three years ago.

Ultimately, your goal in a counseling meeting is to help the client reach a decision that best meets the client's objectives and solves the client's problem. You may find it helpful to write out a plan, so that you and the client are less likely to forget important issues. First, identify the client's objectives. Then list the alternative courses of action, both legal and nonlegal, that have been suggested by your research, your investigation of the facts, and by the client's statements to you. For each of the alternatives, write the pros and cons to clarify, for yourself and your client, the probable legal and nonlegal consequences of each alternative. Then indicate the costs and the likelihood of success of each alternative. You may also want to make notes beside each alternative of questions for the client that can explore the client's feelings about the alternatives and consequences.

Before meeting with the client, think about how to present this material to the client and how the client is likely to respond. Try to anticipate problems. Finally, consider having either a written agenda or an outline to give the client near the start of the meeting.

But make sure that you have significant room to add comments or responses from the client. You do not want to give the client the impression that you have already decided what is best. You have a lot to hear from the client to clarify his objectives and to understand the relative importance to the client of various consequences.

Exercise 13-A

Based on the information in the lawyer's Memo to the File in John Starr's case in Chapter 12, write a plan for a counseling meeting with John Starr. This plan assumes that you have already developed your legal theory (you know what claims would be viable). Your plan could use the format below or another format that you find useful. For your guidance, one alternative has been completed.

JOHN STARR

<u>Objectives</u>: Possibly sue Pennsylvania Deluxe Hotel for negligent infliction of emotional distress based on the incident in which Starr viewed on TV his wife's being shot by Hotel security guard; hold Hotel accountable for pain, stress, disruption to his life (and his wife's life and great aunt's life?); get financial compensation (damages from Hotel); maintain strength of marriage to Jane Starr.

<u>Alternatives</u>:

COURSE OF ACTION #1—DO NOTHING FURTHER

    A. *Pros*

        — no future expenditure of time or money

        — alleviate stress on marriage due to different views on lawsuit between John and Jane

        — maybe put incident behind them and get on with their lives

        — no conflict with Alice [and therefore Jane]

    B. *Cons*

        — no resolution of John's anger at Hotel

        — no possibility of award of damages

    C. *To evaluate pros and cons, what questions would you ask John?*

        — How strongly does he feel about compensation (financial? psychological?) from the Hotel?

        — How strongly does Jane feel that she does not want him to file a lawsuit, that she wants to put the whole thing behind her?

— How strongly does Jane feel that Alice should not be
further distressed? Would refraining from suit end
the stress between John and Jane?

— How much of the stress is due to Jane's new position
(exposure to danger; position of importance)? [be
careful asking this]

COURSE OF ACTION #2—_____

A. *Pros*

B. *Cons*

C. *Questions*

COURSE OF ACTION #3—_____

A. *Pros*

B. *Cons*

C. *Questions*

III. STRUCTURE OF THE COUNSELING MEETING

BECAUSE A CLIENT IS LIKELY to want to quickly hear a
lawyer's assessment of the situation, the lawyer should spend little
time talking about general issues and begin the meeting by
focusing directly on the client's major concerns. Remember the
college senior who visited a doctor for recurrent headaches and
blurred vision. The senior's first question to a doctor who had done
some tests would probably be, "Am I all right?" The law client's
equivalent is probably to ask for a single, bottom line answer.
Often, there is no single answer. However, the lawyer can briefly
summarize the alternatives at the start of the meeting (with an
explanation of the legal basis for the suit), indicate the pros and
cons of each alternative, and then discuss them with the client in
what seems to be the order of importance to the client.

Before discussing the alternatives in detail, however, it would
be useful for the lawyer to summarize the client's objectives as the
lawyer understands them. In this way, if the lawyer is mistaken
about what the client really wants, the client can clarify the
situation at the start. And the lawyer does not waste time
emphasizing what turns out to be of minor importance to the client.

The lawyer's goal in the counseling session is to help the client
decide on a course of action that will best help the client achieve
his objectives. Clients should be encouraged to take an active role
in the process of considering alternatives. However, the meeting is
not likely to follow the orderly format of the lawyer's plan. Rather,

the client, like most people, is likely to bounce from one topic to another before exhausting all of the relevant considerations, go back and forth, and sometimes go in circles. The purpose of the lawyer's counseling plan is not to control the meeting, but to have a reminder of the major issues the lawyer and the client should discuss.

IV. TECHNIQUES OF COUNSELING

ALL OF THE INTERPERSONAL SKILLS important in interviewing the client are equally or even more important in counseling a client. The counseling meeting may very well be stressful for the client and the lawyer needs to be aware of the client's state of mind and concerns. The lawyer should also consider the particular client's level of sophistication and experience with similar problems, his aversion to risk, time pressures the client may be under, and the client's financial concerns. Finally, throughout the meeting, the lawyer's attention should be undivided.

The lawyer is in the best position to predict the legal consequences of each of the alternatives. The lawyer has researched the law and can explain the legal context. This means telling the client how courts have decided similar cases, indicating what issues of law remain unresolved, and suggesting how a jury or a court is likely to view the case. In Mr. Starr's case, for example, the lawyer would need to explain the elements of the tort and, in particular, the element of a sensory and contemporaneous observance of the accident, which Mr. Starr may have difficulty proving because he did not see the shooting in person. The client, however, is the most important predictor of the nonlegal consequences of each alternative. And the client is the only source of the client's values. Mr. Starr may feel that he will not have closure if he does not get some sort of satisfaction from the Hotel.

Throughout the counseling meeting, the lawyer can use different types of questions to advantage. (See Chapter 12.) Open-ended questions will enable the client to respond fully, to play an active role in the discussion and decision-making, and to encourage the client to explore a range of issues. Narrow questions can elicit specific information and clarification. A lawyer may help the client focus on certain issues by summarizing the client's responses in a way that gives the client an opportunity to confirm, clarify, or reject the summary. The lawyer may also need to point out to the client when the client's wishes are in conflict and help the client determine which objectives are paramount.

The client will want to know what the probability of success is for each alternative. Some lawyers suggest that stating the percentage likelihood of success is easier for a client to evaluate [*You have a 70% likelihood of success if you go to trial.*] than a general statement [*You have a pretty good chance to win if you go to trial.*] Another way to express the client's likelihood of success concretely is by stating the odds. For example, a lawyer might say that the client's likelihood of success at trial was 60–40 in favor. But above all, the lawyer must give candid advice. Although no one wishes to be the bearer of bad news, the client's best interest can only be served by the lawyer's honest assessment of the claim.[2]

Finally, a client may have difficulty making a decision and may ask the lawyer not for predictions about consequences, but what the lawyer would advise him to do. Under this circumstance, assuming the lawyer has had an opportunity to review the alternatives and consequences with the client and the client is still undecided, the lawyer should try to give an opinion based on the client's values. For example, the lawyer might say [*Since you feel strongly that the Hotel should have to admit its negligence in hiring the security guard and compensate you for the misery this has caused in your life, since your claim on the merits is fairly strong, and since your wife is willing to go along with your decision, then I think you should file a lawsuit against the Hotel.*] At a later stage in the proceedings of the same case, the lawyer might say [*Since you feel the Hotel has acknowledged its error by offering to settle the case and since you would now like to put an end to the whole incident, I think you should accept the Hotel's $30,000 offer of settlement even though you asked for a much higher amount in the complaint.*]

If the client then asks what you would personally do, you can give your opinion, indicating what the basis for that opinion is. For example, you could say [*Since I personally don't have any immediate financial need and since I don't mind taking a risk, I would wait before accepting the settlement offer.*] Where you feel you could not give a basis for an opinion, do not give one.

---

[2] Section 1 of the Comment to Rule 2.1 on Counseling states in part: In presenting advice, a lawyer endeavors to sustain the client's morale and may put advice in as acceptable a form as honesty permits. However, a lawyer should not be deterred from giving candid advice by the prospect that the advice will be unpalatable to the client.

Exercise 13-B

All of the students in the class completed a counseling plan for John Starr in Exercise 13-A. However, for purposes of this exercise, half of you will play the role of John Starr and half of you will play the role of Mr. Starr's attorney in a 20–30 minute counseling session.

Those of you acting as Mr. Starr should try to put yourself in his position, thinking about his objectives and state of mind. Those of you who are acting as attorney should think about your plan and about counseling techniques in general.

CHAPTER 14

LETTER WRITING

LETTERS MAY BE THE MOST FREQUENT TYPE of writing that lawyers do. Even lawyers whose practice does not require them to write interoffice memos or court documents write letters. In fact, Rule 1.4(a)(3) of the Model Rules of Professional Conduct requires a lawyer to "keep the client reasonably informed about the status of a matter," and clients are quick to complain when their lawyers do not communicate with them enough.

Like office memoranda, the letters that a lawyer writes to or on behalf of a client often require total familiarity with the law, the facts, and their interaction. But letter writing is also the most personal kind of writing a lawyer does and the most stylistically varied because, in letters, you always tailor tone and analysis to individual audiences and specific purposes. A lawyer who begins the letter-writing process by analyzing audience and purpose—the two primary elements of the rhetorical context—is thus in a good position to formulate effective writing strategies.

Given the importance of rhetorical context in letter writing, this chapter begins by discussing the elements that comprise it. Section II then examines five types of letters that lawyers commonly write:

- **client opinion or advice letters,**
- **status letters,**
- **letters to adversaries,**
- **letters to third parties, that is, to parties indirectly but significantly involved in a legal dispute, and**
- **transmittal letters, letters that accompany documents and provide instructions**

Finally, in section III, we discuss the increasing role **e-mail correspondence** plays in legal practice.

I.   ANALYZING THE RHETORICAL CONTEXT

A. Think About Your Audience

WHETHER WRITING MEMORANDA OR LETTERS, you must know your audience or you will be unable to develop effective strategies. But while the audience for law school memos is unvarying—legal practitioners with a generalist's knowledge of the subject matter—the audience for letters is varied and diverse. It is rarely adequate, therefore, to label your audience as "client" or "adversary." Rathe analyze your reader in detail.

A number of factors will help you draw a portrait of your reader.

- Consider your reader's legal experience. Is she a general practitioner, specialist, businesswoman aware of the laws affecting her business, or lay person?

- Determine your reader's level of education and language proficiency. Is he a professor, a high-school dropout, a fluent speaker of English?

- Take into account your reader's physical, mental, and emotional condition. Is your reader emotionally fragile, hostile, or physically debilitated?

- Note the age of reader. Are you communicating with a teenager or with a senior citizen?

Such an analysis will help you make a variety of rhetorical decisions. First, it will help you determine whether a letter is the most appropriate way to communicate with your client. In a number of situations, a phone call or a counseling session in your office may be preferable. Certainly if the client is distraught, personal communication is more suitable. If the matter is complicated or the consequences particularly significant, you would probably want to meet with the client in person to make sure that your client fully understands your analysis and the client's options. And under any circumstances, a personal meeting provides an opportunity for interaction, listening, and discussion that a letter or email cannot provide.

Nevertheless, there are a number of instances where lawyers would write letters to clients giving an opinion or advice.

- Business clients often want letters giving legal advice regarding a transaction.

- A client may be unable to come to the lawyer's office because of distance or infirmity.

- The lawyer may be unable to reach the client by phone.

- A lawyer may want to write to a client in advance of a counseling meeting to set out some issues that will be the basis of their discussion.

- A client may find it helpful to receive a follow-up letter summarizing the options discussed at a counseling meeting so that the client can review the options at leisure.

If a letter or email is in order, an audience analysis will also help you find the level of analysis and detail that is appropriate for your reader. It will help you determine whether you can use terms of art or must stick to plain English. In addition, it will help you make decisions about the kind of personal interaction that is appropriate. Although young lawyers worry that the human touch might make them appear unprofessional, responding to a client's implicit or explicit worries is central to establishing rapport. Clients often need and appreciate a few words of sympathy, reassurance, explanation, and good humor and may be put off by a technocrat.

Of course, the business of audience analysis is complicated by the fact that lawyers often write for multiple audiences. For example, a letter from a defense attorney to an elderly victim of an accident might be read by the attorney's supervisor, the victim's family, the victim's family lawyer, the court, and even the public-at-large

When you have multiple audiences, you probably want to target your strategies at your primary reader—or at the middle range of possible readers. When, however, your audiences have vastly different backgrounds, consider drafting different letters for each or, if appropriate, include your office memorandum for those who might need a more detailed understanding of the dispute. Finally, remember that some letters are read from the file long after they are written. Thus all your correspondence should be accurate and ethical. Although courts rarely review letters, it is wise to write letters as if review was inevitable.

B. Determine the Letter's Purpose

Decisions about content and tone do not depend solely on audience assessment. Equally important is the purpose of the letter. Indeed sometimes your letters to a single individual will differ in tone or content because the purpose of each letter is different. A short note informing a client about a meeting the attorney had with a witness may be, for example, more informal than a letter setting out the client's legal options.

Most letters have at least one of three primary purposes:

- to counsel a client about available options

- to persuade someone to a course of action, or

- to inform someone of something.

The "counseling" category includes letters advising clients about their best legal options. The "persuasive" category includes letters negotiating settlements or letters requesting favors or information. Within the "informative" category fall letters notifying a party of a legal development, letters describing an event, letters analyzing a legal problem, letters denying a request, or letters giving instructions.

Frequently, letters have more than one primary purpose. For example, one common client letter, the advice letter, offers both a general analysis of the client's legal problem and a description of the advantages and disadvantages of each of the client's legal alternatives.

In addition to these primary purposes, an advice letter may also have a host of secondary goals:

- to establish rapport

- to check facts

- to request directions as to how to proceed

- to establish a time-frame for response

Sometimes all these goals work in harmony. Your analysis of the client's problem informs your discussion of the client's alternatives. Sometimes, however, a letter has conflicting purposes. Although you think the claim is strong on the merits, you feel obligated to warn the client about the risk, stress, expense, and prolonged nature of a court trial. Prioritizing and balancing primary, secondary, and conflicting purposes are part of the art of letter writing. You need to organize your document so that your highest priorities receive the greatest stress.

C. Analyze Available Writing Strategies

Once you have examined your audience and purpose, think about what kind of approach would best achieve your purpose with that audience. In other words, you develop a rhetorical strategy. There are three central elements to consider in developing a strategy: persona and tone, treatment of law and facts, and organizational concerns.

1. Writer's Persona and Tone

Because readers form impressions of their lawyers largely on the basis of their letters, it is a good idea to think about how you want to appear to your reader, that is, the image you want to project. In legal writing, your image is limited by notions of professional decorum. Most lawyers' letters are courteous, clear, reasonable, and concise. They avoid invective, exaggeration, sarcasm: displays of anger or contempt are unprofessional and counterproductive. Yet not all legal correspondence should sound the same either. For example, a probate lawyer for a grieving widow might adopt the tone of a "family solicitor"—who is reliable, comforting, and experienced—while a prosecutor writing to a hostile witness might want to adopt a brisk, no-nonsense, authoritative tone.

Tone is achieved partly by the formality of diction and grammar. A letter to a colleague, a long-time client, or a young adult might be informal in tone. You might well use first names in the salutation and signature. Contractions and personal pronouns would be permissible. In fact, personal pronouns are often used to establish solidarity and rapport with clients. Simply by using the first person plural, as in "we need to review your options here," you identify with your reader and establish rapport. Another popular technique is to use the second person singular, as in "you asked me to research possible claims against AC Company." By directly addressing the reader, you bring her into the flow of discourse. Many clients appreciated a "you centered" letter.

Other letters require greater distance and formality. A letter to a business client might resemble an office memorandum in format and tone. To an elderly "old-world" client who needs reassurance, a discursive, leisurely letter might be the most effective: "I trust your recovery will proceed speedily as you continue in the care of your doctors and wife. Meanwhile, we are striving to reach a prompt and equitable resolution in your action against Kent City Taxis and, indeed, have made some progress."

As suggested by the above examples, variations in tone are determined in part by sentence length and diction. A discursive, leisurely letter has a goodly share of long sentences with parallel, coordinate clauses, while a "bottom-line" letter might be short and blunt. But even more important than sentence length is word choice. Good advocates are sensitive to connotation. A prosecutor would say "informant" rather than "snitch" because it has a more favorable connotation. For dramatic effect, he might describe an arsonist's work as an "inferno" rather than a "fire." Defense counsel might refer to a "head-on collision" as a "car accident" to distance the event and describe the victim as "injured" rather than "paralyzed."

Juxtaposition is another powerful way to communicate attitude. By yoking together two antithetical statements, for example, you can express incredulity without actually stating it: "You said the check was in the mail. I have not received it." Or, if you juxtapose bad news with an acceptable alternative, you demonstrate empathy and alleviate your client's disappointment.

Diplomacy is needed even with adversaries, especially when the relationship between attorneys is likely to be long term. Lawyers must be able to confront each other as politely as they do forcefully if they are to serve their clients well. Framing requests or denials of requests indirectly is one important way attorneys can be both civil and effective. For instance, requests framed as orders are often perceived as threatening and hostile, and generate resistance rather than acquiescence: "You must provide us with this information before our next meeting." If this directive is framed indirectly, as a question or declarative statement, it is more likely to achieve the results desired: "Can you provide us with this information in time for us to review it before our next meeting?" A declarative statement is also more effective "We would welcome an opportunity to review this information before our next meeting."

Refusing a demand or request also requires tact. Avoid abruptness. Instead, give reasons why you cannot perform the requested act: "The pressure of work makes it unlikely we can compile the information you want in time for our next meeting."

2. Tailor Your Treatment of Law and Facts to Your Audience

A general desire to present a reader with a comprehensive legal analysis must be balanced against your audience and purpose. For example, in an advice letter, a detailed analysis of authority is probably appropriate if you are writing to a corporation's in-house counsel. Yet many lay clients would be confused by this kind of in-depth analysis and would profit more from a simple application of law to facts. Sometimes, even if your audience has the intellectual sophistication to understand a comprehensive analysis, you would nonetheless be wise to keep your analysis of the issues short—your reader may be suffering under time constraints, for example. Finally, your audience and purpose should determine how thorough your letter should be. When writing to an adversary, for instance, you must make a strategic decision about how much of the facts and your research you wish to share.

3. Choose an Effective Organization

Up to a point, your organization of material in a letter is governed by the conventions of the genre. An opinion letter, for example, has a format somewhat similar to an office memorandum. Yet within these confines, there are many organizational decisions to make.

In letters, as in memos, introductory paragraphs usually define the issues and frequently provide a roadmap informing the reader of the document's organization. Yet many letter writers regard introductory paragraphs as an equally important opportunity to develop a relationship with the reader. Early rapport makes the reader more receptive to later more complicated matters. Thus, the opening sentences might inquire after an injured client's medical progress, acknowledge a harried reader's hectic schedule, or appeal to a hostile reader's sense of fair play. In taking the time to show your concern, you may be able to cement relationships or secure cooperation (but do not overplay this personal side and become chatty).

Strategy is behind a number of other organizational decisions. Should you announce your conclusion up front or lay the groundwork for it first? Generally, readers are anxious to know your conclusion, and thus stating it early is advisable. Should you put your reader on the defensive by opening with a warning or threat, or should you begin with the events that underline the threat? An analysis of the rhetorical situation will help you answer these questions.

II. TYPES OF LAWYER LETTERS

A. Opinion or Advice Letters

WHEN A LAWYER COMMUNICATES her legal analysis and advice to a client, she is writing either a formal opinion letter or an advice letter. A written opinion letter is a formal expression of your belief that a specific course of action is or is not legal, and it most typically involves financial transactions. It is not a guarantee of legal rights, however; it is restricted to its jurisdiction, to the law at the time the letter was written, and to its facts. Moreover, it usually contains a caveat testifying to these limitations. Nonetheless, because clients place great reliance on them, and because opinion letters are the grounds of malpractice actions when they fail to meet established standards, law firms often limit the number of attorneys who can issue opinions on their behalf.

In contrast, advice letters are written by most attorneys. These letters are more informal evaluations of the relative merits of the client's case and of its probable outcome. They are meant to guide clients in decision-making. Indeed, Rule 1.4(b) of the Model Rules of Professional Conduct requires a lawyer to explain "a matter to the extent reasonably necessary to permit the client to make informed decisions regarding the representation."

Because advice letters are more frequently written than opinion letters, we focus on them here. Be aware, however, that advice letters also open an attorney to liability, as well as protect her from it. When you carefully research, analyze, write about a client's legal problem, you are engaged in professional conduct

An advice letter opens with an introductory paragraph that states the issue and conclusion. Often it then summarizes the facts that gave rise to the dispute. The facts are followed by an explanation and application of the law, and this in turn leads to a discussion of the alternatives. Finally, the closing paragraph indicates the next step in the proceedings.

Some attorneys separate these sections with headings, especially when the subject matter is complex or the letter is long. Many times, however, section headings are unnecessary and off-putting, especially when you are writing to a lay client about a relatively uncomplicated matter. Topic sentences and unified paragraphs are good substitutes for section headings in this situation.

1.   The Salutation and Introductory Paragraph

Most lawyers' letter begin formally—with the conventional and professional "Dear Mr. Doe or Mrs. or Dr. or Professor." However, once you have gotten to know your reader well, you may want to adopt a more informal style and address the reader by his first name—"Dear John"—in order to promote a sense of rapport.

After the salutation, the introductory paragraph should, at a minimum, articulate the question that your client asked and that your letter analyzes and answers. The question may be two-sided, involving first, an inquiry into the client's legal position, and second, an inquiry into the legal alternatives.

Frequently your introductory paragraph also provides an answer to the question you pose. Not only are many clients made anxious and annoyed by having to wait for a conclusion in which they have a stake, but many find they can concentrate on the analysis more easily when they know where the discussion is heading. Some few attorneys do defer the conclusion until after the analysis, especially when the legal outcome is unfavorable. They hope their discussion will make the disappointing conclusion understandable, if not entirely palatable. The general consensus seems to be, however, to summarize your conclusion early in the letter—but be careful to indicate your conclusion is an opinion, cogent and reasoned, but not definitive.

Above and beyond framing and answering the issue, most introductory paragraphs also try to set a tone conducive to a good working relationship. Sometimes this is achieved by explicitly sympathizing with your reader: "I know you've been anxious about finding grounds for an appeal." Often you can tie your legal conclusion to an expression of solidarity or sympathy: "I know this has been a difficult time for you, so I am pleased to report that your claim is strong."

The paragraph below begins an attorney's advice letter about a widower's claim against a mental hospital for negligently failing to prevent his wife's suicide while she was a patient there. The widower is a thirty-five-year old architect who is still recovering from his wife's protracted mental illness and eventual suicide.

February 24, ____

Mr. John Braun
114 Garden Place
Heights City, Missouri 1230 _____

Re: Park Crest Hospital

Dear Mr. Braun:

As I promised when we met a few weeks ago, I have researched the grounds for a suit against Park Crest Hospital for its negligent care of your wife. I believe you have a strong chance of winning your case if we went to trial, but another option is to work towards a settlement. There are advantages and disadvantages to these alternatives that I will outline after reviewing both the facts of your case and the law that governs them.

---

2. The Facts

Most advice letters include a summary of the facts similar to that in an office memorandum. This account should be objective, narrated chronologically or topically, and concisely focused on the legally relevant facts. In addition, to protect yourself from liability in the event that other material facts become known at a later date, make it clear in your statement that your opinion is based on the facts stated and might change if you learn additional information. This disclaimer does not absolve you, however, of the responsibility of checking and rechecking the facts before you write your advice letter.

Because my analysis of your suit is based on the facts as stated, it might change if my summary is inaccurate. I would therefore appreciate it if you read the following account for accuracy and completeness and report any mistakes or omissions.

On June 21, ____, the day after her second attempt at suicide, your wife, Rachel Braun, voluntarily checked herself into Park Crest Hospital. Park Crest is a private hospital that specializes in the treatment of mental disorders. After she was admitted, Dr. Richmond, the attending physician, diagnosed Ms. Braun as severely depressed with suicidal tendencies. He ordered that she be monitored closely for any suicide attempt and prescribed a program of anti-depressants and psychotherapy.

For the first 18 days of her hospitalization, your wife was placed on accompany status in a ward for acutely ill patients. Access to this ward was restricted. Hospital personnel could enter and exit the ward only through locked elevator and stairway doors. Visitors could come only once every two weeks. Nurses checked on patients every 20 minutes.

At the end of this period, Dr. Richmond noted in your wife's chart that she showed good response to her treatment. Her mood was brighter, and she seemed less preoccupied and withdrawn. Because of her improved condition, he transferred her to an open ward. Patients on an open ward could leave their rooms and congregate in the halls and lounges. Nurses were present on the ward at all times. Twelve nurses worked 3 eight-hour shifts, taking care of a total of 23 patients.

For the next ten days, your wife continued to improve. She began, and appeared to enjoy, occupational therapy. She socialized with other patients. Dr. Richmond then told her she was well enough to go home. That night, two days before her scheduled release, Ms. Braun was agitated. The nurse noted in her chart that she found Ms. Braun weeping. When the nurse questioned her, Ms. Braun expressed worry about whether she could manage in the "real" world. In response, the nurse administered sleep medication, for which the doctor had left an "as needed" order. The nurse also noted that a visitor, the spouse of another patient, had reported seeing Ms. Braun earlier that day swallowing pills taken from her pocket.

There is nothing in Ms. Braun's chart indicating that any physician acknowledged or responded to these observations of your wife's increasingly disturbed condition. The release order was not rescinded. On her last night at the hospital, the nurses checked your wife every two hours, noting she was sleeping heavily and her breathing was depressed. At 6:30 A.M., your wife was found in her bed, dead of a self-administered overdose of sleeping pills. Ms. Braun had not been searched for contraband when she was first admitted to the hospital, or at any other time.

3. Legal Analysis

Like the discussion section in a memorandum, the analysis section of an advice letter should be organized around the issues. Where there are many issues or subissues, you may want to begin this section with a roadmap orienting your reader to your organization.

As discussed in Part I of this chapter, your analysis of each issue must be tailored to your audience. At a minimum, you want to apply the law to the facts and come to a conclusion. Occasionally, when your client has some legal background or special need for a full discussion, you might decide to provide a full review of legal authority (citing both statutes and cases). Do not go into an extensive analysis of a point if the bottom line is undisputed, however.

Discussion of legal authority tends to be less extensive in letters than in memos. Remember you are writing to a layperson, not a lawyer. Do not use legalese, case analysis, or analogies or distinctions as you do in law school. Many lawyers, however, do not stint their discussion of the relative merits of each party's claims and defenses. Your client will be especially interested in learning the legal arguments supporting his side and wiser for learning those of his opponent. Your client cannot make an informed decision without this kind of full coverage.

> Park Crest's liability for your wife's suicide depends on whether it used such reasonable care as her known mental condition required. The hospital's duty is proportionate to the patient's needs. In examining a hospital's conduct, courts look at the propriety of the medical judgment and at the sufficiency of the nonmedical ministerial care. Park Crest probably breached both duties of care.
>
> The propriety of Park Crest's medical judgment is measured against the skill and learning ordinarily used under the same or similar circumstances by members of the medical profession. Medical judgment includes determining the appropriate level of supervision. The hospital's initial care of Ms. Braun seems to meet this test. At intake she was properly diagnosed and treated. It was appropriate to place her on a closed ward while she was acutely depressed and it was appropriate to move her to an open ward as she improved. Indeed modern psychiatric theory dictates that patients receive as much freedom as is consistent with their safety. Normal interaction is regarded as the best way of restoring the confidence necessary to mental health. Nonetheless, the hospital was negligent in failing to search for contraband at intake and for failing to address, or even to acknowledge, the developing depression the R.N. noted in your wife's medical chart.

> A hospital, however, is not an insurer of a patient's safety. Given that psychiatry is an inexact science and that treatment involves taking calculated risks in the hope that increasing freedom will help the patient, Park Crest will claim it exercised reasonable care in gradually easing her supervision. The absence of any notation that Ms. Braun's depression continued past the restless night supports its contention that it could not have reasonably anticipated Ms. Braun's suicide. However, given your wife's mental history, Park Crest's failure to follow up on the nurse's observations, especially when she noted that Ms. Braun might have been in possession of her own supply of drugs, is a breach of the hospital's duty to safeguard her.
>
> An important issue is whether the hospital's nonmedical ministerial care was sufficient, which is determined by a standard of ordinary care, including the regularity of observation, the number of nurses in attendance, and the safety of the premises. The hospital here cannot be faulted for insufficient staffing or dangerous conditions. The nursing staff could be faulted, however, for its failure to search and seize contraband from your wife. It might also be liable for failing to notify a physician of your wife's depressed breathing, since the nurses had not administered any sleeping medication and depressed breathing is often a symptom of over-medication.

4. Recommendations to the Client

Your legal analysis prepares for your recommendations. Begin by explaining the client's various alternatives—often to file a lawsuit, to begin negotiations, or to suggest defenses. Your job sometimes involves coming up with a plan to protect someone from liability. You may suggest to an employer, for example, that it implement procedures for sexual harassment complaints to prevent future liability. After describing your proposals or a client's alternatives, outline the advantages and disadvantages of each suggestion. If the client has pressed you for an opinion on what he should do, indicate which you think is the best course of action in light of the client's objectives. Remember, however, that the decision about how to proceed is your client's, and it is inappropriate to push too hard for any particular course of action. Thus you should conclude this section by requesting instructions or suggesting that meeting in person may be appropriate to determine the next steps.

> Under either test, therefore, a jury might well find Park Crest breached its duty of care. Were we to go to trial, it is possible you would win substantial monetary relief. However, trials are costly, time-consuming, and ultimately unpredictable. Thus I think you should also consider pursuing an out-of-court settlement with Park Crest. Although negotiations tend to result in lower awards, they have two primary advantages. First, they would save you from the continuing

> stress that will undoubtedly be encountered by litigating your claim. Second, negotiations are likely to succeed. It is in the hospital's interest to avoid the negative publicity that would accompany a trial, and additionally, a settlement is likely to cost both parties less in legal fees and damages than a lawsuit. Thus it is likely we can bring Park Crest to the bargaining table.

5. Closing Paragraph

Your closing paragraph provides you with a second opportunity to demonstrate your personal concern and goodwill. Reiterate, for example, your willingness to be of service. It is also the paragraph in which you inform the client of the next step in the proceedings. If the next step must be taken within a specified time period, be certain your reader is aware of it. "Very truly yours" or "Yours sincerely" are the traditional complimentary closings.

> I suggest we meet to discuss these options, their risks, and their advantages so that you can make a thoroughly informed decision. You also need to phone about any corrections or additions you think need to be made to the statement of facts. Once you have decided how to proceed, we can discuss the next step in the process of compensating you for your tragic loss.
>
> Very truly yours,
> Jane Turner

One final reminder: client letters almost always need to be rewritten. Even if you analyzed the rhetorical situation before you began your letter, writers tend to use first drafts to work through their own thinking. This is natural. Until the subject matter is clear to you, it is difficult to clarify it for someone else. By the second draft, however, you should be writing for the reader, looking for an organization and tone appropriate for just that audience.

Exercise 14-A

Critique each of the following excerpts from letters to Mr. John Starr concerning possible action against the Pennsylvania Deluxe Hotel for negligent infliction of emotional distress. See Exercise 6-A(2) on pp. 161–162.

1. Sample Openings

Do the following introductory paragraphs effectively establish rapport, provide an organizational roadmap, and summarize options?

a.   Dear Mr. Starr:

After carefully scrutinizing the facts of your situation and the relevant laws and cases, I have concluded there is no question that your reasons for wanting to sue Pennsylvania Deluxe Hotel are well founded. However, the courts take many things into consideration when making such decisions. The facts of your case are such that a jury could conceivably find either way on whether or not the Hotel negligently inflicted emotional distress. There are a number of courses of action we can take at this point, including taking your case to court or seeking a settlement. It is my opinion that we first try the latter, to resolve the situation privately by seeking from the Hotel a public acknowledgment of wrongdoing and an apology, and perhaps some compensatory damages. I will explain why I have come to this conclusion after I review the facts of your case and Pennsylvania law pertaining to your situation.

b.   Dear Mr. Starr:

I would like for us to meet on April 30, at 4:00 p.m. in order to discuss your options in dealing with this matter. Before coming to the meeting, I would like you to have an understanding of how the law has treated situations similar to yours.

2.   Sample Presentation of Law

Do these paragraphs clearly communicate the law in terms that are ethical and accurate and that a lay person could understand? Does the attorney appropriately apply the law to the client's circumstances?

To recover for negligent infliction of emotional distress in this state, we have to prove that you are closely related to the victim, that the your distress was severe, that your shock resulted from a single identifiable traumatic event, and that you were near the scene of the accident and that your shock resulted from a sensory and contemporaneous observance of the accident.

We will have no trouble proving the first three elements, although it would strengthen our case if you continued to refrain from working to underscore the severity of your injury. The last requirement is problematic, however. We would have to convince the court that seeing a live action event on TV is the same as seeing it in person. In *Trask v. Vincent,* this prong was not satisfied when plaintiff was in a phone booth with her back to the sidewalk when her husband was floored by a falling window box. She emerged two minutes after the incident to find a crowd around her husband, who was lying on the pavement in a pool of blood. Since you were not even as near the scene as the *Trask* plaintiff, and similarly failed to witness the actual shooting, we may have trouble proving your case.

3. **Sample Presentation of Options**

Do the following paragraphs effectively consider the non-legal implications of each option and convincingly communicate that the decision on how to proceed is the client's?

It may be in your best interest to try to talk with your wife and great aunt before you seek a legal remedy since your aunt's health and your marriage might suffer if you proceed against their wishes. Both parties seem to want to put the event behind them. Moreover, were you to litigate, there is a real chance you could lose since you were not at the scene of the shooting.

Another less stressful option is settlement talks. Since you seem most interested in holding the Hotel accountable for its negligence, we could seek a public statement of accountability and a public apology instead of compensatory damages, though we could ask for some out-of-pocket reimbursement if you wish it. Whatever course of action you decide upon, I will support absolutely.

The ultimate decision on how to proceed is yours and yours alone. Please do not hesitate to call me if you have any questions. I am available to help you. When you've decided what to do, we can discuss the specifics of what the next steps will be.

Exercise 14-B

1. *You are an attorney for Mr. Timothy S. Eliot. Read the following facts and cases. Make an outline of the law relating to covenants not to compete. Then edit the letter to Mr. Eliot that follows the case summaries.*

Facts

Your client, Mr. Eliot, has been a salesperson for Kid-Vid Corporation, which manufactures and sells electronic toys like video games, robots, computers, etc. He is fifty years old, married, has two children (one in college, one in high school), and lives in a four-bedroom house in a suburb of New York City.

Mr. Eliot has been with Kid-Vid for ten years. He sells the Kid-Vid line to department stores and toy store chains all over the country, and he is well known and well respected by the store buyers. Last year he earned $75,000 in salary and commissions. Mr. Eliot has no written employment agreement with Kid-Vid and the company has been having financial problems. Thus, he is looking for a new job.

Mr. Eliot knows from preliminary conversations with other toy companies that finding a good position will be difficult. His age and experience are actually working against him. The big companies usually hire youngsters whom they can train and pay peanuts. Mr. Eliot is set in his ways—which, by the way, work—and he has a family to support. On the other hand, it is time to find something new. Mr. Eliot could wind up on the street.

Recently, Mr. Eliot had lunch with the CEO of Toydyno, Ms. Baer. Toydyno has a novel product, the Knobot. Knobots are amazingly dexterous and articulate robots that can be programmed to play with children. Toydyno wants experienced, savvy, aggressive sales people to put Knobots into toy departments, where Mr. Eliot already has extensive contacts. It also wants salespersons to develop contacts in bookstores, camera shops, and sporting good stores. It doesn't have time to train novices. At lunch, Ms. Baer said she thought Mr. Eliot fit the bill and suggested he come to work for Toydyno. However, one of the terms in the Toydyno contract concerns a covenant not to compete. The covenant provides that if the Employee leaves for any reason,

1) The Employee is prohibited from

    a) selling electronic toys to anyone anywhere,

    b) using lists of customers who buy Knobots from Toydyno for resale to the public, and

    c) disclosing the "computer source codes," which make the Knobots do what they do, or disclosing the Employer's technique for making the "flange-hinges," which give the Knobots digital flexibility.

2) The Employee must turn over all customer lists in his possession. The lists are not merely of the names of customers. They also will include pertinent data regarding credit, merchandise turnover, buying patterns, volume of sales, and merchandise returns. The data will have been gathered by Toydyno personnel, including Employee.

Mr. Eliot has asked you to research this issue in New York and determine if, and to what extent, the courts are likely to enforce such a covenant. He wants to know whether he should negotiate any of the terms of the covenant not to compete.

Case Law

Columbia Ribbon & Carbon Manufacturing Co. v. A-1-A Corp.,
369 N.E.2d 4 (N.Y. 1977)

Defendant Trecker was employed by Columbia Ribbon as a salesman for several years. He signed an employment contract with the following restrictive covenant:

1. The employee will not disclose to any person or firm the names or addresses of any customers or prospective customers of the company.

2. The employee will not, for a period of twenty-four months after the termination of his employment, sell or deliver any goods of the kind sold by the company within any territory to which he was assigned during the last twenty-four months prior to termination.

After Trecker was demoted, he terminated his employment with Columbia Ribbon and took a job with a competitor, A-1-A Corporation. Columbia then sued to enforce the terms of the covenant.

In determining whether a salesman is bound in whole or in part by a covenant not to compete with an employer after termination of employment, the court said that restrictive covenants are disfavored in the law. Powerful public policy considerations militate against depriving a person of his or her livelihood. Thus restrictive covenants are enforced only if they are limited in time and geography, and then only to the extent necessary to protect the employer from unfair competition which stems from the employee's use or disclosure of trade secrets or confidential customer lists. If, however, the employee's services are truly unique or extraordinary, and not merely valuable to the employer, a court will enforce a covenant even if trade secrets are not involved.

The court said that the broad sweeping language of the covenant in this case had no limitations keyed to uniqueness, trade secrets, confidentiality, or even competitive unfairness. The affidavits made no showing that any secret information was disclosed, that Trecker performed any but commonplace services (his work did not require the highly developed skills of learned professionals like doctors or lawyers), or that any business was lost. Moreover, nothing in the purely conclusory affidavits by Columbia contravened the points in Trecker's own affidavit that no trade secrets had been involved in his employment, that he had taken possession of no customer lists, and that all customers were publicly known, or obtainable from an outside source.

Accordingly, Columbia's showing was insufficient to defeat summary judgment. The court therefore affirmed the order below denying enforcement.

Greenwich Mills Co. v. Barrie House Coffee Co.,
459 N.Y.S.2d 454 (App. Div. 1983)

Three salesmen worked for Greenwich Mills, a company that sold coffee, tea, and related products to hotels, restaurants, and stores. When they were hired, they entered into a restrictive covenant with Greenwich Mills. Eventually they left Greenwich Mills and began working for Barrie House, which engaged in a similar business. Their former employer, Greenwich Mills, sought an injunction to uphold the covenant.

In denying Barrie House's motion for summary judgment, the court held that restrictive covenants will not be enforced absent trade secrets or special circumstances, but that knowledge of the precise blends of coffee that various customers of their former employer preferred might be considered a trade secret. Information on the technology and manufacturing process of a product that is unique is a trade secret. The court further stated that any trade secret through which a party might gain an unfair advantage would be sufficient to make a covenant enforceable if it is reasonable in time and area and bans solicitation of former customers rather than a total ban on competition. The court said a trial was necessary to determine whether there were trade secrets justifying an apparently reasonable one year ban on solicitation of Greenwich Mills customers.

Scott Paper Co. v. John J. Finnegan Jr.,
476 N.Y.S.2d 316 (App. Div. 1984)

A regional sales manager signed a restrictive covenant with Scott Paper Company, a paper manufacturer. The covenant provided that the manager would not engage in any work that involved confidential information obtained at Scott within 150 miles of the manager's last assignment for a period of not less than six nor more than twenty-four months. When the manager left, the paper manufacturer sought to enjoin him from using this information.

The court said that confidential information includes any information relating to the company which is not known to the general public, such as pricing and promotional information, customer preference data and buying records, customer lists, product sales records, market surveys and marketing plans, and other business information. The court did not enforce this covenant not to compete, however, because most of this information was outdated or generally known within the industry.

Quandt's Wholesale Distributors Inc. v. Giardino,
448 N.Y.S.2d 809 (App. Div. 1982)

Quandt, a distributor of restaurant food, had salesman Giardino sign a restrictive covenant that provided that for six months following termination of his employment, he would not compete with Quandt in the area to which he had been assigned.

The court held the distributor's six-month, three-county restrictive covenant was reasonable. However, plaintiff distributor made no showing concerning the unfair competition criteria mentioned in *Columbia Ribbon*. Customer names were readily available from directories. Giardino was well-trained and effective, but his services were not unique. Nor had plaintiff suffered an irreparable injury. In fact, five weeks after Giardino left, the sales on his route were greater than what they had been when Giardino left. Therefore, the court held that the restrictive covenant was invalid.

In editing the following letter, consider the following:

1) the audience for the document,

2) the purpose of the document, and

3) the writing techniques adopted to serve that audience and that purpose.

More specifically, assess

- the effectiveness of the writer's tone, particularly in the introductory and concluding paragraphs,

- the strategy, logic, and clarity of the writer's organization,

- the appropriateness of the letter's length, comprehensiveness, and use of supporting legal authority, and

- the need for an objective or adversarial recitation of the facts.

Dear Mr. Eliot,

This letter gives you my opinion of how a New York court would rule on the restrictive covenant contained in your prospective employment contract at this moment in time. I cannot guarantee the court will agree with my analysis. In addition, the law upon which I am basing my analysis is always subject to change by the courts or possibly the legislature. Furthermore, I have written this letter for your benefit only and not for the benefit of third parties. The letter is not to be used for any purpose other than for your information. Finally, I have based my opinion in part on the facts that you gave me at our meeting. If you misstated them then, or have since remembered facts, please let me know since a change in facts might change my analysis.

In determining whether a covenant not to compete is reasonable, courts examine a number of factors. First, an employer has a legitimate interest in enforcing a restrictive covenant not to compete in order to protect himself from unfair competition resulting from the loss of an employee's unique services. Although an employee's extraordinary services can justify the enforceability of a covenant not to compete, enforcement usually is not granted merely on the basis of the uniqueness of the employee's services. Reasonable time and geographic restrictions must be set forth in a covenant in order for it to be enforceable. In *Quandt*, a covenant not to compete that contained reasonable time and territory limitations was not enforced because the salesperson's duties were not extraordinary in nature. The services of an employee who acts merely in the capacity of an effective and well-trained salesperson may be valuable but are not so unique that their loss would result in irreparable damage or unfair competition to the employer. *Quandt's Wholesale Distrib. v. Giardino*, 448 N.Y.S.2d 809, 810 (App. Div. 1982). In fact, in *Quandt*, the sales in the employee's territory were equal if not greater once he terminated his employment.

The salesperson being hired by Toydyno will be expected to solicit new customers to promote the Knobots. However, this is not an extraordinary job requirement that any salesperson would not be expected or able to fulfill. The anticipated duties of this salesperson are not so unique that performance by another individual would cause Toydyno to incur a loss.

Although an employee's skills may not be classified as unique, a restrictive covenant may be enforced in order to prevent the use or disclosure of confidential customer information or trade secrets. It is highly likely that the "source codes" and the technique for making "flange-hinges" would be considered trade secrets. Not only is this information highly technical and probably the result of long hours of costly research, but it is so intrinsically related to the manufacture of the Knobot that its exploitation would cause Toydyno considerable harm. Therefore, it is likely that a court would uphold the provision of the covenant that prohibits you from disclosing this information.

The customer lists that you will be privy to may also be construed as confidential since they will contain business information that might give you an unfair competitive advantage. In *Scott Paper Co. v. Finnegan*, 476 N.Y.S.2d 316 (App. Div. 1984), a regional sales manager employed by a paper manufacturer signed a restrictive covenant prohibiting him from using business information including customer preference data, pricing and promotional information, customer buying records and other business information. When he left his employer and began working for another paper company, his former employer attempted to enjoin him from using this information. The court, however, held that it was either readily available from other sources like distributors in the paper industry or, as was the case with the pricing information, no longer relevant.

It is not clear if the business information on the client lists that you will have possession of would be obtainable from different sources. Assuming that it would not be—particularly the credit information—it is possible that you could gain an unfair advantage were you to use it. Hence, the information will most probably be deemed confidential and you will not be able to keep the lists.

Even though you will not be able to keep the lists, you will be able to maintain your customer contacts. The test applied by the courts in deciding when the identity of a customer is confidential is whether the customer's name is readily obtainable from an outside source. *Columbia Ribbon v. A-1-A Corp.*, 369 N.E.2d 4 (N.Y. 1977). The customer contacts you will make will not be confidential. Your customers will include camera stores, bookstores, and sporting goods stores. Since the identity of these customers can be obtained in any business directory, a court would not consider them trade secrets. For the same reason, your original contacts in department stores in the region could not be construed as confidential either.

There is also the issue of the reasonableness of time and geographic restrictions. Here courts examine their scope and duration as well as a showing of unfair competition. If you were to use or disclose the business information on the customer lists, it would be reasonable only to enjoin you from competing in the area where that information would be relevant. It should be noted, however, that no geographical limitation could prevent you from selling electronic toys or anything else absent your possession and utilization of a trade secret or confidential customer lists.

To sum up, since Toydyno's "computer source codes," and the technique for making "flange-hinges" are trade secrets, the court may prevent you from disclosing or using them. Although you may have to return the customer lists because they contain confidential business information, you will be able to maintain your customer contacts since they are readily obtainable from other sources. Thus, you will be able to compete with Toydyno as long as you do not use any trade secrets or confidential information.

Ultimately, therefore, you should agree to clauses 1(c) and 2. Not only is Toydyno within its rights in demanding this information be kept confidential, but in all frankness, your employment prospects are not so bright that you can flatly reject all restrictions. However, you should not agree to 1(a) and (b), at least in their present form. I will write to Toydyno proposing these terms. Please call me if you have any questions.

Very truly yours,

2.   *Rewrite the advice letter to Mr. Eliot.*

B. Status Letters

Clients want to be kept informed about the progress of their cases and are understandably distressed when their lawyer fails to respond to their inquiries. As one lawyer wrote, when he was a litigant as well as a lawyer:

> There's something wrong with us lawyers . . . when we can't realize the harm we're doing to our clients and to the public, the heartache and frustration and pain we cause to others because we fail to attend civilly and promptly to the needs of others for communication. If we can't take care of a client properly, we shouldn't accept the retainer.[1]

A useful means of communicating the progress of a case is through a status letter to the client. Unlike an advice or opinion letter, which usually occurs at the beginning of a potential transaction or litigation, a status letter is typically sent as matters are proceeding and is intended to keep the client abreast of current developments. A status letter may be sent by traditional mail or by e-mail, and will vary in length depending on the client's case. Typical sections in a status letter are described below:

1. The Introductory Paragraph

The introductory paragraph provides the context of the case, using an appropriate attorney-client tone. In this paragraph, you should connect with the client, showing an understanding of the client's personal situation, and provide a brief summary of the status of the case.

Here is an example of a status letter written to Michael Brown, an eighteen-year-old high school senior who has been charged with possession of narcotics. The previous year, while Michael was in one of his high school classes, a police officer took a police dog through the student parking lot at his school, and the dog alerted at his car. Michael was asked to come to the parking lot by the assistant principal and to open his car. He complied, and the assistant principal searched the glove compartment of Michael's car where he found three ounces of marijuana. Michael's case is now before the state's highest court; two lower courts have denied his motion to suppress evidence. The lawyer writing to Michael has just filed a brief with the court and is awaiting information on the schedule for oral arguments.

> February 21, 20___
>
> Dear Michael,
>
>   I hope this letter finds you well, and that despite understandable concerns about your pending case, you are continuing your studies at Martin Van Buren High School as planned. I am writing to tell you

---

[1] Robert S. Caine, "A Lawyer's View of Being a Litigant," N.Y.L.J. May 1, 1994, at 2, quoted in Stephen Gillers, *Regulation of Lawyers: Problems of Law and Ethics* 74 (9th ed. 2012).

> about the status of your appeal to the Abbott Supreme Court and explain the arguments made in the brief I filed today.

2. Summarize the Context

In the next paragraph, briefly summarize the context of the letter, describing the factual or legal proceedings to date. Keep this paragraph to a reasonable length for easy reading. You will be going into more detail in the following paragraphs.

> As you know from our previous meetings, we are appealing the denial by both lower courts of our motion to suppress the evidence of marijuana found in your car. In my brief to the Abbott Supreme Court, I argued that the evidence of marijuana in your car should be suppressed on the grounds that it was obtained in violation of your rights under the Abbott Constitution and the Fourth Amendment to the U.S. Constitution. In addition to the written arguments in the brief, I will also be making an oral argument to the Court that should be scheduled in the next three to four weeks. Usually, the Court follows with a decision in a month. I am hopeful that the arguments will yield a favorable result so you can continue your plans to go on to college, but the facts are close and so the outcome is not certain.

3. Summarize the Factual or Legal Analysis

If some new factual developments have occurred, describe them here. If reporting on the legal aspects of a case that you have not explained earlier, you should explain the law, using language appropriate to your audience, here an eighteen-year-old high school senior. Depending on your audience, you may need to explain legal terms. If you have already explained your analysis in an earlier advice memo, you need not repeat it in this letter.

> Our first argument was that under the circumstances of your case, a dog sniff is a search within the meaning of the Fourth Amendment and therefore the police needed probable cause (Probable cause means the police had evidence that it was more likely than not that you had drugs in your car.) This is a somewhat difficult argument because some courts have concluded that a dog sniff is not a search when conducted at an airport or at a border, and other courts have held that a dog sniff is not a search at all because it discloses only the presence of illegal substances. However, the U.S. Supreme Court has never stated that a dog sniff is never a search, so this argument is still viable.

> If the court concludes that the dog sniff was a search, our second argument was that the police were so closely involved in the dog sniff

of your car that they needed probable cause to conduct the search. In general, because teachers and administrators must maintain order in the schools, probable cause is not required when school officials alone are conducting a search. They need only act reasonably. However, we argued in your case that the police were so heavily involved in initiating and planning the parking lot search that it was, in essence, a police search, not a search by school officials. Here, we focus heavily on the facts of the case and the active involvement of Police Officer Taylor. He was the one who originally suggested a parking lot search to counter suspected drug use in the high school, and who pressed the principal and assistant principal to agree, even when they had reservations. The State argued in its brief that it was a search by school officials, since the principal approved the search and the assistant principal conducted it.

Even though the lower courts ruled against us on these arguments, the Abbott Supreme Court is not bound by the legal decisions of these courts and will be deciding the legal issues without regard to the lower court opinions.

If the client has been fully informed of the arguments before, another option is to briefly refer to the arguments and only make the point in the final paragraph relating to the standard of review.

4.   The Expected Results and Available Options

Although no lawyer can predict the future with complete accuracy, you may be able to suggest a likely result. And if the result is uncertain, you can state that. Here, also, you may indicate to the client what options are available so that the client can start thinking about how to proceed when the appeal is decided.

Ideally, the Abbott Supreme Court will grant the motion to suppress the evidence of marijuana found in your car. Then the state will have to decide whether to proceed with your case. Since they have no other evidence against you, it is very likely that they will drop the charges. However, if the Court denies the motion, the Court will allow the evidence to be introduced and send the case back to the trial court for further proceedings. This means the state will be allowed to use the evidence of marijuana found in your car against you at trial.

5.   The Closing Paragraph

In the closing paragraph, the lawyer can indicate what comes next, or just reiterate the lawyer's availability to the client.

Since it will take at least several weeks for the Court to decide the appeal, I suggest that you continue with your applications for college. If we do have to go to trial, it will likely not be for a few months. I know it is hard, but at this point you should plan for the best possible outcome. If the time comes to go to trial, we will talk about trial strategy and any other options, perhaps a plea bargain, that may be available.

As always, if you have any questions, please give me a call.

Very truly yours,
Maureen Blake

C. Letters to an Adversary/Demand Letters

Your first letter on behalf of a client may be one informing the opposing party of your client's claims. Frequently this letter explores the possibility of an out-of-court settlement.

The format of such letters may not differ radically from the client advice letter. They too might open with statements identifying the purpose or, in this case, the demands of the letter. They may then go on to summarize the facts and arguments that support the client's claim. Finally, they might close by reiterating the client's demands and the consequences of failing to meet them.

Yet each part of an advocacy letter is informed by your persuasive purpose. Thus your treatment of the subject matter may be quite different from that in an advice letter. In particular, the degree to which you expound on the facts and the law depends on the strategy you have devised for that case.

1. The Opening

It is common to begin a first advocacy letter by identifying yourself as your client's lawyer. After this sort of ritual recital, present your client's claims and demands. In presenting these demands, most lawyers adopt a courteous, reasonable tone. Certainly as long as a compromise is possible, you want to appear cooperative. If negotiation falters, you may decide to assume a firmer, more indignant, or more threatening tone. But at no time should you become so strident and angry that you put your client's case in jeopardy.

2. Factual and Legal Summary

When writing to the opposing party, strategy dictates your treatment of the factual and legal basis of your client's claim. Where your case is strong, a thorough and well-crafted presentation of facts and law may convince the opponent it is better to concede or to compromise than to persist in opposition, especially if you couple your analysis with explicit warnings about your other alternatives.

On the other hand, you might decide not to do your opponents' work for them, believing that they will see the strength of your position only if they do the research themselves. Within the bounds of professional responsibility, you might also decide to withhold facts or to remain silent about legal theories.

3.   Closing

An effective way to close an advocacy letter is to suggest the parties will mutually benefit from a compromise. This conciliatory gesture might be followed by a reminder of the actions you will take if your letter fails to affect this desired resolution. The letter may then end with your demand. To avoid uncertainty and needless delays, be sure to set a date by which the other party must respond and be prepared to act if the party does not.

What follows is the first letter Mr. Braun's attorney wrote to Braun's adversary, Park Crest Hospital. The letter is addressed to the president of the hospital, but an obvious second reader is the hospital's attorney. Both these readers are likely to have fairly broad knowledge of the law governing medical malpractice. The letter tries to convince Park Crest that settlement is its best option.

                                                         March 21, _____

James Jones
President
Park Crest Hospital
3405 South Main Street
Heights City, Missouri 1230 _____

Dear Mr. Jones,

I represent Mr. John Braun in his claim against Park Crest Hospital for breach of its duty to exercise reasonable care to prevent the suicide of his wife, Ms. Rachel Braun, while she was a patient at your hospital. As you know, your liability depends on the propriety of the hospital's medical judgment and the sufficiency of the nonmedical ministerial care. Once you have reviewed the facts of this case, you will realize that Park Crest breached both duties.

The facts that have led to this claim are unfortunate and painful. On June 21, 20, the day after her second attempt at suicide, Rachel Braun voluntarily checked herself into Park Crest Hospital. Upon admission, Dr. Richmond, the attending physician, diagnosed Ms. Braun as severely depressed with suicidal tendencies. He ordered that she be monitored closely for any suicide attempt and prescribed a program of antidepressants and psychotherapy. He did not search her for contraband.

For the first 18 days of her hospitalization, Ms. Braun was placed on accompany status in a ward for acutely ill patients. At the end of the period, Dr. Richmond transferred her to an open ward.

After ten days on the open ward, Dr. Richmond told her she was well enough to go home. That night, two days before her scheduled release, Ms. Braun became agitated. The nurse noted in Ms. Braun's chart that she found the patient weeping. When the nurse questioned her, Ms. Braun expressed worry about whether she could manage in the "real" world. In response, the nurse administered sleep medication, for which the doctor had left an "as needed" order. The nurse also noted that a visitor, the spouse of another patient, had reported seeing Ms. Braun earlier that day swallowing pills taken from her pocket. Regrettably, she took no action other than to record this report. No one searched Ms. Braun for unauthorized drugs. Nothing in Ms. Braun's chart indicates that any physician acknowledged or responded to your nurse's observation that Rachel Braun was becoming increasingly depressed. Certainly, the release order was not countermanded.

On Ms. Braun's last night at the hospital, the nurses checked the patient every two hours, noting she was sleeping unusually heavily and her breathing was depressed. At 6:30 A.M., they found her in bed, dead of an overdose of sleeping pills.

You are well aware that a hospital's liability for the suicide of one of its patients depends on whether it used such reasonable care as the patient's known mental condition required. Courts have held that the determination of the proper degree of supervision is a medical judgment and that the propriety of that medical judgment is measured against the skill and learning ordinarily used under the same or similar circumstances by members of the medical profession. Your failure to search Ms. Braun's person and possessions when she was reported to have an unauthorized supply of drugs is, in light of Ms. Braun's medical history, a breach of your duty to safeguard her from harm. See Stuppy v. United States, 560 F.2d 373 (8th Cir. 1977). Equally reprehensible is your failure to reassess your medical diagnosis after receiving the nurse's report that Ms. Braun was becoming increasingly distressed about her release.

Park Crest was also negligent in its ministerial supervision. The nursing staff as well as the physicians can be faulted for their failure to search Ms. Braun. In addition, the nurses were negligent by failing to notify a physician of Ms. Braun's unusually deep sleep and depressed breathing, given that these are symptoms of overmedication and the staff had not administered sleeping medication to Ms. Braun that evening. See M.W. v. Jewish Hosp. Ass'n of St. Louis, 637 S.W.2d 74 (Mo. App. 1982).

In light of these instances of serious misconduct, I believe a trial court would award Mr. Braun the damages that he justly deserves.

Nonetheless, my client is willing to consider settlement in order to avoid the costs, publicity, and burdens of litigation. Thus, I suggest we meet in an effort to resolve this unfortunate dispute.

I welcome your serious consideration of this request. Please call my office as soon as possible to arrange a meeting. If I do not hear from you by April 18, ____. I will proceed to file Mr. Braun's claim.

> Very truly yours,
> Jane Turner

Exercise 14-C

Using the facts in Exercise 14-B, assume Mr. Eliot has agreed to your course of action. Write an "advocacy" letter to Toydyno introducing yourself and attempting to advance your client's cause.

D. Letters to Third Parties

As an attorney, you will need to write to witnesses, experts, investigators, agencies, and numerous other parties. Sometimes you will be requesting information or favors from them. At other times, you will be informing them of some development. But whatever the occasion, your letters will be stronger if you consider your audience and purpose before drafting them. Keep the following general considerations in mind.

When you are asking the reader to do something for you, you may have to create a little incentive. If you acknowledge the burden you are imposing but then appeal to your reader's good will, you might secure the reader's cooperation: "I realize compiling this information will probably take more time than you can easily afford. Yet Mr. Doe's claim cannot proceed without it." If possible, offer any assistance that could ease the burden. When simple appreciation fails to create incentive, however, a warning might be in order: "I am sorry that I will have to inform your supervisor that my last three requests for copies of Mr. Doe's insurance claims have gone unnoticed."

When you are relaying neutral information, your task is simple. State your news quickly and clearly, and then explain why you are communicating it. Readers like to feel you value their understanding.

More difficult to write are letters conveying bad news, which is often best communicated on the phone or in person. But if you need to do it in writing, try to soften it by first extending one or two courtesies. "I appreciate your reluctance to get involved in a dispute between your employer and a co-worker. Regrettably, you are the only witness to the altercation that occurred on March 13th." After this, state your bad news clearly: "Thus I must inform you that a deposition has been set for . . . ."The temptation to misunderstand is too great to permit even minor evasions. Nonetheless, where possible, look for options or ways to mitigate the effect and soften the blow.

The following is a letter to Ms. Diana Wells, who—while visiting her husband at Park Crest—had observed Rachel Braun taking unauthorized drugs.

September 30, _____

Ms. Diana Wells
123 First Street
Heights City, Missouri 1230 _____

Dear Ms. Wells,

I have just received your letter expressing your reluctance to testify about the events leading to Ms. Braun's tragic suicide.

Let me assure you that I appreciate the difficult position you are in. From your letter, I infer that, having entrusted Park Crest Hospital with the care of your husband, you feel it is imperative to maintain good relations with the hospital's administration and staff. Thus, although you empathize with Mr. Braun's bereavement, you wish to avoid becoming involved in a dispute between them.

If your testimony were not so vital, I would not press you on this matter. Unfortunately, you are an important link in establishing that Park Crest knew Ms. Braun had her own drug supply and failed nonetheless to take steps to prevent her from harming herself. I think you will agree with me that a jury ought to be allowed to determine Park Crest's liability not only because Mr. Braun deserves to be compensated for his painful loss, but because other patients, like your husband, may need to be protected from such fatally negligent conduct.

I suggest that we meet to review your potential testimony. Such a meeting would enable me to prepare you for the courtroom experience and thereby allay some of the natural anxiety you may feel about participating in this trial. I will call you in a few days time to arrange a meeting at your convenience. I would sincerely regret having to subpoena you to obtain testimony that I believe you would freely give in happier circumstances. Let me assure you I will do all I can to minimize the repercussions of your participation.

Very truly yours,
Jane Turner

E. Transmittal Letters

Transmittal letters are cover letters that usually accompany documents and provide instructions to the recipient. Transmittal letters are often quite short, yet it is surprising how badly written and organized many are. These letters should be written clearly and logically. They should not be written in old fashioned legalese, but neither should they be casually thrown together. For example, you need not write "Enclosed herewith please find as per your request two copies of the Anderson agreement. Said agreement should be kept by you in and only in your safety deposit box. I remain yours faithfully." But also, do not write "Here are the copies of the agreement you asked for. Keep them safe. Yours. . . ." A middle ground is the simple, "I am enclosing two copies of the Anderson agreement that we discussed this morning. Please keep the copies in a secure place, preferably your safety deposit box. Let me know if you need any other documents. Yours truly. . . ."

When you write instructions, make sure the recipient understands the purpose of the transaction, and explain the steps in the order that they should be done. For example, "Please read through this agreement to ensure that it is in the form we discussed. If the agreement is acceptable to you, bring it to a notary public. You should sign it in front of the notary at the line marked 'Signature.' Sign your name exactly as it is typed under the line. Write the full date on the line marked 'Date.' The notary will then sign and stamp the agreement. Bring the agreement with you to our next appointment on May 4th."

If the instructions involve several steps or several documents, number them. For example, "I am enclosing the forms you will need to probate your aunt's will:

1. Petition to Admit the Will to Probate and Appoint an Executor

2. Oath on the Bond

3. Waiver of Notice

4. Affidavit of Heirship

5. Petition for Independent Administration."

Then explain in turn your instructions for each document.

III. E-MAIL AND INSTANT MESSAGING

THERE IS NO DENYING E-MAIL AND INSTANT MESSAGING.[2] It is how people make arrangements with friends, and it has become standard practice in business: lawyers report that e-mail is often their preferred method of correspondence with colleagues and clients. But, for a professional, e-mail is as much a curse as a blessing.[3] Though sometimes a boon to time management—there are no time zones, you can answer on your own schedule, you can avoid chit chat and prevent interruption— e-mail also clogs your screen. In addition, e-mail's speed and spontaneity often result in messages and replies replete with miscalculations of tone and ill-considered advice. Thus, many agree that for sensitive matters, phone and face-to-face conversation is more effective because you can monitor reactions and respond accordingly. Moreover, traditional letters may be better suited for complex topics, confidential matters that cannot risk being forwarded, or legal documents that need, for example, signatures and notarization. Certainly, conversations, phone calls, and letters are more confidential.

A. E-mail and Degrees of Formality

Some miscalculation of tone stems from e-mail being a mix of genres. To family or friends, e-mail is like a scribbled note (remember to deposit check on kitchen counter) or postcard (you won't believe what just happened to me while waiting for the bus). To a colleague, an e-mail may be like a memo or voice mail reminder that the meeting is at 4:00 in room 100. To a client, it is often like a business letter.

Each type of e-mail requires a different degree of formality. A message to a friend can be extremely informal (yo ben, can u plz meet me @ 4?). You may use abbreviations, called e-acronyms (TTYL-talk to you later), smilies—strings of characters meant to convey tone (J or:-D, which means 'shock' to the initiated), and a signature that contains a quotation ("*a rising tide floats all boats*"). None of this is appropriate in business e-mail.

---

[2]   A New York Times article reported that a 10 hour BlackBerry blackout produced in users "feelings of isolation, a strong temptation to lash out at company IT workers, and a severe longing, not unlike drug withdrawal." Brad Stone, *Bereft of BlackBerrys, the Untethered Make Do*, N.Y. Times, April 19, 2007, at C4. In another article, a professor of psychiatry uses the term " 'acquired attention deficit disorder' to describe the condition of people who are accustomed to a constant stream of digital stimulation and feel bored in the absence of it." Matt Richtel, *It Don't Mean a Thing if You Ain't got that Ping*, N.Y. Times, April 22, 2007, at section 4, WR5.

[3]   The pros and cons of e-mail are discussed at length in a book on e-mail by David Shipley and Will Schwalbe, *Send: The Essential Guide to E-mail for Office and Home* (Alfred A. Knopf 2007). Anyone who desires further information will find this book invaluable.

A message to a colleague should be 'business casual': "Dear" and "Sincerely" are always appropriate, but you may also use less formal salutations and closings (Hi Paul, Regards Nick). In the business setting, e-mail should be grammatical, properly punctuated and spelled, and use upper and lower-case letters. This is especially important when writing to a supervisor (or one of your professors). An overly familiar message will often be met with a formal reply that sets the relation straight.

---

hey prof,

> when can i c u about my exam?

> > > joe

Dear Mr. Smith:

> I review exams for one month after the grades are published. That time has passed.

> > > Sincerely,
> > > Professor D'Amici

A message to a client, especially if it is essentially an advice or status letter, should probably observe all the rhetorical considerations with which this chapter began. Admittedly, e-mail threads complicate the issue of formality. After several exchanges, it often seems unnecessary to begin each response with a salutation and closing. And indeed, with a co-worker, this may not be necessary; civility with a client, however, never goes amiss.

One peculiar phenomenon of e-mail is 'flaming,' sometimes known as 'online disinhibition effect.' Because it is so easy to fire off an e-mail, messages can be particularly impulsive, offensive, and intemperate. The recipient is often 'enflamed' and relationships can be irreparably damaged. Thus avoid angry, sarcastic, or duplicitous e-mails, ones that are like gossiping behind someone's back. Write, wait, re-read, and re-think before hitting 'send.'

B. E-mail and Confidentiality

E-mail is not a private form of communication. Your institution's e-mail administrator is always able to read messages.[4] Some companies monitor their employees' e-mail, and although less likely, a hacker may read your messages. Most breaches of

---

[4] An e-mail administrator installs, configures, and maintains e-mail server software that is responsible for sending and receiving e-mails to and from an institution. An administrator also maintains accounts on the server for every individual and looks into problem reports when e-mail is not sent or received properly.

confidentiality do not come from these sources, however; they come from mis-addressing the e-mail, forwarding a message, or hitting Reply All instead of Reply. These mistakes in the address field can lead to wide circulation of private matters and waive privilege. As a result, the address field requires the same careful forethought as the message itself.

Most law firms put confidentiality warnings on all their e-mail messages. These warnings inform the recipient that the information is confidential and request a recipient who is not the addressee to destroy the message without copying or forwarding it to another, and to notify the sender of his or her error in mailing.[5] Such instructions are not always followed, and some firms use encryption programs to avoid the problem.

It is also important to remember that e-mail and instant messages are often archived. If a lawsuit arises—even years later—the messages may be available for discovery.[6] E-mail messages could quite conceivably contain evidence of gender discrimination, for example, or evidence about the terms of a contract. E-mailed questions can come back to incriminate you: "Is this way of proceeding common practice? It doesn't seem so to me." Even if the messages are confidential work product, the privilege may be waived. If you want to avoid such eventualities, remember some legal advice should always be delivered in person or by phone.

C. E-mail and Legal Advice

Users of e-mail tend to expect quick replies, at least within the time one would return a voice mail message. Instant messaging has an additional limitation because the sender knows whether the addressee is online.[7] If a client is asking for legal advice, especially advice on a complex matter, it is better to respond by saying you need to give the problem some thought than to offer off-the-cuff counsel. Then, before replying at length, you should research, draft, print, and rewrite your e-mail message just as you would a conventional advice or status letter.

You may indeed have clients who are IM or e-mail addicts. These clients often believe that they will be billed only for the 30 seconds it takes to send back a reply. Because of this, they may

---

[5] Wayne Schiess discusses this in *Writing for the Legal Audience* at 41-44 (Carolina Academic Press 2003).

[6] See, for example, Geanne Rosenberg, *"Electronic Discovery Proves an Effective Legal Weapon,"* N.Y. Times, March 31 1997, at Business 5.

[7] The New York Times reported that businesses fear that "if there wasn't an immediate response," a client might "go look elsewhere for an answer." Matt Richtel, *It Don't Mean a Thing if You Ain't got that Ping*, N.Y. Times, April 22, 2007, at WR5.

bombard you with messages. It is important to clarify that the time it takes to research and respond to e-mail and instant messages is billable time.

D. Formatting Your E-mail

Because of the volume of e-mail lawyers receive, effective formatting is important. It helps the recipient to prioritize which e-mail to read, when to read it, and when and whether a reply is needed. A number of suggestions follow.

1. The Address Field: To, Cc, and Bcc

We have already discussed the care with which you must fill the address field. Use the 'To' field for all the people you are directly addressing. Use the 'Cc' field for those who need to be kept in the loop on the matter. It is both courteous and helpful to let the main recipient know why you have 'Cc'd' the message. In the closing, add a sentence like "I've Cc'd this message to John Estes, who will be taking the depositions." The 'Cc' field can also be used to compliment or reprimand an employee. If you 'Cc' a supervisor on an e-mail that compliments a person's work, it spreads the good word. If you 'Cc' the supervisor on a complaint, it is a reproach and should only be done for serious infractions—otherwise it is a form of "flaming." Finally, treat 'Bcc' with extreme caution. Because it is blind, the addressees of those in 'To' and 'Cc' fields are unaware of the addressee in the 'Bcc' field (unless the recipient hits 'reply all'). Thus, because 'Bcc' is sneaky—and arguably unethical—its use should not be general practice.[8]

2. An Informative Subject Line

Netiquette suggests you always fill in the subject line. In fact, e-mail manuals recommend treating your subject line as a brief summary of the message. Instead of entitling a message "Waiver," entitle it "Smith's Waiver Form Needed by Tuesday." This tells the recipient what the message is about, what action is needed, and when it must be done. With instant messaging, and even e-mails, the subject line sometimes is the entire message: 'reimbursement receipts due 5/15.'

3. The Message Field

E-mail users tend to like short, concise messages, that is, messages the length of a computer screen before scrolling. Admittedly, this

---

[8] Shipley and Schwalbe think there is a limited place for 'Bcc' when writing people outside your firm. For example, if your supervisor wants to be kept abreast of a case but doesn't want direct client interaction, 'Bcc' might be appropriate. Nonetheless, they too think 'Bcc' should be used rarely. *See supra* note 3, at 75.

is not always possible. When you need to write a long e-mail, it may make sense to use an attachment. If you are including an attachment, it is courteous to give the recipient the title of the document and the software program used. If you do not have an attachment, many suggest that you begin with a summary or table of contents, and follow with a notice of when a response is needed.

A summary concisely states the gist and point of the e-mail. For example, you might start with a polite salutation (Dear Mr. Dean) and an opening summary like "This e-mail contains information about the three issues we are appealing in your case, your opponent's reply and our responses, and the date of oral argument."

A table of contents permits the reader to read only the most important sections. For example, in a defamation suit, the table of contents might read as follows:

Table of Contents

- The April 1, 2016 statement was not made of and concerning Mr. Small

- The April 1, 2016 statement is not false or defamatory as to Mr. Small

- The July 31, 2016 statement was not made of and concerning Mr. Small

- Counter-arguments & rebuttals

- Oral Argument on October 11, 2016

Because the recipient may only browse the e-mail, if the sender needs a response by a certain time that needs to be made clear at the beginning: "Please let me know by June 15, 2017, if you are attending the oral argument."

For ease of reading, use short, block paragraphs and double space between each paragraph. Headings, bullets and enumerations can be helpful. Finally, end with a polite closing like "Yours truly" or "Sincerely." The following is an example of e-mail correspondence.

Subject Line: *Smith v. Harmon*, Jan. 17th deadline for subpoenas

Dear Mr. Doe:

I appreciated having the opportunity last week to discuss the timing of responding to, and the scope of documents requested by, the subpoena duces tecum recently served on HFTC Silver Roth, LLC. During that conversation, you agreed to extend the deadline for

HFTC's compliance with the subpoena to January 17, 2017. You also agreed to narrow the scope of the categories of documents requested by the subpoena as follows:

Request Nos. 1, 4, 5, 13 and 14

The relevant time period will begin on January 1, 2017.

Request No. 2

The scope of the requested "communications" will be limited to the subjects identified in the subpoena.

Request No. 3

The requested "meetings" will exclude meetings related to HFTC's acquisitions, as the focus of this request is on meetings related to Credit Agreements.

Requests No. 6, 7, 8, 9

The requested documents will exclude documents related to HFTC's 10Q and 10K filings and U.S. Aggregates' restatement; the focus of this request is on documents related to the Credit Agreements.

Request Nos. 10, 11 and 12

The relevant time period will begin on the first date of the fourth quarter 2017.

    Please let me know if you these changes are not accurate, and thank you again for your cooperation in this matter.

Very truly yours,
John Manfini

4. Replying to E-mails

When replying to an e-mail, put your answer at the top of the correspondence, not at the bottom. The addressee might not scroll down and therefore think you hit reply mistakenly. Also make sure your answers to a message are clear. It may help to quote relevant passages from the original message. For example, if a partner asks you if you are deposing Mr. Johnson on the 14th or the 15th and attending the conference on the 20th, do not reply "yes." Separate your responses: "I am deposing Mr. Johnson on the 12th, not the 14th or the 15th. I do plan to attend the conference on the 20th."

Be very careful when replying to a thread that has a long string of messages beneath your response. If you are forwarding a message to another attorney, for example, check that there is nothing in the thread that is not for the eyes of that recipient. In fact, if the thread does not contain information that the recipient needs, delete the thread.

It is also important to remember that any e-mail message that has been replied to or forwarded may also have been edited. What a person wrote and what you read may differ; this can again create misunderstandings and bad feelings, so before you "flame," get the facts.

5. The Signature Block

Your signature block should give your reader full contact information. This should include your full name, your title, your organization, your address, your phone and fax numbers, and your e-mail address. With this information, the recipient can respond in the manner with which he or she is most comfortable.

6. Reading E-mail

Although it would make chronologic sense to read new e-mails from the bottom up, most readers read e-mail from the top down. Thus, a person who has sent several e-mails on the same subject should alert the recipient to the content of the earlier e-mail—even if it is just to say, "as I mentioned in my earlier e-mail about my conversation with John."

E. A Word on Instant Messaging

Instant messaging is becoming a corporate practice. Employers on the phone with a client use it to get quick answers to questions the client has raised. Because it occurs in real time, it accelerates scheduling and dialogues, and aids in fast brainstorming and problem solving. Instant Messaging also provides a record of correspondence. As a form of communication, it thus carries many of the same benefits and risks of e-mail.

Exercise 14-D

Often when you counsel a client about a proposed transaction, you discuss the transaction with the client in person, rather than by letter. You might, for example, meet with a client about a proposed contract. Review the facts and cases described in Exercise 14-B, in which you are an attorney representing Timothy Eliot in a transaction involving an employment contract that includes a covenant not to compete. Assume that Mr. Eliot is going to come to your office for advice. Plan the counseling meeting.

Ordinarily you would review each of the proposed terms of a contract, even if you do not intend to discuss every term with the client. For purposes of this exercise, the counseling meeting will focus on a single term of the contract, the covenant not to complete.

How would you explain this contract term to Mr. Eliot? What are Mr. Eliot's likely objectives? What options does Mr. Eliot have? What are the pros and cons of each? What are the risks? What is likely to be most important to Toydyno? What aspects of the covenant might be successfully renegotiated?

How would a personal meeting look and sound different from a letter? What kind of relationship would you hope to establish in the meeting? Would the result be the same? Does one method of counseling (by letter or in person) seem to be more effective in this situation? If you decide a meeting with Mr. Eliot in person would be more effective, can a letter play any role in the process?

Exercise 14-E

1. *The attorney handling Larry Kemp's case (see Exercise 2-L) asks you to write to Mr. Kemp answering whether he must pay restitutionary alimony to his former wife. Will you communicate with Mr. Kemp by an e-mail letter? Write an e-mail letter to him.*

2. *Your firm also represents Irving Pick. See Exercise 7-C (3). Write Mr. Pick an e-mail letter advising him whether to include the sculpture in the Nadoff bankruptcy estate.*

3. *Your client Adele Stuart was a tenant at Lake City Apartments. When she moved out at the end of her three-year lease, she removed the curtain rods and curtains that she had put in at the windows of two rooms. The lease did not allow her to remove real property from the apartment. Her landlord will not return Ms. Stuart's security deposit because the landlord claims that the curtains and curtain rods were fixtures. [Fixtures are personal property that become real property because the property became fixed to real property and was used as part of the realty.] Explain to Ms. Stuart in an e-mail letter whether she will get her security deposit back.*

4. *In 2014 your client Joe Peters granted an easement[9] to his neighbor Philip Smith for Smith to park his car on Peters' driveway, which abutted Smith's land. At the time, Smith and his wife had one car, a two-door sedan. The easement provided that Peters would maintain the driveway at his discretion.*

In 2017, the Smiths' adult son came home to live with his parents, bringing his SUV with him that he parked on the Peters' driveway. The Smiths then decided to put an addition on their home and hired a construction crew. The crew parked its heavy truck on the driveway,

---

[9] An easement is an interest in land given by a landowner to another to allow specified use of the land. The holder of the easement is the dominant estate and the land over which the easement is given is the servient estate. The easement is usually conveyed by a deed or some other writing. An easement of a right of way, such as the Peters-Smith easement, is often interpreted to allow reasonable use for a reasonable purpose and not impose an undue burden on the servient estate.

from which it loaded and unloaded equipment, and damaged the black top surface.

Peters has complained to Smith, who replied that the construction would be finished in two weeks, but that his son would live with them indefinitely.

Peters asks you what he "can do about the situation" and asks for a brief explanation soon as a "heads up" to explain to his family. Without doing research (although you may have some information in your property case book) e-mail Peters with a heads up of what this is about.

5. *Your client Adele Stuart received a demand letter from her neighbor's attorney, demanding that she stop using a narrow strip of land between their houses, and remove all equipment on that strip. Adele has been gardening that strip for the last thirty years, since she and her neighbor each moved there. She often leaves her trowel and gardening fork there. The neighbor sold her house last month and the new owners, the Mullins, moved in. Ms. Stuart has FAXED you the attorney's letter, which demands she vacate the strip in one week.*

You will respond to Ms. Stuart that she owns that strip of land by adverse possession.[10] Send her a response by e-mail.

---

[10] Adverse possession requires actual use of the disputed property, and use that is exclusive, continuous, open and notorious, hostile (done as a claim of right to the property) all for twenty-one years.

CHAPTER 15

THE TRIAL BRIEF: MEMORANDUM OF LAW IN SUPPORT OF OR IN OPPOSITION TO A MOTION

I. INTRODUCTION

IN CHAPTER 7 WE EXPLAINED that the purpose of a legal memorandum is to analyze a problem in an objective, exploratory way and to reach a conclusion based on that analysis. When you are writing to a court, however, your purpose is very different. You are then writing as an advocate representing one side in a dispute, and your purpose is not to explore, but to persuade the court to decide the case in your client's favor.

When you have a case before a trial court, you often need to file one or more motions. A motion is a request to the court for a ruling on a legal question. The court will respond to a motion with a ruling called an order. You may make the motion and attach a memorandum of law on your own initiative or the court may request that all parties file memoranda on a legal question that has arisen in the course of the litigation.

A. The Purpose of Trial Briefs

A document written for a trial court (called a trial brief, memorandum of law, or an advocacy memorandum of law) is frequently submitted in support of or in opposition to a motion. Attorneys may also submit a trial brief to present their side of any disputed issue, to summarize the evidence, to support or oppose post-trial motions, and to request particular instructions to the jury. Finally, attorneys may file extensive post-trial briefs at the end of the litigation to present the court with their final arguments based on the facts adduced at trial.

B. Content of Motion Papers

Typically, a motion includes the following documents:

1) A notice of motion. This notifies the other side that a motion has been filed and usually includes a hearing date. Sometimes the notice is combined with the motion.

2) The motion itself, signed by an attorney.[1]

3) A trial brief that supports the motion.

4) Supporting documents, like affidavits.

5) A proposed order (a ruling in your favor that the judge could sign).

The attorney opposing the motion may submit a brief in opposition to the motion, and other supporting documents, such as a proposed order.

Attorneys make motions at many different stages of litigation—before trial, during the trial, or after the trial. Here are some examples of types of motions that may be brought in a single case.

- The plaintiff's attorney may file a motion for a preliminary injunction at the same time that she files the complaint.

- The defendant's attorney may respond to the complaint with a motion to dismiss the complaint for failure to state a claim (known as a demurrer in some state courts).

- If the case proceeds, the plaintiff's attorney may move for certification of a class.

- Either party's attorney may move to compel discovery.

- Either party's attorney may move for summary judgment.

- Either party's attorney may move for judgment as a matter of law at the close of the evidence offered by an opponent at trial.

- The attorney whose client has lost after a trial may enter a renewed motion for judgment as a matter of

---

[1] Fed. R. Civ. P. 11 states:

(a) **Signature.** "Every pleading, written motion, and other paper must be signed by at least one attorney of record in the attorney's name. . . .

(b) **Representations to the court.** "By presenting to the court a pleading, written motion, or other paper . . . an attorney . . . certifies that to the best of the person's knowledge, information and belief, . . .

(1) it is not being presented for any improper purpose, such as to harass, cause unnecessary delay, or needlessly increase the cost of litigation;

(2) the claims . . . are warranted by existing law or by a nonfrivolous argument. . .;

(3) the factual contentions have evidentiary support . . .; and

(4) the denials of factual contentions are warranted on the evidence. . . .

law, or move for a new trial, or move to alter or amend the judgment.

Motions are typically made in writing. (Often this is required by the court rules.) The writing serves various purposes. It gives notice to the opposing party and to the court, it tells the opposing party and the court the grounds on which the motion is based, it gives supporting facts and law, it requests the relief sought, it gives the opposing party time to respond, and it provides a record.

C. The Importance of Court Rules

When you file a motion before a trial court, you need to familiarize yourself with the applicable court rules, whether you are in federal or state court. Often more than one set of rules is relevant. Some rules apply to all courts of a certain type, such as the Federal Rules of Civil Procedure, which govern civil cases in all federal trial courts. Other rules may apply to local court systems, like all trial courts in the Eastern District of New York. Finally, individual judges may issue their own rules.

For example, if you were filing a motion in federal district court in the Eastern District of New York, you would have to be aware of three sets of Rules. Here are some excerpts from these Rules.

1.   The Federal Rules of Civil Procedure:

Rule 7(b)   Motions and Other Papers.

> **(1) In General.** A request for a court order must be made by motion. The motion must:
>
>> (A) be in writing unless made during a hearing or trial;
>>
>> (B) state with particularity the grounds for seeking the order; and
>>
>> (C) state the relief sought.

2.   Local Civil Rules of the United States District Courts for the Southern and Eastern Districts of New York:

Local Civil Rule 6.1. Service and Filing of Motion Papers.

> . . .
>
> (a) On all motions and applications under Fed. R. Civ. P. 26 through 37 inclusive and 45(c)(3), (1) the notice of motion, supporting affidavits, and memoranda of law shall be served by the moving

party on all other parties that have appeared in the action, (2) any opposing affidavits and answering memoranda of law should be served within seven days after service of the moving papers, and (3) any reply affidavits and reply memoranda of law shall be served within two days after service of the answering papers. . . .

(b) On all civil motions, petitions, and applications other than those described in Rule 6.1(a), . . . (1) the notice of motion, supporting affidavits, and memoranda of law shall be served by the moving party on all other parties that have appeared in the action, (2) any opposing affidavits and answering memoranda shall be served within fourteen days after service of the moving papers, and (3) any reply affidavits and memoranda of law shall be served within seven days after service of the answering papers.

3.   The Rules of Individual Judges Motions:[2]

3.A. *Pre-Motion Conference Requests in Civil Cases*

. . . For motions other than discovery motions, in all cases in which the proposed movant is represented by counsel, . . . a premotion conference with the court must be requested before making:

i.   Any motion pursuant to Fed. R. Civ. P. 12 or 56

ii.   Any motion for a change of venue; or

iii. Any motion to amend a pleading pursuant to Rule 15 of the Fed. R. Civ. P. where leave of court is required.

To request a pre-motion conference, the moving party shall file and serve a letter not to exceed three (3) pages in length setting forth the basis for the anticipated motion. All parties served may, but are not required to, serve and file a letter response, not to exceed three (3) pages within seven (7) days from service of the notification letter.

. . . .

---

[2]   Individual Practices and Rules, the Hon. Margo K. Brodie, Eastern District of New York, revised February 2012.

The bottom line is—

Check the rules!

Check the rules!

Check the rules!

Rules cover a variety of points, some substantive and some procedural. For example, Fed. R. Civ. P. 23 establishes the prerequisites for a class action. By contrast, Rule 6 is technical, describing the method for computing periods of time under the Federal Rules. Nevertheless, Rule 6 contains critical practical information:

- On what day do you start counting the time period?

- What if the last day is Sunday?

- What days count as "legal holidays"?

You should become familiar with the applicable court rules at the start of your case. (Most are posted on the Internet.) Failure to do so could be embarrassing or even disastrous. You do not want to go to the courthouse to file a case, only to find that all case documents must be filed electronically. You do not want to miss a deadline for filing an answer to a counterclaim because you thought you had 30 days to file your answer, and the correct period of time is 20 days.

II. THE ATTORNEY AS ADVOCATE

A. Audience

THE AUDIENCE FOR A TRIAL BRIEF is a judge who reads many briefs every day and who decides many cases. A secondary audience is the opposing party. Since judges play the crucial role in litigation, think carefully about what information they need from your trial documents, and how you can clearly and quickly communicate that information. Judges are busy people. They will look to your memorandum for everything they need to decide the motion.

Unless you are told differently for your particular assignment, you should assume the judge is a generalist, that is, the judge sits on a court of general jurisdiction rather than on a specialized court, such as a bankruptcy or tax court. And although a judge most likely is familiar with some aspects of the case, such as procedural rules, you should still include information such as the burden of proof where appropriate.

Your most important task, however, is to introduce your case. The judge probably will know nothing about the facts of your case except those you include in your documents, and may know little specifically about the legal rules and arguments involved, except those you formulate and develop. Therefore, the documents you submit to the court will be its first (and sometimes only) source of this information. Although oral argument is the second source of this information, not all cases are argued before a judge, and those that are may be allotted only a short time.

In addition, remember that trial judges are bound to follow the precedents in that jurisdiction, and want you to tell them, reliably and clearly, what those precedents are. At the trial stage, the legal precedents are probably more important than policy arguments. The judges also want to reach a fair result. You can influence their sense of fairness by convincing them that they would be doing what is right by deciding the case in your client's favor. Finally, since judges do not like to be reversed, you need to convince the court that you have strong arguments on your side.

B.   Persuasive Writing

When you write to a court, you write to inform the court about the case and to persuade, that is, to convince the court to decide in favor of your client.

1.   The Attorney's Appeals to Ethics, Emotion, Reason, or a Combination of All Three[3]

a.   Ethics

Some values that attorneys share come from the special ethical obligations imposed by professional codes of conduct.[4] Indeed, the Code of Professional Responsibility imposes the obligation to maintain "the integrity of the profession."[5] This Code and the Model Rules of Professional Conduct both require candor to the courts. For example, under the Model Rules, an attorney must not make false statements of material fact or law[6] and must disclose material facts and legal authority, even adverse legal authority.[7] Although an attorney also owes the client a duty of zealous advocacy,[8] that duty stops short of inaccuracy. In addition, the lawyer's duty to the court as an officer of the court requires

---

[3]   Aristotle identified three components of oral persuasion: appeals to ethics, to emotion and to reason. They apply to persuasive writing as well.

[4]   States have adopted either the ABA's Code of Professional Responsibility (MC), or the Model Rules of Professional Conduct (MR).

[5]   MC Rule 8.

[6]   MR 3.3 (a)(1).

[7]   MR 3.3 (a)(2)(3). Under § 3.3 (a)(3) a lawyer must disclose legal authority in the controlling jurisdiction that is directly adverse and that is not disclosed by opposing counsel.

[8]   MC Preamble (2).

compliance with court rules. That duty also requires that you show your respect for the court and that you are candid about your case. If the court doubts your candor, it will look to the other attorney to explain the facts and the law.

Your credibility also depends on more mundane concerns. If your work is careless, for example, if you cite cases incorrectly or if you inaccurately describe the decisions you rely on, the court may not trust any of your work. Once you lose credibility with the court, you have not only damaged yourself professionally, but you have injured your client.

b. Emotion

An argument may also appeal to emotion and can be proper and effective, if it is restrained. You can evoke sympathy for your client's suffering, anger at the defendant's cruelty, or respect for the values of fairness and justice. (An emotion that is inappropriate is hostility towards the opposing counsel and parties.) Most important, you should convey your conviction for the merits of your client's case, and positive feelings towards your client. You want to make the judge care who wins the case.

c. Reason

Of course, reason is what we most associate with successful advocacy, and logical exposition is the core of the Argument section in a trial brief, which is analogous to the Discussion in a memorandum.

The term "argument" is not used to mean a pugnacious statement, but means a presentation of reasons that support a conclusion. In the Argument section of the document, you analyze the law and apply the law to the facts of your case as you do in an office memorandum. However, an Argument differs from a Discussion. First, your audience is a court. Second, the purpose of the document is to persuade the court to decide the case favorably for your client. So you will write in a more assertive tone, developing reasons why your client should prevail in order to convince the court to accept your conclusions.

2. Creating the Theory of the Case

An important skill of the advocate is in creating the theory of the case. Your theory of the case is the client's story and the legal framework within which you want the court to understand it.

The theory begins with the overarching context or theme of the case. It is your statement of what the case is really about. A good theory of the case makes the case come alive, winning over your reader or your listener. It will appeal to that person's sense of justice; it will explain all parts of your argument; and it will provide a result that feels correct. In order to develop a theory, start by becoming very familiar with the facts and controlling law. Think about the possible strategies and most appealing presentation you can make. Then give an account of the facts that support the client's legal claim in a persuasive narrative. In other words, link the client's story to the legal theory upon which relief is sought. This should lead logically to the court's ruling in the client's favor.

For example, assume you are representing black and Latino construction workers who have unsuccessfully applied for membership in an all-white construction union. The overarching theme of the case is racial discrimination. The clients' story recounts that despite their qualifications, they were repeatedly denied membership in the union. Your legal theory is that this denial violates the prohibition against intentional race discrimination under Title VII of the Civil Rights Act of 1964. This violation on invidious grounds would logically lead the court to conclude that justice would require a verdict in your client's favor.

Here are some additional examples. Note the opposing theories.

First Example:

The plaintiff in a libel case may stress how the defendant magazine damaged her career and her life by its defamatory story about her, and why there is a minimal social value in protecting the magazine and its sleazy practices.

The defendant's theory of the case, its defense, will stress first amendment values and the important role the media plays in a democratic society; and the leeway it needs to fulfill that task.

Second Example:

A transgender plaintiff alleging discrimination "because of . . . sex" under Title VII of the Civil Rights Act of 1964 would stress that she, a biological male, was fired because she failed to act according to gender stereotypes by presenting herself as a woman.

The defendant company's theory of the case is that Congress did not intend Title VII of the Civil Rights Act of 1964 to apply to anything but the traditional definition of sex and so the transgender plaintiff could not bring a claim under that statute.

Third Example:

In an employment discrimination suit, the plaintiffs' theory of the case may be that affirmative action for blacks and Latinos is necessary to achieve real racial equality after decades of discrimination. The defendant company would characterize such relief as reverse discrimination which harms innocent white employees.[9]

3. Principles of Style

a. Achieving Tone

The tone of your brief should reflect the serious responsibility that you have assumed as your client's advocate. You are not going to place that client at risk by irritating the court, for example, by overstatement, inaccuracy, or informality. Nor are you going to lecture the judges by telling them what they must or must not do. Therefore, avoid imperative sentences, since it is inappropriate to issue commands to a judge. You should also avoid being belittling or sarcastic, especially in regard to other judges. Finally, avoid using exclamation points or italics. Your readers will more readily believe what you say if you sound reasonable.

To be persuasive, you need to sound objective, preserving at least the appearance of neutrality about the facts of the case, but revealing a firm concern and determination that no miscarriage of justice occurs. You want to impress upon the court the thought you have given to your client's problem, your commitment to your client's representation, and your respect for the court. In other words, you want to exhibit candor, conviction, and intelligence to serve your persuasive purpose and achieve an ethical appeal.

Tone in large measure results from the interplay between diction (word choice) and attitude. In the written medium, you can convey tone by skillful use of diction, juxtaposition (or context), and syntax (sentence structure).

b. Diction

Diction is a basic means of conveying attitude or tone. Many words have both explicit and implicit meanings. Select words on the basis of both their denotation (their explicit meaning or stipulated properties) and their connotation (their implicit meaning or

---

[9] For a fuller discussion of this suggestion, see Elizabeth Fajans and Mary R. Falk, *Untold Stories: Restoring Narrative to Pleading Practice*, 5 Legal Writing 3 (2009); Brian Foley and Ruth Anne Robbins, *Fiction 101: A Primer for Lawyers on How to Use Fiction Writing Techniques to Write Persuasive Fact Sections*, 32 Rutgers L.J. 1 (2001); Kenneth D. Chestek, *the Plot Thickens: The Appellate Brief as Story*, 14 Legal Writing 127 (2008).

overtones that have evolved from usage). To refer to a person as an informant, for example, is far more neutral than to label that person a snitch, which connotes double-dealing and self-interest. If you describe police officers "unwarranted placement" of a GPS device, your connotation is that the police were not justified in acting as they did, and that they had no search warrant.

Pay particular attention to verbs because they, without a lot of embellishment, immediately and forcefully characterize an action. "Ogling" connotes a lasciviousness that "staring" does not capture. "Jab" minimizes an action that "wallop" maximizes. Because you want your prose to move, let your verbs, more than your adjectives, describe.

Certainly, an adjective or adverb is sometimes in order, but, one apt adjective is often preferable to a series of them because it focuses the reader on the most telling detail. It is enough to know someone was accosted by a man screaming racial epithets. To add they were bigoted, insulting, and demeaning is unnecessary. If the adjectives do not materially refine the point, they dilute the impact of any given description. Understatement is, therefore, often more forceful than overstatement because of its bare concentration on the essential. It also acknowledges your readers' abilities to grasp your point while allowing them to draw their own conclusions. Similarly you should avoid using qualifiers and intensifiers (very, clearly, possibly, absolutely) since insistence without substance is more irritating than persuasive. For example, to say simply that "this case arises from a tragedy," can be more forceful than "this case arises from a tragedy of a truly and clearly terrible magnitude."

c.   Context

Context and juxtaposition are other good ways to establish tone. Instead of stridently denouncing testimony as incredible, juxtapose conflicting statements and remark on their discrepancy. Similarly, you can juxtapose an opposing argument with facts or precedents that cast doubt on its validity or applicability. In the following example, the prosecution marshals a series of facts to undermine defense counsel's contention that there was insufficient proof that defendant intended to cause damage to the building, an element of second degree arson.

In October 2016, Dick Terney ignited five separate fires on a sofa cushion and on the mattress on which Beth Lot's body was lying. He then fled from the building, leaving the blaze to consume all of the mattress, to char Lot's body beyond recognition as a human being, to create an opaque wall of thick, black smoke from floor to ceiling inside

> the apartment, and to generate heat intense enough to deteriorate the bedroom door. Yet the defense contends the evidence cannot prove beyond a reasonable doubt that Terney intended to damage the building and not simply to destroy his girlfriend's body.

d. Sentence Structure

The principles of good English sentence structure set forth in Chapter 10 and Appendix A apply to persuasive writing. Particularly important are those principles that promote clear and affirmative expression.

1. Active voice is more forceful than passive voice. Active voice points the finger ("The defendant held Ms. White at gunpoint"). However, use passive voice if you want to deemphasize the actor in the sentence ("Ms. White was held at gun point"). Also use passive voice when you want to direct your reader to the facts ("Acting as an arm of the prosecution, hindering the presentation of the defense, and giving unconstitutional jury instructions were acts of judicial misconduct"), and to promote continuity between sentences ("The plaintiff supported his evidence with a 2016 study of environmental hazards. This environmental study was conducted in three counties.")

2. Affirmative sentences are more dynamic than negative sentences.

3. Shorter sentences adequately related to each other are preferable to longer sentences. They flow more fluidly. Long sentences slow the reader down if they contain a series of interrupting phrases or clauses that separate the subject and predicate. However, a series of short, staccato sentences can be abrupt and choppy.

4. Transitional sentences or phrases help your reader comprehend the logical development of your argument.

5. Rhetorical questions are not useful. They raise questions that you should answer explicitly.

e. Quotations

Whenever you use language that is not your own, quote the language exactly, place the words within quotation marks, and cite the source of the quotation. Failure to do so is plagiarism.

Whenever a quotation is fifty words or more, use a block quotation, that is, indent and single space the quote and do not use quotation marks. Place the citation as the first non-indented text after the quotation.

Be selective in choosing quotations. Use them principally for statutory language and statements of the rule of a case or cases, or for particularly apt language that you cannot equal yourself. When you do quote an authority, do not immediately just repeat it in your own words. Instead, tell the reader how the quotation relates to your point. If the quotation is long, however, you help your reader if you forecast its essential point.

Do not employ quotations where you can convey that information just as well or better in your own words. It is often difficult to integrate quotations smoothly, and even if this is done successfully, differences in style may be distracting. Moreover, too many quotations will slow the flow of your argument, and a reader may decide to overlook them. A reader might also ignore a lengthy quotation because the quotation is just too hard to read. Try, therefore, to use your own words, but be sure to supply a citation to the source. (See Appendix A, section C for further information on quotation.)

III. SPECIFIC TYPES OF MOTIONS

A.   The Motion to Dismiss

THE SUBSTANCE OF A TRIAL BRIEF depends on the type of motion it supports or opposes. A defendant's motion to dismiss, for example, may be filed in federal or state court in response to the complaint. Accordingly, this motion is often decided early in the litigation. Sometimes, the motion is based on non-substantive grounds. For example, it may challenge the court's jurisdiction over the case or the adequacy of the service of process on the defendant. Or the motion may challenge the legal sufficiency of the complaint.[10]

To challenge sufficiency, the defendant must accept as true the facts alleged in the complaint. Therefore, the memorandum will not challenge the accuracy of those facts. Instead, the defendant would show that under no set of facts and no interpretation of the law can this plaintiff be entitled to relief. For example, if the

---

[10] *See, e.g.,* Fed. R. Civ. P. 12 (b)(6)." [A] party may assert the following defenses by motion:

   . . . (6) failure to state a claim on which relief can be granted";

   N.Y.C.P.L.R. Rule 3211 (a). "A party may move for judgment dismissing one or more causes of action asserted against him on the ground that . . .

   (7) the pleading fails to state a cause of action."

plaintiff is the legal representative of a minor who claims loss of consortium of a parent, the defendant will argue that no interpretation of the facts regarding his negligence would permit the plaintiff to succeed, because that jurisdiction recognizes only the loss of consortium of a spouse.

The defendant may also move to dismiss if the complaint omits an allegation that is necessary to the case. For example, a plaintiff's claim will be vulnerable to a motion to dismiss if the claim arises under a statute concerning fraud in the sale of securities, but fails to allege that the defendant sold securities.

Because a motion to dismiss responds to a complaint, the defendant's memorandum in support of its motion sets out the plaintiff's claims in that complaint and cites to the paragraphs of the complaint. If the complaint includes more than one claim, organized by counts, the defendants sets out each count of the complaint and identifies the count or counts at which the motion is directed. Each count should be placed under a separate heading of the memo. A defendant may move to dismiss one count of a multi-count complaint, and then file an answer to the other counts.

You can find a sample Motion to Dismiss in Appendix E.

B. The Motion for Summary Judgment

Another common motion is the motion for summary judgment, which may be submitted by either party. A successful motion will dispose of the case or a part of the case obviating the need for a trial on that issue. This motion is generally filed after the parties have completed discovery, that is, they have taken depositions of the parties and witnesses, taken interrogatories of the opposing party, received documents, and received admissions from the other party to remove uncontested issues. Discovery permits the parties to develop the facts and arguments on which their motions are based.

Start by checking the language of the applicable federal or state rule.

Under federal law, Fed. R. Civ. P. 56(a) states:

"The court shall grant summary judgment if the movant shows that there is no genuine dispute as to any material fact and the movant is entitled to judgment as a matter of law."

Many state statutes have similar language. For example, the Florida Rules of Civil Procedure Rule 1.510 (c) states:

"The judgment sought must be rendered immediately if the pleadings and summary judgment evidence on file show that there is no genuine issue as to any material fact and that the moving party is entitled to a judgment as a matter of law."

Because the motion can be granted only if there are no disputed material facts, an important part of the moving party's memorandum is to show why the material facts are not disputed or why any disputed facts are not material. The party opposing the motion, of course, will try to show that there are disputed material facts. Each party weaves a narrative that shows the facts are either disputed or undisputed, identifies the relevant facts of record from sources such as depositions and affidavits, and cites to those sources.

For example, a defendant employer in an Americans With Disabilities Act (ADA) case may move for summary judgment on the ground that the company did not have to provide the disabled plaintiff her requested accommodation. Under the ADA, an employer must reasonably accommodate only known disabilities of the plaintiff and the parties must engage in what the courts call "an interactive process" to determine those accommodations. The defendant would claim that it did not know of the plaintiff's disability at the relevant time. The defendant's memorandum in support of its motion will garner all the facts that are learned from discovery and affidavits relevant to show that no facts are disputed that are material to its knowledge of the plaintiff's disability and that it did not know of the plaintiff's disability.

The plaintiff's memorandum will do the same in order to contradict the defendant's memorandum and emphasize facts that show that the defendant knew the plaintiff was disabled. If the memos reveal disputed facts on that question, the court will deny the motion so that the issue will be resolved at trial. The parties will do the same for the facts regarding whether the parties engaged in an interactive process. Many courts require the parties to list the disputed and the undisputed facts in their memoranda.

1. The Importance of Affidavits

Affidavits are an important part of pretrial motion practice; they set forth relevant facts that the affiant swears to from personal knowledge. Affidavits are often submitted by a party to the suit, but may also be submitted by a third party, such as a witness or an expert. Affidavits must be prepared following the jurisdiction's rules of procedure and they must be completely accurate. The affiant runs the risk of being impeached[11] at the trial by the opposing party over any false statements in the affidavit.

Fed. R. Civ. P. 56(c)(4) requires that "An affidavit or declaration used to support or oppose a motion must be made on personal knowledge, set out facts that would be admissible in evidence, and show that the affiant or declarant is competent to testify on the matters stated." The affidavit thus includes statements that identify the affiant, and that declare the affiant is competent to testify about the facts in the affidavit, and the statements are based on personal knowledge.

The affidavit typically begins "I Jane Doe, being duly sworn, state the following:

1. I am the defendant in this case and have personal knowledge of the facts stated in this affidavit.

2. I am over twenty-one years old and otherwise competent to testify to the matters in this affidavit."

2. Writing the Affidavit

Lawyers usually write the affidavits for their clients to review and sign, but the affidavit is the client's own story. Think about how you want the court to view your client. Write the affidavit in the client's voice, rather than in a lawyer's professional voice or in stilted legalese. Moreover, the affidavit should read well. Use clear sentence structure and organize the facts to tell a coherent story. The body of the affidavit may have topic headings, but not the argumentative ones that you would use in a trial memorandum.

Remember that an affidavit sets forth facts that would be admissible as evidence, not legal conclusions. If Jane Doe is the affiant in the ADA case described above, the affidavit may identify her as the Director of the defendant's Human Resources Department, and go on to say:

"1. I met with the plaintiff in my office on September 6, 2015. At this meeting I authorized the plaintiff to take short-term disability leave for two weeks from September 10–24, 2015.

2. I again met with the plaintiff in my office on October 1, 2015. At this meeting I authorized the plaintiff to use an extra ten minutes as a coffee break.

---

[11] A witness is impeached if her credibility is challenged because she has made conflicting statements of facts.

3. I last met with the plaintiff in my office on October 15, 2015, when she told me that she required a ninety-minute break."

Here, the affidavit is providing facts that are relevant to the defendant's case that the parties engaged in an interactive process to accommodate the plaintiff's disability. But Ms. Doe would not say:

"At these meetings we engaged in an interactive process."

That statement would be a conclusion of law, not a statement of fact. Finally, before the client swears to and signs the affidavit, make sure that the client reviews it carefully so that all the factual statements are accurate.

In a summary judgment motion, the moving party must also show that it is entitled to judgment as a matter of law. Thus in this section, the parties' legal arguments will apply the ADA as interpreted in the Supreme Court and that circuit to the facts of the case. (This requires building arguments in the ways explained in Chapter 11 on arguing questions of law, and, in Chapter 16 on argument in an appellate brief.)

You can find a sample Memorandum in Opposition to a Motion for Summary Judgment in Appendix F.

C. The Motion to Suppress Evidence

Motions are made in criminal as well as civil cases. For example, there are motions for a change of venue, for withdrawal of a guilty plea, for severance of defendants, and to dismiss the criminal complaint. One common motion is the motion to suppress evidence, typically made pre-trial. There, the defendant in a criminal case alleges that certain evidence was obtained in violation of his constitutionally protected Fourth Amendment rights against unreasonable searches and seizures. The defendant would argue that under the exclusionary rule, the evidence cannot be admitted into evidence at trial because it was obtained illegally.

Motions to suppress may be made under either federal or state codes of criminal procedure.[12] Local court rules, and individual standing orders of individual judges must also be consulted. Generally, a motion to suppress consists of the following:

- a notice of motion,

- a motion (the notice and the motion may be combined),

---

[12] F. R. Crim. P. 12(b)3(c); F.R. Crim. P. 47; NY CPL § 710.20.1.

- an affidavit or declaration by the defendant or the defendant's attorney,

- a memorandum of law.

As with civil motions, the notice informs the court and the opposing party of the nature of the motion and the date, time and place the movant asks that the motion be heard. The motion must include the relief sought and the grounds for that relief.

1.   Notice of Motion and Motion

Here is an example of a combined notice of motion and motion in a case where the defendant alleges that the warrantless installation and monitoring of a GPS on his truck violated his Fourth Amendment rights.

SIRS:

PLEASE TAKE NOTICE that upon the annexed affidavit of Elizabeth Mason, Esq., dated January 6, 2017, and upon all the papers and proceedings in this case, the defendant Robert Sloan will move this Court at the federal courthouse, 27 Joralemon Street, Brooklyn, New York, on January 25, 2017, at 10:00 a.m., or as soon after as counsel can be heard. Defendant seeks an order pursuant to Fed. R. Crim. P. 12 (b)(3) to suppress evidence obtained from the warrantless installation and monitoring of a Global Positioning System (GPS) tracking device on defendant Sloan's van. Defendant Sloan argues that the warrantless search violates his rights under the Fourth Amendment of the United States Constitution. In the alternative, defendant respectfully requests a hearing on this motion and such other relief as this Court may deem just and proper.

---

2.   Affidavit or Declaration in Support

A sworn statement, by affidavit or declaration in support, is usually part of the motion papers.[13] This document provides the factual basis upon which the motion should be granted. The defendant in a criminal case, however, typically would not give a detailed factual affidavit at this stage in the proceedings. Such an affidavit could subject the defendant to impeachment at trial if there are inconsistencies or inaccuracies in the facts. More commonly, the defendant's attorney would submit an affirmation or declaration giving background facts which provide the basis for the defendant's motion.

---

[13]   Fed. R. Crim. P. 47(b). "A motion may be supported by affidavit."

Here is a sample attorney affidavit in support of the motion to suppress in the GPS case.

STATE OF ABBOTT   )

) SS:

COUNTY OF KINGS   )

Elizabeth Mason swears under penalty of perjury to the following, except for those statements made on information and belief, and as to those, she believes them to be true.

1. I am an attorney duly licensed to practice in the State of Abbott, and I represent the defendant in this matter. I submit this affidavit in support of Mr. Sloan's motion to suppress evidence.

2. The defendant was indicted by the Grand Jury on December 23, 2015 and charged in a one-count indictment with conspiracy to distribute and possess with intent to distribute 100 kilograms of a mixture containing a detectable amount of marijuana, in violation of 21 U.S.C. §§ 846 and 841(b)(1)(B)(vii) (2016). A copy of the indictment is attached.

3. I have discussed this case with the defendant on numerous occasions and am familiar with the facts. I make this affidavit on behalf of the defendant and in support of his motion for an order suppressing the government's use of all evidence obtained as a result of the warrantless use of a Global Positioning System (GPS) device that was installed on Mr. Sloan's vehicle to track his movements continuously for approximately 22 days. This evidence sought to be suppressed includes, but is not limited to, 100 kilograms of marijuana. This evidence should be suppressed as the fruits of a search conducted in violation of the Fourth Amendment to the United States Constitution.

4. On information and belief, the U.S. Attorney of the Eastern District of Abbott intends to use the evidence against the defendant at trial.

5. On or about November 11, 2015, Drug Enforcement Administration (DEA) Special Agent William Brown, working with DEA Special Agents Robert Allen and Marjorie Brooke, decided to install a GPS on the underside on Mr. Sloan's van. This was done in the dead of night, without Mr. Sloan's knowledge or permission. At the time the GPS was installed, Mr. Sloan's van was parked across the street from his house. See the November 11, 2015 report of Special Agent William

Brown, a copy of which is attached. (Hereafter "DEA 11/11/15 Report").

6. According to the DEA 11/11/15 Report, the agents believed that there was a marijuana ring operating out of the Grand Square Greenmarket in Abbott City where Mr. Sloan operates a stand selling indoor and outdoor plants. Based on information the agents purportedly received from an unidentified "witness," who was told by "someone" that Mr. Sloan could sell that person marijuana for a specific price, they installed a GPS device on Mr. Sloan's van. Based on the monitoring of the GPS, the agents determined that Mr. Sloane made approximately four trips per week to Cromwell Nursery located about 15 miles outside Abbott City in the town of Berring for a total of approximately 12 times during the 22 day period. The agents believe that based on the size and the amount of stock Mr. Sloan had at his stand, he did not need to visit the nursery as often as he did to obtain plants for the Grand Square Green Market. See the December 4, 2015 report of Special Agent William Brown a copy of which is attached. (Hereafter "DEA 12/4/15 Report"). Neither of the two DEA reports indicates whether the agents investigated Mr. Sloan's sales at other markets.

7. According to the DEA 12/4/15 Report, based on information obtained from law enforcement in Berring, a witness had seen some marijuana plants growing in one of the back rooms of the Cromwell Nursery. On December 3, 2015, the Berring police raided the Cromwell Nursery and found over 100 marijuana plants. On that same day, the DEA agents stopped Mr. Sloan as he was driving his van back from Berring. Based on the information they obtained from the GPS that indicated Mr. Sloan was in Berring in the vicinity of Cromwell Nursery, they searched Mr. Sloan's van, without a warrant and without his permission. According to the DEA 12/4/15 Report, the agents found a significant amount of marijuana in the van along with transaction records, and arrested Mr. Sloan.

8. According to the DEA 12/4/15 Report, the GPS was removed from Mr. Sloan's van shortly after his arrest on December 3, 2015, a full 22 days after it was installed. During this time the GPS transmitted the location of Mr. Sloan's van to a police receiver night and day, indicating all of Mr. Sloan's personal and private activities during this entire time period.

9.   On information and belief, at no time before or after the installation or during the monitoring of the GPS did the DEA agents obtain a warrant from any court. Therefore, the installation and continuous monitoring of the GPS on Mr. Sloan's van was an illegal search in violation of his Fourth Amendment rights. But for the information obtained from the warrantless and illegal GPS use on Mr. Sloan's van, the agents would not have known that Mr. Sloan was in Berring on December 3, 2015, and would have had no reason to stop or search Mr. Sloan's van. Therefore, all evidence seized from Mr. Sloan's van, including the marijuana and the records, should be suppressed.

WHEREFORE, affiant asks this Court to suppress all evidence on the ground that it was seized as a result of the warrantless installation and monitoring of the GPS device on Mr. Sloan's van, in violation of the Fourth Amendment's proscription of unreasonable searches and seizures. In the alternative, affiant asks this court to grant a hearing on the legality of the police conduct in this case, and requests such other relief as this court deems just.

Dated: January 6, 2017

/s/ _____

Elizabeth Mason
35 Court Street
Abbott City, Abbott 12345
(999) 788-9999

A supporting memorandum of law in the GPS case would provide the court with the relevant facts of the case and the arguments supporting the grounds for the motion. The motion to suppress will usually include a Preliminary Statement giving the procedural posture of the case, a Statement of Facts, and an Argument. The motion may also contain a Table of Contents and an Introduction that precedes the Preliminary Statement.

IV. COMPONENTS OF A TRIAL BRIEF

THERE IS NO SINGLE REQUIRED FORMAT for the trial brief. You could start by checking the court rules. However, in general, courts require that the moving party set forth both the grounds for the motion with citation to supporting authorities, and the specific relief sought.

The brief may have some or all of the following sections:

• The Caption and Title.

• The Table of Contents.

- The Introduction.

- The Statement of Facts.

- The Question(s) Presented (only in limited situations).

- The Argument.

- The Conclusion.

- Any supporting affidavits or appendices.

A.   Caption and Title

The first page contains at a glance the basic information about the case. The caption includes the name of the court, the names of the parties, the docket number, and the initials of the judge to whom the case has been assigned. It also includes the title of the brief in support of or in opposition to the motion. The cover page will usually contain the same information along with the name, address, and phone number of the attorney. A sample caption and title follows in a case involving a Fourth Amendment challenge to airport screening.

UNITED STATES DISTRICT COURT
SOUTHERN DISTRICT OF JORALEMON

GEORGE HANSON,

Plaintiff,

v.

KIRSTJEN NIELSEN, in her official capacity as Secretary of the Department of Homeland Security, and HUBAN GAWADIA, in his official capacity as Administrator of the TRANSPORTATION SECURITY ADMINISTRATION,	Memorandum in Support of Plaintiff's Motion for Summary Judgment Civ. Action No.c66-2017

Defendants.

B.   Table of Contents

You may have a Table of Contents on the page after the Caption and Title. The Table of Contents provides the court with an overview of the contents of the Memorandum and page references for each section. A Table of Contents may be required by some courts, depending on the length of the memorandum. It generally includes: the Introduction, the Table of Authorities (optional), the

Statement of Facts, the Argument with Point Headings, and the Conclusion.

The Table not only provides the court with page references, it also gives the court a summary of your argument through the point headings.

C. The Introduction

The Introduction is a concise statement which provides a context for the motion and basic information about the case. But it is more than that. Since this section comes early in the memorandum, you use it to catch the court's attention, to summarize your most powerful arguments, and to introduce the court to your theory of the case.

The Introduction also identifies the kind of case, the parties, the nature of the motion, the relief sought, and the reason. The complete procedural history of the case, however, is often included in the Statement of Facts, rather than the Introduction. In general, the Introduction should be less than a page. You are looking for impact, not detail.

The Introduction to a memorandum in opposition to a motion would briefly explain why each basis of the moving party's motion should fail. However, the arguments should be made positively.

The following is a sample Introduction to the Defendant's Memorandum in opposition to George Hanson's Motion for Summary Judgment in the airport screening case. What is the Defendant's theory of the case?

Introduction

Defendants submit this memorandum of law in support of their motion for summary judgment. The Department of Homeland Security and the Transportation Security Administration have implemented new security measures using a backscatter machine. These measures are specifically tailored to detect non-metallic explosives in response to increasing threats of plastic and liquid explosives used for airplane terrorism. The backscatter machine is a physical contact-free device that scans a passenger and ensures that the passenger is not carrying any non-metallic threats. Defendants have adopted the machine to prevent human deaths and mass destruction of property caused by air terrorism.

Plaintiff George Hanson sued defendants Kirstjen Nielsen, the Secretary of the Department of Homeland Security, and Huban Gawadia, the Administrator of the Transportation Security Administration, for violating his Fourth Amendment right to be secure from unreasonable searches and seizures. Plaintiff alleges that defendants' airport security procedures overly intruded on his privacy. Plaintiff was at the Joralemon Airport on his way to Baltimore. He chose to receive a pat-down procedure instead of going through the contact-free backscatter machine. In the process of the pat-down, plaintiff's colostomy bag leaked. Plaintiff asks the court to declare defendants' security measures unconstitutional and to permanently enjoin defendants from using the backscatter machine or pat-downs as primary airport security searches.

Defendants' motion for summary judgment should be granted. Defendants' security procedures advance substantial government interests beyond the normal need of law enforcement. These procedures are anti-terrorism measures designed to prevent the loss of human life and massive property damage. The defendants' procedures were also minimally intrusive on plaintiff's privacy.

Exercise 15-A

Which Introduction to the Memorandum in Support of Defendant's Motion for Summary Judgment is better and why?

1.   The plaintiff filed a complaint on September 1, 2017, alleging that the Allston Protestant Church and College violated her rights under the Americans with Disabilities Act. This memorandum is filed in support of Defendant's motion for summary judgment under Fed. R. Civ. P. 56(a), on the grounds that the suit is barred by the "ministerial exception"[14] to federal employment discrimination laws. This exception bars plaintiff, who is a teacher employed by the church. Plaintiff charged that Allston fired her on the basis of her disability, narcolepsy, in violation of her rights under the Americans with Disabilities Act. However, the First Amendment's Establishment and Free Exercise Clauses bar suits brought by ministers against their churches. By forbidding the 'establishment of religion" and guaranteeing the "free exercise thereof," these clauses ensured that the new federal government, unlike the English Crown, would have no role in filling ecclesiastical offices. The plaintiff is a minister. Therefore, the defendant's motion for summary judgment should be granted.

2.   This memorandum is filed under Fed. R. Civ. P. 56 (a) in support of defendant's motion for summary judgment. The plaintiff has no claim under the Americans with Disabilities Act, because she is a teacher of religion. Numerous courts have precluded these claims under the "ministerial exception." Therefore, the court should dismiss the complaint since there are no material facts at issue and the defendant is entitled to judgment as a matter of law.

Exercise 15-B

Evaluate the following Introductions.

1.   Memorandum of Law in Support of Defendants' Motion for Summary Judgment

Introduction

Come now the defendants by their counsel with their motion for summary judgment. Pursuant to the order of this Court entered July 28, 2017, defendants/counterclaim-plaintiffs Tonetic, Inc. and Dr. Steven Nickel (collectively referred to hereinafter as defendants) submit this Memorandum of Law in further support of their motion seeking dismissal of all of plaintiff's copyright infringement claims on the grounds that, inter alia, in accordance with prior rulings by the Court of Appeals for the Second Circuit, plaintiff's description of

---

[14]   *See Hosanna-Tabor Evangelical Lutheran Church and Sunday School v. EEOC*, 132 S. Ct. 694 (2012).

defendants' software is too vague and insufficient to provide a basis for any injunctive and/or monetary recovery.

2.   Memorandum of Law in Support of Motion of Defendant Pressman, Inc. to Dismiss for Forum Non Conveniens or in the Alternative to Transfer Venue

Introduction

In a classic example of vexatious litigation, plaintiff Davis Corporation has filed this action in California—purportedly based on tort and contract claims that arose in Illinois, will be decided solely by reference to Illinois law, and has little or no connection to California—in an attempt to bully the defendant Pressman, Inc. into dropping or compromising its previously-filed collection action in Illinois state court. Davis Corp. is thwarted by the facts, however. They demonstrate that the Central District of California is not the proper forum for this lawsuit and that the action must be dismissed or, in the alternative, transferred to the Northern District of Illinois, a more appropriate forum for deciding this controversy.

D.   Statement of Facts

The Statement of Facts usually includes both the procedural history of the case as it relates to the motion and the relevant facts. Keep in mind a number of points as you write it. First, the court is dealing with many different matters and cannot be expected to be familiar with the facts of your case. Your Facts must be clear and complete. The court needs to know what the case is all about. Second, you have an ethical obligation to include all material facts, even those that may support the arguments on the other side. But, third, you want to present your facts with your theory of the case in mind. Narrate the facts of your case in such a way that the court will be inclined to decide the motion in your favor, even before you get to the Argument section. Your presentation must be subtle, however, not strident or argumentative.

1.   The Procedural History

The court may be hearing a number of motions on one day. Therefore, always provide a clear history of what has occurred in your case and the grounds for the motion. If your Memorandum contains an Introduction, decide which procedural information should be provided in the Introduction and which in the Statement of Facts. There are no rigid rules. Since the Introduction should be fairly short, detailed procedural content often is more effective in the Statement of Facts. If the procedural history is lengthy, then consider putting it in a separate section.

2. The Opening

When you begin the Statement of Facts, think of how you can introduce the court to your theory of the case, and to start favorably for your client. Here are the opening sentences in opposing Statements of Facts. The defendant has brought a motion to suppress the evidence obtained through the installation and monitoring of a GPS on his car in violation of his Fourth Amendment rights.

> For the Government: "On December 3, 2017, DEA agents arrested Robert Sloan after discovering over one hundred kilograms of marijuana in his vehicle."
>
> For the defendant: "Mr. Robert Sloan is a merchant who operates a stand at the Grand Square Greenmarket in Abbott City selling indoor and outdoor plants."

These opening sentences present the court with two opposing views of the case. Both are accurate, but the choice of the facts gives them their impact.

3. Developing the Facts

After giving the procedural history, you present the facts of the case that support your motion. To do this effectively, you must be familiar with the legal standards that govern the motion you are bringing. In bringing a summary judgment motion, for example, you must show not only that you are entitled to judgment as a matter of law, but also that there is no genuine dispute as to any material facts.

In addition to explaining the legal standard for the particular motion, you should think of how you can present the facts in a way that would be most convincing to the court. Although it is inappropriate in the Statement of Facts to adopt an argumentative tone, it is still possible to arrange facts and choose words in such a way that they incline the court to see the case and the motion from your perspective. Consider using the narrative techniques of storytelling that fiction writers use: setting, character, plot, sequence, point of view, and theme.

- The setting where the story takes place can support your theory of the case. For example, in an employment discrimination case alleging racial discrimination, make it clear that the events occurred in a city that is 25% non-white, but the union itself is all-white. This suggests the existence of discrimination.

- Your client is the main character of the story and should be portrayed positively. Include details that humanize the client, painting him in a positive light, even if the facts are not relevant to the legal issue. Explain, for example, that your client is the devoted father of three, has good performance reviews, and has watched all the promotions going to white union workers. Give the court a sense of the client as a person. Describe opposing characters in a negative light.

- Consider also the plot, which involves the client in a conflict in which he seeks to succeed and struggles to achieve a resolution. Frame the conflict from the client's perspective, narrowly or broadly.

- Choose an appropriate sequence. Often a chronological approach is most helpful in giving the court a clear understanding of what happened in the case. However, you may want to present certain facts out of order to give them greater emphasis, or to organize by topics.

- Although you write the Statement of Facts in the third person, write the story from the client's point of view. Use this approach to include the client's mental processes as well as his concrete acts.

- Finally, the theme of your story should lead to the court's ruling in your favor because the result would be just.

The facts should be complete, consistent with your theory of the case, and coherently presented.

Notice the different approaches taken in the following competing statements of facts in the airport body-scanning case. Each statement illustrates the writer's theory of the case. What choices did the writers below make in terms of narrative order, word choice, and appeal to emotion and reasoning?

For the plaintiff

STATEMENT OF FACTS

On October 15, 2016, George Hanson was on his way to a business meeting in Baltimore, Maryland. As he approached the security check-in point at Joralemon Airport, he duly emptied his pockets, took off his shoes and unpacked his laptop from his carry-on bag. (Compl.¶ 9). He then placed all of his personal belongings on the conveyor belt, which carried the items to the other side of the checkpoint. (Compl.¶ 10).

At that point, a TSA agent ordered Mr. Hanson to step into a body-scanning machine. *Id.* The scanner was equipped with whole-body imaging technology, which allows the government to see underneath any air traveler's clothing. The scanner produces graphic images of the person's naked body and projects them on a computer screen, where they are scrutinized by government agents. The machines expose the contours of the traveler's genitals, private accessories such as body piercings and medical devices, and even sanitary napkins used by women. Previously, the scanners had been used only as part of a pilot program in limited locations and only as a secondary means of screening, rather than on a national scale.

Although the machines are meant to help TSA agents detect nonmetallic explosives, experts have raised doubts on the effectiveness of the technology, noting that the scanners may fail to detect the powerful chemical powder used in the attempted bombings of an American Airlines flight in 2001 and a Northwest Airlines flight on Christmas Day, 2009.

Prior to heading off to the airport, Mr. Hanson had glanced at some body-scan images on TSA, *How It Works,* on the internet, and was also taken aback by their intrusiveness. When he arrived at the screening gate, Mr. Hanson tried to find out if he could instead undergo a different search. A TSA agent refused and told Mr. Hanson he could either go through the scanner or undergo a thorough pat-down. (Compl. ¶ 12). The pat-down resembles a police frisk; TSA agents pat down the passengers' genital area and women's breasts.

Mr. Hanson has suffered from Crohn's disease for more than 30 years and recently underwent an emergency operation necessitating a colostomy. He wears an external colostomy bag that collects his feces from a sizable incision in his abdomen. (Compl.¶ 11). Given his medical condition, Mr. Hanson tried to convey to the TSA agent the humiliation that would accompany either search. However, the agent simply repeated that Mr. Hanson must submit to one of the searches— or "take the next train out of Joralemon." When Mr. Hanson pleaded with the agent and asked whether he really thought Mr. Hanson was a terrorist, the agent replied, "as far as we're concerned you're all terrorists until you pass security." (Compl.¶ 13).

Presented with two awful choices, and not wanting to miss an important business meeting, Mr. Hanson opted for the patdown.

(Compl.¶ 14). At this point, the TSA agent yelled out to another official that "we have a guy with a medical device, take him for a pat-down." The agent said this so loudly, bystanders turned their heads to stare at Mr. Hanson. Hoping to avoid further humiliation, Mr. Hanson slunk off to the side to submit to the pat-down. (Compl.¶ 15).

Mr. Hanson asked the TSA agent to be careful of the colostomy bag, and pointed out exactly where it was on his body. Nonetheless, the agent proceeded with a pat-down so rough that he dislodged the colostomy bag, causing feces to dribble out. To Mr. Hanson's horror, the agent continued with the search. Mr. Hanson stood frozen in his spot, too mortified to utter even a word. (Compl.¶ 16). When the pat-down was finally over, Mr. Hanson was left wet, humiliated and covered in his own feces, stripped of all dignity. Mr. Hanson was forced to abandon his trip, depriving him of significant potential business. (Compl.¶ 17). On December 2, 2017, Mr. Hanson sued defendants alleging they violated his rights under the Fourth Amendment against unreasonable searches and seizures.

For the defendant
STATEMENT OF FACTS

Modern-day terrorists now employ previously inconceivable tactics in their mission of destroying American lives and property. In response to continuing threats of terrorism, the Department of Homeland Security ("DHS") and the Transportation Security Administration ("TSA") have recently implemented new screening procedures at the Joralemon Airport ("Airport"), which provide passengers with an option of choosing between going through a backscatter machine or receiving an enhanced patdown procedure. Compl., ¶ 5. The new security procedures have replaced walk-through metal detectors to "streamline the security process." Striker Aff., ¶ 7. The TSA officers at the Airport still use hand wands, the hand-held metal detectors, but only when the officers deem them necessary, such as when "a passenger is in a wheel chair or is otherwise unable to stand up." *Id.*

The TSA developed the backscatter machine to ensure air travel safety by detecting both metallic and non-metallic weapons and explosives concealed under passengers' clothing. The backscatter machine is a state-of-the-art machine that produces an image resembling a chalk etching, and it does not involve any physical contact with the passengers.

The TSA has adopted extensive and strict measures so that the backscatter machine procedure protects the privacy of passengers. The TSA officer who assists the passenger in the screening process never sees the backscatter image. The officer communicates via wireless headset with another officer in a remote secure resolution room, who has the only access to the image.

Moreover, the image viewed by the remotely located officer is programmed to blur out the entire image, especially the passengers' private parts. The backscatter machine cannot store, print, transmit or save the image, and the program automatically deletes the image from the system once the remotely located officer clears the passenger. *Id.* In addition, officers evaluating the image cannot bring any photo-enabled devices in to the resolution room. *Id.* In order to accommodate passengers who may still feel uneasy about the backscatter machine, the TSA provides passengers with an option to opt out from going through the backscatter machine, and allows them to instead receive the pat-down procedure. The enhanced pat-downs involve a TSA officer patting the outer layer of clothes, and it may include some sensitive areas of the body to ensure the absence of weapons or explosives. Compl., ¶ 4.

On October 15, 2017, at the Airport, plaintiff George Hanson approached Officer Larry Striker's screening station, emptied his pockets, and put his belongings on the X-ray scanner. Striker Aff., ¶ 3. Mr. Hanson was on his way to Baltimore, Maryland for a business trip. Compl., ¶ 9. Officer Striker followed the TSA guidelines and asked Mr. Hanson whether he would like to go through the backscatter machine or instead undergo the enhanced pat-down procedure. Striker Aff., ¶ 3. Officer Striker is a veteran TSA security officer with good standing at the Airport, and has received an extensive training on the new screening procedures. Striker Aff., ¶ 2. Officer Striker informed Mr. Hanson that the pat-down procedure will include sensitive areas of his body, but ensured Mr. Hanson that all of the security officers were trained to maintain "the highest level of professionalism." Striker Aff., ¶ 3.

Having gone to the TSA website and examined the backscatter machine, Mr. Hanson judged that the backscatter machine was too intrusive on personal privacy. Compl., ¶ 12. Mr. Hanson refused to go through the backscatter machine and demanded the hand wand procedure, which was not a part of the standard screening process. Striker Aff., ¶ 4. Showing signs of agitation, *id*, Mr. Hanson said that he has a "medical condition" and would feel humiliated and embarrassed to go through the backscatter machine or receive the enhanced pat-down. Striker Aff., ¶ 5. Officer Striker explained to Mr. Hanson that all passengers must go through either one of the two screening procedures. *Id.* When asked by Mr. Hanson whether Officer Striker thought that Mr. Hanson is a terrorist, Officer Striker responded that all passengers could be suspects until passing the security check. Compl., ¶ 13. Officer Striker assured Mr. Hanson that all the security officers were trained in dealing with "all sorts of medical conditions" and that they would "exercise every caution." *Id.*

After talking with Officer Striker, Mr. Hanson agreed to receive the enhanced pat-down. Striker Aff., ¶ 5. Officer Striker referred Mr. Hanson to another security officer nearby, and notified him of Mr. Hanson's medical condition. Compl., ¶ 15. Prior to the pat-down, Mr.

Hanson showed his colostomy bag, which resulted from a Crohn's disease operation, Compl., ¶ 11, to an officer conducting the pat-down. Compl., ¶ 16. Officer Striker did not notice anything "unusual" with the pat-down that the other officer conducted on Mr. Hanson. Striker Aff., ¶ 6. Unfortunately, Mr. Hanson's colostomy bag came detached and started to slowly leak during the enhanced pat-down, but he never told anyone at the TSA of the leak. Compl., ¶ 16. Mr. Hanson asserts that he felt "humiliated" and cancelled his trip to Baltimore, which caused a loss of a business opportunity. Compl., ¶ 17. However, Mr. Hanson did not impose any restrictions on the pat-down procedure, and although Mr. Hanson had the choice to receive the pat-down privately, he did not request to receive it privately. Striker Aff., ¶ 6.

In his complaint, Plaintiff seeks to permanently enjoin Defendants from continuing to use either the backscatter machine or the enhanced pat-downs as a primary means of screening at airports. Plaintiff also asks the court to declare that Defendants' policy of using the backscatter machine or the enhanced patdowns as a primary means of screening at airports is a violation of the Fourth Amendment of the Constitution.

Defendants moved for summary judgment because there is no genuine dispute as to any material fact and the defendants are entitled to judgment as a matter of law.

These two versions of the facts illustrate the very different impression that can be conveyed when working with the same facts. Mr. Hanson's account emphasizes the TSA's violation of his Fourth Amendment right to be protected from unreasonable searches. The narrative begins with Hanson's good faith efforts to comply with airport security measures and the TSA's insistence on using the highly intrusive backscatter machine as the primary means of screening. In telling details, the writer describes the machine's exposure of "the traveler's genitals, private accessories such as body piercings and medical devices, and even sanitary napkins." Given his medical condition, Mr. Hanson tries to explain the humiliation he will experience if subjected to such a screening, only to be met with the agent's crude response to submit or "take the next train out of Joralemon." The quotation captures the agent's insensitive and unprofessional conduct. The last paragraph ends strongly. An agent subjects Hanson to a pat-down so rough that his colostomy bag is dislodged and feces dribbled out. The scenario is so vivid and upsetting it underscores the level of intrusion and elicits empathy for the plaintiff.

In contrast, the government's narrative opens with reminders of the nature of the terrorist threat. It proceeds to outline the efficacy of the technology and the multiple privacy measures the TSA has taken to ensure the screening is no more intrusive than necessary. In contrast to the plaintiff's facts, the incident with Hanson is neutrally reported. Instead of direct quotation—as when the agent yelled "we have a guy with a medical device, take him for a patdown"—we are simply informed that he was "referred" to another security guard. The tone is dispassionate and factual.

Exercise 15-C

1. *Rewrite sentences (a) and (b) as the criminal defendant's lawyer to use more vivid language. Rewrite sentence (c) as the plaintiff's lawyer.*

    a.   The policeman stood in between the defendant and his car.

    b.   He was experiencing fear of imminent harm to himself from his father.

    c.   At the age of seven years, the plaintiff was involved in an automobile accident, being hit by a car, which resulted in the loss of use of his leg.

2. *Read the following list of facts from a case involving the claim of a biological father for a hearing to prevent his non-marital child from being placed for adoption. The standard for determining the father's right to a hearing is whether the father had established a relationship with the child or a family unit including the child.*

The Facts

— Frank Rock and Mary Hall met in 2007

— Frank and Mary lived together 2008–10

— Baby born 2010

— Mary told people, including welfare office, that Frank was the father

— Frank visited Mary in hospital, after baby's birth

— Frank did not know where Mary and child were after Mary left hospital

— Frank never supported baby

— Mary married

— Frank found Mary in 2016 by hiring a detective

— Mary did not permit Frank to visit the baby

— Mary and husband filed petition for adoption Dec. 2016

— Frank filed petition to establish paternity Jan. 2017

Write a Statement of the Facts of one or two paragraphs for a memorandum of law for Frank, supporting his petition for a hearing, and then write one in opposition to Frank's claim (for the state agency).

E. Question Presented (Statement of Issues)

Some (though not most) memoranda of law include a section in which the attorney states the legal questions that the motion raises. Such a section could either precede or follow the Statement of Facts, could come at the end of an Introduction, or be omitted altogether.

The Question should both focus the court's attention on the issues in your motion and suggest an answer that would support a decision by the court in your favor. If your case raises a factual issue, the Question combines the relevant facts of the case and a legal rule. For example, a person seeking to intervene in an action in federal court, pursuant to Fed. R. Civ. P. 24(b)(1), must file a "timely motion." Therefore, one ground on which to oppose a motion to intervene is that the motion was not timely. A Question Presented raising this issue could be stated as follows:

> Is the agency's motion to intervene timely when it was made more than three years after the action was commenced and almost ten months after the judgment was entered?

To intervene as of right pursuant to Fed. R. Civ. P. 24(a)(2), an applicant must also show a legally protectable interest. A party opposing the motion could state the following:

> Did a preliminary injunction remedying racial discrimination against non-whites create a legally protectable interest under Fed. R. Civ. P. 24(a)(2), for white persons who seek to intervene as plaintiffs to obtain union membership for themselves?

The question in both of these examples focuses on a legal issue that the court must consider in deciding whether to grant or deny the motion (timeliness, legally protectable interest) and is framed in such a way that the attorney's argument is clear. [More detailed suggestions on writing a Question Presented can be found in section III of Chapter 16, on appellate briefs.]

Exercise 15-D

Write a Question Presented for a memorandum for Frank Rock and one for the state opposing Frank's petition. (See Exercise 15-C for the facts.)

F.   Point Headings

The Argument is often divided into sections representing the main legal arguments or the counts in the plaintiff's complaint, although a short memorandum may have only one basic argument. If your argument has more than one section, each section would begin with a point heading. The point heading is a single sentence that combines the issue, the relevant facts, the pertinent legal rules, and the conclusion you want the court to reach. Point headings appear in two places. First, they appear in the Table of Contents, providing an overview and outline of the Argument. Second, they appear in the Argument itself, introducing each section that deals with that legal point.

Depending on the content of your argument, you may have main headings and sub-headings. The main heading gives your conclusion on a specific legal argument. If the argument is complex, you may want to include sub-headings as well. Then the main heading provides the conclusion on the argument and the sub-headings provide the reasons. Avoid repeating the same information in the heading and subheading. In addition, do not overdo sub-headings. Your argument on a particular point may be complete in a single sentence. Moreover, if you have too many sub-headings, your argument could appear choppy. Finally, consider the order of your arguments and headings. If there is a threshold argument, it should go first.

Traditionally, the main headings were written in all capital letters, and the sub-headings are written in ordinary type, underlined, and indented. But there is more flexibility now. Follow any applicable court rules. If there are no rules, then for greater clarity, you may put the main headings in bold, and indent and underline the sub-headings.

Here are two examples of effective Point Headings. Since the content of the arguments is different, the writers have used different formats. In the first example addressing the airport pat-down, the writer has used one main heading, plus sub-headings.

In the second example, dealing with whether the installation
and monitoring of a GPS violated the Fourth Amendment, the
writer has used three main headings.

Suggestions on drafting headings:

1.   Keep headings to a reasonable length. Remember they are a
single sentence.

A.   Headings should not be so short that they omit
important information.

**Not: The DEA Never Conducted Mass
Surveillance.**

**Rather: The DEA used GPS Technology in an
Efficient and Targeted Surveillance of One
Individual's Suspected Criminal Activity.**

B.   Headings should not be so long that they are difficult to
follow and they obscure important information.

**Not: The Use of GPS Technology Violated Mr.
Sloan's Reasonable Expectation of Privacy by**

> Providing Information About His Movements That Are More Thorough Than DEA Agent Surveillance Would Be Able to Accomplish Which Distinguishes the GPS Device From a Beeper Like The One in *Knotts* Since That is a Tool that Merely Enhances Police Surveillance but Does Not Provide the Police With Information They Could Not Get by Traditional Means.
>
> Rather: The DEA Conducted a Search When The Officers Used Prolonged GPS Monitoring, Because GPS Technology Provides Extrasensory Surveillance that Reveals Information Otherwise Imperceptible to Police.

2. Headings should provide the information the reader needs. A case name is usually not sufficient.

> Not: *Knotts* Does Not Govern Because It Involved a Beeper.
>
> Rather: The GPS Technology Used in Mr. Sloan's Case Is Distinguishable from the Beeper at Issue in *Knotts* Because the Beeper in *Knotts* Involved Only Sense-Enhancing Technology.

3. The supporting reason for your conclusion must be included either in the main heading or in its sub-headings.

> Not: DEA Agents Committed a Search in Violation of the Fourth Amendment When They Used a GPS to Monitor Mr. Sloan.
>
> Rather: DEA Agents Committed a Search in Violation of the Fourth Amendment When They Used a GPS to Monitor Mr. Sloan for Twenty-Two Days, Because He Had a Reasonable Expectation of Privacy in the Totality of His Movements.

G. Argument

The Argument is the heart of your brief. In it you provide the facts, citations to authority, and reasoning to convince the court to rule in your favor on the motion.

1. Principles of Persuasion

In the Argument section of the document, you analyze the law and apply the law to the facts of your case as you do in an office memorandum. However, an Argument differs from a Discussion in terms of the audience, which is a court, and the purpose of the document, which is to persuade the court to decide the case favorably for your client. So you will write in a more assertive tone, that is, as an advocate.

Here you develop reasons why your client should prevail in order to convince the court to accept your conclusions. The reasoning that you engage in involves the same types of legal analysis you have been doing all year. For example, you may be applying fairly settled law to the facts of your case. Your conclusions would then depend on how you interpret the precedents and how you analogize and distinguish them. Or, you may initially analyze a question of law, for example, on how to interpret a statute, and then apply that statute to the facts of your case. The difference is that in an Argument you always interpret the law and its application as requiring a conclusion favorable to your client. This is not the place to engage in neutral presentations and even-handed analysis. For example, you would not write, "The courts are divided over how to read these statutes together: one way is unfavorable to the defendant, and one way favorable." Instead, you tell the court how to read the statutes in the way favorable to your client. "The provisions of Statute X must override those of Statute Y because X directly governs the subject matter of this dispute."

Another difference is that you must come to a conclusion, and tell the court what that conclusion should be. An advocate uses the topic sentences to do this, such as the sentence above about Statute X directly governing the dispute. By using topic sentences in this way, you make your argument clear to the court. You then go on to provide the reasons that support your conclusion.

Finally, make your arguments clear before dealing with opposing authority and arguments.

Exercise 15-E

1. *Assume you represent two children in a loss of parental consortium claim (loss of intangibles like love, companionship, solace). Rewrite the following statement so that it is affirmative.*

In all but thirteen jurisdictions that have recently considered the issue, children cannot sue for loss of parental consortium.

2. *Assuming you want an exception to the statute of limitations to apply, phrase more effectively.*

While a mere post-traumatic neurosis is not enough to toll the statute, a "post-traumatic depression" coupled with "severe depressive reaction" has been held to constitute the requisite insanity that tolls the statute of limitations.

> **3.** *Assuming you want to invoke an exception to government immunity from liability, phrase more persuasively.*
>
> Generally a municipality is not liable to an individual for failing to provide police protection. However, there is an exception if the police assume a "special relationship" or "special duty" towards an individual.

2. The Thesis Paragraph

The point heading should be followed by a thesis paragraph introducing that argument. Thesis paragraphs can perform different functions.

> **a. Introduction to sub-sections.** Some thesis paragraphs operate as introductions to a major argument, identifying the reasons supporting the argument which may be dealt with in separate sub-sections. Here is an example taken from a motion to suppress tangible evidence:
>
> > John Eli, the defendant, had a legitimate expectation of privacy in the contents of the rental car he drove because the authorized driver of the car had given permission to Eli to drive it. Under *Rakas v. Illinois*, 439 U.S. 128 (1978) Eli had standing to raise his Fourth Amendment motion to suppress the tangible evidence taken from the car for two reasons: he had the authority to exercise exclusive control over the rental car and the right to exclude others, *Id.* at 143 n. 12, and society recognizes his expectation of privacy as reasonable. *Id.* Thus, Eli had standing to assert his Fourth Amendment right.
>
> **b. Standards for the rule.** Other thesis paragraphs may focus on the standards for the rule governing the particular motion, for example, a motion for summary judgment.
>
> > Carol Sloan brings this suit against Compton, Industries, alleging discrimination because of sex under Title VII of the Civil Rights Act of 1964. Plaintiff claims she was terminated because she is a pre-operative transgender person. Pursuant to Rule 56(a) of the Federal Rules of Civil Procedure, defendant respectfully requests this court grant its motion for summary judgment. First, plaintiff's claim fails because she is not entitled to judgment as a matter of law. Transgender persons are not members of a class that Title VII protects. And even if plaintiff is part of a protected class, summary judgment should still be granted because Sloan was terminated for legitimate non-discriminatory reasons, and without pretext. Second, discovery proceedings have produced all necessary facts and there is no genuine dispute

> as to any material fact. Accordingly, defendant's motion for summary judgment should be granted.
>
> **c. Introduction to a single argument.** Still other thesis paragraphs introduce a major argument in a single section of the memorandum.
>
>> Ms. Sloan has been discriminated against "because of sex" because she, a biological male, failed to act according to gender stereotypes by presenting herself as a woman. The Supreme Court of the United States concluded that a person's failure to conform to sex stereotypes constituted discrimination "because of sex" in *Price Waterhouse v. Hopkins*, 490 U.S. 228, 250–51 (1989). In that case, the Court held that comments that the female plaintiff was too "macho" and should walk, talk, and dress more femininely constituted discrimination because of sex. The Court reasoned that "we are beyond the day when an employer could evaluate employees by assuming or insisting that they matched the stereotype associated with their group. . . ." *Id.* at 235, 251. Here, because Ms. Sloan represented herself as female in both name and appearance, she was discriminated against when she was fired because her image did not match the stereotype of one who is biologically male. Therefore, Ms. Sloan is protected under Title VII as a person who was discriminated against "because of sex."

3. Choosing Precedent

The persuasive power of your Argument will also depend on your choice of precedents. Begin your discussion of the precedents with the strongest cases supporting the proposition you need to advance your argument. Typically, you discuss and apply favorable precedents and come to an affirmative legal conclusion before raising and distinguishing unfavorable precedents.

Several factors are relevant in determining which cases would best promote your argument.

- First consider the weight of authority. Whenever possible, base your argument on previous decisions of the highest court in the jurisdiction of your problem, especially decisions of the Supreme Court of the United States if you are analyzing constitutional or federal issues. Even if that Court has not ruled yet on the particular issue in your assignment, relate your arguments to prior decisions of that Court in analogous areas of the law, and to statements that the Court has made in dicta.

- Besides the decisions of the Supreme Court, the most important cases are always the controlling precedents of the jurisdiction. A court always wants to know the law of the jurisdiction. Rely on these decisions and show how they are consistent with the higher court's decisions and policy. Only after this would you use persuasive decisions on the same point by a court that does not bind your court.

- Choose cases because they are particularly relevant, first as binding authority, then because they are factually similar or the reasoning is otherwise appropriate. The reader should not be wondering why you have chosen a particular case to write about.

Remember the basics of using legal sources. The first step to persuasion is to include information that the court needs in order to understand the issues. Quote the controlling statutory language and tell the court what the cases are about, in whatever detail is necessary. Do not try to analyze a case and also explain the facts within a single sentence. Remember that quotes and case names are not a substitute for thorough explication. A strong argument instead requires you to marshal many sources, to work out their meaning, and to apply those sources carefully to your client's case.

Here are some examples showing effective use of precedent from opposing arguments in a motion for summary judgment. The question of law is whether transgender persons are members of a class protected against employment discrimination "because of . . . sex" under Title VII of the Civil Rights Act of 1964, 42 U.S.C. § 2000e2(a) (2006). The Supreme Court has not decided this question and there is no binding precedent in the Circuit in which the motion was filed. The strongest argument for the defendant employer is that Congress did not intend Title VII to include transgender persons. The writer focuses on the majority of circuit court cases which support the legislative history argument. The attorney for the plaintiff cannot make a legislative history argument. Instead, the plaintiff's attorney must focus on how the original view of Title VII's protections has been expanded in other contexts by Supreme Court decisions.

For the employer:

No legislative history even suggests that transgender persons like Ms. Sloan should be included in the class of persons Congress intended Title VII to protect against discrimination "because of . . . sex." Rather, Congress did not intend Title VII to apply to anything but the traditional definition of sex. *Ulane v. Eastern Airlines, Inc.*, 742 F.2d 1081, 1085 (7th Cir. 1984). Title VII prohibits discrimination "against women because they are women and men because they are men." *Id. Accord Etsitty v. Utah Transit Auth.*, 502 F.3d 1215, 1221 (10th Cir. 2007). In fact, courts have "generally recognized that the major thrust of the 'sex' amendment was towards providing equal opportunities for women." *Sommers v. Budget Mktg., Inc.*, 667 F.2d 748, 750 (8th Cir. 1982). Given the comparatively conservative nature of the Congress in 1964, it is reasonable to assume that any intent to extend protection to transgender persons in the sex discrimination amendment would have generated some recorded debate. *Ulane*, 742 F.2d at 1085. Because that information does not exist, the legislative history provides no support for including transgender persons in the protected class.

For the plaintiff:

The Supreme Court's interpretation of the phrase "because of . . . sex" has expanded the meaning of that term. *See Price Waterhouse v. Hopkins*, 490 U.S. 228 (1989); *Oncale v. Sundowner Offshore Services, Inc.*, 523 U.S. 75 (1998). In *Price Waterhouse*, 490 U.S. at 251, the Court held the phrase to include sex stereotyping, and in *Oncale*, 523 U.S. at 78, the Court reasoned that it applied to same-sex harassment. These applications may not have been contemplated by Congress in 1964 because Congress added sex to the Act the day before it went up for a vote in an attempt to prevent the adoption of the bill. *Ulane v. Eastern Airlines, Inc.*, 742 F.2d 1081, 1085 (7th Cir. 1984). However, as the Supreme Court stated, "statutory prohibitions often go beyond the principal evil to cover reasonably comparable evils, and it is ultimately the provisions of our laws rather than the principal concern of our legislators by which we are governed." *Oncale*, 523 U.S. at 79. And while sex specifically was not discussed in depth by Congress, the "theme of a good deal of the statute's legislative history" is "[t]he intent to drive employers to focus on qualifications rather than on . . . sex." *Price Waterhouse*, 490 U.S. at 251. Accordingly, a broad reading of "because of . . . sex" to include transgender persons is in line with Congress's objectives, and so persons like Ms. Sloan are members of the protected class.

As a particular writing technique, if you want the court to be aware of a number of cases, none of which requires individual discussion, group them together with parenthetical explanations—do not merely string cite.

Since transgender persons do not identify with their anatomical sex, they fit the sex stereotyping theory of gender non-conformance. *Barnes v. City of Cincinnati*, 401 F.3d 729, 737 (6th Cir. 2005). Courts interpreting similar statutes have come to the same conclusion. *See, e.g., Glenn v. Bumbry*, 663 F.3d 1312, 1315 (11th Cir. 2011)(equal protection clause)("A person is defined as transgender precisely because of the perception that his or her behavior transgresses gender stereotypes."); *Rosa v. Park West Bank & Trust Co.*, 214 F.3d 213, 216 (1st Cir. 2000)(holding the Equal Credit Opportunity Act prohibits discrimination based on transgender status); *Schwenk v. City of Hartford*, 204 F.3d 1187, 1202 (9th Cir. 2000)(holding gender discrimination unlawful under the Gender Motivated Violence Act).

4.   Rebutting Counter-Arguments

In addition to affirmatively presenting the arguments that support your position, you need to explain away the points against you. The judges know there is another side to this dispute. If the case were one-sided, it would not have been litigated. Thus, even if you are the party who submits the initial brief, that is, you are the moving party of a motion, your analysis should include rebuttal of the other attorney's arguments. However, if you frame those arguments in the way you want the court to understand them, you help the court understand the case, and may "innoculate" the court against the opposing attorney's memorandum or brief. The topic sentence in which you introduce your response to an argument should focus on your response, rather than a description of the opposing argument. For example,

Rather than:

"Compton, Inc. argues that other female employees would be uncomfortable with Ms. Sloan's use of the women's rest room since she is a transgender person."

You could write:

"Compton, Inc.'s concern is illegitimate and facially discriminatory when it argues that other female employees will be uncomfortable when Ms. Sloan, a transgender person, used the women's rest room."

For other suggestions on rebutting opposing arguments, see Chapter 16, VII E.

V.   CONCLUSION

THE CONCLUSION IS A BRIEF STATEMENT, often one sentence, reminding the court of the relief you are seeking. It is often followed by a phrase like "Respectfully submitted," and then

by the signature and name, address, and telephone number of the
attorney of record. For example,

For the foregoing reasons, plaintiff's motion for preliminary injunction
should be granted.

Respectfully submitted,

_____

Attorney's Name
Attorney's address
Attorney's phone number
Attorney for Plaintiff Jane Doe

Date:

CHAPTER 16

WRITING THE APPELLATE BRIEF

I. INTRODUCTION

BRIEF WRITING IS A RISKY BUSINESS. You need to put your case in its best light, but not in a false light, one that risks the outcome of the appeal and your professional credibility. Thus, brief writing is a balancing act—with high-wire stakes—made all the more challenging by the need to frame the facts and arguments in terms of alleged errors below and the standard of review.

You must frame it this way because an appeal is not a re-trying of a case. Appellate courts do not hear evidence in the case as do trial courts. Rather, an appellate court's review is typically limited to a review of the trial court's decision to determine whether, based on the record, the court below committed error in hearing or deciding the case. Thus appellant's attorney searches the record to determine what errors the lower court may have committed, selects those that have the best chance of convincing an appellate court to reverse the decision below, and on that basis, shapes the facts and arguments as convincingly as possible. In contrast, the appellee's attorney argues in favor of affirming the judgment below and tries to rebut the appellant's arguments.

A. Standard of Review

An attorney must also consider the standard of review that is appropriate to each case. The standard of review that an appellate court uses depends upon a number of factors, including the court itself (federal, state, intermediate appellate, highest appellate), the nature of the case (civil, criminal), and the type of error alleged. It is important, though not always easy, for the attorney to determine the appropriate standard of review given that there is a wide range:[1] Some of the more common standards are described below.

> • **Review of Questions of Law**
>
> An appellate court does not defer to the trial court's decision on a question of law and decides the issue *de novo* (without regard to the lower court's determination).

---

[1] The categories are taken from Ursula Bentele, Eve Cary and Mary R. Falk, *Appellate Advocacy, Principles and Practice* pp. 109 et seq. (5th ed. 2012).

Example: Does the government need a warrant to send a drone over a person's greenhouse?

Example: Does the use of Advanced Imaging Technologies (airport body scans) violate the Fourth Amendment?

- **Review of Questions of Fact**

a) **Jury Trials—**

An appellate court will give great deference to a jury verdict and will generally not reverse that verdict. In civil cases, a jury verdict will be reversed only if it is unsupported by any evidence. If some evidence supports the verdict, however, to get appellate review of the weight or the sufficiency of the evidence, the attorney must have made a timely motion below.

Example: Was the evidence insufficient to support the trial court's finding that an airline did not act "arbitrarily and capriciously" in removing a passenger from a flight who it claimed was "inimical to safety" to make room for airline personnel?

In criminal cases, the verdict will be set aside if the appellate court determines that no rational jury could have found the elements of the crime beyond a reasonable doubt.

b) **Trials by the Court (Bench Trials)**

Findings of fact made by a trial court are also given significant deference, though not as great as that given jury verdicts. Under the Federal Rules of Civil Procedure Rule 52(a)(6), for example, a federal trial court's findings of fact will not be set aside unless they are "clearly erroneous."

Example: Was the trial court's finding that the plaintiff was not promoted because of defendant's discriminatory intent clearly erroneous?

However, even if the error was clear, the court will not order a new trial if the error was harmless, that is, it did not seriously damage or affect the outcome of the case.

- **Review of Mixed Questions of Law and Fact**

The standard of review is difficult to characterize because the courts have not adopted a single approach as to whether these questions should be treated more like questions of law or questions of fact.

Example: Was the plaintiff constructively discharged from his job?

> • **Discretion of the Trial Court**
>
> Trial courts have discretion to determine certain issues. For example, many statutes give the trial judge discretion to award attorneys' fees. A discretionary decision by the trial court may be reversed for abuse of the discretion, for improvident exercise of the discretion, or for a failure to exercise discretion. The extent of the trial court's discretion will depend on the matter at issue.
>
> **Example: Did the trial court abuse its discretion by denying the plaintiff back pay in employment discrimination suit?**

Include a reference to the appropriate standard of review early in your argument section, and, if necessary, an argument as to the correct standard. The standard of review that the appellate court uses can determine the outcome of the case. Therefore, the appellate attorney should be aware of the strength of the issues not simply in terms of the merits, but also in terms of how likely the appellate court is to reverse the lower court's decision given the standard of review applied.

Even if the standard is well settled, there is often room to interpret the standard in a manner favorable to your client if you can support your interpretation with authority. For example, the Michigan Court of Appeals describes abuse of discretion differently in different cases. This gives an advocate the flexibility of arguing for a less restrictive or more restrictive interpretation, depending upon your client.

> *People v. Taylor,* 195 Mich. App. 57, 60 (1992)
>
> This Court finds an abuse of discretion only when an unprejudiced person, considering the facts on which the trial court acted, would say there was no justification or excuse for the ruling.

> *People v. Torres,* 222 Mich. App. 411, 415 (1996)
>
> The standard for reviewing a decision for an abuse of discretion is narrow; the result must have been so violative of fact and logic that it evidences a perversity of will, a defiance of judgment, or an exercise of passion or bias.

The state would argue for the more restrictive interpretation set out in *Torres.*

B. Selecting Issues for Appeal

The first step in preparing an appeal is to review the record closely and research the law carefully in order to narrow the issues to those that are truly arguable. Because you want your brief to be credible, you need to avoid making both frivolous and multiple claims. As the Supreme Court has observed, "a brief which treats more than three or four matters runs serious risks of becoming too diffuse and giving the overall impression that no one claim of error can be serious."[2] In the Court's estimation, if you cannot win on the merits of your stronger points, you will not win on your weaker points; an attorney should, therefore, winnow out the weaker arguments.[3]

In first-year legal writing courses, your teachers may have selected the issues for you. You should be aware, however, of some considerations that go into selecting issues for appeal. Since the facts surrounding each legal issue give rise to initial impressions about your client's claims, appraise the record first from this viewpoint. Then read the decision appealed from carefully, examining each motion or objection made by trial counsel and decided adversely to your client for possible grounds for appeal. After this, research the legal issues thoroughly. Then try to grasp the trial counsel's and the opposing counsel's theories of the case, a way of viewing the facts and the law that will help you to create a story that comports with the evidence and explains the event in a coherent, favorable and plausible way.

On the basis of this initial research, begin to plot out your strategy. Ascertain

- which facts are material,

- which arguments are consequential (that is, which arguments would give your client the greatest relief, like a dismissal of charges), and

- which arguments are persuasive (that is, which are likely to convince a court to rule in your favor but which will not necessarily give your client the same degree of relief, like a new trial or a modified sentence).

---

[2]   *Jones v. Barnes*, 463 U.S. 745, 752 n.5 (1983).

[3]   *Id.* at 751–52. Note also that the Code of Professional Responsibility, DR102A(1), says, "A lawyer shall not bring or defend a proceeding, or assert or controvert an issue therein, unless there is a basis for doing so that is not frivolous, which includes a good faith argument for an extension, modification or reversal of existing law." *See also* Model Rules of Professional Conduct, Rule 3.1.

After you identify those arguments for which there is a basis of appeal, decide which combination of persuasive and consequential arguments would most help your client. You have now, at least tentatively, selected your issues.

C. Ordering Issues

After selecting your issues, you must decide how to order them. Generally, you begin with the most persuasive and consequential argument and move in a descending order down to the least important argument. Because the realities are such that a judge might not read your entire brief, you want to put your most important argument in a prominent place to ensure it will be read and to set a positive tone for your brief. By doing so, you establish yourself as a serious, credible, and thoughtful advocate.

Your organization must also be logical: for example, you need to address threshold issues such as whether the court had jurisdiction first. If you have interdependent issues such that one question must be resolved before another question can be meaningfully addressed, you should treat the initial question before the dependent question. For instance, the court will decide whether a party consented to a search before it considers the argument about whether that party revoked consent.

Other problems will present you with different types of legal questions, for example, a constitutional and a statutory question. Barring special considerations, many practitioners would deal with the statutory question first and the constitutional question second because courts often avoid constitutional issues if the matter can be decided on other grounds. If, for example, a defendant did not violate the statute, then the court need not decide whether it is unconstitutional. On the other hand, some appellate practitioners order issues hierarchically, putting constitutional issue first and arguments based on lesser authority second. For example, counsel for petitioner might begin with the constitutionality of a state statute prohibiting a transgender person from using the bathroom of the gender to which she or he has transitioned because the only satisfactory conclusion for the petitioner would be a decision holding it unconstitutional. In the end, the writer must decide which order is most appropriate to the case.

To check on the order and organization of issues and subissues, many people prepare an outline, which helps to clarify the logical relationships among ideas (rules of outlining are discussed in the section on Point Headings). Once you have decided upon an order, make sure your Questions Presented, Point Headings, and Arguments adhere to that order.

D. Audience

The audience for your brief is an appellate judge, and often, the judge's law clerk. Judges often ask their law clerks to read the briefs and then discuss the case with the judge, or write a memo to the judge about the case. Unlike your legal writing professor, the judge and clerk probably do not know much about the case, and may not know much about that area of law. They depend on the attorneys' briefs to explain the facts and the relevant law and to clarify the issues that the judge must decide. The judge knows the case is not clear-cut or it would not have been litigated and would not have been appealed.

If you are writing the appellee's brief, the appellant's counsel is another audience, one who will not only read it, but also answer it! To inoculate the court against those arguments, try to anticipate and rebut the points you think appellant's brief will make.

II. FORMAT OF AN APPELLATE BRIEF: INTRODUCTORY INFORMATION

A. Title Page

THE TITLE PAGE IS THE OUTSIDE FRONT COVER of your brief. At the top of the page you identify the court to which the case is being appealed and provide the index number to your case. The Title Page also includes the name of the Appellee and Appellant and may identify the Plaintiff and Defendant as, for example, plaintiff/appellee. Under this information, you name the court from which the case is being appealed, the party whose brief this is, and the name and address of the attorney representing that party.

B. Table of Contents

The Table of Contents should contain page references for each section of your brief, including the other introductory tables. These sections usually include the following parts often in the order listed:

- Question Presented
- Table of Contents
- Table of Authorities
- Statement of the Case
- Summary of Argument

- Argument
- Conclusion
- Appendix (if any)

Of particular importance in the Table of Contents are the point headings (and subheadings, if any) for the sections in the Argument. The point headings give the court a quick outline and summary of the content of the Argument and permits the court to find the page at which any particular argument begins.

Lawyers traditionally type the main headings in all capital letters. If the heading is more than two lines, however, all capitals slow the reading process. If the court rules permit, you may prefer to use upper and lower case and bold type. Type the subheadings in upper and lower case. Lawyers traditionally underline the subheadings, but you may omit the underline if the court rules permit.

C.   Table of Authorities

In the Table of Authorities, you provide page references in your brief for the authorities you relied on in the Argument. Ordinarily, you divide the authorities into categories. Put cases in alphabetical order with citations. (If a case is repeatedly cited, use *passim* instead of a page reference.) Then list the Constitutional and Statutory Provisions and the Administrative Regulations. Other authorities may be put under the heading of Miscellaneous, or you may set out other categories.

Some schools will require that their students' briefs conform to the format required by the Rules of the Supreme Court of the United States. Under these Rules, the brief should also include sections entitled Opinion Below, Jurisdictional Statement, and Constitutional and Statutory Provisions Involved. *See* Sample Appellate Brief, Appendix G.

III.   QUESTION(S) PRESENTED

THE QUESTION PRESENTED SETS OUT the legal issues that the parties will argue and provides a factual context that explains how those issues arose (unless dealing with a question of law). Like all other parts of the brief, the Question Presented is also intended to persuade the court of the correctness of your client's position. If you frame the question so that it suggests a response in your favor, you give the court the chance to see the issues from your client's point of view.

Under most court rules, the Questions Presented appear at the beginning of the brief. Thus, they are in effect the introduction to your brief and will be the first part that the judges read. Rule 14 of the Supreme Court of the United States requires that the questions be "short." They should also be understandable, preferably on first reading.

If your topic contains more than one issue, then you must pose more than one Question. Put your Questions in the order in which they will be argued. Each Question should be written in the same form, either as a statement beginning with "whether" or in question form, beginning, for example, with "may" or "does."

Some suggestions for writing the Questions follow.

A. The Questions should include a reference to the constitutional provision, statute, or common law cause of action under which the case arises. Put that reference first, then set out the relevant facts.

For example:

> Did the Metropolitan Police violate the petitioner's fourth amendment right to be secure against an unreasonable search when officers, acting without a warrant, flew a drone past a person's greenhouse that was invisible from the road?

This Question identifies the fourth amendment as the constitutional provision at issue in this case. It tells the court what the case is about. For a lesser known cause of action, for example, one that arises under a statute, you may want to include the operative statutory language in the Question.

> Did a person violate 18 U.S.C. § 1071, which prohibits harboring or concealing a person for whom a federal warrant has been issued, when, on four occasions, he gave a fugitive money and lied to the authorities about the fugitive's whereabouts?

B. Unless you are dealing with a pure question of law, the Question should also provide the facts of the case as they relate to the issue.

The judge must decide each case according to its facts and must apply the established principles of law to those facts. Try, therefore, to avoid "label" or abstract questions that identify the type of action that is before the court but tell nothing about the particular facts of the case.

> Did the police seize the evidence in a search of petitioner's residence that violated his Fourth Amendment rights?

This Question labels the case as a search and seizure problem, but does not indicate the particular nature of the Fourth Amendment problem. The sentence could be the issue in almost every Fourth Amendment case. The writer of this Question should have identified why the police seizure of evidence may have violated the Fourth Amendment.

Also avoid general and vague references to facts that the reader has not yet been given, as in the Question below.

> Under the circumstances of this case, were the petitioner's Fourth Amendment rights violated by the manner in which police secured consent?

Instead, flesh out the "circumstances."

> Was the evidence police seized in a search of petitioner's residence inadmissible on Fourth Amendment grounds when petitioner gave his consent to search only after the police officer implied he had legal authority for the search regardless of consent?

When you provide a factual context, you help the court by defining the particular issue your case poses.

C. Describe the parties in general term rather than identifying them by name.

One consequence of placing the Questions Presented first is that the reader knows nothing about the parties. Therefore, you should identify the parties by general description rather than by name. In the following example, the appellant is identified as a member of the bar, not as "appellant" or by name.

> Do the First and Fourteenth Amendments protect a member of the bar from disciplinary action when she advises members of an organization of their rights and discloses the price and availability of legal services?

D. Do not usurp the function of the court and use the Question Presented to decide the issue by including conclusions of law.

The court's function is to decide the issue; the function of the Question Presented is to ask it. The italicized phrases in these examples are conclusions of law.

> Was the appellant denied his constitutional right to raise his children when they were removed from his custody *without due process of law*?

This appellant has assumed the very point at issue: whether he was actually denied due process when the state removed his children from his custody.

E. Let the Question suggest an answer favorable to your client, but do not overstate the client's case.

Most court rules require that the Question not be argumentative. Probably the best way to write a persuasive question that appears neutral is to incorporate favorable facts without shrill commentary. By doing so, you inform the court about the case, you avoid conclusions of law, and you avoid overstatements, which is a problem in the example below.

Is a private chartered school that is under a blanket waiver from state regulation a state actor for purposes of § 1983 liability when the school is run privately in every way and the teachers and administrators have absolutely no connection with the local school district?

A better Question for the petitioner is:

Does a charter school act under color of law for § 1983 purposes if it receives per pupil funding from the state and its charter required approval from the local school district?

F. Although you should not concede an argument, your Question may pose alternative arguments.

You may appear to concede a contested point in order to raise an argument in the alternative. When you use an alternative argument, you are implicitly saying, "but even if I am wrong on the first point, then the other party still should not prevail because of my arguments on point two." Utilizing this technique, the writer concedes the first point only for the purpose of meeting opposing counsel's next argument.

In the fourth amendment search and seizure problem, for example, the appellant can make an alternative argument: even if he did consent to the search initially, he then withdrew that consent. Appellant admits to the consent only for the limited purpose of making his second argument. Such a Question might look like this:

Even if the petitioner initially consented to a search, is the evidence obtained from that warrantless search nonetheless inadmissible on Fourth Amendment grounds because the petitioner withdrew his initial consent to that search?

G. To make questions readable, keep the subject and verb close together.

Keep the subject of the sentence near the verb since this type of construction is the easiest to understand. Do not separate the subject of the sentence from the verb with a series of interrupting clauses or modifiers. The following question is hard to understand because eighteen words (those modifying the main noun) intervene between the main noun (statute) and the verb.

> Whether a *statute* allowing a child witness in a sex-offense prosecution to testify outside of defendant's presence by one-way closed-circuit television *is* valid under the Sixth Amendment right of confrontation when the statute can be applied only upon a showing of individualized, clear, and convincing trauma to the witness.

The question is more readable if the main noun of the sentence is near the verb.

> *Is* a *statute* valid under the Sixth Amendment right of confrontation if it allows a child witness in a sex-offense prosecution to testify outside of defendant's presence by one-way closed-circuit television when the statute can be applied only upon a showing of individualized, clear, and convincing trauma to the witness?

H. Questions of Law

1. If the issue is a question of law, then you need not include individual case facts, but you need facts that explain the issue, as in the Sixth Amendment question above. The following questions provide the reason the party disputes a statute.

> a.   Did the trial court correctly decide that the New Canaan statute that permits and regulates surrogacy contracts violates the state's public policy because it permits the intended parents to compensate the surrogate?
>
> b.   Does a statute violate an advertiser's First Amendment right to free speech if it bans the advertisement of tobacco products in places offering "family" oriented entertainment?

2. Litigation involving a question of law may also involve a second question—that of the law applied to the particular case. For example, after asking question a. above, the appellee/surrogate may add a factual question, linked to the first question:

If not, is the surrogacy contract between the appellant and the surrogate birth mother invalid as coercive because the birth mother is nineteen-years-old and had no children of her own?

Exercise 16-A

These questions involve whether litigation comes within federal maritime jurisdiction in a circuit in which the vessel at issue must be capable of transportation or movement. Which Question is better? Why?

  1. *Does this litigation concerning petitioner's vessel that is incapable of transportation come within federal maritime jurisdiction?*

  2. *For purposes of federal maritime jurisdiction, is a floating structure that is indefinitely moored, receives its power and utilities only from shore, and has never been used for maritime commerce, a vessel capable of movement or transportation?*

Exercise 16-B

  1. *The following Questions Presented have been prepared for appellant, Alice Bell. Ms. Bell is suing her husband Alan Bell for civil damages under a federal statute popularly known as the federal wiretapping act or Title III of the Omnibus Crime Control and Safe Streets Act of 1968. Alice Bell claims her husband wiretapped her business telephone. Which is the best Question and why? What is wrong with the other Questions?*

   a. Did the trial court err in dismissing Ms. Bell's claim against her husband for damages for using an extension telephone to intercept her private communications without her consent?

   b. Does Title III of the Omnibus Crime Control and Safe Streets Act prohibit the appellee's interception of the appellant's telephone conversations?

   c. Did the trial court err in dismissing the appellant's claim since her husband's unauthorized actions of intercepting her oral telephone communications are clearly prohibited by Title III of the Omnibus Crime Control and Safe Streets Act and do not come within the exceptions to the Act?

   d. Does Title III of the Omnibus Crime Control and Safe Streets Act, which prohibits an individual from intercepting any wire or oral communication, provide a cause of action for a wife against her husband who eavesdropped on an extension telephone and secretly recorded her private telephone conversations?

2. *The following Questions were prepared for a case in which the male plaintiff/petitioner alleged that the defendant Party Time, Inc. violated Title VII's prohibition against gender discrimination by hiring only women. Under Title VII, it is not unlawful to have an employment requirement of a bonafide occupational qualification. Evaluate these questions.*

a. Is Party Time, Inc.'s policy of hiring only female promoters allowed under Title VII of the Civil Rights Act where being female is a bonafide occupational qualification?

b. Whether Party Time, Inc.'s policy of hiring only females for the position of "promoter" constitutes unlawful sex discrimination under Title VII?

c. Under Title VII of the Civil Rights Act of 1964, is womanhood a bonafide occupational qualification to serve on a promotion company's promotional team where the team is defined by female sexuality and a feminine image?

d. Did the respondent's hiring policy violate Title VII because its policy was not reasonably necessary to its business of developing marketing and promotional campaigns for its clients?

3. *Assume you are a prosecutor appealing a pre-trial order suppressing evidence of the photographic identification of a robber by the only eyewitness to a bank robbery. The judge had found the photographic identification procedure conducted by the police was (1) "unduly and unnecessarily suggestive" and (2) the identification itself was not "independently reliable." Your student intern has written two versions of the Question Presented. You find one of them conclusory and both of them unpersuasive and unreadable. Using the information they provide, write a persuasive and readable question.*

a. Whether the court properly suppressed the eyewitness's photographic identification testimony where photographs, each one basically resembling the others, were shown to the witness from which she identified the accused as the perpetrator of the crime without any influence from the police officer, and where during the course of the crime, the witness, who had an excellent opportunity to view the criminal, attentively observed the criminal for about a minute in strong light, thus enabling her to give a detailed description of the criminal that closely resembles the accused, on the ground that the procedure was unduly and unnecessarily suggestive and the identification itself was unreliable.

b. Whether the pretrial photographic identification was unnecessarily and impermissibly suggestive when, weighing the various factors which affected the reliability of the witness's description of the perpetrator against the level of suggestiveness of the photographic procedure, there does not exist, in light of the totality of the circumstances, a substantial likelihood of irreparable misidentification, given the facts that the witness, although terrified, had seen the robber at close quarters and the officer's only comment after she tentatively identified the defendant's photo was that she was "doing just fine, a good job."

IV. POINT HEADINGS

UNLIKE AN OFFICE MEMORANDUM, a brief requires headings that divide the Argument section into its main and subordinate components. These headings, called point headings, are more than just topical headings, such as "the first amendment and commercial speech" or "the consent exception." Instead, they are persuasive summaries of the main arguments of the brief arranged in logical order. A point heading should be a conclusory statement about the legal issue that is favorable to your client.

In addition to a heading for each main argument, many writers use subheadings to introduce the subordinate parts of that argument. When read together—as they appear under the Argument section in the Table of Contents, for example—the headings and subheadings should provide a meaningful outline and summary of the entire Argument section. Because the point headings appear in the Table of Contents at the beginning of the brief, they are the reader's introduction to the substance of the Argument.

A. Organizing Headings in Outline Form

The main point headings should summarize independent, unrelated legal arguments, each of which is an independent ground for relief. These point headings need not be logically connected to each other, although they should be in the order you have determined is the best and most logical order for your issues. Subheadings, however, must relate to the main point heading in a logical and consistent way because they are the components of a single argument. An argument that is subdivided is almost always ordered from the general to the specific. The main heading should state your general contention. The subheadings should supply specific reasons supporting the general contention. Any additional divisions should focus on the specific facts supporting the contention of the sub-heading above it. Thus, the outline organizes all the parts of your argument by how they relate to each other.

You need not achieve symmetry of organization among the major headings of the argument. Even if Section I has two subdivisions, Section II may have three subdivisions, or none at all. Where you do have subdivisions, indent and underline the sub-headings, or follow the court rules, and lay out the divisions in accordance with the established rules of outlining.

---

1. Main issues or grounds for relief are introduced by point headings, which are preceded by roman numerals (e.g., I, II, III).

2. Subissues are introduced by subheadings which are preceded by capital letters (e.g., A, B, C).

3. Divisions of subissues are introduced by subheadings which are preceded by Arabic numerals (e.g., 1, 2, 3) and then lower case letters (e.g., a, b, c).

You should not have single subdivisions, that is, a subissue A without a subissue B, or a subdivision 1 without a subdivision 2. Because a subdivision indicates that the main issue above it is divided into more than one point, you should not use a subheading unless you have at least two entries. If there is only one point to make about issue I, then incorporate your subissue into your dominant point heading. This needs to be done in the following outline of a contempt problem.

I. Paley did not act willfully or intentionally.

    A. Paley did not realize that Spence's trial was scheduled that morning.

II. Paley did not act recklessly.

    A. Paley followed standard office practice.

    B. Paley inadvertently did not record the trial date.

The outline should be rewritten.

I. Paley did not act willfully or intentionally because he did not realize Spence's trial was scheduled that morning.

II. Paley did not act recklessly.

    A. Paley followed standard office practice.

    B. Paley inadvertently did not record the trial date.

When you use subheadings, be careful not to subdivide the arguments excessively since too many subdivisions will break up the flow of an argument. Thus, when the subject matter is not too different, you should avoid using a new subheading for discussions running only one or two paragraphs in length. Instead, incorporate the material in those paragraphs into the text of the preceding or subsequent subheadings and write those subheadings to include the added material. On the other hand, do not be afraid to subdivide a complex argument that depends on several different types of legal support. Without subdivision, it might be difficult for the reader to understand and differentiate the legal arguments being offered.

B. Writing Persuasive Headings

Because point headings provide your reader with an outline and summary of your argument, they should be clear, logical, and persuasive thesis sentences. This requires you to provide the reader with several kinds of information: the issue, the pertinent rule of law, the legally significant facts, and your conclusion on the issue. When you are employing only a single main point heading, include all this information in a single, coherent sentence. When you use subheadings, however, the main point heading need only state your legal contention concerning the application of a rule. The subheadings will supply the reasons for that contention and show their relevance to your client's situation.

A point heading should be one sentence, not a string of sentences. To promote comprehension, try to keep each heading and subheading to a readable length. This is especially important for main point headings because traditionally they are typed entirely in capital letters, which often make for difficult reading. If the court's rules—or your professor's rules—allow, use ordinary capital and lower case letters in bold type. Subheadings are printed in ordinary type and are often underlined. They too should be kept reasonably concise (around 25 words) so that their thesis can be easily absorbed.

1. For factual questions, your headings should not be abstract statements of the law (unless clearly supported by sub-headings that supply reasoning and relevant facts).

Rather they should combine the law with the relevant facts of the case. For example, the following heading is only a statement of the law:

> THE FOURTH AMENDMENT GUARANTEES THE RIGHT OF ALL PEOPLE TO BE SECURE IN THEIR HOMES FROM UNREASONABLE SEARCHES AND SEIZURE.

The heading should demonstrate the law's application:

> THE POLICE VIOLATED MR. BAXTER'S FOURTH AMENDMENT RIGHT TO BE SECURE FROM UNREASONABLE SEARCHES AND SEIZURES BECAUSE THEY ENTERED AND SEARCHED HIS HOME WITHOUT A WARRANT AND WITH THE CONSENT ONLY OF MR. BAXTER'S HOUSEGUEST.

Remember, briefs are written to persuade a court to rule in a particular way, for a particular party, under particular facts; they are not abstract discussions written for the general edification of a judge. If you have not related the law to the facts, your heading is unpersuasive.

2. Unless supported by sub-headings that supply your reasoning, headings should not merely state a legal conclusion favorable to your client but should supply supporting reasons.

The following heading states a conclusion only:

> THE TRIAL COURT'S EXCLUSION OF SMITH'S POSTHYPNOTIC TESTIMONY DID NOT VIOLATE SMITH'S CONSTITUTIONAL RIGHT TO TESTIFY IN HER OWN BEHALF.

The writer should supply some support for this conclusion:

> THE TRIAL COURT DID NOT DENY SMITH'S CONSTITUTIONAL RIGHT TO TESTIFY IN HER OWN BEHALF WHEN IT EXCLUDED HER POST-HYPNOTIC TESTIMONY BECAUSE THAT TESTIMONY WAS UNRELIABLE.

In other words, a persuasive heading should be an explanation, not merely an assertion.

3. For questions of law, do not include the facts of your case, but do supply your reasons.

> ABBOTT'S GRANDPARENT VISITATION STATUTE IS CONSTITUTIONAL BECAUSE IT PROTECTS THE WELFARE OF CHILDREN WITHOUT UNDULY INTERFERING WITH PARENTS'

> FUNDAMENTAL RIGHT TO RAISE THEIR CHILDREN ACCORDING TO THEIR OWN BELIEFS.

4. Headings should clearly articulate relevant legal principles rather than cite cases or statutes.

Do not assume your reader knows the rule of law established in a case or statute. Instead, supply the rule. The following heading is uninformative:

> UNDER THE RULING OF *ROSS v. BERHARD*, 396 U.S. 531 (1970), THE FEDERAL DISTRICT COURT PROPERLY STRUCK A DEMAND FOR A JURY TRIAL IN AN ACTION FOR DAMAGES AND INJUNCTIVE RELIEF STEMMING FROM A NUCLEAR POWER PLANT ACCIDENT.

The heading should be rewritten so that the legal principle established in *Ross* is clear.

> BECAUSE A JURY DOES NOT PROVIDE AN ADEQUATE REMEDY FOR COMPLEX CASES THAT ARE BEYOND ITS UNDERSTANDING, THE DISTRICT COURT PROPERLY STRUCK A DEMAND FOR A JURY TRIAL IN AN ACTION FOR DAMAGES AND INJUNCTIVE RELIEF STEMMING FROM A NUCLEAR POWER PLANT ACCIDENT.

5. Point headings should be easily understood.

Because so much information gets packed into point headings, you often have to work hard to make them intelligible. Two helpful suggestions are to keep the subject of your sentence near the verb and to put the facts and reasoning at the end of the sentence. In the following heading, the author's reasoning intervenes between the subject and the verb.

> A PARENT-CHILD PRIVILEGE, LACKING CONFIDENTIALITY, AN ELEMENT CENTRAL TO ESTABLISHED PRIVILEGES, IS NOT JUDICIALLY RECOGNIZED, AND THE DISTRICT COURT, THEREFORE, PROPERLY DENIED THE DEFENDANT'S MOTION TO QUASH THE SUBPOENA.

The heading should be rewritten:

> A PARENT-CHILD PRIVILEGE LACKS THE ELEMENT OF CONFIDENTIALITY CENTRAL TO ESTABLISHED PRIVILEGES,

> AND THUS, THE DISTRICT COURT PROPERLY DENIED THE DEFENDANT'S MOTION TO QUASH THE SUBPOENA.

6. Prefer active voice instead of passive voice, unless you want to dissociate the subject of the sentences from the action expressed by the verbs. In the following heading, there is no tactical reason for using the passive voice.

> THE PROSECUTORIAL MISCONDUCT WAS SO PREJUDICIAL THAT THE INHERENT SUPERVISORY POWERS OF THE COURT SHOULD BE INVOKED AND THE GRAND JURY INDICTMENT DISMISSED.

This heading could be rewritten in the active voice.

> THE COURT SHOULD INVOKE ITS INHERENT SUPERVISORY POWERS AND DISMISS THE GRAND JURY INDICTMENT BECAUSE THE PROSECUTORIAL MISCONDUCT WAS PREJUDICIAL.

If a party wants to emphasize prosecutorial misconduct by beginning the sentence with that language, the party could still end the sentence in the active voice.

> THE PROSECUTORIAL MISCONDUCT WAS SO PREJUDICIAL THAT THE COURT SHOULD INVOKE ITS INHERENT SUPERVISORY POWERS AND DISMISS THE GRAND JURY INDICTMENT.

The following point headings illustrate the petitioner's and respondent's arguments on Ms. Bell's claim against her husband for unauthorized eavesdropping and wiretapping of her telephone.

> PETITIONER'S POINT HEADINGS
>
> I. ALICE BELL STATES A CLAIM AGAINST HER HUSBAND UNDER THE OMNIBUS CRIME CONTROL AND SAFE STREET ACT, 18 U.S.C. § 2510, BECAUSE HE EAVESDROPPED ON AND SECRETLY TAPE RECORDED HER TELEPHONE CONVERSATIONS FOR SIX MONTHS.
>
> A. The Respondent Secretly Tape Recorded Ms. Bell's Telephone Conversations and Violated the Plain

Language of 18 U.S.C. § 2510, which Prohibits any Person from Intercepting any Wire Communication.

B. The Legislative History of the Statute Supports the Plain Meaning that Congress Intended the Statute to Apply to Private Individuals and did not Intend to Exempt Interspousal Wire Tapping.

II. ALICE BELL STATES A CLAIM UNDER 18 U.S.C. § 2510 BECAUSE HER HUSBAND INTERCEPTED HER TELEPHONE CONVERSATIONS ON HER BUSINESS LINE, WHICH DOES NOT FALL WITHIN ANY EXCEPTION TO THE STATUTE.

A. Because the Respondent's Eavesdropping and Wiretapping were not Conducted in the Ordinary Course of Ms. Bell's Consulting Business, They Were Not Exempt Under 18 U.S.C. § 2510(5)(A).

B. The Respondent Eavesdropped on His Wife's Private Conversations Without Her Consent.

RESPONDENT'S POINT HEADINGS

I. THE COURT PROPERLY DISMISSED PETITIONER'S COMPLAINT BECAUSE HER HUSBAND'S INTERCEPTION OF HER TELEPHONE CONVERSATIONS IS EXPLICITLY EXEMPTED FROM THE PROVISIONS OF THE OMNIBUS CRIME CONTROL AND SAFE STREETS ACT.

A. Mr. Bell Used the Business Extension Phone in the Ordinary Course of Business When He Overheard Conversations Establishing His Wife's Infidelity, and thus, His Conduct Is Explicitly Exempt from the Statute's Provisions.

B. Mr. Bell's Original Conduct was Inadvertent and thus He Did Not Willfully Intercept His Wife's Phone Call, as Required by the Statute.

II. THE PETITIONER'S COMPLAINT WAS PROPERLY DISMISSED BECAUSE MR. BELL'S INTERCEPTION OF TELEPHONE CALLS WAS WITHIN AN IMPLIED EXCEPTION FROM THE OMNIBUS CRIME CONTROL AND SAFE STREETS ACT FOR INTERSPOUSAL WIRETAPS.

A. Congress did not Intend that the Crime Control Act Extend to Disputes Between Spouses Because Domestic Relations is an Area Traditionally Reserved for State Law.

B. The Entire Focus of the Omnibus Crime Control and Safe Streets Act is on Law Enforcement Personnel and Organized Crime.

Exercise 16-C

1. *These point headings were written for an appellant's brief arguing that a person who serves alcoholic beverages in his home (a social host) can be liable for serving a guest who the host knew was intoxicated when the guest later was injured. Which point heading is best for the plaintiff-appellant Joseph Nunn? What is wrong with the other headings?*

   A.   Joseph Nunn states a claim against Samuel Tann for serving him alcoholic beverages under *State v. Small.*

   B.   Dismissing Joseph Nunn's claim against the defendant for serving him alcoholic beverages when he was already intoxicated was error and failed to uphold well-established New Hampshire law providing plaintiff with a claim against the defendant.

   C.   The court below committed error in dismissing this suit because under New Hampshire law the defendant violated his duty to his guest not to serve him alcoholic beverages when the guest was intoxicated, knowing the guest would soon be driving his automobile.

2. *Another issue in the social host problem is whether, if the social host is under a duty not to serve the intoxicated guest, the host may be liable to the guest for the guest's injuries as well as to a person whom the guest injured (the more typical claim). Which is the best heading for the defendant-appellee (the social host)? What is wrong with the others?*

   A.   Even if the defendant had a duty not to serve the intoxicated plaintiff, that duty extends only to innocent parties whom the plaintiff foreseeably injures, not to the plaintiff for the plaintiff's own injuries because the plaintiff must bear responsibility for driving while under the influence of alcohol.

   B.   The defendant's duty, if any, arising from RSA § 175:6 extends only to innocent third parties.

   C.   Legislative policy and social welfare dictate that the intoxicant himself cannot recover for his injuries.

   D.   The fact that the appellant was himself the intoxicated guest at the party and not a third person should bar his recovery for injuries resulting from being served drinks, while obviously intoxicated, by his social host.

3. *The following point headings involve a father (George Carr) who was driving his pregnant wife to a doctor's appointment when he was in an accident. The first issue is whether he is immune to suit brought on behalf of the child (Jason). The child was born with birth injuries from the accident. The appeal is to the Illinois Supreme Court.*

> *Some Illinois intermediate appellate courts had held that, in cases alleging parental negligence in operation of a motor vehicle, the parent is immune from suit only if the parent was driving the car for a family purpose.*

These headings are taken from a good student brief. However, they can be even better. How can you improve them?

I. CARR IS IMMUNE FROM LIABILITY TO JASON BECAUSE PARENTAL IMMUNITY DOCTRINE BARS AN UNEMANCIPATED MINOR FROM RECOVERING DAMAGES IN AN ACTION BROUGHT AGAINST A PARENT FOR INJURIES CAUSED BY THE PARENT'S ALLEGED NEGLIGENCE IN THE OPERATION OF A MOTOR VEHICLE.

    A. Holding Carr Immune from Liability to Jason for Injuries Caused By His Alleged Negligence Is Consistent with the Overwhelming Weight of Authority in Illinois.

    B. Jason Is Barred from Suing George for Injuries Caused By George's Alleged Negligence Because Allowing Such a Suit Would Subvert This State's Policy of Promoting Family Harmony and Preventing Tortfeasors from Benefitting By Their Own Negligence.

    C. Jason Should Not Be Allowed to Sue Carr Because Parental Immunity Is the Rule in a Majority of Jurisdictions, and Any Change in the Doctrine on the Basis of Motor Vehicle Liability Insurance Should Be Made By the Legislature.

V. THE STATEMENT OF THE CASE

LITIGATORS ARE NOT NOVELISTS, but those who are good storytellers often have an immeasurable advantage. This is particularly true when writing the Statement of the Case. The Statement is your one opportunity to focus only on the facts and to present your client's version of those facts so convincingly that a court is ready to rule in your client's favor even before reading the Argument.

The Statement of the Case frequently includes two components: an opening paragraph and a Statement of Facts. The opening paragraph, often called the Preliminary Statement, includes procedural information about how the case got to the appeals court. The Statement of Facts portrays the events giving rise to the litigation from your client's point of view. But remember, a lawyer who knowingly misstates the facts violates the Code of Professional Responsibility.[4] You must not only be accurate about

---

[4] Canon 7, DR7–102A(5) says in pertinent part, "In his representation of a client, a lawyer shall not knowingly make a false statement of law or fact." The Model Rules of

the facts that you include, but you must include all the known material facts so as to avoid giving a distorted impression of the events. If you misrepresent the facts or allow a misleading inference to be drawn, you will lose credibility, and will be quickly corrected by opposing counsel—to your client's disadvantage

The facts in the Statement come from the record, and only the record, so it must be read carefully, If the appeal is from a summary judgment, attorneys read the parties' pleadings, motion briefs, the discovery documents and affidavits, and hearings on the motion. If the case went to trial, they read the record of the trial, carefully, as should you if your assignment includes a record of the litigation below. You may want to prepare a detailed outline, for example, of the documents entered into evidence or witnesses' testimony, to use when you write the Statement of Facts.

Unless your instructions are otherwise, you should include a citation to the record below for all information you take from the record.

A. The Preliminary Statement

Many brief writers begin the Statement of the Case with a brief synopsis of the case that provides procedural information about how the case reached that court. The paragraph usually contains information about the nature of the action, the parties involved, the relief requested, the disposition below, and the grounds for appeal. Procedural history is essential to an appellate judge, who has to know how and why the case is before the court. Make sure you explain the background of procedural issues if your appeal involves any. For example, if you are appealing a judge's refusal to give an instruction to the jury, include in the procedural facts the party's request for the instruction and the judge's denial of the request. Some lawyers also summarize the lower court decision in the opening paragraph(s) as well as the claims and defenses raised in the court below. Others, however, conclude the Statement of the Case with this information (see section IV, C).

Example of a Preliminary Statement

This is an appeal from the decision of the United States District Court for the Eastern District of New York, rendered January 29th, 2016. The defendant-appellant, Bob Stuart, was charged with running an interstate sport betting enterprise in violation of 18 U.S.C. s. 1995 (2006) and with heroin trafficking in violation of 21 U.S.C. s. 841 (2012). Stuart moved for an order pursuant to Fed. R. Crim. P. 12(b)(3)

Professional Conduct, Rule 3.3(a)(1) prohibits a lawyer from making false statements of material fact or law.

to suppress evidence obtained from the warrantless search of his cellphone in violation of his Fourth Amendment rights. (R-1) In the alternative, Stuart requested a hearing on the motion. (R-1) The district court denied the motion on the grounds that the search was incident to a lawful arrest. (R-6) Stuart entered a conditional plea of guilty pursuant to Fed. R. Crim. P. (11)(a)(2), reserving the right to appeal the district court's denial of his motion to suppress. (R-7) Stuart now appeals the district court's decision.

B.   The Statement of Facts

1.   The Theory of the Case and Storytelling

Lawyers will tell you that the best statements of fact are those that flow from the theory of the case. A theory of the case begins with finding in the facts a story that moves the court to hold in your favor and provides the legal grounds for doing so. If, for example, your client is charged with assault and battery, there may be many facts about the suspect's appearance that do not fit with the complainant's description of her attacker, thus triggering the defense of mistaken identity. Facts and law fortuitously meet in a credible and persuasive theory of the case.

A story is unlikely to be convincing unless it is internally plausible: the story cannot have meaningful gaps, and contradictions between a person's stated intentions and actual actions must be accounted for—explained, neutralized, or mitigated. These are better tactics than just de-emphasizing them by burying negative facts in the middle of the fact statement or a paragraph. For example, you may be able to show that a defendant's confession was not voluntarily given, but was coerced or that the perpetrator of a crime planted evidence to incriminate your client or that your client admittedly had a history of petty theft, but that does not make him a murderer.

The story must also resonate with your and other people's experience and knowledge of the world: a promotion went to a less qualified man; a car's backfire triggered a violent reaction from a veteran with post traumatic stress disorder; a homeless man urinated in the street. Explanations like these are genuinely believable and often truthful.

Yet, even if a story is coherent, cohesive, and plausible, an appeals court might not find in your client's favor. That is because in the appellate context, the story is not just about the triggering events, unless the standard is de novo, but also about the events at trial and the lens through which events must be viewed. Thus, an appellate decision may turn on whether a court's findings of fact were "clearly erroneous." If the errors were only arguably erroneous, there would be no reversal. An effective theory of a case on appeal must, therefore, incorporate the case's procedural posture and the standard of review. The story must detail every error if it is to satisfy the standard of review.

On the other hand, appellate courts are also concerned with just results, consistent application, and future consequences and are thus more open to policy arguments than are trial courts. Thus, your theory of the case should also be informed by those concerns. Your facts should show the unfairness that would result, and your arguments should speak to the legal consequences of unfairness and to policy.

2.   Organization

Organization is an important persuasive device. In legal narratives, the default organization is chronology. That is often the clearest, easiest, and most effective organization. Thus lawyers rarely use flashbacks or flash forwards—the stuff of fiction, television, and movie scripts.

But a default organization does not always tell a story that complements the theory of the case. Sometimes you may want to grab the reader's attention and create empathy or antipathy. You can then begin with a compelling action that draws the reader in. This can be followed with background that helps the reader to understand the parties and the events. With perspective established, you can then narrate the events chronologically until they come to a climax, ending with a sense of their significance and subtly pointing the way to the desired legal decision. If you are a prosecutor, for example, you might want to begin with the details of the murder and then backtrack to the events leading up to it.

If there are many issues and the Statement of Facts is somewhat lengthy, you may want to use a topical organization instead of a simple chronological organization. If you divide the facts into topics, you may use short topical headings before each new section, such as the evidence at trial, the rulings of the trial court, and the charge to the jury. These subsections summarize and organize the facts pertinent to a legal issue you intend to address in the Argument section of the brief. If you are including witnesses' trial testimony, include that testimony under the appropriate topic, not in a witness-by-witness summary. You would still organize the facts relevant to each topic chronologically.

Before you write the facts, you may want to identify for yourself the events to be covered and the facts material to them. Work out a structure that frames and maximizes the facts most favorable to your client and that limits the impact of facts damaging to your client. Explain away damaging facts if you can. Otherwise bury them in the middle of a narrative and in the middle of paragraphs and sentences. Juxtapose unfavorable facts with favorable facts. Place favorable facts in positions of emphasis (at the beginning and end of sentences, paragraphs, and the narrative). Finally, allocate space according to importance. For example, as attorney for appellant in a criminal case, you would emphasize, even repeat, facts establishing your client's innocence or the paucity of evidence against him.

3. Persuasive Writing Techniques

Several writing techniques will help you to shape this section of the brief persuasively.

a. *Show, Don't Tell*

The significance of a fact or event may become apparent only after you have put it in a meaningful context: use detail, revealing quotes, and juxtaposition as ways of showing instead of telling.

In the following example, the writer suggests the possibility of police coercion by first quoting the exact words of the officer and then juxtaposing Gonzales's reaction.

> Officer Brown wanted permission to enter and to search the apartment. When Mr. Gonzales refused, Officer Brown threatened to seek a warrant. He said, "I can always go ask for a warrant. I'll leave the other officer outside till I get back." (R.1.) Mr. Gonzales then acquiesced to the search.

Help your reader to visualize the scene using vivid details and images.

> **Do not say:** Threading through the room, Jameson bumped into a woman, spilling his drink on her dress and causing her to fall.
>
> **Say instead:** Barreling head first through the crowded room, Jameson banged into a woman, splashing his Bloody Mary over her white silk dress and knocking her to the floor.

The difference in verbs (threading versus barreling and bumped versus banged) and the visual image of a red stain spreading of a delicate, white dress makes the second example of drunken negligence more memorable than the first.

b.   Tell Your Story from Your Client's Point of View

Your theory of the case is often bolstered by telling the story from the client's perspective. Assume you are representing a client who has been charged with assault and resisting arrest, but the defendant's story suggests other defenses—perhaps self-defense against excessive force. He described the police officers as grabbing him from behind and then choking him and forcing him to his knees. Since the police never identified themselves and he didn't know who was attacking him, he panicked and began to struggle against his attackers in self-defense.

The state will tell a different story: the danger of an arrest situation, a dark alley, a violent suspect who had already assaulted someone. Then while the officers attempted to arrest the defendant, who fit the complainant's description of her attacker, he began kicking and hitting the officers.

Notice the point-of-view here. The defendant has a first person perspective: what he was thinking and experiencing explains his reaction. The state stays out of the defendant's head. It uses a third person perspective: an external description of what happened, shaded with details of the setting that favors the officers by highlighting the objective dangers.

The connotation of words also helps to establish point-of-view. You might choose to call a juvenile offender a "youth" rather than the more appealing "youngster" or use "snitch" rather than the more dignified "informant."

Finally, telling a story from the client's perspective may also require you to de-emphasize unfavorable facts about your client's activities by using the passive voice. Passive voice will create a distance between your client and the activity described in the sentence. For example, instead of saying, "Ms. Fox mailed her letters explaining her legal services to all the people who had signed the sheet," you would say, "The letters explaining her legal services were mailed to the women whose names were on the sign-in sheet." By using passive voice, the writer avoids naming Ms. Fox as the person who mailed the letters.

Another way to de-emphasize your client's conduct is to use the other parties involved as the subjects of the sentences. For example, instead of saying that Mr. Gonzales had the stolen bank money in his apartment where it was found, you can focus on the police activity and say, "The police seized crucial evidence, money stolen from a bank, without a warrant."

You can also emphasize or de-emphasize a fact by using independent and subordinate clauses carefully. An independent clause is a sentence containing a complete thought, such as "Sam Paley is an effective lawyer." That clause can be joined in a sentence with a subordinate or dependent clause, which has a subject, and verb but is an incomplete thought, such as "although Paley's memory is poor." Because a subordinate clause depends on the independent clause for meaning, a reader's attention focuses on the independent clause. Therefore, it is helpful to put unfavorable facts into a dependent clause that is joined to a favorable independent clause, such as "Although Paley's memory is poor, he is an effective lawyer." This sentence leaves the impression of Paley's excellence as a lawyer. If you reverse the information in the clauses, "Although Paley is an effective lawyer, his memory is poor," or "Even if Paley is an effective lawyer, his memory is poor," you emphasize the negative information about Paley's memory. These techniques can also help you demonstrate the lesser of two evils: Although my client is a pickpocket, he is not a murderer.

c. Humanize Your Client

Even if the record for your class assignments does not reveal much personal information about your client, you can help the court view your client as a person deserving of fair treatment by giving favorable details and referring to the client in a dignified way, as, for example, "Mr. Gonzales" rather than "Gonzales" or "Petitioner." This sort of personalization was achieved in the following paragraphs:

> Ms. Maria Fox, the petitioner in this case, was charged by the Attorney Registration and Disciplinary Commission of the State of Illinois for "soliciting employment" in violation of Disciplinary Rule 2–103(A). (R.1).
>
> Ms. Fox has practiced law for ten years and has successfully resolved legal problems for the Northwest Community Women's Organization (NCWO) of which she is a member. (R.2). After Ms. Fox spoke at a NCWO meeting, several members requested her business card. She responded to the requests by sending a card and a letter to the members of NCWO who had attended her counseling session. (R. 3).

You may characterize your client positively even if the client is not an individual. Assume you are appealing a summary judgment decision against a condominium board that was sued by unit owners over a new regulation that limits unit owners' ability to rent their units.

You want to portray the Board members favorably. Your theme is that they provide important service to the building. The Board consists of seven members elected by the unit owners for two-year terms. The current Board members were all elected unanimously. Although they receive no compensation, they meet once a month. They each have shouldered these responsibilities on top of their full-time jobs, and they receive at least one phone call and several e-mails a day from the unit owners to which they must respond.

Even corporate entities can be humanized. Using the Digital Millennium Copyright Act as a defense to a claim of copyright infringement, YouTube's attorney characterized the company this way.

> Since its founding in 2005, YouTube has had a profound impact on culture, politics, and society in this country and around the world. YouTube has afforded political candidates and elected officials a new way to communicate with the public; enabled first-hand reporting from war zones and from inside repressive regimes; allowed unknown performers, filmmakers, and artists to rise to world wide fame; inspired laughter at the antics of dancing babies and skateboarding dogs; let students of all ages audit classes at leading universities; and given creators of all sorts a powerful new way to promote their work to a global audience.[5]

Not only do these details characterize YouTube as a socially beneficial global platform, but they implicitly identify free expression as a core issue.

d. *Frame Events Favorably*

Whenever possible, you want to provide details casting events and actions in a positive way. This can be done in the case mentioned above involving a condominium board that had been sued by unit owners over a new regulation that limits unit owners' ability to rent their units. The law is clear that regulations are valid if they are reasonable. Your theory is that the new regulation is reasonable because its purpose is to maintain the value of the owners' condominiums. The policy restricting rentals was adopted in order to maintain the building's current excellent reputation as a place to live and to maintain the value of the unit owners' investments in their units. Your statement of facts will explain in

---

[5]   Memorandum of Law in Support of Defendant's Motion for Summary Judgment, *Viacom International Inc. LLC v. YouTube Inc. LLC,* 676 F.3d 19 (2nd Cir. 2012).

detail the facts learned through discovery that the condominium is located only two blocks from a mid-size university and that the building's policy is to deter undergraduates from living there to prevent noise and frequent turnover of residents. You also explain in detail that a condominium building acquires a negative reputation in the real estate market if it becomes a rental building. Use these details to show that the new regulation is reasonable.

e. Vary Styles and Sentence Length

After one or more long sentences, a short, pithy sentence or even sentence fragment can have a dramatic impact.

> The condition of the home and the children, ages 2 and 4, tested the imagination: dirty dishes were stacked on the counters, in the sink, on the table where a puddle of milk lay curdling; the trash can was overflowing with pizza boxes, beer cans, and whiskey bottles; pottery shards from an overturned lamp lay on the living room carpet; the children were wandering about in wet sagging diapers. Mother drunk—dead to the world.

Moving from formal language to the vernacular often serves a down to earth truth-telling function.

> Plagiarism dwells at the meeting place of two great human endeavors: literature and the law. It is the source of legal and critical disputes, an example of creativity gone wrong.[6]

Finally, try using tricolons, that is, thoughts presented in a series of three, often parallel, units to give a thought depth and cadence.[7]

> The witness testified that the robber she saw had blue eyes; the defendant's eyes are gray. She testified that he was tall and thin; the defendant is only 5 foot 9 inches and is muscular from lifting weights. She testified that he had a deep voice; the defendant is a tenor.

f. Above All, Be Subtle, Not Heavy-Handed

All the advice given here does not mean that you should write in an openly partisan manner. The Statement of Facts should be written to appear neutral—even if it is not. Partisan

---

[6] Laura Stearns, Comment: Copy wrong: Plagiarism, Process, Property, and the Law, Cal. L. Rev. 514 (1992).

[7] Bruce Ching, *Things in Threes—Utilizing Tricolons—A Linguistic Look*, The Law Teacher 18 (Fall 2008) in Linda Edwards, Readings in Persuasion: Briefs that Changed the World (Wolters Kluwer 2012).

characterizations and partisan choice of language must be subtle, or not attempted at all.

The following paragraphs show how the appellee and appellant might each have presented the facts of the case on appeal. In the initial suit, plaintiff had sued Gothic Memorial Chapel for the negligent infliction of emotional distress, claiming that the defendant's conduct was negligent, that the negligence was the cause-in-fact of her emotional anguish and distress, and that her anguish was severe and disabling. At trial, the court held that the defendant was not liable because, although the defendant had been negligent and Miss Morte had suffered severe emotional distress, her distress was not the result of defendant's actions but of her grief at the loss of her father. The issue on appeal is whether defendant's negligence was the cause-in-fact of plaintiff's distress. Each statement of facts illustrates the writer's theory of the case.

The appellant's lawyer might present the facts as follows. (Procedural paragraphs and citations to the record are omitted.)

On the day of George Morte's funeral, in full view of the decedent's daughter, Maria Morte, the hired bearers of defendant undertaker dropped the coffin in which the body lay, causing the lid to spring open and the corpse to crash to the ground. The employees immediately heaved the dead man's body up and swung it back into the coffin. In the process, they bashed George Morte's head against the side of the coffin, smashing his nose and ripping open his right sleeve and forearm as it caught on the lock mechanism. The funeral party was stunned.

This disruption took place as the pallbearers were loading the coffin onto the hearse for the motorcar procession to the graveyard. Maria Morte was standing less than four feet from the coffin and the hearse. She began breathing rapidly. She felt faint. Her complexion grew ashen and her skin cool and clammy. Among the assembled friends and mourners who immediately attempted to assist and soothe Miss Morte was a physician. He diagnosed shock and made Miss Morte lie down and drink fluids until she felt well enough to accompany her beloved father's body to his grave.

For several months after this incident, Miss Morte suffered from a dramatic loss of appetite and weight. She had trouble concentrating, wept easily, and seemed alternately depressed and anxious. She was frequently awakened by nightmares about graveyards, mangled corpses, and open coffins.

The appellee's lawyer might present the facts as follows.

Plaintiff in this action is an unmarried woman of 58 who for the last several years of her 85-year-old and ailing father's life served as his constant companion and nurse. Her mother had died when she was a child and she had no other surviving relation. Miss Morte had never married and had always lived in her father's house. The relationship between this elderly, dying father and his aging, spinster daughter has been described as exceptionally close.

The accident that is the basis for this action took place as the funeral party for George Morte was preparing to leave for the cemetery. The employees of Gothic Memorial Chapel inadvertently dropped the casket in which the deceased lay as they were sliding it into the hearse, requiring them to recover his fallen body from the ground. In the process of lifting the body back into the casket, the decedent's face and arm were injured.

After the accident occurred, plaintiff appeared shaken. Friends came to her assistance and one of them, a physician, made her rest until she was able to accompany the deceased to his final resting place.

For several months after the accident, Miss Morte suffered from the symptoms of grief and mourning which are the natural aftermath of losing a beloved parent. She lost her appetite, cried easily, felt depressed, and experienced nightmares.

Although most cases will not offer you such dramatic possibilities, these two versions of the facts illustrate the very different impressions you can convey even when working from the same transcript. Miss Morte's account portrays the employees of Gothic Memorial Chapel as negligent and crass. The narrative begins with a detailed description of the pallbearers' actions and the resulting disfigurement to her father. The verbs are evocative (heaved, swung, bashed). The short sentence following the description of the incident puts emphasis on the reaction (the funeral party was stunned). The last paragraph, which describes the rather macabre content of Miss Morte's nightmares, links her distress to the pall bearers' actions. In the middle is buried the somewhat unfavorable fact that Miss Morte was not so distraught as to be unable to proceed to the cemetery. By suggesting that it was only the doctor's administration of the tranquilizer that made it possible for Miss Morte to carry on, this fact is minimized.

Miss Morte's attorney does not dwell in the statement on the close relation of this father and daughter or on her subsequent solitariness because to do so would portray Miss Morte's distress as the natural mourning of an unmarried, middle-aged daughter. On the other hand, appellee's attorney begins with these emotionally significant background facts as a way of minimizing the impact the incident in question had on her mental state. The last paragraph reiterates the idea that Miss Morte experienced nothing more or less than the natural grief of a daughter upon the death of her sole parent. Buried in the middle is the incident itself, which is rather quickly summarized and neutrally reported. The tone factual, word choices impersonal. Miss Morte's reaction to the manhandling is minimized by the suggestion she recovered fairly quickly.

C. The Closing Paragraph

You may end the Statement of the Case by relating the facts back to the legal issue before the court and by giving a short summary of the decision of the court below. The appellee will emphasize the decision of the court below more than the appellant would, since that decision was favorable to the appellee.

Contrast these examples from appellant's and appellee's briefs. Notice that the appellant summarizes the arguments made before the trial court while the appellee summarizes the trial court's reasons for its decision.

Appellant

The defendant appealed his conviction on two grounds. The first was that his consent to the search was not voluntarily given in that he "was coerced into agreement by the threat inherent in Brown's language that a future search was inevitable." (R.2.) The second was that the police seized the evidence after he had clearly indicated a desire to terminate the search. *Id.* A divided court of appeals affirmed the conviction. *Id.* This Court granted certiorari on the question of whether the police officer's search violated the fourth amendment.

Appellee

The United States Court of Appeals for the Twelfth Circuit affirmed the defendant's conviction and rejected the defendant's claims that his consent was coerced. Instead, the court held that defendant's consent was freely and voluntarily given in an attempt to allay suspicion and on the assumption that nothing would be found. (R.2.) The court also found that the defendant's attempt to stop the search was an attempt to "obstruct the search" in the face of discovery of the evidence. *Id.*

Exercise 16-D

---

1. *In the following examples, the defendant is appealing from an appellate court decision affirming the trial court's decision closing the courtroom during the testimony of a thirteen-year-old victim of a brutal assault on the ground that his sixth amendment right to a public trial*

had been violated. Which Statement for the defendant is more persuasive and why? Citations to the record are omitted.

Example A

Daniel McGee was indicted for Attempted Murder in the Second Degree and for Assault in the First Degree on June 15, 2014. Five days prior to the indictment, Mr. McGee allegedly assaulted thirteen-year-old Sheila Merta. Although only the defendant was apprehended, he acted in concert with others not apprehended.

The thirteen-year-old complaining witness, Sheila Merta, had testified before a Grand Jury and in two separate pretrial hearings, although no spectators were then present. During her testimony at trial, Ms. Merta began to cry. The prosecutor suggested the courtroom be closed because Ms. Merta was afraid of the spectators and embarrassed about having to testify to the details of the assault.

The trial judge held an *in camera* hearing to determine if there were sufficient reasons for removing spectators from the courtroom. When the judge asked Ms. Merta if closure would make it easier for her to testify, she responded in the affirmative. Ms. Merta then stated that she knew that McGee's mother, who had been a family friend and was in the courtroom, hated her. The trial judge then closed the courtroom because Ms. Merta was fearful of testifying before the spectators. The judge concluded that closure would assure Ms. Merta's testimony. The trial court weighed the equities and decided that it would not be an injustice upon the defendant to have the testimony of Ms. Merta taken without spectators being present. Defendant took exception to the ruling.

On January 13, 2015, defendant was convicted of assault with a deadly weapon, but was acquitted on the attempted murder charge. On February 12, 2015, McGee was sentenced to a prison term of five to fifteen years for the assault.

The Appellate Court affirmed the trial court's decision that the defendant suffered no Sixth Amendment violation. The defendant was then given leave to appeal to this court.

Example B

The Appellant, Daniel McGee, is a resident of York, who, with other unnamed males, allegedly assaulted Sheila Merta, a young girl from their neighborhood, on June 10, 2014. Only McGee was apprehended and charged with the assault.

On June 15, 2014, the Grand Jury of the County of Kings indicted McGee on two counts: Attempted Murder in the Second Degree and Assault in the First Degree. Prior to the indictment, Merta testified before the Grand Jury and at two pretrial hearings.

At trial, Merta began her testimony, but then paused and started to cry. The prosecutor asked to approach the bench where he suggested the court be closed during Merta's testimony because although she had not been threatened in any way, she was frightened about testifying. The court noted that Merta had already testified before the Grand Jury and at two separate pretrial hearings and indicated that Merta "should be an old pro at testifying."

The defense counsel immediately objected to closure, acknowledging that every witness experienced some fear at the prospect of giving testimony at trial but that this "mild anxiety" was not enough to justify closure of the courtroom.

The trial court held a brief *in camera* hearing with Merta to decide whether to close the courtroom to all spectators during her testimony. The judge asked Merta what was the problem, as she had been a very able witness so far. She answered that she did not know, but felt discomfort at the thought of Daniel's mother and neighbors looking at her as she testified. She did not indicate that she would not testify nor did she express a preference for the courtroom to be closed. The judge asked her if it would help her to testify if McGee's mother and other spectators were not in the courtroom. She replied: "I guess so." The judge then decided to close the courtroom. The defense counsel objected, but the judge interrupted, saying he had made his ruling. Defense counsel's exception was noted for the record, but counsel was not given the opportunity to be heard on the motion for closure. The judge then ordered the courtroom to be closed to all spectators, including defendant's relatives, friends, and the press.

McGee was convicted on the assault charge and acquitted on the murder charge. He was sentenced to an indeterminate sentence of five-to-fifteen years.

On Nov. 13, 2016, the Intermediate Appellate Court affirmed the trial court's decision in all respects and held that there was no sixth amendment violation.

Permission to appeal to this Court was granted to McGee on Dec. 1, 2016. Awaiting appeal, Daniel McGee remains incarcerated pursuant to that judgment of conviction.

2. *In the following exercise, the legal question is whether the testimony of defendant's expert witness on the battered woman's syndrome should have been admitted into evidence because it satisfies the test for relevance in the jurisdiction. Read the excerpts. Then write a Statement of Facts first from the appellant's point of view (Joan Brown), then from the appellee's point of view (the State of Abbott). Assume the procedural history has already been written. Before you begin to write, consider these questions.*

    a.   *Which facts would form the focus of a Statement of Facts written from the appellant's point of view? from the appellee's point of view?*

    b.   *Which facts are legally relevant?*

Excerpt of Testimony by Joan Brown

Q: (by Defense Counsel William Blake): Please give us your name and address.

A: My name is Joan Brown and I live at 600 Boston Place in Abbottsville.

Q: How old are you?

A: I'm 29 years old.

Q: Were you married to the deceased, John Brown?

A: Yes.

Q: How long were you married?

A: Nine years.

Q: Did you have any children?

A: Yes. We have a son who is 8 and a daughter who is 5.

Q: Do you have a job outside of the home?

A: No, I never finished high school, and since the kids were born, I stopped getting waitressing jobs.

Q: Did your husband ever strike you?

A.D.A. Robert Canon: Objection, your Honor. The deceased is not on trial in this case. I fail to see the relevance of this testimony.

Defense Counsel William Blake: Your Honor, the deceased's violence towards Mrs. Brown is highly relevant to her claim of self-defense.

The Court: Objection overruled. You may proceed, Mr. Blake. Q: Mrs. Brown, did your husband ever strike you?

A: After my daughter was born, my husband started to beat me up a lot. Before then, he would push me around sometimes, but after Amanda was born, it got much worse and much more frequent.

Q: Can you be more specific?

A: Once John took me outside the house and beat my head against a tree. Another time he stabbed me in the foot with a pencil.

Q: Were there any other episodes?

A: John pushed me down a flight of stairs in the house and I broke my arm and had to go to the hospital to have it set and put in a cast.

Q: Did you go to a hospital on any other occasions?

A: Last February I went to the hospital because I kept vomiting and blacking out after he beat me. There were a lot of times that he would punch me and shove me around. Sometimes he would hit the kids, too. Then other times he would be peaceful for a while.

Q: Were there any other instances in which you went to see a doctor because of your husband's beating you?

A: Two years ago John hit me in the face with a bottle and I went to the doctor to have stitches because my face was all cut up.

Q: Did you ever leave your husband?

A: Yes, last March I left John after one bad night and took the kids to a Women's Shelter on Foster Street. The next day John came to see me and said that he wanted me to come home and that things would be different. I went back with him. He was nice for a week and then he started pushing me and the kids around again.

Q: What happened on the day of April 28?

A: In the morning on the way out the door, John said he had it with me and that when he got home he was going to really finish me off. He said I humiliated him by going to the shelter. I was petrified all day. I knew he meant it. Whenever he said he would do something to me, he would always do it. Just before I knew John was coming home at six-thirty, I went to the drawer in the bedroom where John kept a gun. I took the gun downstairs, and when John came through the door I shot him.

Q: (By A.D.A. Canon) Mrs. Brown, do you have any family in Abbottsville?

A: Well, my husband's sister lives in Abbottsville, but she and I were never really close.

Excerpt of Testimony of Dr. Susan Black

Q: (By Defense Counsel William Blake) Dr. Black, please tell us something about your background.

A: I am a certified psychoanalyst and have spent many years studying the battered woman's syndrome. I have. . . .

A.D.A. Canon: Objection, your Honor. May we approach the bench?

The Court: Yes, you may. The jury is excused. (The members of the jury exit.) Mr. Blake, for what purpose do you intend to introduce expert testimony on the "battered woman's syndrome"?

Mr. Blake: Your Honor, we believe that expert testimony on the battered woman's syndrome is relevant to Joan Brown's claim of self-defense. The testimony would help the jury understand why she reasonably believed that she was in imminent danger on the day of the shooting and why deadly force was necessary to avoid this danger. In addition, this testimony would explain why she did not leave her husband, despite his brutality.

The Court: Mr. Canon?

A.D.A. Canon: I object to any testimony regarding a so-called "battered woman's syndrome." The testimony is irrelevant as it does not explain why, at the particular time that the shooting took place, Joan Brown reasonably believed that this force was necessary to prevent imminent death or great bodily harm to her. In addition, the jury has already heard extensive testimony from both Joan Brown and her neighbor on the alleged violence of John Brown. I see no purpose in further discussion of this issue.

The Court: Mr. Blake, do you have a response?

Mr. Blake: Yes, your Honor. Dr. Black is a well-known authority on battered woman's syndrome. Her testimony will describe this syndrome and show how, in her opinion, Joan Brown displayed the classic signs of the syndrome. This testimony will explain Ms. Brown's state of mind and support her claim of self-defense.

The Court: Well, I would like to hear from Dr. Black and then I'll make a decision on whether her expert testimony will be admissible. Could you please describe the battered woman's syndrome?

A: Certainly. The battered woman's syndrome is a three-stage form of family "disease". In stage 1, the battering male engages in minor physical abuse and verbal abuse. In this tension-building stage, the woman often attempts to placate the male to avoid more serious violence. Stage 2 is characterized by acute explosions of brutal violence by the battering male. In stage 3, the battering male expresses remorse for his behavior and asks for forgiveness, promising to change. The woman is hopeful during the third stage that her husband will indeed change. This is one reason why she stays with him despite the cycles of abuse. There are other reasons as well. One expert has described the demoralization experienced by some women because they cannot control the violence as "learned helplessness" or "psychological paralysis". They become incapable of taking action to change their situations. Of course, they may also be fearful of what will happen to their children, or fear that their husbands will find them and abuse them even more if they try to get away. And they may not have any money or way of earning a living.

Q: Dr. Black, have you interviewed the defendant, Joan Brown?

A: Yes, I have.

Q: Do you have an opinion on whether Joan Brown is subject to the battered woman's syndrome?

A: Yes, in my opinion, Joan Brown is subject to the battered woman's syndrome.

Q: As a battered woman, how did Joan Brown perceive her situation on the 28th day of April?

A: Joan Brown was terrified that her husband would kill her when he returned from work. He said he would, as he put it, "finish her off," and she believed, knowing him, that he would do it.

> Q: I have no further questions. Thank you Dr. Black.
>
> The Court: I have decided not to admit Dr. Black's expert testimony. I do not think it is relevant to the issue of self-defense in this case. In the state of Abbott, the jury applies an objective standard in evaluating a self-defense claim. According to the Abbott statute, which is not being challenged here, the jury must consider how an ordinary, intelligent, and prudent person would have acted under the circumstances existing at the time of the offense.
>
> The jury may return.

VI. SUMMARY OF THE ARGUMENT

SOME COURTS OR RULES OF PROCEDURE require a Summary of the Argument. This is a short affirmative statement of the reasoning in the Argument. It is often your first opportunity to argue your case to the court and because many busy judges read only the Summary before they hear the case, the impression it leaves is important. The summary should continue your theory of the case, that is, you should explain the way you want the court to understand the case by presenting the law you want the court to apply and your interpretation of how that law applies to the facts. It should include only the arguments favorable to your case. Begin the Summary with an introduction that provides the context of the case and sets out the conclusion you want the court to accept, such as "An employer may hire only women on its promotional staff where womanhood is a bona fide occupational qualification." Tell the court what the conflict is, and the decision of the lower court you are asking it to affirm or reverse. Then frame the rules persuasively and briefly apply them to the facts.

After this introduction, you would generally devote a paragraph to each major argument. Because this section is in fact a summary of *your* argument, however, you can omit less important arguments and rebuttals of counter-arguments. Nonetheless, the summary should be written so that it can be understood on its own. Thus, your major points should explain the controlling rules and apply them to the facts of the case before the court, mentioning succinctly the important policies that support your claim.

Generally, you do not need to refer to specific cases or to give case citations, although sometimes it is necessary to name and cite to a crucial case if that decision controls the analysis of the problem. You should always include relevant statutory language and citations, however. In addition, you should always explain the controlling rules before you apply them.

As a rule of thumb, the Summary should not exceed two pages for a ten-to-fifteen page Argument; one page should be sufficient for most briefs. Finally, since this section summarizes your Argument, most attorneys write it only after they have completed the Argument section. An example follows.

SUMMARY OF THE ARGUMENT

Appellant Michael Jameson's Fourth Amendment right to be free of unreasonable seizure was violated when Police Officer Mugan stopped appellant's vehicle in order to investigate two minor misdemeanors that had occurred the previous day.

Although it is long settled that an officer who has reasonable suspicion of any *on-going* criminal activity may stop a vehicle and briefly detain its occupants in the absence of probable cause, *see e.g. United States v. Moran*, 503 F.3d 1135, 1140 (10th Cir. 2007), an officer who suspects a vehicle occupant of *past* criminal activity may only perform a stop if that criminal activity constitutes a felony. *United States v. Hensley*, 469 U.S. 221, 229 (1985). In *Hensley,* the Supreme Court held that where an officer suspects that a vehicle occupant was involved in a felony, the government's interest in preventing and detecting serious and violent crimes outweighs a vehicle occupant's privacy interest. Where, however, an officer suspects past involvement in a misdemeanor, the balance shifts sharply: an individual's interest in avoiding government intrusion outweighs the public's interest in the investigation of minor offenses. Supreme Court precedent thus logically gives rise to a *per se* bright line rule forbidding investigative stops for completed misdemeanors, and the trial court correctly suppressed the evidence seized as a result of the stop of appellant Jameson's vehicle. *See Blaisdell v. Commissioner of Public Safety*, 375 N.W.2d 880, 883–84 (Minn. 1986).

Moreover, the same result is compelled assuming arguendo that vehicle stops like the one here are not *per se* impermissible, but that case-by-case application of the balancing test applied by the Court in *Hensley* is required. In the case before the court, the public's interest in investigation was minimal: the completed misdemeanors in question were trespassing on a construction site and spray-painting a protest slogan. The government's interest in the remote possibility of apprehending the slogan-painter a day after the incident was outweighed by appellant Jameson's individual privacy interest in avoiding the anxiety, humiliation, and inconvenience of a law-enforcement stop. *See, e.g., United States v. Hughes*, 517 F.3d 1013, 1017 (8th Cir. 2008).

Finally, even assuming that the purpose of the stop was constitutional, the stop was nonetheless a violation of appellant's Fourth Amendment rights because the officer lacked the requisite "reasonable suspicion grounded in specific and articulable facts that [appellant] ... was involved in or wanted in connection with a completed" misdemeanor. *See Hensley*, 469 U.S. at 229. The officer had only the single eyewitness's generic description of the trespasser as a white male in his 30's or 40's dressed in dark blue or brown. The witness apparently had a brief opportunity to view the perpetrator before he drove off in a vehicle that she unhelpfully described as a white sedan in good condition, "possibly a Toyota or a Samsung [sic]." Considered singly and in the aggregate, the circumstances here do not approach those deemed to constitute reasonable suspicion. *See, e.g., Moran*, 503 F.3d at 1139–41.

Exercise 16-E

Father Molloy was convicted in April of willfully transporting firearms across state lines. Last week, he was sentenced to four years in prison. His sentence has been stayed pending his appeal. A summer associate in the firm representing Father Molloy has written the following Statement of Facts drawn from the trial transcript and a brief summary of the applicable law. Read these materials and then write a clear and persuasive Summary of the Argument. The only issue is whether Father Molloy was entrapped as a matter of law.

Statement of Facts

Father Molloy runs a soup kitchen and homeless shelter in the parish house of St. Bridget's Church in Brooklyn, New York. A dedicated and outspoken advocate of the poor and oppressed, Father Molloy is much in demand as a speaker at conferences and rallies all over the country. He first came to the attention of the F.B.I. last winter in connection with the arrest near St. Bridget's of suspected terrorist Seamus O'Rourke. No charges have been filed against Father Molloy in New York, but the investigation continues. When Father Molloy (a law school graduate) took a leave from St. Bridget's to teach a course at a law school in Washington ("Faith, Empowerment, and the Law"), he became a target of Prayscam, an F.B.I. "sting" operation.

Calling himself "Kieran Houlihan," Agent William Smith attended a "Housing Now" rally at which the priest spoke ("We cannot rest until all the oppressed are free—Blacks in South Africa, Catholics in Northern Ireland, the poor and homeless everywhere . . .") and signed up to audit Father Molloy's course.

On February 14, 2011, "Houlihan" approached Father Molloy after class and asked whether he might speak with the priest privately. Smith took Father Molloy to Casey's Pub, where he told Father Molloy that he needed help to save his family in Northern Ireland. Through security leaks, a Protestant terrorist organization had learned the names of all those suspected by British Intelligence of having IRA sympathies. The group was systematically executing everyone on the list. In the town where "Houlihan's" uncles and cousins lived, five people had already been killed, including one of his cousins. His family had begged him to help; the Catholic townspeople needed guns to protect themselves. At that point, Father Molloy said "I can't help you with guns, my son, but my prayers are with you and your people."

After the next class, on February 16, "Houlihan" again sought out Father Molloy. He told the priest that he had been able to obtain two dozen unregistered rifles and had been put in touch with an underground "expediter" who could smuggle them onto a flight from Kennedy Airport to Belfast, where his cousins would pick them up. Now, "Houlihan" said, his problem was to get the guns to New York; he was an illegal immigrant without a driver's license and couldn't take the chance of driving his car 300 miles. "I'm sorry, my son, but I can't drive your cargo to Kennedy for you," Father Molloy replied.

On February 21, "Houlihan" once more took Father Molloy to Casey's. "Houlihan" said he was close to solving his problem: he had arranged to ship the guns to New York on Amtrak, packed in a coffin. At Penn Station, a hearse would pick up the coffin and take it to the "expediter" at Kennedy. But Amtrak would not ship an unaccompanied coffin: would Father Molloy accompany the coffin and see that it was safely delivered to the "expediter"? "This is no easy matter, my son," began Father Molloy. "I know, Father, and I am ready to express my family's gratitude in meaningful terms. We will contribute $5,000 to St. Bridget's shelter if you will help us." Father Molloy stared into his glass without speaking. Finally, he said, "Very well, my son, I'll do it."

Father Molloy was arrested a week later on 33rd Street in Manhattan as he supervised the transfer of a coffin full of Remingtons into a hearse driven by Agent Robert Jones.

At trial, the court refused to find that Father Molloy was entrapped as a matter of law. The question thus became one for the jury. Molloy was convicted. On appeal, the only issue is whether the judge should have found there was entrapment as a matter of law.

Brief Summary of Applicable Law
(Full Citations Are Omitted)

A court will find entrapment as a matter of law only when there was "some evidence" of government inducement to commit the crime charged, and the prosecution failed to prove beyond a reasonable doubt that defendant was predisposed to commit that crime. *United States v. Kelly.*

When the undisputed evidence, with all inferences drawn in favor of the government, indicates to any reasonable mind, "some evidence" of inducement, then the court can determine that there was inducement as a matter of law. *Id.* Inducement is an objective inquiry measuring whether the government's behavior was such that a law-abiding citizen's will to obey the law could be overcome. *Id.* Although government agents may use "stealth and stratagem" to entrap criminals, they may not attempt to lure law-abiding citizens into the commission of crime. *See Sherman v. United States; Sorells v. United States; United States v. Kelly.*

Government agents do not entrap if they approach or solicit the defendant to engage in criminal activity. *United States v. Burkley*. Rather, there must be some undisputed evidence indicating that government agents employed "persuasion, fraudulent representations (beyond offering opportunities to one predisposed to commit a crime), threats, coercive tactics, harassment, promises of reward, or pleas based on need, sympathy," or "friendship" in order to show inducement as a matter of law. *Id.* Thus, in *Sherman*, the Court held that there was inducement as a matter of law when the government informer sought to persuade the defendant to procure narcotics with three repeated pleas based on sympathy and mutual experience as drug addicts. Similarly, in *United States v. Owens*, because the government agent posed as a fellow drug user and resorted to friendship to convince the defendant to sell the drugs, the court found inducement as a matter of law.

However, the mere promise of money is insufficient to show inducement. In *Kelly*, the court did not find inducement as a matter of law even though government agents, posing as businessmen, offered Kelly an initial $25,000 to attend a meeting. It should be noted, however, that in *Kelly*, the defendant did not testify "that his will was overborne by any insistent importunings" by government agents. *Id.*

Once a defendant shows inducement, the prosecution must introduce evidence beyond a reasonable doubt of the defendant's predisposition to commit the crime charged in order to defeat a claim of entrapment. *Burkley*. Thus, the prosecution must prove that the defendant had a "state of mind which readily respond[ed] to the opportunity furnished by the officer . . . to commit the forbidden act for which the accused is charged." *Id.* The defendant's predisposition is determined from the entirety of the events leading up to the commission of the crime. *Kelly*.

When predisposition is at issue, the major inquiry is thus whether the defendant was "ready and willing to commit the crimes." *Kelly*. In *Kelly*, the predisposed defendant was aware of the purpose of the meeting and neither protested nor registered surprise at the initial bribe offer, "coolly" assuring the FBI agents that he would do their bidding, without repeated and insistent government pleas. *Id.*

Predisposition may also be proven by evidence of a defendant's bad reputation, previous criminal convictions, rumored activities, and response to the inducement. *Russell*. However, in *Owens*, although the defendant was a drug user and often in the company of drug sellers, the court found no predisposition to sell narcotics, as distinct from a predisposition to use narcotics. The court indicated that the facts that Owens had no prior record for selling drugs and did not show up the first time the agent requested the drugs tended to support its finding of no predisposition. *Id.*

VII. THE ARGUMENT

A. Introduction

IN THE ARGUMENT SECTION OF YOUR BRIEF, you develop the reasons why your client should prevail. The Argument is divided into sections developing separate claims for relief. These main sections are introduced by dominant point headings introduced by roman numerals. The legal arguments supporting each claim are introduced by subheadings when there is more than one supporting argument. Within each section of the Argument, as in the Discussion section of a memorandum, you need to identify the issue, explain the relevant law, work with the decision from the court below and the most relevant authorities you can find, argue your facts and compare cases, rebut opposing argument, and conclude. All this must be covered within the page limits for a brief set by the court. A brief will not be persuasive if you do not support and explain your arguments. Nor will it be persuasive if you avoid the essential hard questions that the court will want answered.

Organize your analysis carefully. To ensure that the structure of your argument is always apparent, build your analysis in terms of the legal conclusions you want to prevail on each major issue. You set out those conclusions and your reasons for the court to adopt them in headings and subheadings. Then begin each paragraph introducing a new topic with a topic sentence that sets out the proposition that paragraph is advancing rather than with the facts of a case.

The order and focus of your analysis is controlled by your persuasive purpose, namely, to persuade the court to reverse or to affirm the decision below. Your presentation should be responsive, therefore, to the opinion below, the kinds of legal argument you are making independently and in response to the lower court decision (and an opponent's arguments), and the type of support that you have. Each case lends itself to particular kinds of arguments.

- Some arguments may be fact-centered; the rule of law is well established and what alone is at issue is its application to the facts. Then the discussion might focus immediately on the particular facts of the case. After discussing the rule of law, you might even decide to marshal your facts before comparing them with analogous precedents.

- Other arguments are more doctrinal; the issue is primarily a question of law about which precedent controls the case or why a law does or does not extend to a new factual situation or how a statute should be interpreted. Here, your main point is to lead off with the law you think should control and your authority for so arguing.

- Still other arguments are more policy-centered; the contentions involve the purpose of the rule and the social and moral desirability of its end. In contrast to a fact-centered or doctrinal argument, a policy-centered argument may discuss jurisdictional trends and secondary authorities at length.

Thus, the type of argument you are making should influence how much space and emphasis to give to the various steps in your analysis. However, many legal problems, especially those you receive as moot court assignments, may present you with several types of arguments that are not exclusive of each other.

Finally, a brief is a work of advocacy, not objective evaluation. Because rules can be framed more or less restrictively, broadly or narrowly, and facts can be interpreted differently, you need to frame them carefully and bolster your interpretation with the best authority you have.

B. Writing a Persuasive Thesis Paragraph

Because the initial paragraph or paragraphs after a point heading are crucial in a brief, they should not simply duplicate the Summary of the Argument. Although you want to forecast the factual and legal points you will be developing, your first task is to get the court's attention. Thus, you may find yourself writing more creative openings than you would in an office memorandum and using your thesis paragraph to introduce the theory of your case.

The thesis paragraph should also be assertive and informative. You want to explain to the court what your client wants and why. You want to tell the court what the controlling law is and how the court should conclude about the issues in the case. Moreover, you want your points to flow naturally, logically, and inescapably to your conclusion.

The following are thesis paragraphs that illustrate how the theory of the case is set out in different types of legal arguments.

Example of a Thesis Paragraph on a Question of Law

I. A PRO SE ATTORNEY IS NOT ELIGIBLE FOR AN AWARD OF ATTORNEY FEES UNDER THE FREEDOM OF INFORMATION ACT BECAUSE HE HAS NOT INCURRED LIABILITY FOR FEES.

Arnie Frank comes to this court seeking a windfall. He wants this court to award him attorney fees that he has not incurred. Mr. Frank is an attorney, but has no client. Instead, he wants to force the government to become his unwilling client, subsidizing his pursuit of a matter of commercial interest to him. The court below correctly refused to allow him fees, holding that a pro se attorney is ineligible for an award of fees under the Freedom of Information Act (FOIA), section 552(a)(4)(E), which permits a court to award "reasonable attorney fees reasonably incurred" to a plaintiff who "substantially prevails" against the United States.

This court has already determined that a litigant who is not an attorney and who acts pro se is ineligible for attorney fees. *DeBold v. Stimson*, 735 F.2d 1037, 1043 n.4 (7th Cir. 1984); *Stein v. United States Dept. of Justice*, 662 F.2d 1245, 1263 n. 12 (7th Cir. 1981). It has not yet addressed whether a pro se litigant who is an attorney may be entitled to attorney fees under the FOIA. The reasoning of those cases, however, applies equally to Arnie Frank. The court below, moreover, properly followed the overwhelming weight of authority in determining that a pro se attorney could never recover attorney fees under the FOIA, since a litigant must actually incur responsibility for fees before the court may award them.

Many thesis paragraphs begin with a conclusion, as in this fact-based thesis paragraph concluding that a clothing store's dress code policy for female employees violates § 703(a)(1) of Title VII of the Civil Rights Act. Its theory is that the dress code violates Title VII because it requires a "uniform" and applies only to female employees.

Example of a Thesis Paragraph on Application of a Rule to Facts

I.   FIELD BROTHERS' DRESS CODE POLICY VIOLATES TITLE VII BECAUSE IT REQUIRES ONLY ITS WOMEN EMPLOYEES TO WEAR A UNIFORM.

Title VII of the Civil Rights Act of 1964 prohibits the dress code implemented by the petitioner because the petitioner forces its female sales clerks to wear an identifiable uniform, while it permits its male sales clerks to wear their own business clothing. Section 703(a)(1) of the Act declares that it is unlawful for an employer to "discriminate against any individual with respect to his compensation, terms, conditions, or privileges of employment because of such individual's . . . sex. . . ." 42 U.S.C. § 2000e–2(a)(1) (2006). A dress code that requires women to wear a uniform while men may wear ordinary business attire constitutes discrimination in a term or condition of employment on the basis of sex.

You may decide not to begin the thesis paragraph with a conclusion, however, if the facts of the case are particularly interesting or compelling. In the paragraph that follows, a seemingly innocuous action creates such an extreme police over-reaction that the writer begins with it to highlight it. The thesis paragraph begins with facts relevant to the legal issue and ends by tying those facts both to the legal principle upon which the case relies and to the conclusion. Be careful that your thesis paragraph is not merely a narrative of background information, or maudlin, or overdone. It must include assertions about the case. Because the rest of the argument is devoted to explaining the reasons for your assertions and conclusions, a narrative that is not tied to your conclusion is confusing.

Example of Thesis Paragraph Beginning with Facts

I.   THE POLICE ACTED WITHOUT PROBABLE CAUSE AND VIOLATED THE FOURTH AMENDMENT WHEN THEY ARRESTED JOSEPH GOLD AND SEIZED HIS PROPERTY WHEN GOLD PULLED A SHOPPING CART WITH HOUSEHOLD ITEMS DOWN A CITY STREET AT MID-DAY AND REFUSED TO TELL POLICE WHERE THEY WERE OBTAINED.

When two New York police officers saw Joseph Gold pulling a shopping cart down a Brooklyn street at mid-day, they leapt from their car, grabbed him, and demanded to know where he had obtained the items in the cart. The officers' extraordinary behavior had apparently been precipitated by a report from two women that they had seen two suspicious men in the neighborhood, neither of whom fits Gold's description. When Gold's reaction to the police intrusion was to remain silent, the officers then compounded that intrusion with a full-scale arrest—frisking, handcuffing, and placing him in the squad car for transportation to the precinct to await a report of a burglary. In the incident just described, Gold's constitutional rights were violated. On the least possible evidence of crime, Gold was subjected to the greatest possible intrusion on his personal privacy even though such an intrusion can be justified by nothing short of probable cause to believe a crime has been committed. Accordingly, the evidence seized from him under these circumstances must be suppressed. U.S. Const. amends. IV, XIV; N.Y. Const. art. §§ 6, 12.

Similarly in a policy driven argument, you may begin with the policy reasons for endorsing or disparaging a decision or a rule.

> ### *Roe v. Wade* Has Dramatically Improved the Lives and Health of American Women and This Court Should Reaffirm It.
>
> Approximately 1.5 million American women choose to have abortions each year. These women make this choice because they take their responsibilities to existing family members seriously; because they believe that they can escape from poverty; because they believe that an education is important; because they believe that they have talents and skills to offer the world; because they believe that someday they will find the right man to marry and raise a family with; and because they have hopes and dreams of better lives for themselves and those they love. The reasons why women choose abortion are numerous, personal and profound. This Court's decision in *Roe v. Wade* has preserved to women the right to make these critical and highly personal decisions.
>
> In his brief, the Solicitor General asks this Court to overrule *Roe v. Wade* and "return the law to the condition in which it was before that case was decided." Brief for the United States as *Amicus Curiae* in Support of Appellants, at 24 ("S.G. Br."). The condition of the law determines the condition of women's lives. The condition to which the Solicitor General would return us is one in which hundreds of women will die each year from illegal abortions and thousands will have to risk their lives or be forced to endure unwanted pregnancies.[8]

If your argument is broken into subissues introduced by subheadings, place the thesis paragraph after the Roman numeral heading and before the first subheading. An argument that is not subdivided because it involves only one basic assertion should begin with a thesis paragraph that summarizes the legal and factual contentions you wish to establish.

> ### Example of a Thesis Paragraph Introducing Subpoints
>
> MR. STUART'S MOTION TO SUPPRESS EVIDENCE SHOULD BE GRANTED BECAUSE WHEN THE DEA AGENTS SEARCHED HIS CELL PHONE WITHOUT A WARRANT, THEY VIOLATED STUART'S FOURTH AMENDMENT RIGHT TO BE SECURE FROM UNREASONABLE SEARCHES AND SEIZURES, AND THEIR ACTIONS DID NOT FALL WITHIN THE "SEARCH INCIDENT TO LAWFUL ARREST" EXCEPTION.
>
> The DEA'Ss search of Stuart's cell phone was unreasonable because it was conducted without a warrant and does not fall within one of the well-defined exceptions to the Fourth Amendment, specifically the exception for a search incident to lawful arrest. The Fourth Amendment protects individuals from unreasonable searches

---

[8]   Thornburgh v. American College of Obstetricians & Gynecologists, 476 U.S. 747 (1986), Amicus Brief Lynn M. Paltrow, Lyn I. Mille Nat'l Abortion Rights Action League.

and seizures, such as those conducted without a warrant. Searches conducted without a warrant circumvent the judicial process and are per se unreasonable. *Schneckloth v. Bustamonte*, 412 U.S. 218, 219 (1973). Three factors determine whether a search incident to lawful arrest is valid. First, the arresting officer can only search items that are part of the arrestee's person or within the immediate area that fall under the definition of a container. *New York v. Belton*, 453 U.S. 454, 461 (1981). Second, the search must be contemporaneous with the arrest. *United States v. Chadwick*, 433 U.S. 1, 14 (1977). Finally, the search must be conducted only to prevent the destruction of evidence or to remove weapons from the arrestee. *Chimel v. California*, 395 U.S. 752, 763 (1969). Here, Mr. Stuart's Nokia stored a vast amount of private data and was neither a part of Stuart's person nor a container. The Nokia is therefore entitled to protection under the Fourth Amendment. Moreover, the search was not contemporaneous with the arrest because it occurred forty minutes after Stuart's arrest and in a different location. Finally, once the phone was in the DEA agent's possession, the agents faced no threat to their safety or evidence. Thus, Stuart's motion to suppress evidence should be granted.

After this thesis paragraph, the writer should go to subheading A and focus on the first prong of the test.

These examples of thesis paragraphs not only preview the writer's theory of the case, they all include the rules that control the litigated issue. The FOIA paragraph included the statutory language about attorney fees, the dress code paragraph included the relevant language of Title VII, the fourth amendment paragraph included the probable cause requirement., the abortion law paragraph the decision in *Roe v. Wade*, and last paragraph the test for a search incident to an arrest.

Exercise 16-F

The following thesis paragraphs introduce the State's arguments to the Second Circuit that there is no sixth amendment violation when a closure order enables a frightened witness to testify. Which example is better and why? What is wrong with the other example?

a.   The sixth amendment provides an accused with the right to a speedy and public trial. Nonetheless, a court has the discretion to bar the public when it decides there is an interest sufficiently compelling to justify closure. *United States ex rel. Lloyd v. Vincent*, 520 F.2d 1272 (2d Cir.), *cert. denied*, 423 U.S. 937 (1975). Although closure is usually upheld only if the psychological well-being of a sex crime victim is at stake, *United States v. Hernandez*, 608 F.2d 741 (9th Cir. 1979), and Merta was only the victim of an assault, she is a minor. Moreover, Judiciary

Law § 4, which gives a court the discretion to close the courtroom during specifically enumerated crimes (divorce, sex crimes), extends to any victim likely to be embarrassed or humiliated during testimony and Merta falls within that class of witnesses that the statute seeks to protect. Also the order was not too broad because the defendant's family was the source of Merta's embarrassment. Finally, the findings were adequate because the court identified the reason for closure and the interest served. *United States v. Brooklier*, 685 F.2d 1162 (9th Cir. 1982).

b.   The trial court properly closed the courtroom during the testimony of Sheila Merta, a thirteen-year-old assault victim who said the spectators frightened her. While the sixth amendment provides that a defendant in a criminal prosecution has the right to a public trial, that right is not absolute when a court concludes that other interests override a defendant's right to an open courtroom. *United States ex rel. Lloyd v. Vincent*, 520 F.2d 1272 (2d Cir.), *cert. denied*, 423 U.S. 937 (1975). In reviewing whether closure was proper, a court must determine the following: 1) whether the party advancing closure established an overriding interest; 2) whether the closure order was no broader than necessary; 3) whether the court examined reasonable alternatives to closure; and 4) whether the trial court made adequate findings in the record to support closure. *Waller v. Georgia*, 467 U.S. 39 (1984). The trial court's order in this case satisfied the *Waller* test. The psychological well being of a young victim of a brutal assault is an interest sufficiently compelling to justify closure; the closure was limited to Merta's testimony; there were no reasonable alternatives to closure; and the findings made during an in camera hearing were sufficient to support closure. Therefore, the appellate court's order upholding the defendant's conviction should be affirmed.

C.   Framing Law Affirmatively

1.   Framing Law in Questions of Fact

As we saw earlier in the section on standard of review, rules can often be formulated broadly or narrowly, depending upon which favors the client's position.

> **State:** A drone is another example of permissible police use of technology to augment their senses if they reasonably suspected criminal activity.
>
> **Defense:** A drone is more than a sense-enhancing device like a beeper because it can be an enormous invasion on an individual's privacy.

Often your formulation of a rule is most likely to be accepted if there is primary authority upon which you can rely or reasonably extend. For example, assume the term "interrogation" is defined in two decisions in your jurisdiction. The first states that "custodial interrogation" means questioning initiated by law enforcement officers after a person has been taken into custody." The second states that "under *Miranda,* the term 'interrogation' refers not only to express questioning but also to any words or actions on the part of the police that are reasonably likely to elicit an incriminating response." If you were representing the defendant, you would adopt the phrasing of the second decision to argue that under *Miranda*, a conversation between two officers about the whereabouts of a gun discarded near a primary school that was made within the defendant's hearing was a ploy as likely to elicit an incriminating response as a direct question and was therefore an interrogation.

If primary authority doesn't exist, you may have to rely on persuasive authority or secondary authority that supports your formulation of the rule.

2. Questions of Law

If your case involves a question of law, analyze it using the strategies explained in Chapters 2, 3, and 11. The strategies of statutory interpretation, for example, include inquiring into the statute's plain meaning, legislative history, and policies. It also may require using the canons of construction. As an advocate, marshal these arguments to interpret the language favorably for your client.

In the example that follows, the writer uses a plain meaning analysis, buttressed by analysis of the legislative purpose behind § 1963 of the Racketeer Influenced and Corrupt Organization Act (RICO). The example follows a thesis paragraph that concluded that the district court correctly denied appellant's pretrial motion for an order excluding the attorney's fees owed by appellant from forfeiture to the government under RICO. The RICO statute prevents an appellant from transferring criminally obtained assets to third parties in order to prevent forfeiture.

The meaning of § 1963 of the Racketeer Influenced and Corrupt Organization Act (RICO), 18 U.S.C. §§ 1961–68 (2006), is unambiguous and does not exempt attorney's fees from forfeiture. Under § 1963(c), title to forfeitable property vests in the government at the time the criminal act was committed, rather than upon conviction of the defendant. Thus, the government may seek a special verdict of forfeiture of tainted assets that were transferred to a third party after the act but before conviction. § 1963(c). The only way a third party may vacate or modify such an order is to show at a post-conviction hearing that he was "a bona fide purchaser for value" of such property "reasonably without cause to believe it was subject to forfeiture." *Id*.

Because under the plain meaning of the statute Congress exempted only two groups of people from the reach of third party forfeiture, tainted attorney fees are forfeitable. Parties who have acquired title to assets before the commission of a crime are exempt from forfeiture. This group would hardly encompass an attorney in the pretrial stage of a criminal proceeding. Parties who are "bona fide purchasers for value reasonably without cause to believe that tainted assets are subject to forfeiture" are also exempt. § 1963(c). An attorney who "purchased" tainted proceeds in exchange for legal services could not be a bona fide purchaser under the statute. An attorney would necessarily be on notice of forfeiture after reading the client's indictment.

The general legislative purpose behind RICO forfeiture also supports a plain meeting interpretation of § 1963. In *Russello v. United States*, 464 U.S. 16 (1983), the Court noted that the broad goal of RICO forfeiture provisions was to strip organized crime of its economic base and separate the racketeer from his illegally gotten gains. *Id*. at 26, 28. The relation-back provision of § 1963(c) furthers that goal by preventing pre-conviction transfers of forfeitable property. A construction inconsistent with the plain meaning of the statute would undermine this goal by allowing a RICO defendant to utilize what may be the fruits of racketeering activity to finance his criminal defense. *See In re Grand Jury Subpoena*, 605 F. Supp. at 850 n.14.

If the question of law is one that asks the court to adopt a new rule, then your strategies involve liberal use of analogy to existing rules and of policy. This example uses historical material and persuasive authorities.

A de facto spouse's right to sue for damages for loss of consortium is the next logical step in the evolution of the doctrine of consortium. Under the early common law, only the husband or father could sue for loss of services of a member of his family. Courts now recognize that wives as well as husbands may bring claims for loss of consortium. In permitting a wife to bring a loss of consortium claim, the New York

Court of Appeals identified the wife's loss as arising out of the personal interest she has in the marital relationship. *Millington v. Southeastern Elevator Co.*, 239 N.E.2d 897, 899 (N.Y. 1968). The husband in *Millington* had been paralyzed from the waist down as a result of an elevator accident. The court reasoned that the woman's "loss of companionship, emotional support, love, felicity, and sexual relations are real injuries" that altered their relationship "in a tragic way." *Id.* In coming to a similar conclusion, the California Supreme Court focused on the shattering effect of a husband's disabling accident on the quality of his wife's life when her husband was transformed from partner to invalid. *Rodriguez v. Bethlehem Steel Co.*, 525 P.2d 669, 670 (Cal. 1974).

Susan Wilson has suffered damage identical to that suffered by a wife whose husband has been injured. Although she was never legally married to John Webster, the stability and significance of their relationship indicates that her emotional suffering will be as great as that of a married woman. Susan Wilson's commitment to her relationship is apparent from its nine-year duration and shared parental obligations, and demonstrates that her loss was no less real than that of Mary Rodriguez, a bride of only sixteen months. Moreover, she has lived with and cared for John Webster since the accident and likely will continue to do so. The circumstances of Susan Wilson's relationship compel a finding that she, like the plaintiff in Millington, has suffered in a "tragic way" as a direct result of the injury sustained by her de facto spouse. *See Millington*, 239 N.E.2d at 899. Accordingly, her consortium rights should be recognized and protected.

D. Choosing and Arguing Precedent

Although you will likely find many precedents relevant to your case, it would be unusual to find one that is dispositive in the jurisdiction of your assignment. If there were one, the case would have been settled, probably well before trial or the motion appealed from. So you probably will have to use the several types legal arguments that you have been learning and that are explained in Chapter 11, and discuss the policy or policies behind the relevant cases to show how a decision in your client's favor will further these policies.

1. Choose Cases Carefully

You should choose the most relevant precedents and be selective; don't drown the court in short references to many cases and string cites that will require the court to do the work of winnowing down the cases to find the most relevant ones. Instead, choose the cases that offer the most favorable analogies to your case, and explain why those decisions apply. Synthesize the point from those cases that you want to argue should control.

Many students rely primarily on quotations from an assortment of cases: they write a conclusory sentence, follow it with a quotation supporting that conclusion and then write that "therefore" that applies to their client's case. A relevant quotation is good support, but does not alone make your case. Instead, you should build your argument more thoroughly. Supply the facts of the precedent cases so you can explain how they apply or do not apply to the facts of your case. Explain the courts' reasoning in precedent cases so you can later argue that reasoning requires a particular outcome in your case because a decision in your favor will implement the policies in those cases. Remember that policy arguments and arguments explaining the consequences of their decisions are important to appellate level courts.

2.　Use Cases to Assert Your Point

Topic sentences also can be extremely important. Use the topic sentences introducing an issue to make the point of your argument, for example, by describing your synthesized rule. They should not be written in the kind of objective, narrative style you use for an office memorandum, but should make a point favorable to your client. In addition to synthesizing cases by their facts, you may synthesize their policies. For example, a topic sentence in a brief opposing Freedom of Information Act (FOIA) attorney fees for pro se attorneys might be, "The same policies that have convinced this court to decline to award attorney fees to a pro se litigant who was not an attorney apply to an attorney who acts pro se." Then go on to explain the policies.

If you list the topic sentences of each paragraph, you should have an outline of your argument.

The following (condensed) paragraphs are on the first part of the *Lemon* test, which requires showing the statute has first a secular legislative purpose; second, the principal or primary effect neither advances nor inhibits religion; third, the statute does not foster an excessive government entanglement with religion. The writer explains that the Supreme Court has almost always accepted the state's declared legislative purpose, and has not inquired further into purpose. The writer synthesized the cases to explain them favorably for the School Board client, and used that persuasive synthesis as the topic of these paragraphs. The paragraph begins with the writer's conclusion, and then summarizes the writer's interpretation of the important cases (the synthesis), before distinguishing the opposing cases:

The purpose of the Sioux Falls Policy and Rules is a secular one: to foster understanding and mutual respect of different religions by exposing students to the various religious cultures and traditions in the world. The court need not inquire behind this statute's stated secular purpose and the lower courts correctly did not do so. Indeed, this Court has consistently accepted a state's avowed purpose. In *Wolman v. Walter*, 444 U.S. 801 (1979), the Court upheld provisions of an Ohio statute authorizing aid to non-public, primarily parochial schools. The Court's entire inquiry into legislative purpose consisted of a single reference to "Ohio's legitimate interest in protecting the health of its youth." *Id*. at 836.

In the last twenty-five years, the Court has inquired beyond the stated legislative purpose only twice, for reasons that do not apply to the Sioux Falls Rules. In *Stone v. Graham*, 449 U.S. 39 (1980), the Court held that the state violated the establishment clause by requiring public schools to post the Ten Commandments in each classroom. And in *School District v. Schempp*, 374 U.S. 203 (1963), the Court held that the state violated the establishment clause by requiring Bible reading every morning in the public schools. The Court found that the purpose of these statutes was "plainly religious" even though each state had justified them on secular grounds. None of the factors that compelled the Court to look beyond the stated legislative purpose in *Stone* and *Schempp* exists in the present case. There are four important distinctions. [analysis of the distinctions followed].

To summarize the second part of the Lemon test, the writer again synthesized the cases and concluded that in cases involving public rather than private schools, the courts analyze only the principal effect of a regulation, not every direct effect:

As long as the principal or primary effect of a regulation neither advances nor inhibits religion, then that regulation is valid under the second part of the *Lemon* test. In cases involving public schools, the Court has always looked to the primary effect of a regulation rather than to every effect. "The crucial question is not whether *some* benefit accrues to an institution as a consequence of the legislative program, but whether its *principal or primary effect* advances religion." *Tilton v. Richardson*, 403 U.S. at 679 (emphasis supplied). The primary effect of the Sioux Falls Policy and Rules neither advances nor inhibits religion. Rather its primary effect is to effectuate the school district's secular purpose.

The cases involving aid to parochial schools provide the exception to the general rule that the Court will invalidate a regulation only if its principal or primary effect advances religion. Because of the character of these institutions, the Court's analysis must be particularly intensive. In those cases only, the Court has invalidated statutes with "any direct and immediate effect of advancing religion,"

> *Committee for Public Education v. Nyquist*, 413 U.S. at 783. Since the Sioux Falls District Public School has no religious mission, this type of inquiry is unnecessary.

Remember strategic use of cases may require you to interpret a precedent narrowly or broadly. If you want to distinguish a case, interpret it narrowly, that is, limit the holding of the case to its particular facts. For example, in the Sioux Falls Rules case, the respondent School District distinguished several cases by interpreting them to apply only to parochial schools, not to public schools. The respondent limited the holdings by considering the contexts in which the cases arose. If you want to analogize a case, characterize the facts and holding more generally so that your case falls under it.

Exercise 16-G

A graduating high school student, Tim Jefferson, has sued in federal district court seeking to declare unconstitutional and to permanently enjoin the inclusion of prayer at graduation. The school board of Tim's school had authorized student elections to permit students to decide whether to include a voluntary, nonsectarian, student-led prayer in their graduation ceremony. By a majority of one, the students voted to have such a prayer.

The most recent decision on this issue is *Lee v. Weisman*, 505 U.S. 577 (1992). In *Lee*, a middle school principal had invited a member of the local clergy to offer a nonsectarian and nonproselytizing prayer at his school's graduation. The Court said that the principal's invitation represented governmental coercion to participate in religious activities, a form of establishment of religion barred by the First Amendment.

1. Assume you are representing Tim Jefferson. Write a sentence or two interpreting *Lee* broadly so that it is analogous to your case.

2. Assume you are representing the school board. Interpret *Lee* narrowly to distinguish it from your case.

Exercise 16-H

The following paragraphs, which are addressed to the United States Supreme Court, argue that Fields Brothers' dress code requirements for employees are illegal under Title VII with respect to the "terms and conditions" of employment because different standards apply to men and women employees. Which example uses case law better and why?

Example A

This Court has consistently held that, under Title VII, an employer cannot impose one requirement on male employees and a different requirement on female employees. *See, e.g., Phillips v. Martin Marietta Corp.*, 400 U.S. 542 (1971). By imposing the requirement that female employees must wear a store uniform, but that male employees need not, Fields Brothers violates Title VII by discriminating against women in their "terms and conditions of employment." *See Carroll v. Talman Savings Ass'n*, 604 F.2d 1028 (7th Cir. 1979).

Dress codes that impose burdens on employees of only one sex are suspect because they can be based on offensive sexual stereotypes and thus violate Title VII. In *Carroll*, the employer had imposed its dress code because it had decided that women tended to follow fashion trends and dressed improperly for work. *Id.* at 1033. Thus, the employer in *Carroll* issued clothing to women employees consisting of a choice of five pieces. The court found the clothing constituted a uniform and held that Title VII prohibited the defendant's practice of requiring females to wear these uniforms. *Id.* at 1029. The court stated that the dress code was based on an improper stereotype that women exercised poor judgment in selecting work attire but men did not. *Id. See also EEOC v. Clayton Fed. Savings Ass'n*, 25 Fair Empl. Prac. Cas. (BNA) 841 (E.D. Mo. 1981) (requiring only female employees to contribute to and wear uniforms is prima facie evidence of actionable discrimination under § 2000e–2(a)).

Example B

In two cases on point to the case at bar, the courts held that employers who imposed a dress code requirement only on female employees violated Title VII. *Carroll v. Talman Savings Ass'n*, 604 F.2d 1028 (7th Cir. 1979); *EEOC v. Clayton Federal Savings Ass'n*, 25 Fair Empl. Prac. Cas. (BNA) 841 (E.D. Mo. 1981). The dress code in *Carroll* required women to wear a uniform that consisted of choices among five items: skirt or slacks, jacket, tunic or vest. Male employees were required to wear ordinary business attire. *Carroll*, 604 F.2d at 1029–30.

The United States Court of Appeals for the Seventh Circuit held that the employer's requirement that women but not men wear a uniform violated § 703(a)(1) with respect to "terms and conditions of employment." *Id.* The court remanded the case for the entry of summary judgment for the female employee plaintiffs. A district court has followed the Seventh Circuit and held that a dress code imposed on female employees only is prima facie evidence of discrimination under § 703(a)(1). *Clayton Federal*, 25 Fair Empl. Prac. Cas. at 843.

Exercise 16-I

Read these case summaries carefully and write a persuasive topic sentence that synthesizes the cases to explain how the cases apply to the facts. Write a topic sentence first for one party and then for the other.

Facts: A child, Bart was born in 2014 to Carole Darin who was married and lived with her husband, your client Gerald Darin. Gerald is listed as the father on the child's birth certificate. Carole and Michael Hahn had had an extramarital affair for some two years before Bart was born and blood tests show to 98.5% probability that Michael is the father.

When Bart was four months old, Gerald moved to New York from California for business. Carole remained in California and lived with Michael for five months, although she and Bart visited with Gerald a few times. Michael held Bart out as his child. Carole then returned to her own home, but when Bart was two she lived with Michael again for eight months. Carole has now reconciled with Gerald and they are living together again and have a child of their own. Michael has filed an action to be declared Bart's father and for visitation. California law imposes a presumption rebuttable only by the husband that a child born to a married woman is the child of the marriage. Michael claims that the presumption infringes his due process rights to establish paternity.

Case A

The state of Illinois brought a dependency proceeding on behalf of two minor children living with their father, Stanley. The mother and father had never married but had lived together with their two children for eighteen years. The mother died. The state declared the children wards of the state under an Illinois statute that provided that children of unmarried fathers, upon the death of the mother, are declared dependents, without a hearing as to the father's fitness as a parent.

The court held that Stanley was entitled under due process to a hearing as to his parental fitness before his biological children could be taken from him.

Case B   ✦

Ardell Thomas had a nonmarital child that she raised in her own home. Ardell never married the biological father Quinlen and never lived with him. The father visited the child from time to time and brought gifts. Ardell married, and when the child was eleven, her husband petitioned to adopt. Quinlen opposed the adoption. The state statute provides that only the mother's consent is required for adoption of a nonmarital child who has not been legitimated. Under the statute, the father has no standing to object.

The court held that Quinlen's rights under the due process clause had not been violated because he had never taken any responsibility for the child, never acknowledged her, and never lived with her in a family unit.

Case C

The unmarried mother and the natural father, Caban, of two children lived together for five years, representing themselves as husband and wife. Caban was named on the children's birth certificates as their father. He and the mother supported the children. The mother moved out with the children to live with another man, not telling Caban where they were. The mother married one year later, and after two years her husband petitioned to adopt the children. Caban learned of their whereabouts only one year after their marriage and visited them several times. State law permits an unwed mother, but not an unwed father, to block an adoption by withholding consent.

The court held that Caban was entitled to a hearing to determine parental unfitness before his rights as a parent could be terminated.

E. Arguing Your Facts

To make your brief convincing, argue your facts thoroughly. Regardless of whether you argue your facts before or after you analyze supporting authority, paint your facts in such a way as to elicit a favorable application of the law. Stress facts that align your case with favorable precedents. Stress facts that show injustices to your client. After you have dealt with your strong facts, work with damaging evidence. You should not ignore unfavorable evidence, as the opposing counsel will certainly present that evidence, and present it in a worse light. Instead, put that evidence forward briefly and provide an exculpatory explanation if possible. Emphasize both exonerating facts and mitigating facts. If possible, demonstrate the irrelevancy of facts that distinguish your case from favorable precedents or that show your client as unworthy. If you cannot do that, explain that while your client is flawed, that does not mean he is guilty of the crime with which he is charged: My client may be forgetful, your Honor, but he is not wantonly negligent.

1. Emphasize Favorable Facts

Treat favorable evidence in depth. Do not describe supportive incidents in broad terms; parade them in detail.

Example (Citations to the Record Omitted)

The Supreme Court has said that, in the best of circumstances, "[t]he vagaries of eyewitness identification are well-known [and] the annals of criminal law are rife with instances of mistaken identification." *United States v. Wade*, 388 U.S. 218, 228 (1967). In Moore's case, the conditions made an accurate identification impossible and the court's description of the identification testimony as "highly reliable" is simply unrealistic.

The robbery took place in a parking lot on a dark October night. The complainant never identified Derek Moore as one of the robbers. The most he could say was that Moore "would fit the description" of one of the tall youths. Indeed, the complainant previously testified that Moore was not one of the robbers. Thus, the People's contention that Moore was one of the youths who committed the robbery depended solely upon the testimony of the Smith brothers, Tom and John, who claimed to have seen him at the robbery scene.

Although John Smith asserted that he had seen Moore climb the parking lot fence, this witness admitted on cross-examination that he had been fifty to sixty feet away and had only seen half of the person's face. Tom's identification testimony is also questionable. From a distance of ten to fifteen feet, through the dark, he said he saw Moore's face for a "split second." Although he asserted that this brief view was sufficient for him to recognize Moore, whom he had never seen before, he could not see whether the hood of Moore's light-colored jacket was up or down. Nor was he able to see an identifying mark on Moore's forehead—a two-inch keloid scar. In sum, it is hard to imagine a less reliable identification that would still result in a prosecution.

---

2. Minimize Unfavorable Facts

You can exploit paragraph structure to highlight favorable material and subordinate damaging material. Positive information should be advantageously located at the beginning and end of paragraphs. Damaging material should be buried in the middle of paragraphs—and sentences—and described generally. In this way, negative information is framed by the positive and is, to some degree, neutralized by the context.

Example (Citations to the Record Are Omitted)

Upon seeing two white males round a corner armed with tire irons and chains, Derek Moore believed that he was about to become the victim of a racially motivated assault. Because Moore knew nothing of the robbery these two youths had just witnessed, this assumption on his part was entirely reasonable. So was his decision to run in the opposite direction. The fact that the district court found the Smiths unassailably truthful in asserting that they had a different motive for chasing Moore is irrelevant to Moore's belief. It is also believable that the Smiths might well have shouted racial epithets at someone they assumed had committed a robbery outside their very window. Thus, these stories do not actually conflict, and there is a plausible and exonerating explanation for why Moore took to his heels.

The examples above focus on the facts that reflect the theory of the case. The paragraphs may be followed with analogies to cases that support that theory. Alternatively, you may first summarize favorable cases and then weave your comparisons to precedent into your analysis of the facts. You should also try to distinguish your facts from unfavorable cases.

Compton's concern that its female employees will be made uncomfortable by a transgender person's use of the women's locker room is not Compton's real reason for terminating Ms. Sloan's employment. It is just another way of stating that the company disapproved of her gender non-conformity, which is discrimination based on sex stereotypes. In *Etsitty v. Utah Transit Authority*, a transgender person was terminated because of her employer's fear that her use of the public women's restrooms would give rise to the employer's legal liability. The court affirmed the grant of summary judgment reasoning that the employer's fear of legal liability was a legitimate nondiscriminatory reason for its termination of the plaintiff. However, Compton was not dealing with public restrooms as the defendant in *Etsitty* was. Moreover, Compton never stated it feared liability as a reason for terminating Ms. Sloan. It only suggested her use of the women's locker room made other employees uncomfortable.

Exercise 16-J

Which example uses facts more persuasively as to whether an employer discriminates on the basis of sex when the store issues business suits to its women clerks only? (Citations to the record are omitted.)

a.   Fields Brothers' dress regulations distinguish between the sexes but do not discriminate on the basis of sex because the distinctions are not based upon immutable sex characteristics nor do they impinge on a fundamental right. Summary judgment in favor of Fields is consistent with that two-prong test to determine sex discrimination in employment.

Fields Brothers' distinctions between male and female employees are not discriminatory as to conditions of employment because clothing styles are not immutable characteristics of a sex but can be changed at will like hair length. For that reason, a sex-differentiated hair length regulation was held not discriminatory. The employee was able to change his hair length in order to comply with his employer's regulations. The respondent in this case could easily have worn one of the suits issued to her and could have complied with the dress code. Her desire to wear her own choice of suit is not an immutable characteristic. Nor does Fields' code impinge upon an employee's fundamental rights such as marriage and child rearing. In cases in which regulations impinge on female employees' fundamental rights, the employers did not impose any restrictions on male employees. Fields, however, imposes dress regulations, albeit different ones, on its male sales clerks.

b. The Fields Brothers adopted a dress code policy for both male and female sales clerks in 1999. The store sells conservative business clothes and its customers are predominantly business people of both sexes. The store's president has explained in his affidavit that the store's management policy is to cater to its customers' preferences for conservatively dressed sales clerks. All members of the store's sales staff are therefore required to wear appropriate business attire.

The court below differentiated between the "uniforms" that the female clerks are required to wear and the "ordinary business" attire required of male clerks. In reality, there is no difference. The male clerks' suits are as much "uniforms" as the female clerks' suits. Male business attire has developed over the years into a recognized uniform of shirt, tie, suitcoat, and suit pants. A male clerk who deviated from this attire would not be appropriately dressed. Design of female business attire, on the other hand, is a relatively new industry, and the same similarity of appearance has not yet developed. The store's decision to supply its female clerks with suits was an attempt to solve the problem created by this difference.

The court also emphasized that female clerks must wear a patch with the store logo on their suits while the men are issued a pin. Yet no real difference exists between a patch and a pin. If a patch makes a business suit a uniform, then so does a pin. All sales clerks wear conservative business suits and the store logo; all are treated alike in the "terms and conditions of employment."

F. Rebutting Opposing Arguments and Authority

Establishing your own argument requires rebutting opposing argument. Yet you do not want to overemphasize those opposing arguments by setting them forth in all their untarnished glory and then scrambling to recoup your losses. Instead, address the argument opposing counsel is likely to make implicitly rather than explicitly, by answering it as you present it. In other words, make your counter-argument affirmatively and as an integral part of your case, rather than as a separate section devoted only to counter-argument.

When you rebut your adversary, avoid topic sentences that overemphasize the other party's arguments. Weak introductions frequently include statements like

- It is (has been) argued that . . .
- Respondents assert . . .
- The courts rejecting this claim have said . . .

Such expressions highlight the opposing argument by opening the paragraph with it. For example,

> It has been argued that awarding a child damages for loss of consortium would result in speculative and uncertain damages. However, damages for injuries sustained by the Jones children are no more difficult to ascertain than they are in other classes of injury involving intangible losses where the courts have allowed recovery.

If the author of this example had simply omitted the first sentence, her topic sentence would have focused on the reason why the opposing argument is not sound. She would have suggested the avenue her opponent would take, without unduly emphasizing it.

> Damages for injuries sustained by the children in this case are no more speculative than they are in other classes of injury involving intangible losses where the courts have allowed recovery.

Or again, in arguing that the first amendment's guarantee of freedom of association protects not only activities of an organization but also the activities of attorneys who assist that organization, the petitioner should not say:

> One may argue that *Trainmen, Mine Workers,* and *United Transportation Workers* can be distinguished from petitioner's case since in those cases the union was the party charged with violating a statute, while in this case the party charged with violating the statute is the attorney. However, the Court has held that lawyers accepting employment under a constitutionally protected plan of referral have a constitutional protection like that of the union which the state cannot abridge. *Trainmen v. Virginia,* 377 U.S. at 8.

A more effective advocate might say:

> This Court recognizes the right of an organization to request an attorney to assist its members in asserting their legal rights. In *United Mine Workers* and *Brotherhood of Railroad Trainmen,* the Court held that a state could not proscribe a range of solicitation activities by

> unions seeking to provide low cost, effective legal representation to their members. Lawyers who accepted employment or acted at the request of these unions were also protected because their actions helped the unions further their members' rights.

Although you should deal with supporting authority first, you must disclose authority in the controlling jurisdiction that is directly adverse. This is an ethical responsibility imposed by the American Bar Association's Code of Professional Responsibility Disciplinary Rule 7–106(b). The Model Rules of Professional Responsibility, as adopted by each state, also require an attorney to disclose legal authority in the controlling jurisdiction known to be directly adverse to the position of the client if opposing counsel does not disclose it.[9] Although your opponent probably will find and include these contrary decisions, you should address them anyway. There are also strategic reasons to acknowledge unfavorable law. Your brief will be taken more seriously if you go below the surface to rebut adverse authority with reasonable arguments. By doing so, you show the strength of your client's position. Moreover, if you are the appellant, you may "inoculate" the court to opposing counsel's argument by putting it in a context favorable to your client. In addition, you assist the court by setting out the conflict and in doing so, add to your credibility.

It is important to remember that not every argument can be rebutted on its face. For example you may not be able to meaningfully distinguish the facts. In this situation, you may need to concede one argument but argue that another type of argument outweighs the importance of the first. Assume, for instance, that an old Supreme Court case excluded domestic relations cases from diversity jurisdiction, but the statute actually gives Federal courts jurisdiction over "all civil actions." In a battle between the text of the statute and the precedent, the Supreme Court in *Ankenbrandt v. Richards*, 504 U.S. 689 (1992), allied itself with its precedent, reasoning that where Congress failed to alter the Court's earlier decision, it was likely that decision reflected congressional intent.[10].

There are a number of other ways to minimize the significance of an unfavorable precedent and to convince a court that a rule should not be extended to include the circumstances of your case.

---

[9] Model Rules of Professional Conduct 3.3(a)(2) say, in pertinent part, that an attorney shall not "fail to disclose to the tribunal legal authority in the controlling jurisdiction known to the lawyer to be directly adverse to the position of the client and not disclosed by opposing counsel."

[10] We thank Wilson Huhn for bringing this example to our attention in *The Five Types of Legal Argument*, 2nd ed., 189–191 (Carolina Academic Press 2008).

- You could explain, for example, that the reasoning of an unfavorable decision does not apply to your facts and would, therefore, create an injustice unless an exception was made.

- Or you could ask a court to overturn a decision because it is no longer sound public policy given changes in society.

- You might examine developments in allied fields that support changes in the field of law with which you are concerned.

- You could also demonstrate that, as a practical matter, a rule is not working well—it is too difficult to administer or too vague.

- As a last resort, you could argue a case was poorly reasoned.

You might also need to diminish the impact of an unfavorable statute. Here you might try to show that

- the statute does not control the subject matter of your case,

- the language of the statute is ambiguous enough to permit a construction more favorable to your client, or

- the statute is unconstitutional.

Chapter 11, on questions of law, explains these strategies of argument.

Finally arguing in the alternative is a different type of counter-argument. Here, for the sake of argument, you concede one point only to follow with another argument showing why your client should nonetheless win. Thus, you might first argue that your client never consented to a search, and then argue that even if she did, she revoked that consent.

The following paragraphs are representative examples of arguments attempting to neutralize adverse decisions. The examples are based on the following problem.

Stone v. Eagle

The parents of Juliet Stone, an infant born with severe birth defects, brought a wrongful life action on behalf of the infant against an obstetrician. They allege he negligently failed to inform them that the mother's age made her fetus vulnerable to an increased risk of Down's Syndrome and that amniocentesis, a procedure by which the presence of Down's Syndrome in the fetus can be discovered, was available to her. John and Mary Stone allege that they were deprived of the choice of terminating the pregnancy and that they would have terminated the pregnancy if they had known their child, Juliet, would be born with Down's Syndrome. The suit is for damages to the child. (Wrongful life claims are distinguishable from wrongful birth claims. In a wrongful birth claim, the parents, on their own behalf, sue the physician whose alleged negligence resulted in the birth of an unwanted or deformed child.)

Defendant moved for summary judgment and dismissal of Juliet Stone's wrongful life action on the grounds that she failed to state a claim upon which relief could be granted. The court granted the motion on the grounds that Juliet Stone had not suffered a legally recognizable injury. It reasoned that no life could not be preferable to an impaired life, that neither the court nor a jury would be able to ascertain an appropriate measure of damages, and that defendant did not cause Juliet Stone's impairment. In fact, she could never have been born a healthy child.

In appealing the dismissal of her wrongful life claim, Juliet Stone must overcome the fact that most courts, like the district court in her case, have rejected actions on behalf of infants who have attempted to sue for wrongful life. Recently, however, a few courts have permitted partial recovery in wrongful life claims, allowing the infant to recover as special damages the extraordinary medical expenses which the infant's condition would require.

Example 1: Precedents are not followed universally

The California Supreme Court has recognized wrongful life as a new cause of action. *Turpin v. Sortini*, 31 Cal. 3d 220, 643 P.2d 954, 182 Cal. Rptr. 337 (1982). The *Turpin* court held that a doctor was liable for negligently depriving expectant parents of information that they needed to determine whether birth would be in the best interest of a severely malformed fetus. *Id.* The court approved of a lower court decision, *Curlender v. Bio-Science Laboratories*, 106 Cal. App. 3d 811, 165 Cal. Rptr. 477 (1980), recognizing the claim of an infant plaintiff afflicted with Tay-Sachs disease. This child suffered mental retardation, blindness, pseudobulper palsy, convulsions, muscle atrophy, susceptibility to other diseases, and gross physical deformity. The *Turpin* court recognized that the child in *Curlender* had a "very limited ability to perceive or enjoy the benefits of life, [and that] we cannot assert with confidence that in every situation there would be a societal consensus that life is preferable to never having been born at all." *Id.* at 229, 643 P.2d at 963, 182 Cal. Rptr. at 346.

Example 2: Precedents conflict with sound public policy

Two fundamental tenets of tort law are to provide a remedy for every wrong committed and to deter future harmful conduct. Both these goals are furthered by recognizing a claim for wrongful life. Social interests are advanced when a physician's duty to an unborn child extends to providing expectant parents with the genetic counseling and prenatal testing that enables them to make informed decisions about what is in the best interest of the fetus. The wrongful life claim complements professional practice by requiring all physicians to exercise proper diligence and skill in caring for patients both living and unborn. *Curlender v. Bio-Science Laboratories*, 106 Cal. App. 3d at 828, 165 Cal. Rptr. at 487. Because physicians have the medical expertise and knowledge to detect fetal abnormalities, they should be responsible for testing for them and counseling parents about them. Neither the state nor the parents should be burdened with the care and maintenance of children suffering from detectable genetic malformations while the physician who failed to exercise diligence and skill remains immune from liability.

Example 3: Precedents are inconsistent with trends in related fields

Many of the issues in a wrongful life action have been recognized in other medical malpractice actions. The prenatal injury cases have established an unborn child's right to sue. The wrongful birth action has recognized proximate cause and imposed liability on physicians for negligence in counseling and testing for genetic defects. The right to die cases have given the individual a right of self-determination which overrides social assumptions about the sanctity of life. These extensions in tort law reflect its responsiveness to changing social values and establish grounds for recognizing a wrongful life claim.

Exercise 16-K

1. *Identify these writers' techniques for minimizing unfavorable precedents or facts. Evaluate each writer's success.*

Example 1   The court below relied heavily on *Carroll v. Talman Savings Ass'n*, 604 F.2d 1028 (7th Cir. 1979). Yet *Carroll* is the only decision from a court of appeals that has held a dress code discriminatory. Not only is the case ten years old, but it was decided only by a 2–1 vote over the vigorous dissent of the respected Judge Vest.

Example 2   In *Carroll*, the court overturned an employer's sex-based dress code policies which required its female employees to wear a uniform but permitted male employees to wear a wide variety of attire, including sport coats and leisure suits. The *Carroll* dress code is easily distinguishable from the one required by Fields, where both men and women must dress in conservative business suits. In fact, in *Carroll*, the court said that Title VII does not prohibit uniforms in the workplace but only requires that a "defendant's similarly situated employees be treated in an equal manner." Fields Brothers accomplishes the very thing that the court suggests: it treats its employees equally.

Example 3 Fields Brothers has urged that the proper comparison is to cases involving personal grooming regulations in which the courts have held that grooming standards, such as hair length regulations for male employees that differ from the permitted hair length for females, did not constitute sex discrimination under Title VII. In *Knott*, for example, the court permitted reasonable grooming standards for its employees that included minor differences for males and females that reflected customary grooming styles.

These grooming codes are markedly different, however, from Fields' dress codes. First, Fields' disparity of treatment between the sexes is more severe. Fields requires female clerks to wear a clearly identified uniform in a limited style and color range while permitting male clerks their own choices. In *Knott*, each sex was required only to meet a customary standard of good grooming. The limitations on their grooming were minor. Second, grooming regulations merely maintain a standard of conventional grooming for employees to follow. In *Knott*, men with long hair were unconventional and inappropriately groomed for their employer's business. Fields Brothers, however, fired the plaintiff for wearing her own conventional and entirely appropriate business suit because it was in a different dark color from the one issued. Finally, some courts have justified grooming regulations because they are not based on immutable characteristics. This Court, however, has never limited the reach of Title VII to regulations based on immutable characteristics but has inquired more broadly as to whether the employer imposed disparate treatment on male and female employees.

Example 4 Although several courts have recognized an exception to Title III for interspousal wiretapping, some federal courts have held that a cause of action exists between spouses for violation of the Act. In *Jones v. Jones*, the court applied Title III to a husband who had tapped a telephone at his estranged wife's residence, and in *White v. White*, the court held that there is a cause of action for a wife whose husband had hired an investigator to tap her telephone. In these cases, however, the parties had

Example 5

gone beyond a domestic dispute. In *Jones*, the parties were already estranged. The telephone was located outside of the marital home. In *White*, a third party to the relationship was the agent of the intrusion. Neither of these cases involved the special nature of an ongoing domestic relationship within a marital home.

Those courts that have decided that Title III does not apply to interspousal wiretapping have misinterpreted the policy behind the statute. As the legislative history shows, Congress repeatedly heard testimony about the frequent use of electronic surveillance between spouses in divorce cases. In fact, one committee witness, echoing the testimony of others, said that "private bugging can be divided into two categories: commercial espionage and marital litigation." Several Senators stated in the Congressional Record their understanding that the bill prohibited private surveillance.

2. *Rewrite Example 2 so that the paragraph begins more persuasively.*

3. *Rewrite Example 3 so that the paragraph begins more persuasively.*

4. *Rewrite Example 4 so that the paragraph begins more persuasively.*

VIII. CONCLUSION

THE CONCLUSION IS VERY BRIEF. It is not another summary of the arguments. Instead it specifies the relief that the party is seeking. It is followed by a closing, like "Respectfully Submitted," and then your name and address as attorney of record.

IX. THE APPELLEE'S BRIEF

MANY ATTORNEYS WHO REPRESENT appellees underestimate the importance of the appellee's brief. They reason that because they won in the court below, and because more cases are upheld on appeal than are reversed, all that remains to win again is to explain the lower court's decision to the reviewing court. Indeed, many attorneys believe that because the appellant often turns their arguments against them, the less said the better. Careful attorneys, however, never rest on their laurels. A good appellee's brief requires the same care and creativity as an appellant's brief.

The opinion below is, of course, strong authority in your favor. It is generally advantageous, therefore, to refer to that opinion and to choose quotes from it. Do not, however, rely upon it exclusively, especially if the opinion is poorly reasoned. Because lower court opinions, especially in a moot court problem assignment, often need bolstering, you should argue your case in the way that you think is most effective. You need not confine yourself to the structure of the decision used by the court below.

In appellate practice, you would always begin by reading the appellant's brief carefully and outlining the appellant's arguments. You would also read the cases that the appellant relies on if you are not already familiar with them and update those cases. Make sure that you meet each of the appellant's arguments in your own brief. Except for clearly frivolous points, which you should label as such, you cannot afford to ignore the appellant's weak or strong arguments. Give the judges your side of each point. Dispose of the appellant's weaker arguments quickly. (Be sure to cite to the appellant's brief if you refer to the appellant's argument.)

You need not confine yourself to the structure used in the appellant's brief. The appellee's Argument section may be organized completely differently from the one in the appellant's brief. If the appellee has stronger arguments for one issue than for another issue, the Argument section should begin with the appellee's strong issue, not the appellant's strong issue. Put your best argument in the most prominent position in the brief. Emphasize your main points; do not be defensive.

Indeed, as counsel for the party that won below, your brief should sound confident and convincing. The Questions Presented, Statement of Facts, Summary of the Argument, and Point Headings should all reflect the appellee's orientation rather than the appellant's. As a general rule you should put your side's view of the case first in every section and then refute the appellant's view rather than put the appellant's viewpoint first and leave your reader waiting to hear your client's arguments. (See section VII, E for suggestions on how to handle opposing arguments.)

You should also choose those arguments that will create sympathy for your client. While some student advocates are hesitant to do that when representing the government, the effective attorney will find ways to present the client's point of view sympathetically, regardless of the particulars of the case.

In other words, an appellee's brief should not be a negative document that merely argues against the appellant's brief, but should be an affirmative document.

There may be some significant differences between moot court programs and the situation you would face writing the appellee's brief in practice. In an actual appellate case, you would have the benefits of the appellant's brief, the briefs already written for lower courts, and the complete record when you write your own brief. Typically a case that reaches a supreme court has been briefed at least once before. The attorneys know their opponent's arguments and their own weaknesses well. You would know exactly which arguments your opponent relied upon and you could play off your opponent's choice of cases and words.

In moot court programs, however, the parties may not have briefs submitted to lower courts and the appellee may not have the appellant's brief. You may only have the opinion below, the references in that opinion to the arguments raised by each side in the lower courts, and an abbreviated record to help you frame your arguments. In that case, imagine an appellant's brief written by an opposing counsel. Decide how you would write the appellant's brief, and, however hard it is to tear apart your own arguments, respond in a positive fashion by asserting the appellee's best arguments and rebuttals.

Finally, you should note that in a true case, the appellant might have a parting shot. After the appellee's brief has been filed, the appellant may file a reply brief. The appellee, then, must choose arguments as carefully as the appellant did to avoid giving the opposing counsel an opportunity to tear apart the appellee's arguments unanswered in writing. In moot court, however, the appellee's brief is usually the last written word.

Editing Checklist: Brief

I. **Questions Presented**

    A. Do the questions combine the legal claim and the controlling legal principles with the key facts that raise the issues?

    B. Are the questions framed so as to suggest an affirmative answer?

    C. Are the questions persuasive without being conclusory?

    D. Do the questions read clearly and succinctly?

II. **Point Headings**

    A. Do the Point Headings provide a sound structure for the Argument section of the brief?

    B. Do the headings set out legal contentions favorable to your client and support those contentions with reasons and relevant facts?

C. Do the headings have a conclusory tone favorable to your client?

D. Are the headings clearly and concisely written?

E. Is each heading a single sentence?

III. Statement of the Case

A. Did you include the procedural history?

B. Are the facts set forth in a narrative that will be easy for a reader unfamiliar with the case to follow?

C. Is the statement complete, accurate, and affirmative?

1. Are all essential facts included and irrelevant facts omitted?

2. Are unfavorable facts included without being overemphasized?

3. Are favorable facts effectively placed in positions of emphasis?

4. Is the statement accurate?

5. Are record references included for all facts?

D. Does the statement include any legal conclusions or editorializing that properly belongs in the Argument section?

IV. Summary of the Argument

A. Did you answer the Question Presented?

B. Did you summarize from the Argument the main reasons for your answer?

C. Can the Summary be understood on its own?

V. Argument

A. Organization

1. The Thesis Paragraph

a. Does each issue under a point heading begin with a thesis paragraph setting forth in affirmative (and conclusory) terms the major contentions?

b. Does the thesis paragraph present an integrated statement of the theory you are putting forth?

c. Is its length proportionate to the argument?

2.   Large-Scale Organization

     a.   Is each ground for relief a separate point heading?

     b.   Is the Argument organized around issues and subissues?

     c.   Wherever possible, is the first issue the one most likely to succeed? Are all points under it arranged in order of strength?

3.   Small-Scale Organization

     a.   Is each new topic introduced by a topic sentence that synthesizes your argument?

     b.   Is each issue or subissue developed clearly and logically?

     c.   Is your argument made before the opposing argument is countered, i.e., do you make effective use of the positions of emphasis?

     d.   If the topic sentences of each paragraph were arranged in an outline would a strong skeleton of the argument emerge?

     e.   Does each paragraph advance the argument?

     f.   Are there genuine transitions between paragraphs?

     g.   Do the sentences within a paragraph coherently relate to each other and the topic?

B.   Analysis

1.   Are the facts of the case argued effectively?

2.   Are the authorities cited appropriately described, explained, and applied?

     a.   Are the rules of law stated clearly, accurately, and affirmatively?

     b.   Are the facts of cases which are helpful to your client presented as consistent with the facts of your client's case, insofar as this is possible?

     c.   Are "harmful" cases adequately distinguished or explained?

     d.   Is the decision appealed from either supported or criticized?

3.   Are policy arguments effectively made?

4. How have the arguments of the opposition been answered?

    a. Have you made sure that opposing arguments are not treated defensively?

    b. Are affirmative counter-arguments made convincingly?

5. Is the argument logical, internally consistent, and thoroughly developed?

VI. Language

1. Is the language clear, concise, and chosen for persuasive impact?

2. Is an otherwise persuasive brief marred by technical errors such as spelling and grammatical errors?

Chapter 17

Oral Argument

STUDENTS APPROACH MOOT COURT oral argument with either excitement or trepidation. Some students look forward to it because they believe they are better oralists than writers. They welcome the chance to impress the court with their interpersonal skills and ability to think on their feet. For others, the first oral examination of their legal knowledge of a complex problem, while standing alone and in public, is daunting. Yet litigators regard oral argument as a welcome chance to speak directly to judges about the case, the client, and the stakes.

I. PURPOSE OF ORAL ARGUMENT

ORAL ARGUMENT BEFORE A JUDGE or panel of judges is not about delivering an uninterrupted, rousing speech, such as you might hear at a debating society. Admittedly, you want to convince the court of your commitment to your client and the merits of the case. But conversation, not speechifying, is the best way of doing that. For practicing attorneys, oral argument is an opportunity to

- focus the court on the facts, rules, and policies that are favorable and dispositive,

- address any questions that are troubling the court in order to clear up its misunderstandings or doubts, and

- motivate the court in a way hard to accomplish in a written, less personal brief.

If you can accomplish these three things, your oral argument should go well.

These goals are common to both trial and appellate advocates. Nonetheless, oral argument at the trial level differs in several ways from oral argument at the appellate level.

A. Oral Argument in the Trial Court

The trend in appellate courts is to either reduce the length of oral argument or, even more frequently, to decide cases on the basis of the briefs, without any oral argument. This is less true at the trial court level. Since trial courts often have a heavy docket and judges often do not have law clerks, oral argument is an efficient way to handle a large number of motions, the source of most oral argument in trial courts.

Local rules and practices dictate the scheduling of oral arguments in trial courts. Some courts hear pre-trial motions once or twice a week or month, on "Motion Days." Some courts set aside time for motions in the morning. But whatever the schedule, the judges are likely to hear enough motions in a row that they need to move through them expeditiously.

After a brief round of argument, for simpler, often pre-trial, motions—like a motion to amend a pleading, to quash or compel discovery, or to admit or suppress evidence—judges will often rule from the bench. For oral argument on more complicated, dispositive motions—like a summary judgment motion, preliminary injunction motion, or motion to dismiss—a court might take the motion "under advisement," until the court has read the briefs. When your motion is based on a federal (or state) rule, keep the elements of the rule in mind when preparing for and making your argument.

In addition to pre-trial motions, advocates argue motions during and after trial. These may arise from evidentiary matters or may request, for example, specific jury instructions or judgment as a matter of law. Post-trial motions may focus on recovery of costs or judgment notwithstanding the verdict.

Whether pre-trial or trial, oral argument at this level is less formal than in appellate courts. You argue before a lone judge for as long as you have something to say and the judge is willing to listen. Moreover, there is no single chance to make your points. Often both parties go back and forth until the judge has heard enough. In addition, since the process is less formal, trial lawyers sometimes exhibit less decorum than do appellate lawyers. They interrupt each other or posture more. Good judges, however, maintain control over their courtrooms to ensure each party has the opportunity to make its case.

B. Oral Argument in the Appellate Courts

Appellate courts, as mentioned before, tend to rely on the detailed analyses that are in advocates' briefs. The judges often come to oral argument with questions about the troublesome aspects of the case and with presuppositions about the case's outcome. Nonetheless, good advocates can reassure judges and rebut presumptions, often changing a judge's mind.

Appellate arguments are made in front of a panel of judges and follow a formal procedure.

- The appellant or petitioner stands at the podium before a panel of judges and argues and answers questions for a set period of time, usually 10 to 30 minutes.

- When the appellant sits down, the appellee or respondent follows suit.

- Finally, if the appellant has reserved time for rebuttal—often 1 to 3 minutes—he or she returns to the podium to correct whatever misstatements the appellee may have made or to refocus the court on a core, determinative issue.

While arguing, the attorneys are kept apprised of the time by the clerk or bailiff, who holds up a time card or flicks a light on the podium—usually green to start, yellow when a few minutes are left, red to stop. If the speaker is in the middle of a point when time is up, it is common to ask whether she may finish answering the question or whether she may conclude. The court will usually give permission. Remember also that while judges interrupt the speaker with questions, the parties may not interrupt each other or the judges.

Although trial and appellate argument differ in formality, they also have much in common. In both, you must prepare carefully, argue the facts and the law thoroughly, and give a persuasive presentation. Thus, although the rest of this chapter focuses on appellate argument, much of its advice is equally applicable to the trial advocate.

II. PREPARING THE ARGUMENT

THERE IS NO SUBSTITUTE for solid preparation. Begin by reviewing all the material you used to write the brief. Then select the two or three issues you think will probably control the judges' decision. Also work on your theory of the case or your theme, a "take" on your client's claim that cuts to the core and plays to the judges' sense of fairness and compassion. After this, outline your argument.

A.   Review Materials

Renew your familiarity with the Record on Appeal. Make sure you are clear about the procedural facts, as well as the legally significant facts and the appropriate standard of review. If the court should ask you about a detail, you should know the facts so well you can tell whether the fact comes from the complaint or the record.

Then reread your brief and your opponent's. Tab any section you think your opponent or judge may refer to. Identify that party's best issues and your best. These are the issues that will probably be the foundation of the court's decision. Finally, reread cases and relevant secondary authority. If time has elapsed between the time you submitted the brief and oral argument, update your research.

B.   Select Issues

Oral argument is not a spoken version of the written brief. You do not have the time, nor is this the place, to argue every point of your case. Instead, crystallize the issues. Select and make the two or three arguments that you think will probably control the judge's decision for or against you and that will make the court want to rule in your favor. These are the points you will keep returning to if the court's questioning takes you astray. In selecting arguments, keep a few other things in mind.

- Do not try to make complex arguments. Oral argument is a poor time for explaining subtle intricacies of the law or of case analysis. Leave that for your brief. Arguments based on fairness, simplicity, and common sense are often more effective than those based on esoteric complexities.

- Choose among the types of arguments you included in your brief, for example, policy arguments, doctrinal arguments, and arguments based on the equities of the facts of your case. Remember, though, that these arguments are not mutually exclusive. You can focus on doctrinal arguments and yet humanize the case by relating these arguments to your client's situation. You should also choose among consequential and persuasive arguments and decide which ones to stress.

- Once you have selected your main points, determine how to rebut your opponent's. If there are adverse cases, decide in advance how you will distinguish them or diminish their importance. But remember, although you want to address your opponent's weak points, you do not want to be defensive and use up your time explaining why your opponent's position is wrong before you make clear why you believe your position is right.

- Anticipate the questions that the court will ask and determine your answers. The court will probably ask about obvious weaknesses in your case. Therefore, know how to meet those weaknesses. You also need to think through your case so that you know which points, if any, you can safely concede and why these points are not dispositive.

- Finally, be prepared to deal with the implications, especially the policy implications, of the result you seek. These considerations are important to the court and should be incorporated into your outline. For example, a judge may ask, "If we decide in your favor, what will happen if. . . ."

C. Pick a Theme

Choose a theme for your case. A theme should be rooted in law and fact, capture the court's attention, and garner its sympathy or sense of fairness. It often stems from the facts, as in the following example.

> Your Honor, this case involves a widowed grandmother who is trying to adopt her orphaned five-year-old granddaughter in the face of a social services law that prohibits unmarried people from adopting or fostering children, a statute that violates her 14th Amendment rights.

When there is a compelling social goal, the theme may be policy based.

> This case asks whether the government's interest in fighting air terrorism justifies the use of backscatter scanning machines at airports when all possible privacy measures have been taken.

At other times, the theme may focus on law.

> Despite the petitioner's claim she is an independent filmmaker entitled to the reporter's privilege, the funding for her film on a death row inmate was secured with the help of the very death penalty clinic representing the inmate. This violates the Second Circuit's independence standard, which was established to promote the free flow of unbiased, truthful information.

Once you have chosen a theme, return to it often to drive home your arguments. It helps the court to keep its eye on the ball, on what is truly at stake for the parties or the nation.

D. Outline Your Argument

After you review materials and select your theme and arguments, plan your outline.

You should not read your argument from notes, so try to prepare a short outline with clear headings that will jog your memory about the points you want to make. Avoid writing out your arguments since this will tempt you to read your notes rather than the judges' faces. You want to be looking at the court so you can assess and adapt to their reactions and responses. So create an outline in list or bullet form and put the headings in bold so you can find them easily, as in the example below.

Backscatter machines do not violate the reasonableness test for suspicionless searches for three reasons

1. **Air terrorism is a severe threat to humans and property**

    •   a plane itself can be turned into a weapon

    •   de-arming a terrorist is necessary to prevent a plane from being used as a weapon

    •   there have been multiple terrorist attacks in the air

2. **The search procedure had extensive privacy measures**

    •   Passengers faces are blurred

    •   Images are deleted when passengers cleared

    •   Transportation Security Administration agents viewing the scans are in locations far from passengers being scanned

3. **No alternative measure is adequate**

    •   magnometers & hand wands cannot detect non-metallic weapons.

There is, however, one exception to the outline rule. You may want to prepare the beginning of your argument in more detail to get you started at the time when you are likely to be the most nervous. In this introduction, you should greet the court, introduce yourself and your client, and set out your roadmap. However, even this introduction should be memorized, not read. Practice it repeatedly until you know it by heart.

Some people advise that you prepare two arguments. One is the outline of the crucial points you must include even if the judges give you little time to make your own presentation. The other is the longer talk to use if the bench is cold, that is, if your judges ask few questions and you must fill your time with your own presentation.

In either event, many advise that your outline not be longer than two pages stapled into the inside of a folder. This will prevent you rifling through pages trying to find your place or the information you need. On the back of the folder, you can attach a list of important cases, briefly summarized and cited, that you can refer to if the court questions you about them. But remember, although you may wish to refer to crucial cases in your argument, you should limit the number of cases you mention. Use your time in oral argument to concentrate on facts, reasoning, analysis, and policy. Your brief contains the cases and the citations. Thus, do not give the reporter citations to cases that you mention unless the court requests them. Reading case citations impedes the conversation with the bench and wastes time.

III. STRUCTURE OF PRESENTATION

A TYPICAL ORAL ARGUMENT HAS FIVE PARTS.

1. An Introduction

2. A Statement of Theme and Roadmap of Issues

3. A Summary of Facts (in some Moot Court competitions)

4. An Argument

5. A Conclusion and Prayer for Relief.

Each part is discussed in this section.

A. Introduction

A standard introduction which both appellant and appellee can use is, "Good morning/afternoon, Your Honors, my name is_____, counsel for the _____ (appellant/appellee or petitioner/respondent)." In some Moot Court programs, students are advised to preface this statement with "May it please the Court." If your Moot Court rules provide for rebuttal, the appellant should reserve time for rebuttal during this introduction.

B. Theme and Roadmap of Issues

1. The Appellant

After the introduction, the appellant should set the theme and issues. For example, an appellant might begin as follows.

> This case is here on the defendant's motion for summary judgment. The issue is whether TSA agents violated my client's Fourth Amendment protection against unreasonable searches and seizures when they, without a warrant or individualized suspicion, forced him to undergo either an invasive pat-down or body-scanner search.

Then, before launching into your roadmap, tell the court the relief the client is looking for:

> The Court should deny defendant's motion for summary judgment because this type of suspicionless search is unreasonable.

After this, the appellant can begin the roadmap, setting out the main points.

> **Backscatter searches and pat-downs are unreasonable for three reasons**
>
> 1. Subjecting millions of Americans to an intrusive search as a primary means of screening is unreasonable.
>
> 2. Backscatter searches are intrusive because they allow agents to view intimate details of passengers' bodies and enhanced pat-downs have agents physically touching a passenger's private parts
>
> 3. Absent a concrete danger, the TSA should use less intrusive methods as a first line of screening before opting for highly intrusive methods.

This brief outline helps the judges follow the development of the argument. Moreover, the outline gives a framework within which to work and to which it is useful to return, especially in the face of interruptions by questioning from the judges. After giving the judges the legal context of the appeal and an outline of the main arguments, the appellant should present the first argument.

2.   The Appellee

Like the appellant, the appellee must also introduce himself and the party he is representing. But the appellee is not tied to the same format as the appellant. He need not state the issue or recite the facts unless there is some reason for doing so—for example, to correct the appellant's version of the facts. Instead, the appellee might open with vivid facts, a rejoinder to one of the appellant's conclusions, or a persuasive statement of the theme or issues that will capture the courts' attention. If the appellee is the prosecutor in a particularly vivid criminal case, for example, the appellee might follow the introduction by saying, "Your Honors, the defendant has been tried and convicted by a jury of the first degree murder of his wife of fifteen years who was pregnant with his third child at the time of her murder." Or the appellee might begin with the thematic issue: "Your Honors, the issue is whether the government's interest in fighting air terrorism justifies the use of body scanners at airports when all possible privacy measures have been taken and the consequences of lack of surveillance can be as grave as the 9/11 tragedy."

This persuasive opening is usually followed by the appellee's roadmap. In general, the appellee's argument should not be a point by point refutation of the appellant's argument. Instead, appellees should present their arguments in the order most effective for the client. However, an appellee should listen carefully to the appellant's argument and be ready to change the presentation to meet the appellant's points. Flexibility is essential. An appellee should also listen carefully to the questions that the judges ask the appellant. In this way the appellee may learn which aspects of the case particularly concern the court and speak to those issues.

C. The Facts

1. Appellant

In Moot Court competitions, it is common, after the opening, for the appellant either to give a brief recitation of the facts or to at least ask if the court wants a short recital. In practice, this is not typically what lawyers do and what judges permit since time is short. Often the judges have read the briefs and are familiar with the facts. However, if the court asks for a summary, if the facts are central to resolving the dispute, or if the facts are expected in your Moot Court argument, then the appellant would give a short factual review.

Generally, a chronological narrative is the clearest organization. Do not be too detailed and do not characterize the facts inappropriately: an accurate, objective narrative of the facts supporting your conclusion works best, as in the example below.

Mr. Hanson recently underwent an emergency operation for Crohn's disease. He now has a colostomy bag. When Hanson explained to the TSA agent at the airport that both a back scanner search and pat-down would be humiliating given his condition, the agent said he had to choose one method. Hanson opted for the pat-down. It was performed so roughly the bag was dislodged, leaking urine and feces. Hanson had to cancel his business trip so he could return home to clean up. He now

---

asks the court to declare these measures unconstitutional as primary
airport security searches.

2. The Appellee

The appellee is not required to recite the facts, and where the
opponent's version was essentially truthful, the appellee can
simply weave significant facts into the argument. Where, however,
opposing counsel misrepresented events or omitted relevant facts,
he or she may need to correct the record and tell the story from the
client's perspective.

D. The Argument

The Argument section is where both attorneys try to prove that the
authorities and equities require a decision in their favor. Both
parties should begin with their strongest argument. Not only does
it put their case in its best light, but it is the best chance of
ensuring that argument gets the time it deserves. Once judges
start with questions, other points may get short shrift.

If your strongest argument is a factual issue, begin by
explaining the law in the light most favorable to your client and go
on to apply it to the facts, showing how it implicates or exonerates
your client. When dealing with a question of law, explain why a
statute's plain language does or does not result in an
interpretation favorable to your client. Then show how legislative
intent or policy support your claim.

In moving through your points, remember that the judges'
questions may force you to depart from your roadmap. If you have
not finished your first argument and a judge interrupts with
questions about your second point, answer the questions and then
say, " "Your Honors, one last point about the first issue." If the
judges' questions on your second point enabled you to make your
fundamental arguments on that issue, you should not repeat them
after you finish your argument on the first point. Because you need
to manage your time, go straight to your last issue instead, saying
something like "since we covered the second issue during
questioning, I turn now to the last issue." Brief transitions like
these make it easier for the court to follow the argument.

Despite your best intentions, time may run out before you have
made all your arguments. If you are fortunate enough to have a
few moments left, try to summarize your last points quickly. If you
do not have the time to do even that, admit your time is up and
rest on your brief for the arguments you were unable to make.

On the other hand, do not worry about finishing before your allotted time is up. If you have made all your essential points, simply thank the court for its attention and sit down.

E. Rebuttal

The appellant's rebuttal is the last word in the oral argument. The appellant should not include new information not made during the main presentation, nor rehash what has been said. Instead, the appellant should use the time to rebut important points, not the small details, that the appellee seems to have raised, or to correct significant errors in the appellee's presentation or to shore up those arguments that were weakened by the appellee or the judges' questioning. In other words, use the time to go for the big points. For example, if the appellee based her argument on a theme that she repeated with persuasive effect, the appellant could begin by redefining that theme in order to negate, or at least weaken, its impact.

In sum, although oral argument can be quite stylized, there is still a good deal of room for varying the format of the presentation. Your main concern as an advocate should be that the court knows what the issues are and gets the important information it needs to understand your version of the case.

F. Prayer for Relief

Both parties should close the argument with a prayer for relief, such as "For the reasons stated, appellant respectfully requests this court to reverse the judgment of the court below" (or use the specific name of the court below). You may want to briefly remind the court of one central point before you state the prayer for relief, but you must not irritate the court by dragging out the argument or by giving lengthy summaries once your time has elapsed.

IV. QUESTIONS BY THE COURT

AN ORAL ARGUMENT IS A CONVERSATION with the court, not a speech or a debate. The purpose of oral argument is to give the judges the opportunity to ask questions. Yet nervousness makes many first-year students react to questions as if they were unwarranted interruptions or attacks. Instead of responding this way, you should use the questioning as an opportunity to find out the judges' thinking on the issues in the case and to resolve any problems the judges may have in deciding the case in your favor.

A. Types of Questions

Judges frequently ask three types of questions: questions asking for information, friendly questions and adversarial questions.

- **Questions asking for information.** Sometimes a judge is simply requesting information or clarification about the record, the law, or an argument you have made. If you are well prepared, these are non-threatening questions to answer.

- **Friendly Questions.** It is important to remember that some questions are friendly. For example, if you have lost your train of thought, a judge will sometimes ask a question to put you back on track. Sometimes, a question invites you to speak on a matter that the judge knows is on the court's mind. She is giving you the opportunity to address that concern. Often a judge who agrees with your position will ask a question that advances your argument in the hope your answer will persuade others on the bench. These questions are a good opportunity to agree with the judge and promote your case.

- **Adversarial Questions.** Inevitably courts will ask challenging questions about troublesome aspects of your case—sometimes in a less than friendly or polite tone. Even these questions can be helpful, however, because they allow you to show that those weak points are not as damaging as they might appear, or are not dispositive.

Whether neutral, friendly, or hostile, judges will question you about the strength of your authorities—which you must be able to analogize or distinguish accordingly—and about the policy implications of a decision in your favor. Prepare for these questions. Because a judge may ask you a series of hypotheticals to determine the limits of your claim, think in advance of the impact a decision in your favor will have on future cases. If you want to prove a decision in your client's case will not create a slippery slope, show how the decision can be limited to a few cases similar to your own. Alternatively, you may want to argue that for justice to be done and the public to be served, a new rule is needed. Be prepared to discuss the type of rule best suited to the problem. Would a bright line rule or a factors test work, or should decisions be made on a case by case basis?

B. Formalities of Questioning

Always remember that you are in an appellate courtroom and are expected to conform to the customs of the courtroom.

To begin, always act with decorum and civility. Address the judges with their proper title, as "Your Honor" or "Justice."

Listen to a judge's question without interruption and answer immediately. Always listen to a judge's entire question before responding. Then answer the judge's question directly and immediately—do not tell a judge you will answer the question later. Instead answer the question, even if, as will often happen, the question takes you away from your prepared outline. In that event, return to the structure of your argument when you have completed your answer. If you can, use your response as a means of returning to the topic you had been discussing.

Admittedly, returning to your argument is not always easy or possible, either because the judge has jumped ahead or has returned to an earlier point, or because the judge has decided to take you down the slippery slope. Try not to allow yourself to be led too far afield, but do not openly resist a line of questioning. If you must abandon your outline, do so until the line of questioning ends or a subsequent question offers you an avenue of escape. When you have the opportunity, there is nothing wrong in saying "Now, Your Honors, returning to my earlier point. . ." or "Your Honors, moving on to the next issue. . . ."

Determine in advance what you can concede. Sometimes a judge will pursue a line of questioning that culminates in the request that you concede a point in your argument. Think carefully before conceding. Some points are peripheral and your arguments may be weak. Therefore, you may want to concede that point to maintain your credibility if a concession in no way diminishes your other arguments. Beware of conceding a point that is necessary for your case, however.

Never indicate that you think the judge's question is unwise or irrelevant. If you disagree with a judge's statement, such as a judge's description of a case holding, do so politely. For example, you can say, "Your Honor, my reading of the case, which seems to differ from yours, is that. . . ." Some lawyers preface their disagreement with a phrase like "With all due respect, Your Honor."

Be candid. Do not evade or misrepresent your case's weak points, but decide how you can limit their importance. You gain the court's confidence by knowing the law and presenting it fairly. If, by evasion or lack of candor, you lose the court's confidence, the judges will look to the other attorney to find out what the case is really about. Make sure you quickly correct any mistake or misstatement you may have made. Your frankness and integrity are essential.

Ask the court to clarify confusing questions and admit when you do not know the answer to a question. Even if you have prepared your argument carefully, you may have difficulty responding to some questions. Respond to a confusing question by requesting a clarification from the court. If you are asked a question and cannot think of an answer, or if the question relates to an area of law with which you are not familiar, first try to give a partial answer that in some way responds to the court's question and gives you a moment to think. If the court is still not satisfied, you would be better off simply saying that you do not know the answer rather than wasting the court's time giving an uninformed response. If you are asked about a case that you did not read or cannot remember, simply say that you are not familiar with the case. The judge may stop the line of questioning there or may explain the case to you and ask how it relates to your case.

V. STYLE OF PRESENTATION

THERE IS NO ONE SINGLE WAY to present an oral argument. Instead there is a wide range of successful, yet different, styles. Your presentation will depend on your personality, skills, imagination, and your reactions to speaking in public and being questioned by a panel of judges. There are some points on which everyone agrees, however,

Do not read your argument. Instead, maintain a conversational tone. Speak without notes as much as possible. Look at the judges when you deliver your prepared remarks and when you answer their questions. Be polite but not subservient. Do not punctuate your argument with phrases like "I think," "I believe," or "The Appellant would argue," thereby characterizing your statements as just your opinion. Instead, just state the arguments themselves.

Speak clearly and slowly (nervousness tends to speed up a person's pace). But do not speak in a monotone. Vary your tone to give emphasis to your statements and to maintain the judges' interest.

Stand straight and avoid distracting body movements and facial expressions. Avoid using extravagant gestures or overly casual movements, like slouching over the podium. Do not roll your eyes or grimace when opposing counsel or a judge is speaking. Unprofessional conduct reflects badly on you, not on other parties in the courtroom. You should also try to maintain a professional attitude even if you believe opposing counsel or a judge is being unfairly harsh or demeaning to you.

Look at the judges instead of at your notes, and concentrate on the judges' questions. The best oral arguments are those in which advocates know their case inside out and have a dialogue with the judges in response to their inquiries.

Dress professionally. A conservative suit is customary.

Most importantly, your speaking style should also convey conviction on behalf of your client's cause. If you are not convinced that your client should win, the court will not be either. As an appellate advocate, your argument may be the last step between your client and imprisonment or a burdensome damage award or fine. Your oral skills and legal ability may win the day.

CHAPTER 18

LAW SCHOOL EXAMS

I. INTRODUCTION

YOUR FIRST LAW SCHOOL EXAMS can be a daunting experience, especially if your semester grade depends on the one final exam. But if you come to the exam well prepared and are ready to expend the effort that an exam requires, you should not be overwhelmed by the experience. By this time in your educational career, you probably have developed your own style for taking exams.

The traditional law school exam is made up of essay questions. The professor will give you questions made up of a hypothetical set of facts for you to analyze. You will have to identify the legal issues, supply the controlling law, and apply that law to the facts of the exam questions. Calling on your knowledge of the relevant case law, you should write as full an answer as you have time for. This sounds something like the memoranda assignments that you completed during the semester. However, a very important difference is that the exam assignment is like the discussion section only—you do not set out the facts separately, or craft an issue statement. You also do not write a separate summary section. Your aim instead is to get as much relevant analysis in each exam answer as you can, but not to repeat. You rarely will earn more points by repeating.

Although we have not used what is known as the IRAC formula in this book, you may have noted that IRAC is well suited to an exam answer: Issue (the issue in this question is . . .”), Rule (a contract requires an offer, an acceptance, and consideration), Analysis (Mr. X's letter to Y may not have been an offer because . . . in that way X's letter is like the letter in <u>A v. B</u>, except that A's letter included . . . another problem with X's letter is that . . . .), and a Conclusion (I conclude that X's letter was not an offer, but even if it was, B's letter was a counteroffer and the parties did not enter into an enforceable contract).

II. STARTING THE EXAM

A GOOD PRACTICE is to start by reading through the whole exam, and note whether the professor has provided time allocations, or point allocations, for each question that you can use to measure your time. As you read, try to get an idea of the main issues in each question. This is useful in at least two ways. You may see that the first question is more difficult for you or leaves you cold, but that you can tackle the second question easily. Then start with the second question. You need not answer the questions in the order they appear on the exam. Start with one that you are most comfortable with and most prepared for to get your adrenaline flowing. This will help you take on the rest of the exam. You want to work with as high energy as you can muster (some students bring chocolate bars to eat for this purpose). Be sure to number your answer to correspond with the exam question number or subpart.

Another reason to read through the whole exam first is that you will get an idea of what the issues are in all the questions. This will help you budget your time. So, you may be answering the first question and are not sure if consideration is an issue. If you are reaching the time limit for that question, but you know that consideration is a main issue in the second question, it is likely that it is not important in question one. You may want to include a short analysis of that issue in the first question if you have some time, just to cover yourself. If time is running out, you made your choice of what to omit judiciously.

III. WRITING THE EXAM ANSWER

A. Getting Started

ONCE YOU GET STARTED, be sure to check your time. Don't shortchange the time you have left for the last question because you went way overboard in terms of time on another question. Your professor probably allocates points to each question and your very good answer to question two cannot make up the zero points for question three. If you have taken essay exams before, you probably have developed your own style of answering essay questions and you should continue to do what works best. For example, some people, after they read through a question, will identify the issues and first write or type out a complete outline of an answer for themselves, and then rework the outline before they begin their full answer. Others need to start writing right away, again letting their adrenaline carry them, and they write their way into the exam question. They may keep an outline in their head or write down in a margin or scratch paper an outline, key words and concepts they want to include as they go on. The best advice is to use whatever method works for you.

Make sure that you answer any specific questions. For example, a hypothetical may end with "should the court grant the defendant's motion to dismiss?" Answer the question, but remember that the implied instruction is "discuss," or "analyze," or "explain." Your analysis or explanation will be more important than your "yes" or "no" answer.

When you reach the end of your time for the exam, don't waste it by writing something like "I see my time is up . . ." Use those seconds instead to get in one or two more sentences analyzing the issues or an outline of information that you haven't covered.

B. Use the Facts

Most exam questions will include the specific facts that you need to analyze the issues and to stimulate your discussion. The professor usually has spent a great deal of time thinking about which facts to include, and to provide the material you need to analyze both sides of an issue. Your job is to recognize and use the relevant facts. One indication of a good exam answer is the writer's acute sense of relevance, that is the ability to identify those facts on which the question turns. So you would identify which language in X's letter to Y looks like an offer, and which language clouds the issue, or which language in Y's response may be a counteroffer, and why. You should also identify which language is analogous to or different from language in one or more cases that you read on that issue.

We offer one caveat about the cases to which you refer. Your analysis and responses to issues will always be based on cases (unless you are analyzing statutory language alone) or at least on your understanding of an area of law developed through reading cases. And your professor may have spent more time in class on certain cases than on others. If so, use those cases where you can. However, you probably will find that you do not include as many case descriptions and explanations in your written responses as you thought you would, or that you used in office memoranda or briefs. Where you do rely on particular cases, identify them by name if you can. If you cannot remember the name of the case, describe it. Do not include citations.

Another caveat is about the facts in the question. Do not make up facts, especially ones that will introduce a new issue to the problem. In very rare situations, you may be sure that some important fact was omitted, or that one of the parties was identified incorrectly. In that case, you can make an assumption and identify it as an assumption. For example, you may say "assuming that you meant Charles and not David . . . ." Before you do that, however, reread the question carefully to make sure that it had to have been Charles.

C. Organize Your Answers

Your professor will not expect a perfectly organized discussion. Students have been known to add at the end of an answer a paragraph that should belong well before the end because it adds to the analysis of an earlier issue, but the student did not have time to move the paragraph to its proper place. For example, she thought of a factual comparison or a counterargument after she had moved on to another question or issue. The professor is not likely to cross out the paragraph and to not give credit for that addition. It is important, however, to identify which question or which issue that added last paragraph responds to. If your school uses Examsoft or a similar program, use it to move the paragraph to its proper place.

However, the better organized your answer, the better the professor can identify your response. Organize the way you would organize an issue in a memorandum discussion: if the cause of action you identified requires proof of elements, organize by the elements, for example offer, acceptance, consideration, or the elements of a completed gift: the donor's intent to give, delivery of the item of gift, the donee's acceptance. If the cause of action is analyzed by certain factors, organize by going through the factors. Make sure to include counterarguments. The facts of an exam question will rarely be straightforward, with all facts aligned towards one answer. You show your understanding of the law and the relevant facts by your ability to analyze all sides of the argument.

D. Include Policy

The exam question may also be the vehicle for you to include policy issues. Has the existing legal rule been criticized, and for what reasons? Does it lead to inequities or inefficiencies? As a policy matter, how does the present rule work in the exam hypothetical? If the jurisdictions you have studied use different rules (and the exam hypothetical takes place in a fictitious jurisdiction), explain and apply each competing rule. Has your professor emphasized either rule and criticized others? You should include that analysis. You are writing the exam answer for that professor and that course. You will get a better understanding of how to write the exam for your professor if your professor has given a mid-term or sample exam question near the end of the semester. Take the sample exam even if you have not yet studied for the course. You will acquire important information. And listen carefully when the professor analyzes a good answer or provides a sample answer.

IV. OPEN BOOK EXAMS

AN OPEN BOOK EXAM may sound like a gift from heaven, but don't let yourself be fooled. It requires the same preparation, learning the material of the course, careful reading of the exam questions, and monitoring your time as does a closed book exam. If you are not ready when you come into the exam room, no amount of page turning will get you that winning grade. On the positive side, you can bring in your outline, but you probably won't have time to go through a long outline to answer each question. And you don't want your exam answer to read as if you're just skimming through the casebook table of contents. A better choice is to bring in a key word outline and a list of important concepts. Preparing these outlines will provide a good review, for a closed book as well as an open book exam. But use these lists and outlines in the exam to refresh your memory and ensure that you write complete answers, not to furnish the starting point for your answers. If the course involved statutes, then bring in the statutory sections, or mark the pages in your casebook for those sections.

Remember that the more time you spend looking through the casebook or through the materials you brought with you, the less time you will have for writing your answers.

V. MULTIPLE CHOICE EXAMS

MULTIPLE CHOICE EXAMS can be more difficult than students anticipate, and it is hard to give advice because they can vary among professors. You have probably taken multiple choice exams as an undergraduate, and know that they are rarely simple. Most professors spend a lot of time so they do not make the choices too easy, but do not make them too difficult and time consuming. It is important to read all the choices carefully. Typically, it is easy to eliminate one or two choices, but it may be difficult to decide between the remaining choices, each of which has some plausibility. Read the facts of each choice to see if they differ in ways that are relevant to the issue; the point of the question will depend on them. For example, if the issue is defamation, do the plaintiffs in the questions differ as to whether they are public figures or not. Or in a landlord-tenant question has the defendant a sublet or an assignment?

VI. A LAST WORD

MOST FIRST-YEAR LAW STUDENTS face their first round of exams with trepidation. It gets easier after that. Knowing what to expect helps your preparation—as does the knowledge that familiarity breeds relief.

Come prepared for the exam, stay as calm as you can, and don't think about the exam after it is over. Instead, go on to the challenge of preparing for your next exam.

Your hard work should pay off.

Appendix A

Grammar, Punctuation, and Quotation

INDEX

A. Punctuation

1. Comma Usage

Some comma rules seem arbitrary, but others help the reader to identify the parts of a sentence and see their relation. For example, commas help a reader to recognize introductory material, interrupting material, and afterthought material.

a. When an introductory word, introductory phrase, or dependent clause comes first, put a comma after the introductory material to separate it from the rest of the sentence.

You may omit the comma only if the introductory phrase is short and cannot be misread.

Introductory Word:

Therefore, the statement was defamatory.

Introductory Phrase:

To establish economic duress, plaintiff must show three elements.

Introductory Clause:

If a court decides that a contract is unconscionable, it may refuse to enforce it.

Comma for Clarity:

To clarify, the element requires a showing that the plaintiff involuntarily submitted to a person in authority.

---

b. Surround nonrestrictive, interrupting words or phrases with commas.

A nonrestrictive element contributes information to the sentence but can be omitted without altering the meaning of the sentence.

Example:

Jessica Stone and Michael Asch, while in their senior years at college, met and fell in love.

---

c. When a phrase follows an independent clause like an afterthought, put a comma before it. If a dependent clause follows an independent clause, put a comma before the dependent clause only when the dependent clause is nonrestrictive (that is, the dependent clause gives information that is descriptive but not essential to the sentence).

If the meaning would change, the clause is restrictive and you should not use a comma.

Example:

The court reversed, saying the evidence was insufficient.

Non-restrictive Example:

The court affirmed the decision, although there was a dissenting vote. (comma needed)

Restrictive Example:

The plaintiff will agree to settle if the defendant accepts these conditions. (no comma—the condition is essential)

---

d. Do not surround restrictive phrases or clauses with commas. A restrictive modifier identifies or narrows the word it modifies and is essential to the sentence.

Restrictive Example:

Briefs that explain away damaging facts have a good chance of success.

Non-restrictive Example:

The issue, which has always been controversial, was whether execution constitutes cruel and unusual punishment.

---

e. "Which" and "who" can be restrictive or nonrestrictive, but it is preferable to use "which" only for non-restrictive phrases. "That" always introduces restrictive modifiers.

"Which" cannot refer to persons. Use "who."

Restrictive:

Lawyers who bill on a contingency fee basis earn less.

Non-restrictive:

Lawyers, who are officers of the court, must obey court rules.

---

f. Separate the elements of a series with commas.

Although a comma before the conjunction joining the last element is optional, most grammar and usage books encourage its use because a comma before the conjunction connecting the last element can clarify the number of units you have in the series and their proper division.

Serial Comma Example:

Since then, Mrs. Pascal has been suffering from depression, insomnia, recurring nightmares, and severe weight loss.

Ambiguous Series without a Final Comma:

He sent the job application letter to the following stores: Borders, Barnes and Noble and Waldenbooks.

Ambiguity Erased with Final Comma:

He sent the job application letter to the following stores: Borders, Barnes and Noble, and Waldenbooks.

---

g.   Put a comma before a coordinating conjunction—and, but, or, nor, for, yet—when the conjunction is connecting two independent clauses (unless the sentences are short).

Example:

A statute must provide fair warning to the public of the nature of the proscribed conduct, and it must provide explicit standards for the application of the statute by the people enforcing it.

---

h.   Do not put a comma before a coordinating conjunction when that conjunction is forming a compound subject, verb, or object.

Compound Subject Example:

During a traffic stop, drivers and passengers are not free to leave (no comma before "and passengers.")

Compound Verb Example:

The wrench flew out of Smith's hand and hit plaintiff in the mouth (no comma before "and hit").

Compound Object Example:

Counsel labeled the charges ridiculous and the decision laughable (no comma before "and the decision laughable").

---

i. Do not use a comma to separate a complex or compound subject from its verb. You may want to avoid long, complex subjects by rephrasing your sentence.

> **Example:**
>
> A physical injury sustained by a minor as a result of cruel or inhumane treatment or a malicious act is child abuse (no comma after the complex subject "A physical injury sustained by a minor as a result of cruel or inhumane treatment or a malicious act").
>
> **Rephrase:**
>
> It is child abuse if a minor sustains a physical injury as a result of cruel or inhumane treatment or a malicious act.

j. You may put a comma before a phrase or a word you wish to highlight.

> **Example:**
>
> The vice-president had called for the meeting, then missed it.

k. Commas (and periods) are put inside quotation marks but outside parenthesis and brackets. (If the parenthetical material is a complete sentence, however, the period goes inside the parenthesis.)

> **Example: Quotation Marks**
>
> Once we recognize that "designed for use" means "intended by the manufacturer," court's application seems reasonable.
>
> **Example: Parenthesis**
>
> Given the limitation on length (20 pages), we dropped that discussion.
>
> **Example: Complete Parenthetical Sentence**
>
> Given the limitation on length, we dropped that discussion. (The brief could not be longer than twenty pages.)

2. Semicolon Usage

a. Connect two independent clauses with a semicolon when they are not linked by a conjunction.

> **Example:**
>
> Her moods wavered between depression and hostility; she often expressed a wish to die.

b. When a conjunctive adverb (however, hence, therefore, etc.) or other transitional expression links two independent clauses, put a semicolon before the conjunctive adverb and a comma after it.

> **Conjunctive Adverb:**
>
> Bills are admissible if they comply with CPLR § 4533a; however, judges can relax those standards.
>
> **Transitional Phrases:**
>
> A defendant may waive a formal defect by a guilty plea or by a failure to object at trial or on appeal; on the other hand, a defendant may always challenge a fatal defect by a writ of habeas corpus.

c. When elements in a series are long or contain internal punctuation, use a semicolon to separate the elements.

> **Example:**
>
> This section of the statute outlines three steps: first, the jury must decide the full value of the injured party's damages; second, they must decide the extent, in form of a percentage, of each party's negligence, with a total of all percentages of negligence of all parties equal to 100; third, the judge must mold the judgment from the jury's findings of facts.

d. Semicolons and colons go outside quotation marks.

> **Example:**
>
> Professor Doe took issue with the legitimacy argument made in "Authentic Authorities"; Professor Smith did not respond.

3. Colon Usage

a. Colons are used to introduce enumerations or lists, but you should not put a colon between a verb and its complement. Finish the sentence before the colon, as in the example below.

Examples:

Not: He wrote: three memoranda, two letters, and one brief.

But: He wrote three memoranda, two letters, and one brief.

Or: The contractor made three demands: first, Charo must fire Smith; second, Charo must enter an exclusive distributorship agreement with Champlow; third, Charo must fly to N.Y. to sign a contract to this effect.

---

b. Colons may be used to introduce and highlight a formal statement or example.

Example:

The jury had been out for twelve hours: this may account for the defendant's edginess.

---

c. Colons are used to introduce a long quotation.

4. Em-dashes

Use an em-dash to keep parts visible and to prevent reading what is an interrupting modifier or an afterthought modifier as a series, that is, use an em-dash to set off a modifier with internal commas. One could also use a parenthesis.

Not: His qualifications, education, employment history, character references, were put forward.

But: His qualifications—education, employment history, character references—were put forward.

Or: He forwarded his qualifications—education, employment history, character references.

Or: His qualifications (education, employment history, character references) were put forward.

Or: He forwarded his qualifications (education, employment history, character references).

B. Grammar

1. Agreement Between Subjects and Verbs

A verb must agree in number with its subject.

a.   If the subject is singular, the verb must be singular.

> The fifth **amendment guarantees** due process of law.

b.   If the subject is plural, the verb must be plural.

> These **amendments guarantee** due process of law.

c.   A verb must agree with the subject, not with a noun in a modifier.

> A long **list** of numbers **is** available.

d.   If 2 singular subjects are connected by an **or** or **nor**, the verb is singular.

> Either **John** or **Jane is** willing to speak to the professor.

e.   If 2 plural subjects are connected by **or** or **nor**, the verb is plural.

> Either **1st-year students** or **2nd-year students are** registering on Friday. I cannot remember which.

f.   If one singular and one plural subject are connected by **or** or **nor**, the verb agrees with the nearer form.

> Neither **Joan** nor her **classmates want** to rewrite the memorandum.

g.   Compound nouns, that is, nouns connected by **and**, take plural verbs unless the compound noun is singular in meaning.

> **1.**   **Property and Torts are** her least favorite subjects [compound noun].
>
> **2.**   **Trusts and Estates is** her favorite subject [singular meaning].

h.   Collective nouns like *government, corporation,* or *court* are usually singular.

> The Board meets in secret.

i.   Singular Indefinite Pronouns (which don't refer to a specific person or thing) are singular: anybody, anyone, each, either, every, everybody, neither, nobody, no one, somebody, something.

> **Everyone is** seated.

j.   Plural Indefinite Pronouns take plural verbs: both, few, many, several.

> **Both contain** errors.

2.   Agreement   Between   Pronouns   and   Their Antecedents

Just as subject and verb must agree in number, so subjects and pronouns must agree in number and person.

This line, for example, was the lead into an ad for a well-known Chicago store:

EVERYONE HAS THEIR PRICE

"Everyone" is singular, and "has" is singular. But "their" is plural and does not agree with the subject to which it refers. Of course, in correcting the "their," the copy writer should try to rewrite the ad without using sexist language. The writer could try "his or her" or could look for some other construction that attracts less attention. You could try an article, for example.

EVERYONE HAS A PRICE

The following rules govern subject-pronoun agreement.

a.   If the antecedent is singular, the pronoun is singular.

> **table/it**

b.   If the antecedent is plural, the pronoun is plural.

> **chairs/they**

c. If the antecedent is everyone, everybody, each, either, neither, nobody, one or anyone, the pronoun is singular.

> **Everyone** should take his or her coat.

d. If the antecedent is two nouns joined by and, the pronoun is plural.

> **John and Jane** want to go. **They** leave tomorrow.

e. If the antecedent is two plural nouns joined by **or** or **nor**, the pronoun is plural.

> **Neither the Does nor the Smiths** want to go, so we will not wait for **them**.

f. If one antecedent is singular and one plural, the antecedent agrees with the nearer noun.

> When you finish **the brief or the letters**, bring **them** to me.

g. Collective nouns usually need the singular pronoun.

> **The jury** rendered **its** verdict.

h. If the antecedent is singular and neuter (neither masculine nor feminine), the pronoun is it or its.

> **The court** recessed for lunch. **It** returned at 1:00 P.M.

3. Ambiguous Pronoun Reference

a. Avoid Vague Referents. If the pronoun is **this, that, it, such,** or **which** and refers to a preceding noun or statement, the relationship between the pronoun and the noun should be clear.

"This" is best used in combination with a noun so that it is absolutely clear what the "this" refers to.

> **Example:**
> The defendant traveled west on Main Street at fifty miles per hour. This violates the law.

Since the "this" could refer to traveling west as well as to the rate of speed, the word "this" needs a noun.

> **Rewrite:**
> This rate of speed violates the law.

    b. If the pronoun can refer to two preceding nouns, make it clear which noun the pronoun refers to.

> **Example I:**
> The parent corporation and the subsidiary, which places great emphasis on loyalty, have a singularly responsive relationship.
>
> **Rewrite:**
> The parent corporation, which places great emphasis on loyalty, has a singularly responsive relationship with its subsidiary.
>
> **Example II:**
> Jim talked to John while he waited for the elevator.
>
> **Rewrite:**
> While Jim waited for the elevator, he talked to John.

    c. The referent or antecedent for every pronoun should be present in the sentence or, at least, in the preceding sentence.

   4. Apostrophe Usage

Apostrophes are used to indicate possession or contraction.

    a. Singular possessive nouns are formed with **'s**.

> The court's decision

    b. If a singular possessive noun ends in **s**, add an **'s**. (Some writers use an apostrophe only.)

> James's plea

    c. Plurals not ending in s take an **'s**.

> Women's rights

d.   Plurals ending in stake an apostrophe.

> The associates' employment handbook

e.   The possessive case of two closely linked nouns is formed by the addition of a single **'s** if, and only if, one thing is possessed by both.

> The brother and sister's apartment, but the brother's and sister's casebooks)

f.   *Note an important exception: possessive pronouns are not formed with apostrophes.* For example:

> "It's" is the contraction of "it is."
>
> The possessive form of "it" is "its."
>
> "Who's" means "who is."
>
> "Whose" is the possessive form of who.
>
> "You're" means "you are."
>
> "Your" is the possessive form.

g.   The plural of names is not formed with apostrophes.

> James = Jameses
>
> Smith = Smiths

h.   Do not follow a possessive noun with an appositive—a noun that describes the noun next to it. A noun is not the equivalent of a possessive noun or possessive pronoun. Rewrite the sentence using 'of.'

> **Not:** The court rejected the defendant's, Board of Parish Life, free exercise argument.
>
> **But:** The court rejected the free exercise argument of the defendant, Board of Parish Life.

5.   **Sentence Fragments and Run-Ons**

a.   Sentence Fragments

A sentence must have a subject and a predicate. Most sentence fragments do not result from the absence of a subject and a predicate; rather they are the result of punctuating a dependent clause as a sentence. A dependent clause does not express a complete thought and must, therefore, be combined with an independent clause.

> **Not:** Even though his contributory negligence may diminish damages.

Either add a comma and finish the sentence with an independent clause or omit "even though."

> **But:** Even though his contributory negligence may diminish damages, he will recover.

b. Run-On Sentences

There are two kinds of run-on sentences. First, there are those in which two complete sentences are joined with a conjunction, but with no punctuation before the conjunction (fused sentence). Second, there are those run-on sentences in which two complete sentences are joined by a comma instead of a semicolon (comma splice).

> **Fused Sentence Example:**
>
> Personal service upon Multitech Associates was not proper and Village Realty's suit will therefore be dismissed.
>
> **Rewrite:**
>
> Personal service upon Multitech Associates was not proper, and Village Realty's suit will therefore be dismissed.
>
> **Comma Splice Example:**
>
> Multitech had not designated Sue Johnson to accept summons, she had neither express nor implied authority.
>
> **Rewrite:**
>
> Multitech had not designated Sue Johnson to accept summons; she had neither express nor implied authority.

C. Use of Quotations

Keep quotations short. But if you do use a long passage of fifty words or more, you must set out the quote in block form, that is, indented and single spaced. You do not use quotation marks when you set out a quote in block form. Put the citation as the first non-indented text after the block quotation.

When you do use quotations, it is important to use them accurately. You must quote material exactly as it appears in the source from which you quote. You may alter the quote, but if you do, you must indicate the alterations. Use these devices.

1. **Ellipses**

    a. Indicate omissions with an ellipsis (these are three periods with a space between each). Do not indicate omissions from the beginning of the quote. When an omission indicated by an ellipsis occurs in the middle of a sentence, there should be a space before the first ellipsis point and after the third point. When an omission indicated by ellipsis points occurs at the end of the sentence, you must add a fourth point, which is the period for the sentence. There is a space after the last quoted word when you are omitting part of the quoted sentence.

    > **Examples:**
    >
    > "Defendant's testimony about the crash scene and the road supervisor's description of the right of way. . . are more than enough evidence from which to find plaintiffs were lawfully on the property."
    >
    > And
    >
    > "Defendant's testimony about the crash scene and the road supervisor's description of the right of way are more than enough evidence. . . ."

    b. Omit punctuation marks that were before or after the omitted material unless they are grammatically necessary, as they are in the following example.

    > "When the court uses the term 'lawfully on the defendant's property,'. . . it means the plaintiff was in a location that is consistent with its reasonably expected use."

    c. When you omit a whole paragraph, center three ellipsis points on a new line with spaces in between each. Then go to a new line, indent, and proceed with the cited source.

2. **Brackets**

    a. Use brackets to show the addition of a letter, changes of case, a clarification, or an editorial comment. Put your own version inside the brackets.

> **Examples:**
>
> "[L]awfully on the property means. . . the plaintiff was in a location that is consistent with its reasonably expected use."
>
> Or
>
> The court said, "he [the defendant] must have known the gun was loaded."

In the first sentence, the writer used lawfully to begin a sentence. The writer had to capitalize the "l." The capitalization of "L" indicates the writer has omitted the beginning of the sentence in the original source. The writer of the second sentence decided to clarify the referent for the pronoun "he."

b. If you have altered a quote by omitting a letter, use a pair of brackets with nothing inside them.

> "The conduct is consistent with its expected use[]."

c. Use "[sic]" to indicate that you have quoted accurately and that the original contains a mistake.

> **Example:**
>
> "The statue [sic] applies to tort actions only."

3. Emphasis

You may use italics (the preferred method in a quotation) or you may underline to add emphasis, but you must explain your additions after the citation. Use this device sparingly.

> **Example:**
>
> "The statute *applies to tort actions only*." *Jones v. Smith*, 510 S.E.2d 53 (Fla. 1980) (emphasis added).

If the italics or underlining is part of the original quotation, note that in a parenthesis (emphasis in the original).

4. Capital Letters and Quotations

a. Begin a quotation with a capital letter if it is introduced by a colon or if the quotation is syntactically independent of the rest of the sentence.

> **Example:**
>
> As the judge said, "The motion is denied."
>
> **Example:**
>
> The testimony of the plaintiff was explicit: "At all times, I was free to leave the site of the polygraph examination."

b. If the quotation is a syntactical part of the sentence, do not capitalize the first letter.

> **Example:**
>
> He said that the cross-examination was "almost finished."

Exercise A-1: Grammar and Punctuation

Correct the grammar and punctuation errors in the following sentences.

1. Every decision concerning the children were made jointly.

2. It is unlawful in N.Y. to confine a person against their will.

3. The filing fee violates Doone's right to be heard in court, therefore, this fee requirement should be invalid.

4. The aerial surveillance was a concentrated search undertaken for the express purpose of observing defendants activities.

5. Olympia Department Store denied they had committed outrageous acts.

6. As a general rule the court will refuse to enforce that part of the contract that is unconscionable.

7. The District Court following a hearing denied defendant's suppression motion.

8. A sufficient connection between the litigation and the forum state exist; therefore, the court possesses jurisdiction over the defendant, and they should hear the case.

9. Based on aerial surveillance, the police entered the premises seized certain evidence and arrested the three defendants.

10. The requirement, that interrogatories be answered by the production of the relevant documents, was not met.

11. CPLR § 3124 requires disclosure "if a person, without having made timely objection, fails to answer interrogatories".

12. The superintendent's answer was insufficient and the protective order was unjustified.

13. Neither defendants nor plaintiff contest the facts.

14. The court said it would make it's ruling in the morning.

15. Ms. Lattimore discussed Ms. Smith when she went to the restroom.

16. We did not offer him the job (given his lack of qualifications.)

17. The court said that "the actor disregarded the probability that severe distress would follow. . ."

18. Once we recognized that "designed for use" means "intended by the manufacturer", the court's application seems reasonable.

19. The court denied the defendant's motion because they had not filed in time.

20. Given his lack of qualifications (no field work experience) we did not offer him the job.

21. There is no reason to strike burdensome interrogatories if they are ". . .necessary to a resolution of defendant's affirmative defense."

Exercise A-2: Grammar and Punctuation

Correct the errors in the following sentences.

1. The Board's refusal to act makes them liable.

2. When Jane Edwards sought to end the harassment her complaints were disregarded. First by her supervisor then by the Personnel Sub-Committee, and finally by the Board itself.

3. Church's are free to enter into contracts.

4. The statute does not begin to run if the defendant ". . . through fraud or concealment causes the plaintiff to relax his vigilance . . ."

5. Rev. Bryant who is sixty-five refers to himself as "the rock'n roll preacher".

6. After careful consideration I believe your sexual harassment claim is solid.

7. The Board failed to act therefore it will be held liable.

8. Jane Edwards threatened to complain to the Minnesota Department of Human Rights after which she was fired.

9. If there is no invocation at graduation, their right to free exercise of religion is violated.

10. He had a contractual agreement with Healthdrink Inc. not to discuss Healthdrink and it's deceptive advertising.

11. The first amendment protects churches from state intervention in church affairs and thus the court is unlikely to order your reinstatement.

12. Her complaints were ignored by Bryant by the Personnel SubCommittee and then by the Board.

13. The chain of events, described in Mr. Miller's testimony, suggest an act of robbery.

Exercise A-3: Review Exercise—Coherence, Grammar, and Style

Diagnose errors and revise.

(1) "First, the conduct must be extreme and outrageous". (2) In <u>Davis</u> the court argued that if the tactics' used by the creditors have involved the use of abusive language, repeated threats of ruination of credit and threats to the debtor's employer to endanger his job, recovery could be sustained, citing authorities and previous cases in other jurisdictions. Id., at p. 407. (3) It is clear that based on these tests liability could be established by the various tactics used by the Department store. (4) Disregarding, for now, the fact that Augusta the plaintiff herein didn't actually owe money, the employee of the credit department used abusive language such as "four-flushing bitch," sent letters with statements threatening to report Augusta's delinquency to the credit rating bureau which, if done, would substantially hurt her credit rating and, in addition, on numerous occasions threatened to report her "refusal" to pay to her employer which might be construed by a reasonable person as a serious impairment to her continued employment. (5) An argument that could be made by Olympia, at this juncture, is that some meaningless speech from a collection department employee would hardly be considered oppressive or outrageous. (6) One only has to look at the aforementioned decisions to see that the store's position is weak at best. (7) In finding only one instance of outrageous conduct in Davis, the number of extreme actions here are clearly distinguishable. (8) The second factor involves the foreseeability by the store that the severe emotional distress will occur. (9) "Liability extends to situations in which there is a high degree of probability that the severe distress will follow and the actor goes ahead in conscious disregard of it" is a direct extraction from the courts opinion. Davis, *supra*. (10) This standard can be used as a basis for the instant situation, thus, the letter written by Augusta to the store's president is evidence that the store knew of the situation in

April, and the harassment was not stopped nor correcting the billing error. (11) If a letter to the store's president is not sufficient information, establishing foreseeability, and consequences that might result from the store's continued actions then what is?

APPENDIX B

CITATION EXERCISES

Rewrite these citations correctly. If the correct form requires information you do not have, such as a page number, indicate the information with an underline.

1. Claims under the Age Discrimination in Employment Act may be proven with disparate impact analysis. U.S. v. City of Jackson, 544 U.S. 228 (2005) at 230.

2. Marsh v. Metropolitan Housing Institute, 6 Fed 3rd 9 (CA2 1992).

3. There are three possible scenarios with police involvement in searches of students on school property. See In re Angelia D.B., 564 N.W.2d 682 (Wisc. 1997), State v. Tywayne, 993 So.2d 251 (Fla.), In re Josue T., 989 P.2d 431 (Alaska Sup. Ct 1997).

4. The court held that the Fourth Amendment had been violated. Abel v. Grant, 470 F.Supp. 2d 133 (Pa. 2007). It concluded that the police lacked probable cause. Abel, at 135.

5. In Ryan v. Quinn Brothers Corporation, 318 N.E.2d 6 (NY 1964), the court held that the defendant had violated the statute. See New York General Obligations Law, chapter 12, section 4. However, the plaintiff received only nominal damages. Ryan, supra on page 10.

6. Title 15 section 552 of the United States Code permits a court to award fees "reasonably incurred" to a successful litigant [my emphasis]. One court has interpreted this phrase broadly. Black v. Jones, 300 F.3d 402 (2003).

7. Spring v. Mason, 2006 WL 238755.

8. Psychiatrists have testified that anti-psychotic medication is an essential part of treatment for schizophrenia. United States v. Weston, 255 F.3d 873 (D.C. Cir. 2001), United States v. Arena, 2001 WL 1335008 (S.D.N.Y.). The risk of side-effects can be controlled. Id. at 875.

9. For this exercise, give the correct citation for page 223 in the book Understanding Criminal Law by Joshua Dressler. The fourth edition was published in 2006.

10. For this exercise, give the correct citation for the law review article "Does the Commerce Clause Eclipse the Export Clause?" The author is Claire R. Kelly. The article appeared in volume 84 of the Minnesota Law Review in 1999, starting on page 129.

SAMPLE OFFICE MEMORANDUM

TO: Leslie Smith, Supervising Attorney

FROM: Law Assistant

DATE: June 10, 2017

RE: *Brian Kay v. Jemma Martin* Motion to Quash Service of Process

Question Presented:

1. Under Ohio law, whether a motion to quash service of process on the basis of fraud would succeed when a friend and former business partner asked our client, a resident of Pennsylvania, to come to Ohio to visit a hospitalized friend, but served our client on a contract dispute while he was in Ohio.

2. If so, whether the former business partner gave our client a reasonable time to leave the jurisdiction before serving him when our client remained in Ohio for 4½ hours after the hospital visit in order to see his sister, and was served in the airport while he was waiting for his flight home.

Brief Answer:

1. Probably not. Our client cannot prove that Jemma Martin's sole purpose in inviting him to Ohio was to serve him with process when their hospitalized friend did in fact ask to see him and Kay visited that friend.

2. No. If the invitation to visit was a ploy, then Martin did not give Kay a reasonable time to leave after their discussion and hospital visit, and service could be quashed.

Statement of Facts:

Brian Kay, our client, had been in business in Philadelphia with Jemma Martin, a college friend, for two years following their graduation. Kay still resides there. After the business closed, Martin claimed that Kay owed her $8,000. Kay denied the debt, saying he had made an equal investment in equipment and supplies.

On April 30, 2017, Martin, who had moved to Cleveland, Ohio, called Kay to tell him that their mutual friend, Carl Dawson, had been in a car accident and was in the hospital in Cleveland. Dawson had asked Martin to arrange a visit with Kay, who agreed to meet Martin at the hospital the next day so that they could visit Dawson together. The two met in the hospital lobby, but when Martin said that Dawson had been sent for x-rays, they decided to get some coffee while they waited. While they were in the cafeteria, Martin told Kay that he had to repay the money he owed her. Kay denied the debt, repeating that their losses were equal. After going back and forth on the matter for a while, Kay suggested they go to see Dawson.

Kay visited Dawson until 5:30 p.m., and then Martin offered to drive Kay back to the airport to make the 7:00 plane back to Philadelphia. Kay declined, saying he had arranged to dine with his sister and take the last shuttle at 10 p.m.

After meeting with his sister, Kay was waiting in the airport terminal around 9:30pm when he was served with the summons and complaint in Martin's suit for the debt. When Kay arrived in Philadelphia, he called Martin. She told Kay that she had hoped that they could have resolved the issue without litigation, but after their discussion at the hospital, it was clear that was not going to happen. Kay asked Martin why she did not mention the lawsuit on the phone when she called about Dawson's accident. Martin replied that she knew Kay would come to Cleveland to see their friend, but not if he had known that she intended to serve him with process if their talks failed.

Discussion:

A court will quash service of process upon Kay if Jemma Martin's invitation to come into the jurisdiction to visit a mutual friend was a ploy to obtain service upon him. In Ohio, "personal service obtained upon a defendant who is induced to come within the jurisdiction of a court through trickery, fraud or artifice is an abuse of process and will be set aside upon proper application." *Guzzetta v. Guzzetta*, 137 N.E.2d 419, 420 (Ohio Ct. App. 1956). If a person has been enticed by fraud into the jurisdiction, he cannot be served until a reasonable time has elapsed after he conducted his business there. *Suhay v. Whiting*, 96 N.E.2d 609, 611–12 (Ohio Ct. Com. Pl. 1950). Martin's desire to bring the two friends together was probably not simply a ploy for luring Kay into the jurisdiction for the sole purpose of suing him. The visit with Dawson was a genuine reason for the invitation. However, if Martin deceived Kay because she had a second motivation that she intentionally concealed, then Martin did not give Kay a reasonable time to leave since he departed within hours of the visit, and service should be quashed.

A court will quash service on the basis of fraud if the plaintiff intended to trick the defendant at the time she invited the defendant into the jurisdiction. *Guzzetta*, 137 N.E.2d at 421. The invitation must be part of a plan to get the defendant to come into the jurisdiction, "the sole purpose" of which is to attempt service. *Id*. However, if the invitation was "extended in good faith and for the purposes stated," service will not be quashed. *Id*. The court presumes "honesty of motive and purpose unless the circumstances and facts are sufficient enough to satisfy the mind that the acts relied upon were fraudulent." *Id*. at 422–23; see also *Commercial Mut. Accident. Co. v. Davis*, 213 U.S. 245, 256–57 (1909) (quoting Missouri law). Further, service is not objectionable simply because the defendant comes to the jurisdiction as a result of some act of the plaintiff's. *Suhay*, 96 N.E.2d at 611. The plaintiff must have acted fraudulently. *Id*.

The plaintiff must have formed the intent to lure the defendant before she issues the invitation. In *Guzzetta*, the plaintiff had invited the defendant into the jurisdiction to see their daughter. While defendant was in the jurisdiction, the plaintiff learned that he had remarried and was expecting a child. Worried that these developments threatened her financial security, plaintiff served him for unpaid alimony. *Guzzetta,* 137 N.E.2d at 420. The court held she did not act fraudulently because she did not decide to serve him until after he was in the jurisdiction. *Id*. at 421. Further, the court held that the plaintiff's lawyer had acted in good faith when he arranged for service upon the defendant because the lawyer had set up his meeting with the defendant prior to knowing that his client wanted to serve the defendant. *Id*.

In *Davis,* the Court also found the service unobjectionable. *Davis*, 21 U.S. at 257. The plaintiff invited the defendant insurance company into the jurisdiction hoping they could settle an insurance claim. He served the defendant when they were unable to resolve their dispute. *Id* at 250–251. The defendant claimed the invitation was a trick to bring the company's agent into the jurisdiction in order to serve him. However, the Court did not quash service, holding that there was no clear error in the lower court's finding of no fraud. *Id*. at 257. The plaintiff's invitation to negotiate the claim was not issued in bad faith; rather the plaintiff acted with a bona fide attempt to settle. *Id*. The mere fact that service of process had been prepared before the defendant entered the jurisdiction did not negate the plaintiff's hope not to have to use it. In contrast, in *Suhay*, the court quashed service of process. The plaintiff's lawyer had ordered a delivery of slag in order to bring the defendant into the jurisdiction precisely so he could be served. *Suhay*, 96 N.E.2d at 609, 613. The court held that service could be quashed because the delivery order was a ploy to bring the defendant into the jurisdiction. *Id.*

When Martin invited Kay to come to Ohio she acted in good faith at the request of their hospitalized friend and for the purposes stated. She may indeed have had mixed purposes, the other one being her desire to settle her financial dispute with Kay, but nothing suggests she had arranged or decided to serve Kay beforehand. Moreover, if there is a question of plaintiff's motive but no facts show fraud, service is valid. *Davis*, 213 U.S. at 245. However, Kay's case is distinguishable from *Davis* in one key respect: the agent in *Davis* knew he was entering the jurisdiction to discuss an insurance claim, but Martin admitted she did not tell Kay she would sue him if their talks failed because she knew he would not come to Ohio if he knew. Even though Martin may have genuinely wished to reunite her two friends, she concealed her second motive, and this is similar to the facts in *Suhay*, where the plaintiff's delivery order was a clear trick. Nonetheless, if serving Kay was not Martin's sole purpose in bringing him to Ohio and the court will presume honesty of motive and purpose unless the circumstances and facts sufficiently satisfy the mind that the acts defendant relied upon were fraudulent, Martin will probably prevail on this issue since she had an honest motive and had not definitively decided to serve Kay.

If the court were to find Martin fraudulently enticed Kay to come to Ohio, it would then determine whether she gave Kay a reasonable amount of time to leave the state after concluding the business for which he came. *See Suhay,* 96 N.E.2d at 612. Nonetheless, a person is not granted "eternal immunity from service in Ohio. A reasonable time to return is all he can ask." *Id.,* citing *Jaster v. Currie,* 198 U.S. 144, 148 (1905). In *Suhay,* the plaintiff served the defendant immediately after the defendant's third of five deliveries of slag. 96 N.E.2d at 613. Since his business had not yet been concluded, the court quashed service. In contrast, in *Jaster v. Currie*, the court held upheld service because the defendant had lingered in the jurisdiction for two days after he had completed his business and had stayed too long. *Jaster,* 198 U.S. at 148.

Martin probably did not give Kay a reasonable time to leave, although she did not serve him until after the 7:00 p.m. shuttle departed. No case defines reasonable time, but a court would probably find that Kay did not linger when he spent three hours in Ohio so he could have dinner with his sister. His hospital visit with Martin was delayed by his friend's medical procedures and so his visit with his sister was delayed. Moreover, three hours fall far short of the two days in *Jaster*, 198 U.S. 144.

<u>Conclusion:</u>

Since Martin had a good faith reason for inviting Kay to Ohio, a court is unlikely to find she acted fraudulently when she invited him and will uphold service. If she acted fraudulently, however, the court will probably not find Kay lingered unreasonably in Ohio and will quash service of process.

SAMPLE OFFICE MEMORANDUM

To: Mary Appleby, Esq., an attorney practicing in Philadelphia

From: Law Associate

Re: Intervention of Right—Fed. R. Civ. P. 24(a)(2)

Date: November 15, 2017

Statement of Facts: Six white members of Local 444 seek to intervene as of right in an employment discrimination suit filed against Local 444 by our clients, a group of minority workers. Local 444 is divided into an A branch and a B branch. Membership in the A branch provides higher hourly wages and increased job security. B branch members must apply to Local 444 to gain entry into the A branch. The proposed intervenors have been members of the B branch for more than five years.

The minority workers had filed suit in federal district court for the Eastern District of Pennsylvania on February 13, 2014, under Title VII of the Civil Rights Act of 1964, 42 U.S.C. §§ 2000e et seq. (2012). They alleged that the union engaged in discriminatory employment practices in its A branch admission process. The workers claimed that they applied for membership in the A branch, but that they were refused admission based on their race and national origin, although they met the job requirements.

The case went to trial in May 2015, and the court entered a preliminary order on January 6, 2016, holding that Local 444 violated Title VII by illegally and intentionally denying minority workers admission to the A branch based on their race and national origin. The preliminary order mandated, among other things, that Local 444 adopt a non-discriminatory admission policy, and that the A branch have no less than 25% minority membership by 2020. The goal could be met through a combination of direct admission to the A branch and apprenticeship training. Local 444 appealed the 25% plan to the Court of Appeals for the Third Circuit on February 3, 2016. The district court entered a final judgment on July 29, 2016, affirming its finding of race discrimination and adopting an Affirmative Relief Plan that included the 25% requirement.

On September 1, 2016, six white B branch members moved to intervene as of right in the suit. They allege that, despite their qualifications, the union denied them admission to the A branch because of the union's practice of favoritism in the admission process. The white intervenors maintain that requiring the union to admit a significant number of minorities into the A branch in the coming years and implementing the 25% plan would further limit their opportunities for A branch admission.

The Third Circuit affirmed the 25% plan on October 15, 2016. The motion to intervene is currently before the court.

Question Presented: Will a court grant the white union workers' motion to intervene as of right under Fed. R. Civ. P. 24(a)(2) in a Title VII employment discrimination suit, where the motion accused the union of preferential treatment based on favoritism in its A branch admission process, the motion was filed during the pendency of an appeal, and the white B branch members make no claim based on race discrimination?

Conclusion: The white workers' motion to intervene as of right under Fed. R. Civ. P. 24(a)(2) in the Title VII employment discrimination suit should be denied because, although their interests are not adequately represented by the parties to the suit, their motion was not timely, and their intervention would require adjudicating interests that Title VII does not protect.

Applicable statute:

Fed. R. Civ. P. 24(a)(2): Intervention of Right.

> On timely motion, the court must permit anyone to intervene who. . . (2) claims an interest relating to the property or transaction that is the subject of the action, and is so situated that disposing of the action may as a practical matter impair or impede the movant's ability to protect its interest unless existing parties adequately represent that interest.

Discussion: Six white B branch members seek to intervene as of right under Fed. R. Civ. P. 24(a)(2) in a Title VII discrimination suit filed by minority construction workers against Local 444. In order for the court to grant the motion to intervene as of right, the white B branch members must prove that their motion was filed in a "timely" fashion, that their interest in the suit relates to "the property or transaction that is the subject of the action," that their interest may be impaired or impeded by the outcome of the suit, and that the parties to the suit do not "adequately represent" this interest. *See* Fed. R. Civ. P. 24(a)(2). All four elements of the Rule must be proven. *Liberty Mut. Ins. Co. v. Treesdale, Inc.*, 419 F.3d 216, 220 (3d Cir. 2005). The burden of proving each element falls on the intervenor. *Michaels Stores, Inc. v. Castle Ridge Plaza Assocs.*, 6 F. Supp. 2d 360, 364 (D.N.J. 1998). Although the white

B branch members' interest is not adequately represented by the parties to the suit, their motion to intervene as of right should be denied because it was not filed in a timely fashion. Moreover, the intervenors failed to establish that their interest is related to the subject matter of the suit or that it might be impaired by the outcome of the litigation, because their interest is not one legally protected by Title VII.

Intervention as of right provides a non-party to a lawsuit with an opportunity to inject itself into the suit when the parties, in pursuit of their own objectives, might significantly interfere with the non-party's legally protected interests. *Kleissler v. United States Forest Service*, 157 F.3d 964, 971 (3d Cir. 1998). In judging whether each element of intervention is met, the Third Circuit applies a flexible set of standards, rather than rigid definitions and formulaic rules. *Id.* Pragmatic considerations are important when assessing the merits of intervention, with the costs to the litigation itself weighed against the benefits of judicial efficiency. *Id.* at 970. The unique facts of each case also play a key role in a court's evaluation of a motion to intervene. *Id.* at 972.

The first element of a successful motion to intervene as of right requires that the motion be "timely" filed. Fed. R. Civ. P. 24(a)(2). The timeliness of the filing is assessed using a "reasonableness" standard. *Princeton Biochemicals, Inc. v. Beckman Coulter, Inc.*, 223 F.R.D. 326, 328 (D.N.J. 2004). Whether a motion is accepted as "timely" is based on three factors: the phase of the litigation when the motion was filed, any prejudice to existing parties that might result from the delayed filing, and the proposed intervenor's reason for not filing earlier. *In re Cmty. Bank of N. Va.*, 418 F.3d 277, 314 (3d Cir. 2005).

A motion filed during the earlier stages of the suit, especially before discovery ends, helps ensure that the parties' rights and claims are not damaged by granting intervention. *Michaels*, 6 F. Supp. 2d at 364. In *Michaels*, the motion to intervene in a lease dispute was timely as it was filed less than two months after the suit was filed. However, a motion need not be submitted at the outset of the litigation to be timely. Although early intervention is favored by the courts, intervention has nonetheless been granted when filed even after the liability phase of a lawsuit. *Princeton*, 223 F.R.D. at 328–29. However, the intervenors must have a reason for the delay. In *Princeton*, for example, in a patent infringement suit, the intervenor was not informed it might be the true owner of a patent until the night before a copyright infringement suit began regarding that patent. Accordingly, the intervenor required time to investigate whether it did in fact have a claim of ownership. *Id.*

Here, the actual timing of the white B branch members' motion is late in the litigation (two years after the suit was filed, eight months after the 25% plan was first set out in the preliminary order, more than a month after a final judgment was rendered, and during the pendency of Local 444's appeal of the 25% plan). However, this alone is not enough to disqualify the motion.

A second factor is whether the timing of the motion is prejudicial to the parties. In *Princeton*, no party claimed prejudice because of the brief time between the proposed intervenor's learning of its alleged rights in the patent and its moving to intervene. 223 F.R.D. at 328 n.3. But a longer period may also be permitted. In a case alleging a violation of condominium by-laws, although four years elapsed between the filing of the suit and the motion to intervene, the court held that timeliness would not bar the proposed intervenors. *Mountain Top Condo. Ass'n. v. Stabbert Master Builder, Inc.*, 72 F.3d 361, 370 (3rd Cir. 1995). The court reasoned that the critical question was whether proceedings of substance on the merits had occurred. In that case, since the parties had not completed discovery nor filed dispositive motions, they had not been prejudiced. *Id.*

In the Local 444 case, although the motion does not require relitigation of whether the A branch admissions policy discriminated based on race, intervention could cause prejudice. It would further delay the affirmative order providing relief to those who had been the victims of race discrimination more than two years ago, and distract the court from the question of whether the defendant had violated federal law prohibiting race discrimination.

Moreover, the white B branch members' motion for intervention as of right fails to meet the third factor of the timeliness element: a satisfactory reason for the delay in filing. In *In re General Motors Corp. Pick-up Truck Fuel Tank Products Liability Litigation*, 134 F.3d 133, 140 (3d Cir. 1998), the court denied a motion to intervene in a suit alleging a defect design in the fuel system of GM trucks. Certain GM truck owners did not move to intervene until four months after the court granted provisional certification of a nationwide class and almost two months after they had received notice of the proposed settlement. The court noted that the proposed intervenors had "offered no explanation . . . except that they had no basis to intervene until they found out that the class counsel had reached a provisional settlement . . . ." *Id.*

Similarly, the B branch members offered no explanation as to why they did not file their motion until more than two years after the suit was filed, a suit of which B branch members of Local 444 would be aware. They may claim that they did not understand how the lawsuit would affect their interest in non-discriminatory admission to the A branch until the court delineated the 25% plan in the preliminary order. They might have further delayed filing until they were able to investigate how the plan in its final form would affect their opportunities. *See Princeton*, 224 F.R.D. at 329. But even if this is true, the extremely long delay in filing their motion to intervene appears to represent an instance of the "wait and see" approach explicitly disapproved by the Third Circuit. *Kleissler*, 157 F.3d at 974. Although waiting to file until after a final judgment may be an efficient strategy for the intervenors, it slows down the litigation process and promotes attacks on the ruling in the original suit, both of which contribute to inefficiency in the judicial system as a whole. *Id.* Since the courts seek to avoid these problems, *id.* at 969, the intervenors will not satisfy the timeliness element because they have not produced a satisfactory reason for their delay.

The second element of a satisfactory motion for intervention as of right requires the proposed intervenor to claim "an interest relating to the property or transaction that is the subject of the action." Fed. R. Civ. P. 24(a)(2). This element has been recognized by the Third Circuit as the most important of the four in assessing a motion to intervene as of right. *Kleissler*, 157 F.3d at 972. As with all of the elements, there is no single test or strict rule as to what constitutes an acceptable "interest"; rather, the interest is evaluated against a set of standards to determine whether it is "sufficient." *Liberty*, 419 F.3d at 220. The facts surrounding each interest play a key role in this judgment. *Kleissler*, 157 F.3d at 972.

Perhaps, most important, an intervenor's interest must be legally recognizable and defendable, and directly related to the subject of the suit. Weak, peripheral, or vague connections between the interest and the lawsuit will not suffice. *Kleissler*, 157 F.3d at 972; *United States v. W.R. Grace & Co.-Conn.*, 185 F.R.D. 184, 189 (D.N.J. 1999). The interest must be grounded in a statute, constitution, administrative regulation, contract, or the common law. *W.R. Grace*, 185 F.R.D. at 189.

However, although an interest arising out of one of these sources of law is necessary for intervention, that does not by itself guarantee that a court will allow intervention. The interest also must be one protected by the particular subject of law on which the lawsuit is based. Thus, in *Liberty*, an insurance compensation case, the Third Circuit denied a motion to intervene because the law on which the intervenors based their statutorily-created interest in insurance compensation did not apply to their situation. The court noted that the law on which they relied applied only to parties that legally declared bankruptcy, which the defendant had not done. Thus, the law did not provide them with a remedy. *Liberty*, 419 F.3d at 222–23.

In the Local 444 case, the intervenors' interest in the suit is focused on preventing the union from making employment decisions based on preferential treatment of "favored" members, not based on race. Accordingly, their interest has no basis in the "property or transaction that is the subject matter" of the suit: race-based discrimination prohibited by Title VII. The relevant section of this statute states:

It shall be an unlawful employment practice for a labor organization—

> (1) to exclude or to expel from its membership, or otherwise to discriminate against, any individual because of his race, color. . .or national origin;

> (2) to limit, segregate, or classify its membership or applicants for membership. . ., in any way which would deprive or tend to deprive any individual of employment opportunities, or would limit such employment opportunities or otherwise adversely affect his status as an employee or as an applicant for employment, because of such individual's race, color. . .or national origin;

> . . . .

42 U.S.C. § 2000e–2(c)

This language makes it clear that Title VII is not a remedy for the type of "discrimination" that the intervenors accuse the union of practicing.

Accordingly, granting the motion to intervene will burden the court with the task of adjudicating two unrelated interests in a single suit. *Cf. Kleissler*, 157 F.3d at 970. In addition, denying the motion does nothing to prevent the proposed intervenors from filing their own suit. They could allege the violation of their rights under an appropriate statute, either under the Landrum-Griffin Act, 29 U.S.C. § 401 et seq. (2012), or the Taft-Hartley Act, 29 U.S.C. § 141 et seq. (2012), or allege the union's violation of the duty of fair representation. *See generally Liberty*, 419 F.3d at 223.

The B branch members might claim that they have a right to admission to the A branch under the court-ordered Affirmative

Relief plan which mandates a non-discriminatory admissions policy. However, that plan was designed to require admission to the A branch free from the race discrimination which for so long had characterized the union's practices. B branch members are free to seek admission based on their qualifications and will be considered on the merits, without the "favoritism" that they allege existed. To the extent that they might have competition now from the minority workers who will be eligible based on the 25% goal, they are asserting an economic interest, which does not support intervention as of right. *Mountain Top*, 72 F.3d at 366. For these reasons, the proposed intervenors' interest in the lawsuit is "legally unprotectable," and fails to satisfy the second element. *In re Cendant Corp. Sec. Litig.*, 109 F. Supp. 273, 278 (D.N.J. 2000).

The third element of a successful motion for intervention as of right requires that the intervenor be so situated that "disposing of the action may as a practical matter impair or impede the movant's ability to protect its interest." Fed. R. Civ. P. 24(a)(2). The requirements for satisfying this element are set relatively low: the intervenor only must prove that this legally protectable interest "may" be impaired. *Princeton*, 223 F.R.D. at 329. This practical impairment is established when the outcome of the suit might have a real, direct, and negative impact on its interest. *Liberty*, 419 F.3d at 226–27. Marginal and secondary effects on the intervenor's interest are not enough. In *Michaels Stores, Inc.*, for example, a chain of retail stores had contracted with a tenant to take over the lease in the tenant's property in a shopping plaza. A competing store in the same shopping plaza with similar products moved to intervene, based on an exclusivity clause in its contract. The court granted the motion, concluding that disposition of the action would impair the competing store's interest. *Michaels*, 6 F. Supp. 2d at 365. Similarly, the intervenors proved impairment where a party would be deprived of the full benefits of owning a patent, and the ownership of the patent was the subject of the lawsuit between two other parties. *Princeton*, 223 F.R.D. at 329.

These cases show that any impact the Title VII employment discrimination suit might have on the white B branch members' interest fails to satisfy the impairment element. The court-mandated, 25% minority membership plan was aimed at ending the union's race-based discriminatory practices. While this plan might reduce the white union workers' opportunities for admission into the A branch, it will not affect their interest in opposing the union's alleged practice of offering preferential treatment to "favored" union members. Such an interest cannot, as a practical matter, be hindered in such a way as to warrant granting a motion for intervention as of right.

The final element of a successful motion for intervention as of right is that exiting parties do not "adequately represent that interest. Fed. R. Civ. P. 24(a)(2). To prove inadequacy, the intervenor must show that his interest "may be" insufficiently represented. *Mountain Top*, 72 F.3d at 368. The burden of proof for establishing inadequate representation is "minimal." *Id.* Courts have recognized three general forms of insufficient representation by parties: when the intervenor and the party have opposing interests, when the parties to the suit collude against the intervenor's interest, and when the parties fail to satisfactorily defend or advocate on behalf of the intervenor's interest. *Ass'n. for Fairness in Bus., Inc. v. New Jersey*, 193 F.R.D. 228, 231 (D.N.J. 2000). Any of these types of inadequate representation will satisfy this element.

For example, when the narrow interests of the parties to the suit fail to take the intervenor's legally protected and potentially impaired interests into account, intervention is warranted. *Id.* In *Ass'n for Fairness*, the beneficiaries of a state-sponsored affirmative action program were permitted to intervene as defendants on the ground that the state of New Jersey, charged with defending the program, had broader interests and was considering sacrificing that affirmative action program to preserve other programs. *Id.* at 231–32. Similarly, in *Princeton*, the intervenor successfully proved that his interests were inadequately represented because neither party to the patent infringement suit stood for its interests in promoting public education and ensuring compliance with its Patent Policy. 223 F.R.D. at 329. *Cf. Michaels*, 6 F. Supp. 2d at 365.

In the Local 444 case, assuming arguendo that the B branch members have a legally recognizable interest, the B branch members could satisfy this element. Neither the minority union members nor Local 444 would adequately represent the intervenors' interest in preventing the union from providing preferential treatment to "favored" union members. Although neither party was completely adverse to the intervenors' interest, this interest was absent from the litigation. The suit dealt solely with race-based discrimination under Title VII. When neither party attempts to advocate on behalf of the intervenors' interests, it is generally understood that the interest was inadequately represented. *Michaels*, 6 F. Supp. 2d at 365. Accordingly, one of the forms of inadequate representation "may have been" present in this case. *See id.*

However, even if B branch members' interests were inadequately represented by both the plaintiffs and the defendant, their motion to intervene will not succeed, because they cannot prove the remaining elements of the Rule.

SAMPLE MEMORANDUM IN SUPPORT OF A MOTION TO DISMISS

IN THE CIRCUIT COURT OF COOK COUNTY, ILLINOIS
COUNTY DEPARTMENT, LAW DIVISION

PARK, INC., <u>et al.</u>,	)	
Plaintiffs,	)	No. 86 L 22939
v.	)	N.W.
DAVID RYAN, <u>et al.</u>,	)	
Defendants.	)	

MEMORANDUM IN SUPPORT OF MOTION TO DISMISS
COMPLAINT AS TO WRIGLEY HOUSING, INC., JOE
SAYERS, ANN CHRISTIE, AND MARGARET JAMES

INTRODUCTION

Plaintiffs PARK, INC., a real estate management company, and its President, Earl Marple, have sued more than thirty individuals and organizations active in the tenants' rights movement in the West Park section of Chicago. Plaintiffs' four-count complaint purports to state claims for libel and slander. On December 22, 2016, defendants Wrigley Housing, Inc., Joe Sayers, Ann Christie and Margaret James, filed a motion to dismiss the complaint as to those defendants pursuant to Rule 2–615 of the Illinois Rules of Civil Procedure. This memorandum is submitted in support of those defendants' motion to dismiss.

STATEMENT OF FACTS

Plaintiff Park is a corporation engaged in the business of managing and developing real estate. (Complaint ¶ 1.) Park has developed and manages more than 500 rental units in the West Park area of Chicago. (Complaint ¶ 12.) Plaintiff Marple is President of Park, and has been in the real estate business since 1989. (Complaint ¶¶ 1, 9.) This case arises out of a dispute between Park and Marple, on the one hand, and the West Park Tenants' Committee ("WPTC"), the Professionals for Better Housing ("PBH"), and Alderman David Ryan, on the other hand, concerning Park's real estate management practices. (Complaint ¶¶ 16–22.)

In April 2016, WPTC convened a meeting of tenants and former tenants of Park and of representatives of other tenants' rights organizations and block clubs, in response to complaints about Park's rental policies and practices. (Complaint ¶ 22; Exhibit A.) Park's tenants continued to meet, to distribute literature to Park tenants, and to picket at Park's rental office and at Marple's home. (Complaint ¶ 22.)

Plaintiffs allege that the communications published by WPTC and PBH were defamatory. (Counts I and II.) Specifically, in Count I, they allege that a newsletter attached as Exhibit A to the complaint contains the following defamatory statements:

> That in August 2015 (or on or about said time) there were complaints regarding Park as to "giant rent increases"; "failure to refund security deposits and pay interest"; "chronic heat and hot water problems"; "intimidation of tenants"; and "outrageous set of move-out policies."

(Complaint ¶ 30.)

Plaintiffs allege that a leaflet attached as Exhibit B to the complaint contains the allegedly defamatory statement that "the WPTC wanted to meet with Park 'to discuss the state investigation of Park.' " (Complaint ¶ 28.) They also allege that leaflets attached to the complaint as Exhibits C and D libel Park and Marple by stating, inter alia, that Park's tenants want to meet with Marple to discuss "problems relating to his mismanagement of ten buildings in West Park with nearly 500 apartments" and, specifically, "lack of water," "lack of heat," "poor building security," "unfair security deposit deductions," "lack of smoke detectors," "unresponsiveness to requests for repairs," "failure to pay security deposit interest," "electrical problems," "roaches," "intimidation and harassment of tenants," "infrequent garbage pickup," and "outrageous move-out policies." (Exhibits C–D; Complaint ¶ 31.) Plaintiffs allege that Exhibits A, B, C and D were authored by WPTC and PBH and that the authors "were one or more of the following Defendants," with Christie included on a list of thirteen names. (Complaint ¶ 25.)

In Count II, plaintiffs allege that various defendants, including Christie, picketed the offices of Park's rental agent. (Complaint ¶¶ 47–48.) Plaintiffs claim that various picket signs and oral communications included defamatory statements that Park and Marple were "in housing court," did not supply heat in their buildings, had a policy "not to return security deposits," "made bogus deductions" from security deposits, and that the buildings managed by Park had roaches. (Complaint ¶ 49.)

Counts III and IV concern a letter sent to the limited partners of Park on or about October 1, 2006. (Complaint ¶ 64.) The letter indicates that it was endorsed by Alderman Ryan and a number of tenants' and housing rights groups, including Wrigley Housing. (Exhibit E.) Plaintiffs allege in Count III that the letter contains the following allegedly defamatory statements:

A. Evidence exists documenting continuous complaints by tenants about maintenance problems and the indifferent handling of these complaints by Park, Inc.

B. City inspection reports detail numerous instances of housing code violations in Park, Inc. properties.

C. Park is not repairing housing code violations and is not making repairs in a workmanlike manner.

D. Numerous outgoing tenants have complained about not receiving proper disbursement of their security deposits.

E. Most tenants have not received the requisite interest on their security deposit.

F. The buildings show serious signs of mismanagement and distress.

G. Many tenants are not renewing their leases with Park, Inc. because they cannot deal with habitually poor management.

H. The buildings are developing high vacancy rates and falling into disrepair.

ARGUMENT

The plaintiffs' complaint must be dismissed because the communications complained of in Counts I, II, III, and IV are not defamatory per se under Illinois law. Even assuming that the statements are defamatory, Illinois law grants them a qualified privilege. Furthermore, plaintiffs' prayer for punitive damages is unsupported and must be stricken from the complaint. Finally, the complaint contains no allegations concerning defendants Sayers and James and should be dismissed as to those defendants.

I. ALL COUNTS MUST BE DISMISSED BECAUSE THE COMMUNICATIONS COMPLAINED OF ARE NOT DEFAMATORY PER SE.

Under Illinois law, the defendants' statements are not defamatory per se. To be considered defamatory per se, the language must be so obviously and naturally harmful to the person to whom it refers that damage is a necessary consequence and need not be specially shown. *Owen v. Carr*, 113 Ill. 2d 273, 274, 497 N.E.2d 1145, 1147 (1986); *Sloan v. Hatton*, 66 Ill. App. 3d 41, 42, 383 N.E.2d 259, 260 (4th Dist. 1978). Four classes of words, if falsely communicated, give rise to an action for defamation without a showing of special damages:

1.   Those imputing the commission of a criminal offense

2.   Those imputing infection with a communicable disease

3.   Those imputing inability to perform or want of integrity in the discharge of duties of office or employment, and

4.   Those prejudicing a particular party in his profession or trade.

Fried v. Jacobson, 99 Ill. 2d 24, 26, 457 N.E.2d 392, 394 (1983). With respect to corporate plaintiffs, moreover, the alleged libel must assail the corporation's financial or business methods or accuse it of fraud or mismanagement. *American International Hospital v. Chicago Tribune Co.*, 136 Ill. App. 3d 1019, 1022, 483 N.E.2d 965, 969 (1st Dist. 1985); *Audition Division, Ltd. v. Better Business Bureau*, 120 Ill. App. 3d 254, 256, 458 N.E.2d 115, 118 (1st Dist. 1983).

To determine whether particular language constitutes libel per se, Illinois courts apply the rule of innocent construction:

a written or oral statement is to be considered in context, with the words and the implications therefrom given their natural and obvious meaning; if, as so construed, the statement may reasonably be innocently interpreted as referring to someone other than the plaintiff it cannot be actionable per se. This preliminary determination is properly a question of law to be resolved by the court in the first instance.

Chapski v. Copley Press, 92 Ill. 2d 344, 347, 442 N.E.2d 195, 199 (1982). Thus, the court must examine the statements here within the context of the surrounding circumstances and events, and judge the words accordingly. Id.; *Sloan v. Hatton*, 66 Ill. App. 3d at 43, 383 N.E.2d at 261. Moreover, the trial court is required to make this determination in the context of the entire publication. *Chapski*, 92 Ill. 2d at 345, 442 N.E.2d at 199.

The following emerges clearly from an examination, in context, of Exhibits A through E to the complaint: As Exhibit A shows, tenants of buildings owned and managed by Park were meeting and organizing in early 2006. It is clear from Exhibits B through E that the tenants' goal was to meet with Park and Marple to discuss various problems the tenants perceived.

> "To plan other direct action to get Park to meet with us" (Exhibit B)

> "We want to meet with Earl Marple to discuss and get action on these problems" (Exhibit C)

> "Quite simply we want Park to meet with us and begin to address our legitimate concerns" (Exhibit D);

> "Therefore, we are asking that (1) you attend a special meeting of the West Park Housing Forum. . . and (2) that you encourage Mr. Marple to attend this meeting also" (Exhibit E, at 3).

Thus, the context of the communications here was clearly a dispute between tenants and a landlord about the manner in which he was managing his buildings.

Chapski requires that, in ruling on a motion to dismiss, the trial court must review the allegedly libelous documents to determine, as a matter of law, whether they are subject to a reasonable non-defamatory construction; if so, the documents are not actionable even if they may also be subject to a reasonable defamatory construction and even if the party receiving the communications understood them in a defamatory sense. *Chapski*, 92 Ill. 2d at 345, 442 N.E.2d at 199. Following this mandate, Illinois courts have repeatedly dismissed libel cases after finding that the statements complained of were susceptible of a reasonable innocent construction. *See, e.g., Meyer v. Allen*, 127 Ill. App. 3d 163, 165, 468 N.E.2d 198, 200 (4th Dist. 1984); *Audition Division, Ltd. v. Better Business Bureau*, 120 Ill. App. 3d at 257, 458 N.E.2d at 119; *Cartwright v. Garrison*, 113 Ill. App. 3d 536, 537–40, 447 N.E.2d 446, 447–50 (2d Dist. 1983).

Rasky v. CBS, Inc., 103 Ill. App. 3d 577, 431 N.E.2d 1055 (1st Dist.), *cert. denied*, 459 U.S. 864 (1982), is particularly relevant to this case. The *Rasky* plaintiff was a landlord whose building maintenance and business practices were criticized by a number of tenants' groups and a state representative, among others; CBS News then broadcast a news program describing the controversy and interviewing tenants. The appellate court, affirming dismissal of the case, held that the derogatory remarks by the news media and community groups could be interpreted innocently.

> The overall thrust of the CBS news telecast was that citizens in the community were bitterly opposed to the

way in which they perceived that plaintiff managed his buildings and that, through their representatives, they intended to explore available legal remedies for redress. In that context, the report noted that Edgewater citizens: have accused plaintiff of being a "slumlord"; have previously taken legal action against him; claim he does not make repairs. In our opinion, the CBS news telecast, taken as a whole, is capable of an innocent construction and cannot be considered defamatory as a matter of law.

103 Ill. App. 3d at 577, 431 N.E.2d at 1059.

The communications complained of in this case, read as a whole and in context, amount to no more than the statements found to be nondefamatory in *Rasky*. The thrust of Exhibits A through E is that numbers of citizens were "bitterly opposed to the way in which they perceived that plaintiff[s] managed [their] buildings and . . . intended to explore available legal remedies for redress." *Id*. In that context, Exhibits A through E may reasonably be construed innocently and thus may not sustain an action for defamation.

Furthermore, it is not libel per se to state that complaints have been filed about a business. *See, e.g., Audition Division, Ltd. v. Better Business Bureau*, 120 Ill. App. 3d at 254, 458 N.E.2d at 119; *American Pet Motels, Inc. v. Chicago Veterinary Medical Ass'n*, 106 Ill. App. 3d 626, 628, 435 N.E.2d 1297, 1300 (1st Dist. 1982). Illinois courts have reasoned that a statement that customers have complained about a business is not equivalent to a statement that the business is incompetent, fraudulent, or dishonest. Thus, the statements complained of in Exhibit A—that in August 1985 there were a variety of complaints regarding Park (Complaint ¶ 30)—are not defamatory, as a matter of law.

Under Illinois law, it is also not libel per se to state that a plaintiff's business activities are under investigation. *Cartwright v. Garrison*, 113 Ill. App. 3d 536, 539, 447 N.E.2d 446, 450 (2d Dist. 1983); *see also Spelson v. CBS, Inc.*, 581 F. Supp. 1195, 1205 (N.D. Ill. 1984), *aff'd mem.*, 757 F.2d 1291 (7th Cir. 1985). Thus, the statement complained of in paragraph 28 of the complaint (that the WPTC wanted to meet with Park "to discuss the state investigation of Park") is not defamatory per se, as a matter of law.

In short, when considered as a whole and in context, the statements in Exhibits A through E are susceptible of a reasonable innocent construction, and do not constitute libel per se.

II. THE COMMUNICATIONS COMPLAINED OF ARE ENTITLED TO A QUALIFIED PRIVILEGE UNDER ILLINOIS LAW.

Even assuming, arguendo, that this Court finds the statements complained of defamatory, they are nonetheless not actionable, because they are privileged under Illinois law. Certain communications, even if false and defamatory, are afforded special protection—a qualified privilege—because the law recognizes their social importance. The elements of this qualified privilege are (1) good faith by the defendant, (2) a legitimate interest or duty to be upheld, (3) publication limited in scope to that purpose, and (4) publication in a proper manner to proper parties. *See, e.g., Edwards by Phillips v. University of Chicago Hospitals*, 137 Ill. App. 3d 485, 488, 484 N.E.2d 1100, 1104 (1st Dist. 1985); *American Pet Motels, Inc. v. Chicago Veterinary Medical Ass'n*, 106 Ill. App. 3d at 630, 435 N.E.2d at 1301.

The face of plaintiffs' complaint demonstrates that the privilege applies here. First, the defendants had a good faith, legitimate purpose for the communications challenged: to address a matter of shared concern—the availability of decent, affordable, safe housing in the West Park community—and to assist one another in dealing with problems they perceived in the management practices of one large landlord. The documents themselves, a newsletter and leaflets, show that defendants' purpose was entirely legitimate, *i.e.*, to meet with Park to discuss those problems.

Moreover, the statements in Exhibits A through E were limited in scope to furthering these common concerns. The newsletter describes community efforts to improve housing conditions. (Exhibit A.) The leaflets and letter to Park's limited partners are directed at the goal of meeting with plaintiffs to discuss certain perceived problems in Park's rental units. (Exhibits B, C, D, E, at 3.)

Finally, the statements here were communicated in a proper manner and to proper parties. The newsletter and leaflets were distributed to Park's tenants and to other residents of the West Park community interested in improving their housing conditions. (Complaint ¶¶ 31, 54B.) Exhibit E was addressed only to the limited partners of Park. (Complaint ¶ 64.)

Similarly, the statements complained of in Count II, which concern the picketing of Park's rental agent, are privileged under Illinois law. The persons making these statements spoke in good faith and in the interest of promoting good rental housing; they limited their statements to Park tenants and prospective tenants; and they made the statements in furtherance of their purpose to persuade plaintiff to meet with them to discuss their perceived problems and complaints. (See Exhibit D: "Why we're picketing Park/Rental Express" . . . "Quite simply, we want Park to meet with us and begin to address our legitimate concerns . . . .")

Under these circumstances, the qualified privilege clearly applies to all the communications complained of in plaintiffs' complaint, requiring dismissal as a matter of law, absent factual allegations that defendants abused the privilege. *See, e.g., American Pet Motels*, 106 Ill. App. 3d at 626, 435 N.E.2d at 1302.

III. PLAINTIFFS FAIL TO STATE A CLAIM FOR PUNITIVE DAMAGES.

Punitive damages may not be recovered unless a defendant has acted with actual malice. *Gertz v. Robert Welch, Inc.*, 418 U.S. 323, 349–50 (1974). Plaintiffs here seek an award of punitive damages based solely upon the bald assertion that defendants acted "maliciously, willfully, and with a conscious disregard for the rights of Plaintiffs." (Complaint ¶¶ 32, 52, 55, 60, 67, 71.) Bare allegations of actual malice in a complaint, however, do not suffice; "rather, conclusions of malice and intent must be clothed with factual allegations from which the actual malice might reasonably be said to exist." *L.R. Davis v. Keystone Printing Service, Inc.*, 111 Ill. App. 3d 427, 433, 444 N.E.2d 253, 262 (2d Dist. 1982). Because plaintiffs do not adequately plead actual malice, their prayers for punitive damages should be stricken from the complaint.

IV. THE COMPLAINT DOES NOT CONTAIN THE NECESSARY FACTUAL ALLEGATIONS CONCERNING CERTAIN INDIVIDUAL DEFENDANTS AND SHOULD THEREFORE BE DISMISSED AS TO THOSE DEFENDANTS.

Finally, the complaint should be dismissed as to certain of the individual defendants because it contains no allegations of wrongdoing on their part. The complaint contains no factual allegations whatsoever concerning the conduct of defendants Sayers and James, and should therefore be dismissed in its entirety as to them. Counts III and IV, which concern the letter to Park's limited partners, contain absolutely no allegations that defendants James, Sayers, or Christie participated in the composition or publication of that letter, and should therefore be dismissed as to those defendants. Additionally, Count II, alleging defamation based on picketing the office of Park's rental agent, is devoid of any allegations concerning the conduct of defendants

James or Sayers, and should therefore be stricken as to those defendants.

Finally, plaintiffs fail throughout to allege defamation with sufficient particularity. In actions for libel and slander, a plaintiff is held to a high standard of specificity in pleading. *Altman v. Amoco Oil Co.*, 85 Ill. App. 3d 104, 106, 406 N.E.2d 142, 145 (1st Dist. 1980). By contrast, plaintiffs here allege, for example, that the authors of Exhibits B, C and D "were one or more of the following Defendants," including defendant Christie in a list of thirteen names. (Complaint ¶ 25.) Unless plaintiffs can amend to specify the personal involvement of each named individual, the complaint should be dismissed as to those individual defendants.

CONCLUSION

For the foregoing reasons, defendants Wrigley Housing, Inc., Joe Sayers, Ann Christie and Margaret James respectfully request that this Court enter an order dismissing the complaint with costs, or, in the alternative, dismissing them as defendants in this case.

WRIGLEY HOUSING, INC.,
JOE SAYERS, ANN CHRISTIE
AND MARGARET JAMES

By: _____

Their Attorney

SAMPLE MEMORANDUM IN OPPOSITION TO A SUMMARY JUDGMENT MOTION

IN THE CIRCUIT COURT OF COOK COUNTY, ILLINOIS LAW DIVISION

TREY ALVARADO	)	
Plaintiff	)	No. 0000
v.	)	
MICHAEL BREWER	)	
Defendant.	)	

Plaintiff's Memorandum in Opposition to Defendant's Motion for Summary Judgment

Introduction

This case involves defamation per se appearing in defendant's book about steroid use among professional baseball players. The defendant, Michael Brewer, authored *Baseball's Dark Side,* a book describing steroid use among professional athletes in Major League Baseball ("MLB"). (Def.'s Aff. 2). The book was written in 2005 and published in early 2006. (Def.'s Aff. 3). One chapter of the book is specifically about pitchers, including the plaintiff Trey Alvarado. Trey Alvarado is a successful pitcher for the Chicago Cubs. In this chapter, Brewer makes clear that Alvarado's improved professional performance from the 1998 to 1999 season was due to steroid use. Defendant has moved for an order of summary judgment on the ground that his statements can be innocently construed.

The flap copy of *Baseball's Dark Side* describes the book as a nonfiction account of steroid use in the MLB. An excerpt about Alvarado in the chapter reports that, "After three years of mediocre performance, Trey Alvarado inexplicably surged to stardom in his 1999 and 2000 seasons with the Chicago Cubs. Alvarado went from a rarely used benchwarmer to a twenty-two game winner, including a no-hitter". (Pl.Ex. A at 54). The book then compares Alvarado's statistics from the 1998 and 1999 seasons, stating, "Alvarado attributes his improved performance to a new weight

505

training and practice routine, and to the team's new pitching coach, but one has to wonder if such dramatic changes could really result simply from training." (Pl.Ex. A at 55). The author then states, "Just prior to the 1999 season, Alvarado was seen on many occasions in the company of Dr. Ryan Henderson. Everyone who is anyone in professional baseball knows that Dr. Henderson is the go-to guy if you want to start juicing." (Pl.Ex. A at 56).

Alvarado filed a complaint on August 21, 2006, alleging that the statements authored by Brewer are false and defamatory per se. Specifically,

1. Alvarado does not and has never used steroids. Alvarado has blood and urine tests from the time period in question proving that he was not using steroids.

2. Alvarado saw Dr. Henderson only once for a legitimate sports injury—a strained rotator cuff.

3. Alvarado's improved performance was a result of his improved physical condition, his increased practice time, and the attention of the team's new pitching coach.

(Pl. compl. at 3)

Defendant Brewer has moved for summary judgment asking that the court rule that his statements fall within the exception to defamation per se because they can be innocently construed. The defendant's motion is now before the court. This memorandum is in opposition to that motion.

Argument

The defendant's motion for summary judgment should be denied. First, the record shows that there is a genuine issue of material fact regarding the frequency and purpose of Mr. Alvarado's visits to Dr. Henderson. Second, defendant Brewer is not entitled to summary judgment as a matter of law. His statements concerning Mr. Alvarado are defamatory per se and cannot be given an innocent construction. Even if the statements could be innocently construed, the court should abandon the innocent construction rule and instead apply a rule of reasonable construction to these statements.

Under Illinois law, summary judgment should be granted only where "the pleadings, depositions, and admissions on file, together with the affidavits, if any, show that there is no genuine issue as to any material fact and that the moving party is entitled to a judgment as a matter of law." 735 ILCS 5/2-1005(c). Although "the summary judgment procedure is to be encouraged as an aid in the expeditious disposition of a lawsuit, it is a drastic means of disposing of litigation and therefore should be allowed only when the right of the moving party is clear and free from doubt." *Purtill v. Hess*, 489 N.E.2d 867, 875 (Ill. 1986). In determining whether a genuine issue of material fact exists for summary judgment purposes, a court must construe the materials of record strictly against the movant and liberally in favor of the non-moving party. *Harlin v. Sears Roebuck and Co.*, 860 N.E.2d 479 (Ill. App. Ct. 2006).

First, the record shows that there is a genuine issue of material fact. The parties disagree as to the frequency and purpose of Alvarado's visits to Dr. Ryan Henderson, who is now deceased. Defendant wrote that the plaintiff "was often seen in the company of Dr. Ryan Henderson," whom the defendant described as the "go-to guy if you want to start juicing." (Def. Exh. A). The plaintiff's affidavit, however, states that he paid one office visit to Dr. Henderson for a second opinion on his rotator cuff injury. (Pl. Aff. at 5).

Mr. Alvarado's relationship with Dr. Henderson is material to this claim because the defendant states that Alvarado was in the doctor's company several times and implies that Alvarado received steroids from the doctor. Accordingly, Alvarado's affidavit raises a disputed material fact and defendant's motion must be denied.

Second, the defendant is not entitled to judgment as a matter of law. The record clearly supports plaintiff Alvarado's claim for defamation per se. A statement is considered defamatory per se if "the defamatory character" of the statement "is apparent on its face and when the words used are so obviously and materially harmful that injury to the plaintiff's reputation may be presumed." *Dunlap v. Alcuin Montessori School*, 698 N.E. 2d 574, 580 (Ill. App. Ct. 1998). The elements of defamation are that (1) the defendant made a false statement about the plaintiff, (2) the defendant made an unprivileged publication of that statement to a third party, and (3) this publication caused damages to the plaintiff. *Seith v. Chicago Sun-Times*, 861 N.E. 2d 1117 (Ill. App. Ct. 2007); *Solaia Technology, LLC v. Specialty Publ'g Co.*, 852 N.E.2d 825, 839 (Ill. App. Ct. 2006).

Because Alvarado is alleging defamation per se, however, he is required to plead or prove only the first two elements. *Seith*, 861 N.E.2d at 1126 ("It is well established that if a plaintiff alleges that a statement is defamatory per se, he need not plead or prove actual damages to his reputation; statements that are defamatory per se are thought to be so obviously and materially harmful to the plaintiff that injury to [his] reputation may be presumed.").

In Illinois, five categories of statements, if falsely communicated, give rise to a cause of action for defamation per se: (1) statements imputing the commission of a crime; (2) statements imputing infection with a loathsome communicable disease; (3) statements imputing an inability to perform or want of integrity in performing employment duties; (4) statements imputing lack of ability or that otherwise prejudice a person in his or her profession or business; and (5) statements imputing adultery or fornication. *Fried v. Jacobson*, 457 N.E.2d 392, 394 (Ill. 1983). The defendant's statements about Trey Alvarado are defamatory per se in that they falsely impute that Mr. Alvarado committed a crime (illegal drug use) and that he lacked integrity in performing his employment duties. Moreover, the statements prejudice him in his profession.

The Illinois rule is that even if an allegedly defamatory statement falls into one of the recognized categories of words that are actionable per se, it will not be found actionable per se if, read in context, it is capable of a reasonable innocent construction. *Bryson v. News America Publ'ns, Inc.*, 672 N.E.2d 1207, 1215–16 (Ill. 1996). However, Illinois courts narrowly construe the innocent construction rule, and it does not apply here. In *Bryson* the defendant used the word "slut" in a magazine article to describe plaintiff. The defendant argued that the word had several meanings, some of which, like bully, are not defamatory. The court read the word in context of the article, however, giving the words and their implications their natural and obvious meaning. The article included false descriptions of the plaintiff's sexual proclivities, and included statements in the article that intensified the sexual implication of the word "slut." Thus, the innocent construction rule did not preclude plaintiff's defamation per se claim against the author and publisher of the article.

Most recently, the Supreme Court of Illinois held that statements in a book about a well-known criminal defense attorney read in context could not be innocently construed, and that the lower courts had strained to find an innocent meaning when the defamatory meaning was far more probable. *Tuite v. Corbitt*, 866 N.E.2d 114 (Ill. 2007). The defendants had written a book about their experiences with organized crime in the Chicago area. The book included a discussion of the plaintiff's representation of a criminal defendant. They wrote that the attorney required a very large retainer fee, that they believed that he had it "all handled," and that it was a "done deal" that they would be acquitted. The plaintiff denied the book's statements about his role and alleged

that the statements were defamatory per se in that they falsely
implied that he would use the retainer to bribe judges and others
in order to assure the client's acquittal. The court held that the
statements could not be innocently construed to mean that the
clients believed only that they were getting the best legal
representation. Given the book's overwhelming focus on organized
crime and corruption in the criminal justice system, the
statements defamed the plaintiff by imputing criminal
wrongdoing, lack of integrity and an inability to perform his
professional duties. *Id.* at 128.

Illinois law precludes a court from employing the kind of
unwarranted naiveté that the lower court had exhibited when it
read the statements about the plaintiff Alvarado as
complimentary. In the context of the defendant's entire book, that
court's reading was unreasonable. Trey Alvarado's claim is similar
to that of the plaintiff in *Tuite*. Both books implied wrongdoing
rather than accusing the plaintiff outright. Nevertheless, the
statements are clearly defamatory given the context, the subject
matter and the purpose of the book, and the implications about the
plaintiff Alvarado that his improved pitching performance would
be inexplicable were it not for his association with a doctor known
to have supplied steroids to athletes.

The context of a statement is critical in determining its
meaning, so it is vital that the statements in Brewer's book
referring to Alvarado be read as a whole. When so read, those
statements are defamatory per se. A given statement may convey
entirely different meanings when presented in different contexts.
Chapski v. Copley Press, 442 N.E.2d 195 (Ill. 1982). Brewer's book,
Baseball's Dark Side, purports to be a nonfiction "tell all" about
"what really went on in the years before MLB implemented stricter
drug testing policies." (Def. Ex. A at 1). *Baseball's Dark Side*
consists of stories about players' drug use. Brewer describes them
as blights on baseball's long, illustrious history. Brewer intended
to and did write about Alvarado in this context. Brewer falsely
implies that Alvarado met with Dr. Henderson on more than one
occasion for the purpose of obtaining illegal steroids. Additionally,
Brewer falsely implies that Alvarado's improved performance from
the 1998 to 1999 and 2000 seasons was due to something other
than Alvarado's intensive training regimen. (Ex. A at 2.) When
read in context, these statements clearly convey the message that
Alvarado was using steroids to improve his professional
performance. There can be no innocent meaning to his words. To
apply the innocent construction rule in this case, the court would
have to strain to find an unnatural meaning for Brewer's
statements when a meaning that is defamatory is far more

reasonable. This the court may not do. *See Tuite*, 866 N.E.2d at 123; *Bryson*, 672 N.E. 2d at 1217. Brewer's book is not about amazing turnarounds in baseball; it is about drug use in baseball. It would be an unreasonable reading that Brewer intended to convey a story about Alvarado's baseball skills given the context of the book as a whole. It is far more reasonable to believe that Brewer intended to convey a story about drug use.

Brewer's statements concerning steroid use are thus false and fall within the categories of statements that Illinois law deems defamatory per se: Brewer's statements impute the commission of a crime, his statements prejudice Alvarado in his profession, and they impute a lack of integrity in performance of his duties. Thus, they are defamatory per se. The court should deny Brewer's motion for summary judgment because, as a matter of law, Brewer is not entitled to judgment.

Alternatively, should this court determine that the defendant's statements could reasonably be given an innocent construction, the court should abandon the innocent construction rule in favor of a rule of reasonable construction, that is, it should ask whether the defendant's words may reasonably be interpreted as defamatory.

The innocent construction rule, first adopted in dicta in 1962 in *John v. Tribune Co.*, 181 N.E.2d 105 (Ill. 1962), was intended to protect freedom of speech and to mitigate the harshness of defamation law's strict liability. However, given the developments in first amendment jurisprudence of the United States Supreme Court since *John*, the rule is no longer needed. *New York Times v. Sullivan*, 376 U.S. 254 (1964), imposed the requirement that public officials plead and prove actual malice (that is, the defamatory statements were made with either knowledge of their falsity or with reckless disregard of their truth or falsity). *Curtis Publ'g Co. v. Butts*, 388 U.S. 130 (1967), further insulated defamation defendants when the Court extended the application of the actual malice standard to public figures, and then in *Gertz v. Robert Welch Inc.*, 418 U.S. 323 (1974), to limited public figures. Moreover, *Gertz* abolished the possibility of strict liability in defamation cases involving private figures and required that private plaintiffs prove at least negligence. Statements that are opinion or hyperbole also insulate a defendant from some defamation claims. *Milkovich v. Lorain Journal Co.*, 497 U.S. 1 (1990). Finally, defendants are protected if they come under a qualified privilege. *Kuwik v. Starmark*, 619 N.E.2d 129, 134 (Ill. 1993) (where defendant is protected by a qualified privilege, plaintiff must prove that the defendant either intentionally or recklessly published the material knowing it was false or with reckless disregard of its falsity).

Thus, as Justice Thomas recently stated, "the [innocent construction] rule is wholly insensitive to the complex context and sensitive balance between the public's interest in free speech and the individual's interest in his good name, unsullied by falsehood." *Tuite*, 866 N.E.2d at 133 (concurring in part and dissenting in part). It is a "thumb on the scale" for the defendant where none is needed. *Id.* For this reason, an overwhelming majority of the states have repudiated the rule in favor of a reasonable construction rule. The latter does not suffer from the innocent construction rule's inherent flaw, namely that it deprives the jury of the determination of whether a defendant's statements could reasonably be innocently construed. If a court has already decided as a matter of law that a statement cannot reasonably be construed innocently, then no jury could determine otherwise on the innocent construction claim. There is nothing for the jury to decide. "In theory, though apparently not in actual practice, the plaintiff should then be entitled to judgment as a matter of law. Alternatively, the judge should be compelled to enter a directed judgment or judgment notwithstanding the verdict if the issue is submitted to the jury and the jury determines otherwise." Linda Malone & Rodney A. Smolla, *The Future of Defamation in Illinois after Colson v. Stieg and Chapski v. Copley Press, Inc.*, 32 DePaul L. Rev. 219, 277 (1983).

The reasonable construction rule does not suffer from these defects. Under the reasonable construction rule, the court first determines whether there is any reasonable way to interpret the statement in a defamatory manner. If the statement can reasonably be so interpreted, the case proceeds, and the jury must ultimately decide if the statement was actually defamatory. *See Tuite*, 866 N.E.2d at 136 (Thomas, J. dissenting in part).

While prior decisions should not be overruled without "good cause," Illinois courts have found "good cause" where the prior decision in question proves to be unworkable or badly reasoned. *People v. Sharpe*, 839 N.E.2d 492 (Ill. App. Ct. 2005). *Stare decisis* is not an "inexorable command." *Chicago Bar Ass'n v. Illinois State Board of Elections*, 641 N.E.2d 525 (Ill. App. Ct. 1994). That Illinois courts have struggled with the application of the innocent construction rule shows it is unworkable. For example, in *Chapski v. Copley Press*, the court recognized the "inconsistencies, inequities and confusion that are now apparent from the interpretations and applications of the rule as originally announced in *John* . . . . [W]e are persuaded that a modification of the innocent-construction rule would better serve to protect the individual's interest in vindicating his good name and reputation." 442 N.E.2d. at 198. *See also Newell v. Field Enterprises, Inc.*, 415 N.E.2d 434 (Ill. App. Ct. 1980); *Garber-Pierre Food Products, Inc. v. Crooks*, 397 N.E.2d 211 (Ill. App. Ct. 1979); *Moricoli v. Schwartz*, 361 N.E.2d 74 (Ill. App. Ct. 1977).

Conclusion

Plaintiff requests this court to deny defendant's motion for summary judgment. The record reveals a disputed material fact. Moreover, defendant's statements are defamatory per se and cannot be innocently construed.

TREY ALVARADO

BY: _____

His Attorney

SAMPLE APPELLATE BRIEF

In the

NEW YORK STATE COURT OF APPEALS

Michael Jameson,

Defendant—Appellant,

v.

People,

Plaintiff—Appellee

On Appeal From

New York State Supreme Court,
Appellate Division, Second Division

BRIEF FOR THE DEFENDANT—APPELLANT

Michael Jameson

Rose M. Lerman-Falk

Attorney for the Plaintiff—Appellant

QUESTION PRESENTED FOR REVIEW

1. Whether the Fourth Amendment's guarantee against unreasonable seizure was violated when police stopped appellant Michael Jameson's vehicle to investigate two misdemeanors committed on the previous day.

TABLE OF CONTENTS

TABLE OF AUTHORITIES

Cases

Statutes

Miscellaneous Authority

OPINION BELOW

The opinion of the New York State Supreme Court, Appellate Division, Second Department, rendered on October 16, 2016 (Roswell, J.), reversing the order of the Supreme Court, Queens County (Keats, J.), rendered on April 12, 2016, suppressing tangible evidence.

JURISDICTION

On January 11, 2017, Michael Jameson was granted leave to appeal to the New York State Court of Appeals pursuant to § 460.20 of the Criminal Procedure Law (Smith, J.).

STATUTE INVOLVED

The right of the people to be secure in their persons, houses, papers, and effects, against unreasonable searches and seizures, shall not be violated, and no Warrants shall issue, but upon probable cause, supported by Oath or affirmation, and particularly describing the place to be searched, and the persons or things to seized. U.S. Const. amend IV.

STANDARD OF REVIEW

All of the issues presented on this appeal are reviewable de novo.

PRELIMINARY STATEMENT

On March 15, 2016, Michael Jameson was indicted for possession of one kilogram of marijuana in contravention of New York Penal Law § 429.25. He moved in Supreme Court, Queens County, to suppress the tangible evidence on the ground that it was the fruit of a violation of the Fourth Amendment. On April 13, 2016, the court granted his motion. The People thereupon sought and were granted permission for interlocutory appeal to the Appellate Division, Second Department, pursuant to N.Y. Crim. Proc. Law § 221.25. On October 17, 2016, that court reversed the suppression order. On January 11, 2017, this Court granted Michael Jameson leave to appeal from the decision of the Appellate Division.

STATEMENT OF THE CASE

A hearing on appellant Jameson's motion to suppress the drugs seized from his vehicle on February 7, 2016, was held in Supreme Court, Queens County, on March 25, 2016. The sole witnesses were Police Officer Thomas Mugan of the Seagrove-East Seagrove Precinct and Detective Arnold Staab of the New York City Joint Anti-Terrorism Taskforce. The court found the hearing testimony entirely credible; the facts are undisputed.

In the early morning of Saturday, February 6, 2016, Officer Mugan investigated a report of a trespasser in the sparsely populated beach community of East Seagrove, New York. (R. 3)[1] The woman who had called in the report told him that minutes before, she had seen a man (white, average build, thirties to forties in age, dark hair, wearing a dark blue or brown coat) across the street, where a golf course and resort were under construction by the Strutt Organization. He was marking the walls of the partially constructed club house with spray paint, but very soon got into his car and drove off. (R. 4–5) The woman told the officer that the car was white, a sedan, and in good condition. Noting that she "wasn't too good at cars," the woman said she thought the vehicle was Japanese, "maybe a Toyota or a Samsung [sic]." (R. 6) It had New Jersey license plates, a circumstance that the officer conceded was "not too unusual," given that the New York-New Jersey border was ten miles from East Seagrove. (R. 7, 18) The woman was too far away to see the license plate number. (R. 7)

After speaking with the woman, the officer proceeded to investigate at the construction site. On the wall facing the street someone had painted the words "RESIST STRUTT" with Day-Glo orange spray paint in letters two or three feet tall. (R. 8–9) The officer testified that the perpetrator would have been charged with two misdemeanors, criminal trespass and making graffiti. (R. 10)

Detective Staab testified with respect to the painted slogan. The Strutt Organization is a large multi-national corporation specializing in the construction and operation of luxury resorts, golf courses, and casinos. "Resist Strutt" is an international network of groups opposed to Strutt's employment, financial, and construction practices as well as its ties to anti-democratic regimes abroad. (R. 20–21) Although the main activity of the group is non-violent protest, there have been some scuffles with law enforcement resulting in the arrest of demonstrators, and one arson attempt against a Strutt property in Crimea was attributed to Resist Strutt activists. (R. 22)

---

[1]   Numbers in parentheses refer to pages of the record on appeal.

On the morning of February 7, a day after the graffiti incident, Officer Mugan was on motor patrol about a mile from East Seagrove when he saw a white Toyota sedan heading toward the town. It had New Jersey license plates and was driven by a "thirty-ish" dark-haired white man in a dark coat. (R. 12) There was nothing in itself unusual about the presence of an adult white man in the majority white area, but suspecting that the driver might be the trespasser from the morning before, the officer pulled the Toyota over. He approached the vehicle, and when the occupant opened the window, the officer smelled stale marijuana smoke and saw a clear plastic bag on the rear seat filled with what the experienced officer recognized as marijuana. (R. 13–14)

The officer arrested the driver, appellant Michael Jameson, who was subsequently indicted on charges of possessing a kilo of marijuana. (R. 15) Appellant was not charged with the misdemeanors, however; the eyewitness was unable to identify him as the man she saw at the scene. (R. 25–26)

On April 13, 2016, the hearing court granted appellant's motion to suppress the marijuana seized from his vehicle as the fruit of an unconstitutional stop. Ruling from the bench and citing *United States v. Hensley*, 469 U.S. 221, 229 (1985), the court applied "a *per se* rule that police may never stop an individual based solely on reasonable suspicion of perpetration of a completed misdemeanor." The court further articulated two alternative bases for its suppression order. First, the court noted that were it not to adopt a *per se* rule, but rather, to employ a case-by-case balancing of interests, it would conclude that "the public's interest in finding a trespasser who painted a protest slogan on private property was outweighed by Michael Jameson's individual interest in free passage on a public thoroughfare and in going about his business free from government intrusion." Second, the hearing court concluded that even had the vehicle stop for investigation of a misdemeanor been constitutional, the officer had an insufficient factual basis for the stop. According to the court, "the arresting officer lacked sufficient articulable facts which, singly or aggregated, gave him reasonable suspicion to stop defendant Jameson's vehicle. The facts he testified to could describe the vehicle and appearance of many innocent travelers in the area." Thus, "under the totality of the circumstances, as a matter of law, the facts here simply do not constitute the requisite reasonable suspicion that defendant Jameson was the person seen by the eyewitness."

The prosecution requested permission to appeal the suppression order, certifying that the suppression order left it without adequate proof to proceed with the case. Permission for an interlocutory appeal to the Appellate Division, Second Department was granted, and on October 16, 2016, in a 3-to-2 decision, that court reversed the hearing court's order.

In its decision, the Appellate Division majority rejected the hearing court's conclusion that United States Supreme Court precedent supported a bright-line rule prohibiting vehicle stops for the investigation of completed misdemeanors. Noting that in *Hensley*, 469 U.S. at 229, the Supreme Court held that vehicle stops to investigate completed felonies were constitutional, the appellate court dismissed as "patently absurd" the implication that stops related to completed misdemeanors were therefore *per se* unconstitutional; the issue of stops to investigate misdemeanors had simply not been before the Court, and its silence could therefore not be taken as a ruling on the issue.

The majority also rejected the hearing court's alternative holding that society's interest in finding the perpetrator of the specific misdemeanors in this case was outweighed by Michael Jameson's privacy interest. On the contrary, according to the appellate court, "[h]e was subjected to nothing more than a stop of his vehicle, a common, ordinary, everyday event." In contrast, however, "the state had a substantial interest in investigating the crimes here: trespass always carries a possibility of violence if the trespasser is discovered, and the spray painted slogan itself has been connected to violent activities."

Finally, the Appellate Division held that the arresting officer indeed possessed a reasonable suspicion that Michael Jameson had perpetrated the misdemeanors; since it authorizes only minimal intrusion, reasonable suspicion is accordingly a minimal quantum of evidence.

The court concluded that the evidence of the eyewitness as to the trespass and graffiti painting of the Strutt property provided the requisite particularized and objective basis for a stop.

Two dissenters disagreed with all of the majority's conclusions, agreeing with the hearing court on all three issues presented. *Inter alia,* the dissenters voiced concern that to permit investigative stops for completed misdemeanors was "a further and dangerous step down the increasingly broad and slippery path of disrespect for Fourth Amendment values."

SUMMARY OF THE ARGUMENT

Appellant Michael Jameson's Fourth Amendment right to be free of unreasonable search and seizure was violated when Police Officer Mugan stopped appellant's vehicle in order to investigate two minor misdemeanors that had occurred the previous day.

Although it is long settled that an officer who has reasonable suspicion of any *on-going* criminal activity may stop a vehicle and briefly detain its occupants, in the absence of probable cause, *see, e.g., United States v. Moran,* 503 F.3d 1135, 1140 (10th Cir. 2007), an officer who suspects a vehicle occupant of *past* criminal activity may only perform a stop if that criminal activity constitutes a felony. *United States v. Hensley,* 469 U.S. 221, 229 (1985). In *Hensley,* the Supreme Court reasoned that where an officer suspects that a vehicle occupant was involved in a felony, the government's interest in preventing and detecting serious and violent crimes outweighs a vehicle occupant's privacy interest. *Id.* Where, however, an officer suspects past involvement in a misdemeanor, the balance shifts sharply: an individual's interest in avoiding government intrusion outweighs the public's interest in the investigation of minor offenses. Supreme Court precedent thus logically gives rise to a *per se* bright-line rule forbidding investigative stops for completed misdemeanors, and the trial court correctly suppressed the evidence seized as a result of the stop of appellant Jameson's vehicle. *See Blaisdell v. Comm'r of Pub. Safety,* 375 N.W.2d 880, 883–84 (Minn. 1986).

Moreover, the same result is compelled assuming arguendo that vehicle stops like the one here are not *per se* impermissible, but that case-by-case application of the balancing test applied by the Court in *Hensley* is required. Here, the public's interest in investigation was minimal: the completed misdemeanors in question were trespassing on a construction site and spray-painting a protest slogan. Society's interest in the remote possibility of apprehending the slogan-painter a day after the incident was outweighed by appellant Jameson's individual privacy interest in avoiding the anxiety, humiliation, and inconvenience of a law-enforcement stop. *See, e.g., United States v. Hughes,* 517 F.3d 1013, 1017 (8th Cir. 2008).

Finally, even assuming that the purpose of the stop was constitutional, the stop was nonetheless a violation of appellant's Fourth Amendment rights because the officer lacked the requisite reasonable suspicion that appellant had been involved in a completed misdemeanor. The officer had only the single eyewitness's sparse and generic description of a white male trespasser driving a white sedan. The circumstances here are closely analogous to those found not to constitute reasonable suspicion, *see, e.g., People v. Yiu C. Choy*, 173 A.D.2d 883 (2d Dept. 2012), and do not remotely approach those deemed constitutional. *See, e.g., Moran*, 503 F.3d at 1139–41.

ARGUMENT

I. **THE APPELLANT'S FOURTH AMENDMENT GUARANTEE AGAINST UNREASONABLE SEIZURE WAS VIOLATED WHEN THE POLICE STOPPED HIS VEHICLE TO INVESTIGATE COMPLETED MISDEMEANORS.**

The police stop of appellant Michael Jameson's vehicle doubly violated the Fourth Amendment guarantee against unreasonable seizure: the purpose of the stop was improper and the factual predicate for it was insufficient. *See* U.S. Const. amend. IV; *United States v. Hensley*, 469 U.S. 221, 229 (1985); *United States v. Arvizu*, 534 U.S. 266, 277–78 (2002). The decision of the Appellate Division reversing the order suppressing the fruit of this illegal stop should not be permitted to stand; when it ruled that motorists could be stopped to investigate completed misdemeanors and when it held that police had reasonable suspicion that appellant was the perpetrator of the misdemeanor, that court misinterpreted and misapplied rulings of the Supreme Court of the United States.

In 1968, in the landmark case of *Terry v. Ohio,* the Supreme Court created an exception to the Fourth Amendment's requirement that seizure of the person be based on probable cause, ruling that a police officer may stop and briefly detain an individual if the officer has "reasonable suspicion" to believe that the individual is committing a crime. 392 U.S. 1, 20–21(1968). The Court reached this conclusion by balancing the government's interest in crime prevention against the individual's privacy interest. *Id*. The *Terry* rule has since been extended to vehicle stops, which must accordingly be based on a reasonable suspicion of criminal activity. *See Delaware v. Prouse*, 440 U.S. 648, 663 (1979). When the legality of a *Terry* stop is challenged, a reviewing court must examine de novo the events that led up to the stop to determine whether the "historical facts, viewed from the standpoint of an objectively reasonable police officer, amount to reasonable suspicion." *Ornelas v. United States,* 517 U.S. 690, 696, 699 (1996). Although the facts need not "rule out the possibility of innocent conduct," the totality of the circumstances must form "a particularized and objective basis" for a stop. *Arvizu,* 534 U.S. at 277–78.

It was long believed that, by their nature, *Terry* stops should apply only to on-going or imminent criminality. In 1985, however, the Court ruled in *United States v. Hensley* that "if police have a reasonable suspicion, grounded in specific and articulable facts, that a person they encounter was involved in or was wanted in connection with a completed felony, then a *Terry* stop may be made to investigate that suspicion." 469 U.S. 221, 229. As in *Terry,* the Court reached its conclusion by weighing governmental and individual interests. The Court conceded that the Government's interest in investigating a completed crime is less substantial than the interest in crime prevention and that "[p]ublic safety may be less threatened by a suspect in a past crime who appears to be going about his business than it is by a suspect who is currently in the process of violating the law." *Id.* at 228–229. Nonetheless, because waiting until probable cause was obtained might enable the felon to flee and remain at large, the Court concluded that law enforcement interest outweighed the individual's privacy interest. *Id.* at 229.

Neither the ruling nor the reasoning in *Hensley* supports the Appellate Division's conclusion that police may make vehicle stops for the purpose of investigating completed misdemeanors, and even were such stops constitutional, the stop here, based solely on an eyewitness description of a generic white man in a generic white car falls far short of the particularized and objective basis required for a *Terry* stop.

A. **Under the Fourth Amendment, vehicle stops to investigate completed misdemeanors are *per se* unreasonable.**

The constitutional issue presented here is one of first impression in this state. In *United States v. Hensley,* the Supreme Court held that individuals could be stopped and detained by law enforcement upon reasonable suspicion of having committed a felony; it follows from that ruling that no such stop may be made to investigate a completed misdemeanor. *See Gaddis v. Redford Township,* 364 F.3d 763, 771, n.6 (6th Cir. 2004); *United States v. Roberts,* 986 F.2d 1026, 1030 (6th Cir. 1993). This conclusion is supported, first, by the historical division of crimes into felonies and misdemeanors. Second, when the privacy interests of individuals are weighed against the governmental interest in apprehending the perpetrators of petty offenses, the balance favors individual rights.

The bright-line felony/misdemeanor distinction is as old as the common law. The qualitatively different blameworthiness of the two is inherent in the etymology of "felony" itself, "an old word meaning wicked or treacherous." *See* J.H. Baker, <u>An Introduction to English Legal History</u> 425 (2d Ed. 1979). The distinction between felony and misdemeanor is underscored by the punishment incurred by perpetrators: felonies were punishable by death and misdemeanors by fine or forfeiture. Although most felonies are no longer capital offenses in most jurisdictions, a distinction based on the nature and severity of sentencing endures. *See generally,* Rachel S. Weiss, *Defining the Contours of United States v. Hensley: Limiting the Use of Terry Stops for Completed Misdemeanors,* 94 Cornell L. Rev. 1321, 1338–1342 (2009). Felonies are often defined, as in New York, as infractions punishable by more than a year of incarceration. *See, e.g.,* N.Y. Penal Law § 10.00(5). Misdemeanors are punished by a year or less of incarceration, or by fines, probation, or community service. Significantly, felons and misdemeanants serve their custodial sentences in different institutions—local jails for the latter, compared to the more ignominious sequestration in state or federal penitentiaries for the former. Given the historical pedigree and persistence of the felony/misdemeanor distinction, the clear implication of *Hensley* is that *Terry* stops for completed misdemeanors are *per se* unconstitutional.

Even if the felony/misdemeanor distinction in itself is not conclusive, application of the balancing test used in *Terry* and *Hensley* demonstrates the impermissibility of stops like that in this case. To determine the reasonableness of seizures "that are less intrusive than a traditional arrest," the Supreme Court weighs "the gravity of the public concerns served by the seizure, the degree to which the seizure advances the public interest, and the severity of the interference with individual liberty." *Blaisdell,* 375 N.W.2d at 883, quoting *Brown v. Texas,* 442 U.S. 47, 50–51 (1979), aff'd on other grounds, 381 N.W.2d 849 (Minn. 1986). As the Supreme Court acknowledged in *Hensley,* the interest in investigating completed crimes is by its nature less compelling than the interest in preventing crime. But that interest is weaker still for misdemeanors—crimes long regarded as less blameworthy and less threatening to an ordered society than felonies and punished far less severely.

Moreover, it is difficult to see how vehicle stops would meaningfully advance any legitimate public concern. A stop is unlikely to produce anything but the driver's name—information that could be obtained by a license-plate check. Even granting that occasionally there might be circumstances in which such a stop serves the public interest in investigation and apprehension, such circumstances are unlikely to "arise. . . in a misdemeanor context with sufficient frequency to appreciably advance the public interest. . . ."*Id.*

With respect to the other side of the scale, the interference with individual liberty, the Supreme Court has long recognized that the "minimal" intrusion of a *Terry* stop is nonetheless a real psychological and physical intrusion. Such a stop is "normally effected 'by means of a possibly unsettling show of authority[,]. . .interfere[s] with freedom of movement, [is] inconvenient,. . .consume[s] time [and] may create substantial anxiety." *Prouse,* 440 U.S. at 657. In addition, extending the reach of *Terry* carries with it risks of legitimizing a technique for harassment and for conscious or unconscious racial and ethnic profiling. *Cf. Blaisdell,* 375 N.W.2d at 883, citing *Terry v. Ohio,* 392 U.S. at 37 (Douglas, J., dissenting). Thus, when the potential for interference with "the right of every individual to the possession and control of his own person," *Union Pac. R.R. Co. v. Botsford,* 141 U.S. 250, 251 (1891), is weighed against the government's interest and the likelihood that that interest will be advanced, "the limited benefits to the public interest resulting from warrantless stops to investigate past misdemeanors do not outweigh the intrusion on the 'motorist's right to free passage without interruption.' " *Blaisdell,* 375 N.W.2d at 883–84, quoting *United States v. Martinez-Fuerte,* 428 U.S. 5443, 557–58 (1976).

A bright-line rule forbidding stops like the one here is thus the clear implication of *Hensley. Gaddis,* 364 F.2d at 771, n.6. Although it is true that the Supreme Court has on occasion expressed a preference for fact-specific rather than bright-line rules, *see Hughes,* 517 F.3d at 1017, citing *Ohio v. Robinette,* 519 U.S. 33, 39 (1996), it is equally true that the Court does not hesitate to make bright-line rules where they are appropriate. Indeed, *Hensley* itself is just such a rule: officers may stop individuals upon reasonable suspicion of a completed felony, period. Just as the serious nature of most felonies justifies such stops, so the minor nature of most misdemeanors forbids them.

Finally, the two dissenters in the Appellate Division believed that to permit investigative stops for completed misdemeanors would be to take "a further and dangerous step down the increasingly broad and slippery path of disrespect for Fourth Amendment values." They are not alone in their concern that *Terry* is being extended far beyond what the Court intended, or could have imagined, and, further, that its incremental extension over the past decades has not meaningfully improved the prevention or detection of crime. *See generally,* Jeffrey Fagan, *Terry's Original Sin,* 2016 U. Chi. Legal F. 43 (2016).

B. **Assuming arguendo that vehicle stops for the investigation of completed misdemeanors are not *per se* unreasonable under the Fourth Amendment, but should be determined on a case-by-case basis, the stop here was impermissible, because the appellant's interest in free movement outweighed the public interest in the investigation of minor property damage committed a day earlier.**

Should this Court decline to impose a bright-line rule forbidding *Terry* stops for the investigation of completed misdemeanors and instead apply a case-by-case balancing of interests, appellant should nonetheless prevail. *See Hughes,* 517 F.3d at 1017; *Moran,* 503 F.3d at 1141–43, *United States v. Grigg,* 498 F.3d 1070, 1076–77(9th Cir. 2007). When "the nature and quality of the intrusion on personal security" are weighed against "the importance of the governmental interests alleged to justify the intrusion" here, *Hughes,* 517 F.3d at 1017, the balance favors appellant Jameson.

In *United States v. Moran,* for example, the perpetrator was believed to be armed and twice entered on occupied private property. The police believed that he would return. Noting that perpetrator was more like an "individual in the process of violating the law or a suspect fleeing from the scene of a crime than a 'suspect in a past crime who now appears to be going about his lawful business,'" the Tenth Circuit concluded that the underlying crime "posed an ongoing risk to public safety" and, therefore, implicated the strong governmental interest in "solving crime and bringing offenders to justice." 503 F.3d at 1142–3, quoting *Hensley,* 469 U.S. at 228. Characterizing traffic stops as brief and non-intrusive and any intrusion on the defendant's personal privacy as minimal, the court held that governmental interest outweighed privacy concerns.

In *United States v. Grigg,* the Ninth Circuit emphasized that courts "must consider the nature of the [completed] misdemeanor offense in question," taking into account "the potential for ongoing or repeated danger (e.g., drunken and/or reckless driving), and any risk of escalation (e.g., disorderly conduct, assault, domestic violence)," as well as the availability of "alternative means to identify the suspect." 498 F.3d at 1081. The perpetrator in that case, however, had violated a local noise ordinance by playing his car stereo very loudly, a non-violent offense which, even if repeated, posed no danger to the public. Balanced against the minimal public interest in his apprehension, the defendant's privacy interests prevailed, and his detention was held to violate the Fourth Amendment. *Id.*

Here, appellant Jameson's privacy interests likewise prevail. The misdemeanors in question neither involved nor threatened violence. The perpetrator trespassed on a construction site early on a weekend morning in order to spray-paint a protest slogan, presumably choosing a time when the site would be unoccupied. Having painted his message, he left. There was no reason to believe that he would return, nor was there reason to believe he was armed. As in *Grigg*, there was no potential for ongoing danger or for escalation. *Id.* Moreover, it was not until some 24 hours later that Officer Mugan detained appellant Jameson, a "suspect in a past crime who... appear[ed] to be going about his lawful business" rather than a fleeing suspect. *Moran*, 503 F.3d at 1142–3. Finally, instead of stopping appellant, the officer could have furthered his investigation by checking the license plate number to determine the owner of the vehicle. In sum, appellant Jameson's Fourth Amendment right to go on his way free of interference or restraint outweighed society's interest in investigating graffiti painting and apprehending the perpetrator.

C. **Assuming arguendo that the public interest in investigating the misdemeanors outweighed the appellant's privacy interests, the stop was nonetheless a violation of his Fourth Amendment rights, because, with nothing but the eyewitness's generic descriptions of the perpetrator and his vehicle, the officer lacked the requisite reasonable suspicion that appellant was the perpetrator.**

If this Court should decide that stopping appellant Jameson's vehicle in order to investigate a completed misdemeanor was legitimate, the tangible evidence seized from appellant's vehicle should nonetheless be suppressed: even were the officer's purpose constitutional, he lacked the reasonable suspicion that is the minimum quantum of evidence required for a vehicle stop. *See Prouse*, 440 U.S. at 663. Where a defendant challenges a finding of reasonable suspicion, the Supreme Court requires reviewing courts to look at the "totality of the circumstances" of each case to see whether the detaining officer has a "particularized and objective basis" for suspecting legal wrongdoing. *Arvizu*, 534 U.S. at 273–74. With respect to the requirement of a particularized basis for suspicion, the courts of this state have repeatedly warned that "[v]ague descriptions or generic descriptions of a suspect which could apply to numerous individuals cannot form the basis of reasonable suspicion." *People v. Ransom*, 9 N.Y.S.3d 595 (N.Y. Crim. Ct. 2015) ("description of four black males at a particular location in a predominantly African-American neighborhood is not out of the ordinary"); *accord, People v. Stewart*, 41 N.Y.2d 65, 69 (1976); *Choy*, 173 A.D.2d at 883.; *People v. Morrow*, 97 A.D.3d 991 (3d Dept. 2012); *People v. Dubinsky*, 289 A.D.2d 415 (2d Dept. 2001); *Matter of Rubin M.*, 271 A.D.2d 291 (1st Dept. 2000).

The descriptions of appellant Jameson and his vehicle that led to the stop of his vehicle twenty-four hours after the event were generic and vague. The eyewitness described a white man of average build, aged somewhere between thirty and fifty years of age. He had dark hair and wore a dark coat. The man drove off in a white sedan that the eyewitness, who admitted that she "wasn't too good at cars," thought was a "Japanese" car, "maybe a Toyota or a Samsung [sic]." Given that the eyewitness appeared to believe that Japanese cars have a distinctive appearance and that she also apparently believed that the Korean electronics manufacturer Samsung makes Japanese cars, her description of the vehicle make was less than reliable. The car had New Jersey license plates, which was unremarkable, given that the New York-New Jersey border was ten miles from the area where the misdemeanors and stop occurred. The eyewitness was too far away to see the license plate number. A day later, on patrol a mile from the construction site, the officer saw a white Toyota with a New Jersey license plate driven by a "thirty-ish" white male with dark hair and a dark coat and stopped appellant Jameson.

On analogous facts, New York courts have found reasonable suspicion lacking. For example, in *People v. Brooks*, 266 A.D.2d 864 (4th Dep't 1999), where defendant's vehicle was stopped "based entirely upon information that a robbery had been committed by three black males in a green automobile," the court held that "[s]uch sparse and general information does not support a reasonable suspicion." Similarly, in *Choy*, 173 A.D.2d 883, a robbery victim's description of assailants as "four young male Orientals, dressed in dark clothing," was "insufficient to give a police officer reasonable cause to follow, stop and frisk two young male Orientals, dressed in dark clothing, three tenths of a mile away, two hours after the crime." Finally, in *Dubinsky*, 289 A.D.2d at 416, reasonable suspicion was similarly absent where officers were looking for robbery suspects described as two white males, 15 to 16 years old, "wearing dark jackets that might be black or blue," and the defendant was stopped fifteen minutes later walking in the direction of the crime scene. Similarly, under the totality of the circumstances, Officer Mugan lacked the particularized and objective evidence constituting a reasonable suspicion that appellant Jameson, a white man in a white car in a predominantly white area, committed misdemeanors a day earlier. The hearing court correctly held that the vehicle stop violated his Fourth Amendment guarantee against unreasonable seizure, and the decision of the Appellate Division should accordingly be reversed.

12

INDEX

References are to Pages